Sodom

ON THE THAMES

CORNELL UNIVERSITY PRESS

ITHACA & LONDON

Sodom

ON THE THAMES

SEX, LOVE, AND SCANDAL

IN WILDE TIMES

MORRIS B. KAPLAN

First published 2005 by Cornell University Press

Printed in the United States of America

Library of Congress Cataloging-in-Publication Data

Kaplan, Morris B.
    Sodom on the Thames : sex, love, and scandal in Wilde times / Morris Kaplan.
        p. cm.
    Includes bibliographical references and index.
    ISBN-13: 978-0-8014-3678-9 (cloth : alk. paper)
    ISBN-10: 0-8014-3678-8 (cloth : alk. paper)
    1. English literature—England—London—History and criticism.
2. Homosexuality and literature—England—London—History—
19th century.   3. Homosexuality, Male—England—London—
History—19th century.   4. London (England)—Social life and
customs—19th century.   5. Sex customs—England—London—
History—19th century.   6. English literature—19th century—
History and criticism.   7. Scandals—England—London—History—19th century.   8. Symonds, John Addington, 1840–1893—
Sexual behavior.   9. Wilde, Oscar, 1854–1900—Trials, litigation,
etc.   10. London (England)—In literature.   11. Sexual orientation in literature.   12. Sex customs in literature.   I. Title.
    PR8477.K37 2005
    820.9'353—dc22   2005008833

Cornell University Press strives to use environmentally responsible suppliers and materials to the fullest extent possible in the publishing of its books. Such materials include vegetable-based, low-VOC inks and acid-free papers that are recycled, totally chlorine-free, or partly composed of nonwood fibers. For further information, visit our website at www.cornellpress.cornell.edu.

Cloth printing   10 9 8 7 6 5 4 3 2 1

frontispiece: *"The Sluggard," Frederic Leighton (1895)*

With love and gratitude,

this book is dedicated to the memory

of my mother, Sylvia Kaplan Radolan,

of my teacher, Don Gifford, and

of my friend, Mary Wood Lawrence

CONTENTS

Sodom

ON THE THAMES

"What's a nice guy like you doing in a place like this?" This well-worn come-on was not redeemed by the fact that it was a question addressed to me—by me. It kept going through my head as I almost compulsively traversed the circuit, sometimes returning to the same venue four or five days in a given week. This went on for almost ten years. I was drawn back to London every summer, occasionally during term breaks, and for two sabbatical leaves. What was it that had such a powerful hold on me? Nothing in my background had prepared me for this state of affairs. What had drawn this retired trial lawyer and committed professor of philosophy into an obsessive pursuit of historical research in the National Archives at Kew and elsewhere?

It all began with a glimpse of two very different objects of desire in late Victorian London: a pair of elaborately dressed feminine figures and some teenage boys in uniform. First, Fanny and Stella, who paraded around the West End's streets, theaters, and arcades followed by groups of admiring men, until the police saw fit to halt their promenades and expose them as Frederick Park and Ernest Boulton. Their arrest and trial in 1870–1871 for "conspiracy to commit sodomy" and to "solicit" others to do so captured public attention like few before it. Newspapers detailed the evidence against them, which recirculated in the form of penny pamphlets and even made its way into a popular limerick. Their photographs were displayed in shops, their private letters printed in the papers, and their attendance at a drag ball in the Strand was eventually featured in a privately published pornographic novel.

Then, two decades later, telegraph delivery boys employed at the central post office admitted to moonlighting as prostitutes at 19 Cleveland Street, a brothel patronized by middle- and upper-class men, including aristocrats, members of Parliament, and perhaps even the grandson of Queen Victoria. The status of the clients led the radical press to accuse the Conservative government of a cover-up: questions were asked in Parliament and an MP was suspended from the House of Commons for declaring he did not believe the prime minister's explanations. Lord Arthur Somerset, the son of a duke, fled the country under threat of prosecution, while another nobleman sued the editor who had named him for criminal libel. In the trial that followed, John

Saul, who described himself as a "professional sodomite," testified that he had picked up the noble lord in Leicester Square and had taken him back to 19 Cleveland Street for sex.

I was introduced to these figures by the historian Jeffrey Weeks in a wonderful essay, "Inverts, Perverts, and Mary-anns: Male Prostitution and the Regulation of Homosexuality in the Nineteenth and Early Twentieth Centuries," which devotes a couple of paragraphs to each scandal, conveniently providing the numbers of the files in the Public Records Office, London, where more details could be found. When the opportunity arose to participate in a summer seminar for college teachers called "The Culture of London, 1850–1920," sponsored by the National Endowment for the Humanities, I developed a proposal. Why not? I had been a trial lawyer in New York for more than ten years, so I felt better prepared than most to deal with court records. In my first book, *Sexual Justice: Democratic Citizenship and the Politics of Desire,* I analyzed the regulation of sexuality and argued for historicizing both the forms of desire and the norms that governed them. London in the late nineteenth century was the site of an increasingly visible male homosexuality and of notorious legal persecution. The archives might provide material for a test case; the research might even yield an article. Besides, it was a chance to spend six weeks in London at the federal government's expense. How could I lose?

It never occurred to me that I would encounter characters so fascinating and stories so compelling that I would spend almost ten years trying to learn more about them. Why had these episodes received so little attention? In part, the answer was simple: they had been eclipsed by the trials of Oscar Wilde in 1895. That scandal and the figure at its center cast an enormous shadow well into the twentieth century, dominating discussion of the legal status of homosexuality in Britain and the United States and shaping popular images of the male homosexual.

What happens if we push Wilde away from center stage? I decided to examine conditions of life for men who loved men and attitudes toward same-sex desire during the decades preceding his prosecution. Wilde's trials did not occur in a vacuum. What cultural configuration enabled his case to become so spectacular? How does private sexual conduct become the subject of political conflict? Is there something especially provocative about sex between men? What about less visible forms of social control than criminal prosecution?

My investigation led from the well-publicized scandals involving legal proceedings to much quieter incidents involving the departure from Eton Col-

Sodom on the Thames

lege in the 1870s of two highly respected teachers. William Johnson resigned under a cloud of suspicion and changed his name to Cory, while Oscar Browning was fired for a technical breach of the rules that no one accepted as the real cause. Many believed that both men had behaved improperly with their students. In the absence of a public record, collected private correspondence between one of these teachers and a former student became my primary source. There I encountered a third set of intriguing figures and relationships: teachers at elite public schools who remained closely connected to former pupils as they ascended the "greasy pole" to political power; circles of young men entangled in romantic attachments with one another that matured into lifelong friendships; men at the center of the British establishment with wives, children, and boyfriends into the bargain; a beautiful youth who converted to Roman Catholicism and took holy orders only to wind up in Sicily with a succession of houseboys who were also intimate companions.

The files on the legal scandals at the Public Records Office (now the National Archive at Kew) led me to the British Library newspaper collection at Collindale, where I encountered a diverse and contentious late Victorian press that not only covered the episodes in great detail but also editorialized about their connections with social class, urban culture, and moral decline. The relatively new practice of publishing "letters to the editor" gave voice to a range of "public opinion." Secondary scholarship and serendipity led me to other references to these incidents in private correspondence. The proceedings against Boulton and Park, which began with their arrest leaving the Strand Theatre in late April 1870, culminated in their trial before the Lord Chief Justice and a special jury at the Queen's Bench, Westminster Hall, in May 1871. The legal theory under which these sons of respectable middle-class families were charged was so problematic that an unusually detailed record survives in the archive: a two-thousand-page handwritten verbatim transcript of the trial as well as copies of all the depositions taken from witnesses at the magistrate's court and the texts of thirty or more letters that were entered into evidence.

Whereas no such legal record remains from the Cleveland Street affair, that matter was so politically sensitive that the files remained sealed until 1976, when scholars fresh from the disclosures in the Watergate scandal and in search of an earlier cover-up produced two books. Indeed, the files are replete with correspondence among the highest officials about how to proceed with a sexual imbroglio that might implicate Prince Albert Victor, grandson of Queen Victoria and second in line to her throne. Their concern with public opinion is manifest not only in their repeated references to the press but also in the official collection of newspaper clippings about the affair. More to my purpose, the file includes statements made to police by the telegraph delivery boys and the "professional sodomite" John Saul; these are far more candid than anything in the published accounts of the case. The historian H. Montgomery Hyde also relied on correspondence addressed to Reginald Brett, a friend of the nobleman who had fled to France in the wake of the scandal. It includes letters from Lord Arthur Somerset's family and from friends concerned about their own links to the house on Cleveland Street. Brett, a well-connected civil servant, ignored requests to destroy the letters, eventually having them bound in a leather volume titled "The Case of Lord Arthur Somerset."

As it turns out, "Regy" Brett had been a student of William Johnson Cory, who resigned in disgrace from Eton in 1872. He had kept in touch with his teacher until his death in 1892, and with his former Eton boyfriend, Charles Williamson, known as "Chat," until his own death in 1930. The son of a successful barrister and judge, Brett eventually launched a political career, serving briefly in Parliament, working actively behind the scenes in Liberal Party politics, and becoming a high-level official in the Ministry of Works, which made him a close adviser and confidant to several generations of the royal family. When his father died, he became the second Viscount Esher.

During his long public career, Brett accumulated a massive archive of correspondence and working papers, now housed at Churchill College, Cambridge. He also saved his journals and much of his personal correspondence with friends and family. Perhaps surprisingly, given the unorthodox character of his intimate life, Esher wished to preserve this material as a legacy for his sons. Eventually he had the letters and journals typed and bound, and added occasional notes to identify participants and occasionally record afterthoughts. He saved the letters he had received from Cory, as well as his teacher's journal for the year 1868. In 1923, he published *Ionicus,* a memoir of Cory partially based on this collection. Regy's correspondence with Williamson reveals that he had saved his friend's letters as well, at one point having them bound in several volumes. After Esher's death in 1930, Chat seems to have destroyed his own letters. However, Regy's replies to Chat after 1889 have been preserved. Together these letters and journals have allowed me to construct an overlapping but fragmentary and interrupted narrative of their shared experience at Eton and its impact on the lives and loves of the three friends.

These three episodes—the prosecution of Fanny and Stella, the friendships formed around Cory at Eton, and the Cleveland Street affair—are the sub-

Sodom on the Thames

jects of parts 1 to 3 of this book. The characters and stories interweave in some surprising ways. A continuing counterpoint is provided by the life and letters of John Addington Symonds. Symonds was a man of letters who wrote massive tomes on the Italian Renaissance and ancient Greece as well as poetry and essays. He also published the first sustained defenses of male same-sex love in English. Married and the father of four daughters, he took several working-class men in Switzerland and Italy as his lovers and maintained long-term relationships with them. His erotic life is chronicled in many surviving letters and in the extremely candid *Memoirs*, written between 1889 and his death in 1893, but not published until 1984. Only four-fifths of Symonds's material is included in the published volume: I was allowed to examine the original manuscript and a full typescript in the London Library.

The second, somewhat unlikely, commentary is provided by the text of a pornographic novel privately published in 1881. *The Sins of the Cities of the Plain, or the Confessions of a Mary-ann* includes an elaborate account of the drag ball attended by Boulton and Park, which graphically presents a final orgy. The book also offers briefer accounts of sex among the boys and with their teachers at boarding school. Quite remarkably, the eponymous "Mary-ann" is named "John Saul" and bears more than a passing resemblance to the historical individual who testified some years later in the Cleveland Street affair. Here too, a visit to the archives became necessary. Although a version of the book is published and marketed as gay pornography, it departs from the original in some interesting and historically revealing respects. Copies of the 1881 edition are available for inspection from the "cupboard" of sexually explicit materials at the British Library, but only at designated desks under the surveillance of the staff.

Oscar Wilde has resisted my efforts to push him off the stage. The appearance of new evidence forced me to reexamine his case in part 4. Frankly, when I began this research, I did not think I would have anything to add to the voluminous commentary already available on Wilde's life, work, and persecution. It seemed unlikely that anything new would emerge for the historical record. However, two recent discoveries are particularly pertinent to my concerns in this book. Merlin Holland, Wilde's grandson, has recently published a more extensive transcript of the Queensberry libel trial than that previously available.[1] In addition, in June 2001 Christie's offered for sale a fifty-page document that included thirty witness statements for the defense: "The manuscript contains the evidence of the Marquess of Queensberry and 29 others, eleven of them young men directly alleging 'indecent behaviour.'"[2] This item brought the unanticipated sum of £44,650 from an anonymous private collector. Holland had access to these documents and judiciously uses them in his notes. (Neil McKenna's *The Secret Life of Oscar Wilde* uses them even more extensively.)[3]

The more complete record of the libel case shows how deliberately Sir Edward Carson, Queensberry's lawyer, played off public memories of the earlier scandals. Although his cross-examination of Wilde remains central to the drama, the new text shows how the lawyer set up the future criminal prosecutions and established a template for the press coverage. He weaves references not only to the house on Cleveland Street (which had been in the news only five years earlier) but also to the cross-dressing and flagrant publicity associated with Fanny and Stella, whose trial had taken place in 1871. Newspaper reports and editorials fleshed out these allusions. My final reason for concluding with Wilde is found in the epilogue, where I present in some detail the treatment of the affair in the editorials and correspondence in *Reynolds's Newspaper.* The debate found there is far more wide-ranging than anyone might expect and is not discussed in recent scholarly accounts of the press coverage. Since it touches on many themes central to this work and introduces new elements that were to become prevalent in the twentieth century, it seems fitting to end there.

The heart of this book is its characters and their stories. I have allowed them to speak for themselves as much as possible. Although they have affinities with gay men, bisexuals, transgendered people, boy-lovers, and pedophiles, they resist easy assimilation to contemporary categories. The diversity of social types and forms of self-understanding on display, even within this limited time and locale, is striking. Because the archives have yielded such rich, complex, and divergent accounts, I have tried to respect the language and conceptual frames of the period. I have quoted at length from primary sources to offer a firsthand experience of material that is not easily accessible, especially in North America. Some individuals involved in these incidents are highly literate and articulate; the unlettered voices sometimes audible in the court records or newspaper accounts can also be eloquent. The lawyers whose arguments survive and the newspapers that comment on these affairs often present conflicting interpretations. The differing perspectives and the wide range of references complicate any simple story about "late Victorian attitudes" toward male homoeroticism. Endnotes identify the sources of these quotations and contextual information: I have not used them to engage other scholars. However, I have benefited enormously from the secondary literature, some of which I discuss briefly in the "Suggestions for Further Reading."

Some readers, impatient with the obscurity of "postmodern" theory, may welcome this return to storytelling, while regretting the number of loose ends and my reluctance to reach conclusions about the sexual identities of the characters. What did they really want? Weren't most of them closeted homosexuals who would have been happier in a more enlightened age? Aren't some of them pedophiles whose pursuit of boys should be frankly condemned? More theoretically inclined readers may object to my method as a naïve attempt to recover voices "hidden from history" in the service of an anachronistic identity politics. Don't I know how very different the past is from the present? Haven't I heard of the discursive or "linguistic turn" that challenges any attempt simply to capture the "experience" of others? How do archival research and the construction of historical narratives contribute to the debates in lesbian/gay/queer studies and in the history of sexuality as they have developed in the last few decades?

I am under no illusion that I have simply recovered "authentic" voices previously "hidden from history" and uncontaminated by their cultural contexts. Legal proceedings, from police interrogations to courtroom testimony, impose their own language, categories, and constraints. Newspaper accounts deploy their own sense of what the public requires or can bear to hear. Editors need to sell papers as well as advance their own cultural and political agendas. Private letters capitalize on the shared educational backgrounds and social assumptions of the correspondents. None of these media is free from discursive shaping and constraint. Moreover, each medium bleeds into the others. Both the forms of same-sex desire and the cultural contexts in which they appear are arenas of contestation. There is plenty of disagreement on offer. No single ideology rules. Radical politics, moral purity campaigns, and conservative defenses of the social order offer competing perspectives and demand different social responses. At the same time, some viewpoints are surprisingly unrepresented in the public debate: the new sexology and liberal toleration do not appear until very late in the period. In the interstices of institutional constraint and ideological conflict, individual voices are sometimes vivid and original. Some of the ideas and values being expressed and debated seem familiar, others quite strange.

I have tried to keep my own interpretations to a minimum. This project no doubt came into being because of its resonance with contemporary sexual politics. Some gay, bisexual, transgendered, or otherwise queer readers may well identify with the characters or stories that follow. For others, these figures and the worlds they inhabit will seem quite alien. They move through a man's world pervasively structured by hierarchies of gender and social class.

However, some of these men resisted dominant norms of masculinity and challenged social inequality. In a concluding section, "Telling Tales," I discuss the role of narrative in the history of sexuality and reflect in more theoretical terms on my research. The characters, stories, and relationships represented here irreducibly intersect sexuality, gender, and social class as well as a plurality of discourses within which same-sex desire may be defined and judged and a broad scope of erotic engagements.

The mobility of eros and the diversity of its manifestations are oddly reflected in the very existence of the archives from which these tales have been gleaned. It would be a mistake simply to take for granted the historical record without reflecting somewhat on the personal desires and institutional interests that led to its preservation. Today, all legal proceedings are transcribed by court reporters and maintained to be used in appeals and other proceedings, whereas the Boulton and Park transcript is almost unique among late Victorian legal documents. (Our record of the Wilde trials was pieced together from newspaper accounts and lawyers' notes.) How does eros become socially troubling? What judgments led newspapers to cover that trial and the Cleveland Street affair in such copious detail, while giving rather less attention to other contemporary events with broader social effects? How is individual desire linked to memory and the production of written texts? What complex desires led Symonds to write so lovingly about his affair with Angelo Fusato, while leaving to his literary executor the decision whether to publish? What could Regy Brett have been thinking when he preserved so much of his intimate correspondence for his sons? What conflicting desires led Regy to collect the letters from his Eton boyfriend in bound volumes, and Chat to destroy them after Regy's death? I do not attempt to answer these questions in the stories that follow but want to suggest here the continuing resonance between love in its many forms and the efforts we take to memorialize it, to preserve eros in the archives.

Let me conclude this introduction with a confession. Long before Michel Foucault described its mode of operation, confession seemed an appropriate vehicle for sexual discourse. In carrying out this research, I described my work to friends as remote from my own experience and from our contemporary situation. I spoke proudly of my effort to recover the distinctive differences of another time, place, and form of life. However, I was fooling myself, if not them. This work is very much informed by the contexts, both political and personal, in which it was written.

First, the political. I began the research after completing *Sexual Justice: Democratic Citizenship and the Politics of Desire*. That book takes its starting point from the decision of the U.S. Supreme Court in *Bowers v. Hardwick* (1986) that homosexuals have no constitutional right to privacy that would protect them against state laws outlawing sexual acts between members of the same sex. I argued that this decision conflicted with decades of civil rights progress and effectively ratified a condition of second-class citizenship for lesbians and gay men. Full equality requires not only the abolition of sodomy laws but also the prohibition of discrimination based on sexual orientation and the legal recognition of same-sex intimate relationships.

Since then, the Supreme Court has overturned a Colorado constitutional amendment that prohibited civil rights protection for homosexuals and, more recently, explicitly reversed *Bowers* to invalidate a Texas law that criminalized homosexual conduct. Today debate rages about gay marriage in Massachusetts, while it has been legislated in the Netherlands, Spain, Belgium, and Scandinavia, as have civil unions in France, Germany, and Vermont. Conservatives in the United States support a constitutional amendment to ban same-sex marriage, and similar state referenda made it a central issue in the election of 2004. Some critics of marriage demand the creation of alternatives for heterosexual couples, while others worry that recognition of same-sex partnerships will further stigmatize other sexual minorities. The movement for lesbian and gay equality has been divided by differences in economic position, social class, and political attitude: "Log Cabin Republicans" square off against the members of "sex panic" who protested then Mayor Giuliani's closing of sex clubs in New York. "Queer" politics has proliferated to include transgendered people, bisexuals, sadomasochists, boy-lovers, and others.

When I began this research, sex scandal seemed a matter of historical interest; its contemporary resonance lay in the social status and self-understanding of same-sex desire. Since then, the politics of sexual morality has resurfaced dramatically. Heterosexual acts took center stage in the affair involving President Clinton and Monica Lewinsky: the details were aired by a "special prosecutor" and in congressional impeachment proceedings. In the nineteenth century as well, alleged affairs with women destroyed the Liberal politician Sir Charles Dilke and the Irish Nationalist Charles Stewart Parnell. All these episodes had political effects well beyond the careers of the individuals involved. As the fate of two prominent Republican congressional leaders charged with extramarital affairs in the wake of the Clinton scandal demonstrates, the charge of sexual irregularity is a double-edged sword. In Britain, under New Labour, one cabinet member was forced to resign after giving police conflicting stories about an alleged robbery by a man he met at a notorious gay cruising ground, while another survived by coming out before newspapers could publish revelations by a former lover. No party, ideology, or sexual orientation can claim a monopoly on moral rectitude. The scandals charted here reinforce that insight and dramatize the power of sexuality to mobilize public opinion and set in motion unpredictable political processes.

At a more personal level, only recently did I recognize how closely these stories touch my own life. My desires have been profoundly influenced by my education at all-male elite institutions in New England in the 1960s, and I did not really come into gay life until I moved to New York City in the 1970s. No doubt the historical Eton of the 1860s and London of the 1870s and after differ greatly from my places and times. Still the "fantasy echoes" of my own erotic history help explain what so engaged me in the archives. My attachments to these figures have vacillated between desire and identification. I'm not about to track those trajectories in detail here. The glamour of Stella's public performances, the commitment of Cory's pedagogy, the devotion of Regy and Chat, the camp defiance of John Saul, the relentless intellectualizing and moralizing of J. A. Symonds, the urban fantasies of *The Sins of the Cities of the Plain* each exerted its own fascination, at least for a time. If this book reaches any conclusion, it is that eros may attach itself to an astonishing array of phenomena and that fantasy plays a crucial role in the process—as much now as then. My erotic adventures in the archives have been a source of great pleasure. I hope the narratives that follow offer some pleasure to readers as well.

In the spring of 1865, the twenty-five-year-old John Addington Symonds had moved to London with his bride of some months and was living on Albion Street near Hyde Park. Walking home from an evening out with friends, Symonds passed through an alley that joined Trafalgar Square with Leicester Square and that took him past some barracks. Wearing evening dress, Symonds was approached by a "young grenadier" who spoke to him:

> I was too innocent, strange as this may seem, to guess what he meant. But I liked the man's looks, felt drawn toward him, and did not refuse his company. So there I was, the slight nervous man of fashion in my dress clothes, walking side by side with a strapping fellow in scarlet uniform, strongly attracted by his physical magnetism. . . . He broke abruptly into proposals, mentioned a house we could go to, and made it quite plain for what purpose. I quickened my pace, and hurrying though the passage broke away from him with a passionate mixture of repulsion and fascination.[1]

This episode was by no means Symonds's first discovery of his desires for other men.[2] *Memoirs*, in which he recounts this tale, reveals that he entertained intense erotic fantasies about men from early childhood. These desires coexisted with a relentlessly demanding morality. During his school days at Harrow, he keenly disapproved of the sexual antics of other boys, while recognizing the direction of his own yearning. He later played an important role in events that led to the resignation of the headmaster Dr. C. J. Vaughan as a result of his involvement with one of the students. As he approached adulthood, "Johnny" repeatedly found himself in love with younger men. He courted a chorister from the Bristol Cathedral with whom he exchanged caresses and love letters, even a kiss. When he confided in his father, a distinguished medical doctor, he was warned off on the grounds that such a friendship across class boundaries could only result in unhappiness for both.[3]

At Oxford, with no such social divide, Symonds continued to develop crushes on other men, pursuing them in search of romantic friendship. He was quite conscious that there was a sexual component to his interest. Symonds's writings reveal that some of his friends routinely indulged such appetites and that his own urges were strong. On graduation, his election as a fellow of Magdalen College was compromised by the campaign of an acquaintance, who circulated excerpts from Symonds's private letters and poems that appeared to express his erotic attraction to other men. Although cleared of any wrongdoing, Symonds had to defend himself at a meeting of the college, where two of his letters were "strongly condemned."[4] The personal crisis provoked by this scandal contributed toward ruining Symonds's health. At his father's direction, he sought medical advice and excruciating "treatment" to overcome his desires. He dedicated himself successfully to the project of finding a wife "on Doctor's orders" (Papa's as well), hoping to be released from their powerful grip. Still, Symonds wrote of the encounter with the grenadier: "The thrill of contact with the man taught me something new about myself. I can well recall the lingering regret, and the quick sense of deliverance from danger, with which I saw him fall back. . . . The longing left was partly a fresh seeking after comradeship and partly an animal desire the like of which I had not before experienced."[5]

If Symonds was already aware of his desire for other men and of its intensely sexual nature, what had he discovered in his encounter with the grenadier? What was the danger from which he had been delivered, and what "the lingering regret"? Symonds himself illuminates the matter with another London scene. Walking through "the sordid streets," gripped by an ill-defined depression, he meets, not a man, but an image: "At a certain corner, which I well remember, my eyes were caught by a rude *graffito* scrawled with slate-pencil upon slate. It was of so concentrated, so stimulative, so penetrative a character—so thoroughly the voice of vice and passion in the proletariat—that it pierced the very marrow of my soul." In the margin of his manuscript, Symonds is explicit: "'Prick to prick, so sweet'; with an emphatic diagram of phallic meeting, glued together, gushing."[6] The powerful response provoked by the drawing takes him back to his brief encounter with the soldier: "The wolf leaped out: my malaise of the moment was converted into a clairvoyant and tyrannical appetite for the thing which I rejected five months earlier in the alley by the barracks."

Symonds had hoped that his marriage and hard work would banish such longings. But they had returned even more strongly: "The vague and morbid craving of the previous years defined itself as a precise hunger after sensual pleasure, whereof I had not dreamed before save in repulsive visions of the night."[7] Such "visions" had haunted him from his earliest years. Now his desires were reflected back to him by other men abroad in the city, and were even written on its walls. The objects of his longing seemed to walk the streets

Sodom on the Thames

beside him. Later he would read this moment as a revelation of relentless needs with which he must "constitute a working compromise": "I know that obscene graffito was the sign and symbol of a paramount and permanent craving of my physical and psychical nature. It connected my childish reveries with the mixed passions and audacious comradeship of my maturity. Not only my flesh, but my heart as well, was involved in the emotion which it stirred."[8] His effort to make sense of his desires for other males lasted a lifetime, producing a body of work that stands as the first sustained defense of love between men to appear in English.

Although Symonds is best known for his promotion of conceptions of "sexual inversion" articulated by Continental sexologists, he was a very complex product of the elite education of his day. His apologies for same-sex desire drew on a variety of sources. His studies of the cultures of ancient Greece and the Italian Renaissance reached a wide readership; he championed the work of Walt Whitman and other "Arcadian" writers; toward the end of his life he collaborated with Havelock Ellis to promote a "psychological" understanding of sexuality. Throughout his work he invoked ideals of "noble pederasty" and democratic comradeship among men. His *Studies of the Greek Poets* (1873) is already replete with homoerotic implications for those who choose to see them; in 1883, he privately published *A Problem in Greek Ethics,* which celebrated pederasty as an ethical institution. Even the diaries and letters incorporated in his *Memoirs* are shaped by literary tradition. In his youth, he kept Plato's *Phaedrus* on the shelf by his bed, alongside *The Confessions* of Augustine.[9] In a letter to a friend detailing his inner turmoil, he writes: "Out of this History I have often thought that, if I lived to do nothing else, I should write confessions wh w. be better for the world to read than Rousseau's and not less interesting. I sometimes think I am being trained for this."[10] Symonds imagined his memoirs as a case study for future, less prejudiced generations. Because of their extraordinary candor, Symonds directed his literary executor to consider the sensibilities of his surviving wife and four daughters in deciding whether to publish. In due course, the manuscript was deposited in the London Library, available only to scholars who received special permission. Not until 1984 did Phyllis Grosskurth produce an edition that includes about four-fifths of the material. Even so, Symonds's literary and historical studies often returned to the theme of male love. His comment on his own poetry could be applied to all his work: "I find it wholly impossible to say anything that is not grossly autobiographical." Learned and eclectic, driven by a relentless will to self-understanding and self-justification, he ransacked the heritage of Western civilization for acceptable models of love between men.

What light do the urban scenes above shed on his efforts to forge an ethic of desire? What happens if we read them as exemplary tales? The encounter with the grenadier develops contrasting images of the "strapping fellow in scarlet uniform" and the "slight nervous man of fashion in . . . dress clothes." Despite the manifest difference in social class, they are bound together by the attraction felt by the one and the commercial interest of the other. But Symonds cannot close the deal: torn by a "passionate mixture of repulsion and fascination," he rushes away. His flight settles nothing, since he continues to feel both relief at his "delivery from danger" and "lingering regret." What does he really want? He is split between "seeking after comradeship" and "an animal desire." What about the grenadier? This icon of masculinity interrupts the erotic fantasy by speaking for himself—making Symonds an offer he cannot afford to accept. Not yet. Symonds reads the graffito as a gloss on his encounter with the man. He emphasizes the social distance between himself and the soldier: the drawing on the wall is "the voice of vice and passion in the proletariat."[11] The virility of the object cannot be more evident: "'Prick to prick, so sweet'; with an emphatic diagram of phallic meeting, glued together, gushing." The image is one of mutual satisfaction, but Symonds positions himself passively before it: the drawing had "so penetrative a character . . . that it pierced the very marrow of my soul." His desires terrify him: "The wolf leaped out . . . a clairvoyant and tyrannical appetite." His vague malaise has become a "precise hunger after sensual pleasure." But Symonds cannot easily satisfy this hunger. He is made very uncomfortable when another man expresses an interest in him. In an earlier letter to a friend whose feelings he does not reciprocate, he states baldly: "I am not a woman." Symonds links his inner conflict to a dilemma inherent in reciprocal male love:

> If you yearn after the grace etc wh you seem to see in me, I admire the generosity, unselfishness, purity of imagination, & sympathy with good wh I know you to possess. Externally grateful, I am inwardly at war—the sport of a hundred wild desires wh you probably have never felt. This will explain why I love to have you near me. You do me good by giving me what I have not got. If I have at times felt your society irksome it is because my nature is at root male & passionate—I do not want to have strong affection given me wh I cannot return in kisses & all else that belongs to love—& great kindness suggests to the beast within me ineffable desires.[12]

Why should Symonds not be able respond to strong affection with "kisses & all else"? He seems unable to imagine erotic love without an asymmetrical division of roles. He is troubled by the need to draw boundaries not only be-tween acceptable and unacceptable desires but also between himself and other men. Where does romantic friendship end and shameful vice begin?

The streets of London proclaimed "the sign and symbol" of Symonds's fantasies and offered opportunities to meet others who shared them. How-ever, the aim of his desires is not simple. Writing the year before his London experiences, he confesses:

> Out of these Diaries & out of my memory of a continual battle, in wh the one thought ever present was "Oh that I cd get Love, that I cd cease to be alone, or die!" . . . in wh the outer world at last came rudely like a great blast of wind to make my strife more arduous and painful, opening my se-cret parts to daylight & imposing on me scornfully the burden under wh already secretly and by myself I was staggering.[13]

"Inwardly" he is at war with himself: his desires collide not only with social barriers but with each other. Commenting on a painting by Simeon Solo-mon, he writes: "[He] might make a better picture of Amor and Libido: Lust dying of the breath of Love."[14] The "outer world" of the city opens his "se-cret parts to daylight," exposing inner chaos. The dynamic at work here is pro-foundly unsettling. It is one thing when Symonds acknowledges he has yearnings that must be controlled, quite another when a virile fantasy steps out of the shadows to proposition him. Scenes of casual but reciprocal at-traction transform Symonds's erotic universe and himself along with it. The world becomes an arena of exciting possibilities where a passing look may of-fer the promise of bliss:

> I remember, for example, today, as though it had been yesterday, how sev-eral years ago a young man in a shirt and trousers, stretched upon a para-pet below the Ponte di Paradiso at Venice, gazed into my eyes as I moved past him, lifted his head, then rose upon his elbows, and followed me till I was out of sight with a fixed look which I shall remember if we meet in the next world.[15]

In the same mood, he declares: "I long to meet with a man, a comrade, the first face and hand responsive to my own. Why? I do not know." During a trip to the Continent with his sister, Symonds describes this longing in letters written home — to his pregnant wife. He adds: "All this has nothing to do with the ties, inviolable and sacred, which bind me to my home, and make me feel my center there in you."[16] Does Symonds really know what he wants? Would everything have ended "happily ever after" had he been able to settle down with the boy on the Ponte di Paradiso(!)? Is it so hard to imagine him writing the same letter home to a male partner that he wrote to his wife? Is there something inherently restless in male desire that resists domestication?

Symonds sometimes divides the world between those men who love men and those who do not. But he also divides "Arcadian" love between those for whom it is a vehicle of aspiration and those to whom it is an itch to scratch. Symonds's attitudes reflect both his Protestant upbringing and the "moral purity" movements of his time: he could be lacerating in his judgments of ethical failings in erotic matters. Despite his affiliations and advocacy, Symonds rejects easy divisions between "us" and "them" no matter how congenial they sometimes appear. Same-sex desire may be noble or base, spiritual or carnal, intensely romantic or casually pleasurable, ethically inspiring or morally corrosive, love or lust. Desire may lead in diverse, sometimes conflicting directions: toward romance, friendship, excellence, knowledge, service, pleasure, power, vice. The aspirations that fuel the highest human accomplishments are entangled with temptations to the basest indulgence. Erotic love has the potential to do great good or evil. Like other students at public schools and elite universities, Symonds is powerfully influenced by his study of Greek culture.[17] It is not enough for him to show that forms of same-sex desire were accepted in classical Greece; Symonds insists they were central to its greatest achievements.[18] Yet powerful desires bring the risk of corruption. Just as Greek love could degenerate into the practice of sodomy, medieval courtly love could lead to adultery.[19] Sometimes Symonds sounds a note of terrible caution, as when he warns Benjamin Jowett, master of Balliol College, that it is dangerous to teach Plato's erotic dialogues to undergraduates.[20] Yet he was relentless in his efforts to make public the history of male love.

Symonds could not accept the elitism of ancient ethics. He argued that male desire unmasks not only individual denial and social repression but also conventional forms of inequality. Desires that cross class boundaries might hold the promise of political transformation. Symonds celebrates the "Calamus" section of Whitman's *Leaves of Grass* for its democratic ethic of male comradeship. Writing to Edward Carpenter, the socialist and feminist who lived openly with his male working-class partner, Symonds declares:

> The blending of Social Strata in masculine love seems to me one of its most pronounced, & socially hopeful, features. Where it appears, it abolishes class distinctions, & opens by a single operation the cataract-blinded eye to their futilities. In removing the film of prejudice & education, it acts like

the oculist & knife. If it could be acknowledged & extended, it would do very much to further the advent of the right sort of Socialism.[21]

However, such utopian moments are always situated in ongoing struggles to forge a self and share a common life. Symonds sometimes called the love of men that he shared with so many of his friends *l'amour de l'impossible*. Life in the city exacerbated his sense of himself as divided, torn by conflicting desires and aspirations. Symonds explicitly links inner restlessness and urban possibility in a letter to a friend written shortly before his meeting with the young grenadier: "Today has been wet, and I have had some opportunity of seeing how dreary it is possible for London to look, without sun, without shops, without movement. Within and without have been equally dismal. I begin to think I must be like . . . a greedy and restless animal wh is kept polished and bright to receive all the images that may be reflected on its surface. I vary so painfully with the circumstances in which I am placed." The city's vacillations between brilliance and darkness, mobility and stagnation, provoke an equally diverse inner life: "It makes me of one man a thousand so that I am not I, but a thousand bubbles, reflecting various colours in their perfect spheres and then becoming nought as briefly as they sprang into existence."[22]

Symonds's narratives of his encounters with the young grenadier and the "rude graffito" show how entangled social reality and erotic fantasy may become in an urban setting. For a man of means, a "gentleman of fashion," Victorian London could indeed be a "city of dreadful delight." In 1865, Symonds was not yet ready to act on his desires and follow the soldier. Others were not so timid, or the grenadier would never have approached him in the first place. Twenty-first-century readers may become impatient with his moralizing, but one contemporary wrote to a former boyfriend, praising Symonds's *Life of Michelangelo* as "walking—oh, so nimbly—over the forbidden ground of the friendships with Thomas Cavalieri and others." In 1892, Reginald Brett worried, in a tone that echoes Symonds's own concerns: "I am told that his character has suffered a little of late years by the *audacity* of his *behaviour.* Have you heard anything about him?" (emphasis in original).[23] As "a walker in the city," Symonds observed London's opportunities for erotic adventures and personal transformation. His writings demonstrate some of the ways that men of his time might have understood their desires for other men outside the legal, moral, and religious condemnation of acts of "sodomy." Despite Symonds's progressive aspirations, his use of models of Greek love and democratic comradeship tended to denigrate the potential of love between men and women. Although he saw a political advantage in promoting psychological conceptions of "sexual inversion" as an inherent condition inclining some individuals toward others of their own sex, he refused to see the condition as pathological or degenerate. Equally important, he worked to overcome the implication that erotic desire for men was necessarily feminine; although he introduced Continental sexology to a British audience, he had no sympathy for the view that men who loved men harbored "a woman's soul in a male body." For Symonds, "sexual difference" involved crossing boundaries of age, social class, and nationality. (Eventually he would form long-term erotic friendships with younger Swiss and Italian workingmen.) Such desires reinforced rather than compromised one's masculinity. Some Victorian gentlemen shared his ethos and inclinations, while others understood their same-sex desires quite differently. Symonds's relentless self-observation and social analysis during a life that spans almost the entire period covered by this book offer an important and continuing counterpoint to other voices in the stories that follow.

PART ONE SEX IN THE CITY

1. "MEN IN PETTICOATS"

The presence in London of sites where men looking for sex with other men might congregate was not new in the 1860s. However, this underworld might have become more easily accessible to men such as Symonds who did not set out deliberately in search of it. This enhanced visibility reflected both the proliferation of urban forms of life and the emergence of a heightened consciousness of erotic possibility among middle-class men. Symonds's narrative of his encounters unsettles any easy division between private and public domains: the urban landscape he charts is at once personal fantasy and social reality. Occasionally, the police would interrupt such casual encounters between men in squares, parks, and public lavatories, leading to prosecutions for sodomy, attempted sodomy, or "indecent assault." The visibility of female prostitution had become a subject of increased public concern as the nineteenth century progressed, and young working-class men willing to exchange sexual favors for ready cash were also not hard to find: guardsmen had a special reputation in that regard. Sometimes these episodes became police matters when complaints of assault were countered by allegations of attempts at blackmail.

"Molly Clubs," where men looking for other men gathered, date back to the beginnings of the eighteenth century.[1] Perhaps the most notorious was "Mother Clap's Molly House." The constable who brought charges against it in 1726 testified:

> I found between 40 and 50 Men making Love to one another, as they call'd it. Sometimes they would sit on one another's Laps, kissing in a lewd Manner, and using their Hands indecently. Then they would get up, Dance and make Curtsies, and mimick the voices of Women. . . . Then they'd hug, and play, and toy, and go out by Couples into another Room on the same Floor, to be marry'd, as they call'd it.[2]

There were men dressed as women: "Some were completely rigged in gowns, petticoats, headcloths, fine laced shoes, furbelowed scarves, and masks; some had riding hoods; some were dressed like milkmaids, others like shepherdesses . . . and others had their faces patched and painted and wore very expensive hoop petticoats, which had been very lately introduced."[3] Most often the "marriage" was nothing more than a one-night stand, but there are some reports of longer-term relationships. In 1728, a blacksmith called "Moll Irons" wed a butcher attended by two "bridesmaids": "Princess Seraphina the butcher of Butcher Row and Miss Kitten (alias Mr. Oviat, 'who lately stood in the pillory')."[4] More puzzling are reports that some of the mollies enacted mock childbirths surrounded by their friends.

These clubs had been known to exist since around 1700 and their owners and patrons were intermittently prosecuted by representatives of the Societies for the Reformation of Manners and officials sympathetic to their cause. These trials could have dire consequences: Of those arrested at Mother Clap's establishment, "three men had been hanged at Tyburn, two men and two women had been pilloried, fined and imprisoned, one man had died in prison, one had been acquitted, one had been reprieved, and several had been forced to go into hiding."[5] These cases received considerable publicity in newspapers and pamphlets; public outrage at those arrested sometimes erupted into fatal

Sodom on the Thames

violence. The last such scandal, involving the "Vere Street Coterie" in 1810, led to a near riot when the London crowd went after six men sentenced to the pillory: "The first salute received by the offenders was a volley of mud, and a serenade of hisses, hooting and execration, which compelled them to fall flat on their faces in the caravan. The mob, and particularly the women, had piled up balls of mud to afford the objects of their indignation a warm reception."[6] Whereas earlier, most mollies came from the working class, those caught up in the Vere Street affair represented a broader social mix. Some men of wealth were believed to have bribed their way out of trouble.[7]

By the middle of the century, such scenes were long forgotten. Those Molly Clubs that survived were pretty much left to their own devices. The mollies were content to entertain themselves. Their notoriety resulted from the efforts of reforming moralists, often aided by individuals with grudges to settle, to clean up particular neighborhoods. Something important happened when these figures of flagrant effeminacy and suspect desire emerged from protected enclaves and began walking the streets openly. This "coming out" challenged conventional assumptions about gender and sexuality, domesticity and publicity, commerce and pleasure. *The Yokel's Preceptor,* a London publication of the 1850s, warns visitors to the city of new dangers, thus whetting the appetites of those with unconventional tastes or restless desires:

> The increase of these monsters in the shape of men, commonly designated margeries, poofs, etc., of late years, in the great Metropolis, renders it necessary for the safety of the public that they should be made known. . . . Will the reader credit it, but such is nevertheless the fact, that these monsters actually walk the streets the same as whores, looking out for a chance![8]

The guide identifies parts of the city that offered such sights and opportunities, including the Strand, the Quadrant, Holborn, Charing Cross, Fleet Street, St. Martin's Court. The author mentions individuals who plied their trade in these parts, one of whom, known by a woman's name, kept a "fancy woman" of his own. He paints a vivid portrait of their gathering places, appearance, and distinctive gestures: "They generally congregate around the picture shops, and are to be known by their effeminate air, their fashionable dress. When they see what they imagine to be a chance, they place their fingers in a peculiar manner underneath the tails of their coats, and wag them about—their method of giving the office."[9] It is hard to imagine Symonds responding to such a sign the way he did to the young grenadier or the phallic graffito. The spectacle of Victorian London offered and inspired a variety of erotic possibilities.

The most notorious incident combining gender transgression and same-sex desire is the case of Ernest Boulton and Frederick Park in 1870–1871.[10] Their flagrant appearance on the scene as "Stella" and "Fanny" was discomfiting enough to get them arrested. Boulton and Park, the sons, respectively, of a stockbroker and a judge, were initially charged with offending "public decency" by repeatedly parading about London's West End dressed in women's clothes and followed by groups of young men. Both their respectable social origins and their very public promenades distinguished them from the mollies of earlier times. The case received extensive publicity that revealed how powerfully the "men in petticoats" amused and troubled the imagination. Witnesses claimed to believe they were women, responding to them as especially flagrant—and attractive—female prostitutes.

Agitation about street prostitution in England's cities and concern about the threat of contagion had been marked in the preceding years. The Contagious Diseases Acts of 1864, 1866, and 1869 tried to control the spread of venereal disease among the armed forces by authorizing both police and physicians in selected naval ports and army garrisons to detain women suspected of being "common prostitutes." These women were subjected to intrusive medical examinations and could be confined in hospitals against their will for up to six months. After their release, their health was regularly monitored. If they failed to cooperate, they could be jailed. This intense regulation of young women and the apparent approval of male sexual license generated increasing opposition from moral reformers, early feminists, and political radicals who condemned the disproportionate impact of the acts on the working classes. Public agitation led to the repeal of these provisions in the 1880s. As for London, visitors from abroad frequently commented on the large number of streetwalkers offering their services at the city's center.[11] The display of sexual opportunities in public spaces was seen as a threat to bourgeois domestic virtue, a threat embodied in women whose "painted faces" disguised the contagion they carried.

To these dangers Fanny and Stella added subversion of the "natural" order of sex and gender. At the same time, the two young men appeared in court as scions of the respectable upper middle class, represented by distinguished barristers who claimed they were performers who had allowed their youthful pranks to get out of hand. Prosecution efforts to show that they earned their living as prostitutes were confounded by evidence about their income and class status. Ironically, the attempt to discipline and punish these privileged miscreants became a spectacular performance before an audience greater than any they might have imagined.

The case began with Boulton's and Park's arrest at the Strand Theatre in late April 1870 and culminated in their trial before the Lord Chief Justice and a special jury at the Queen's Bench, Westminster Hall, in May 1871. After an extended hearing in the Bow Street Magistrates Court that attracted crowds of onlookers and extensive press coverage, they were indicted and tried for "conspiracy to commit the felony" of sodomy. It turned out that the authorities had been watching Fanny and Stella for more than a year. After taking the pair into custody as they left the theater in full drag, accompanied by a young swell, police searched their rooms and confiscated a large quantity of women's apparel, jewelry, photographs, and personal letters. The police surgeon subjected the two to intrusive physical examinations analogous to those authorized by the Contagious Diseases Acts for suspected female prostitutes.[12] Their letters revealed the existence of a circle of friends who shared a coded language, played fast and loose with gender norms, and raised suspicions about deviant desires and sexual practices. Police traced two of their correspondents to Edinburgh, where they conducted similar searches leading to the indictment of Louis Hurt and John Safford Fiske. Witnesses were produced who had seen Fanny and Stella in drag at theaters and restaurants, at the annual Oxford-Cambridge boat race on the Thames, and at a fancy dress ball. On several occasions authorities had ejected them from the Burlington Arcade, the Alhambra Theatre, and other public places because of the commotion they created. Boulton and Park generated a pervasive confusion about their gender. Although newspapers proclaimed righteous indignation at their behavior, they could not disguise their fascination with these exotic figures. Hugh Alexander Mundell, the "idle" gentleman and son of a barrister arrested with them, admitted that when first he met them, they wore men's clothes; still, he insisted he had taken them to be women in disguise. When they protested they were men, this young man-about-town simply refused to believe them. Of course, there is no reason to accept the self-serving testimony of an admirer—given under the threat of legal prosecution. Fanny's and Stella's ambiguous displays of feminine and masculine characteristics may have been among their principal charms.

The public attention paid to the case of Boulton and Park suggests that the appearance of men in women's clothes around the West End was still a novelty. Cross-dressing was not established in the public mind as an indication of same-sex sexual desire. When he charged the defendants with "conspiracy to commit the felony" of sodomy in addition to the less serious "offense against public decency," the prosecutor undertook to establish that link. Sodomy had been defined as a capital crime by the Buggery Act of Henry VIII in 1633 and remained one until 1861, when the penalty was reduced to life imprisonment. (No executions for sodomy are reported after 1836.)[13] Judges had defined the "sin not to be named among Christians" as anal intercourse, regardless of the sex (or species) of the partner, and required proof of penetration. As both active and passive partners were equally guilty, this evidence was not easy to find. The more frequent charges were "attempted sodomy" and "indecent assault."[14] Until the 1830s, men convicted of these crimes could be exposed in the "pillory" where, as in the Vere Street case, angry crowds might vent their outrage by hurling garbage and offal at them. Some were permanently injured or mutilated by these expressions of community morality.[15] Against this background, the decision to charge Fanny and Stella with felonies seriously raised the stakes, mobilizing family and friends in support of the accused men. It also heightened public interest in the story.

The way of life and intimate relations of Boulton, Park, and their friends were subject to intense and protracted scrutiny and were reported in extensive detail in the major newspapers under headlines such as "Men in Petticoats," "The Gentlemen Personating Women," or "The Young Men in Women's Attire." More extravagantly, others announced "The 'Gentlemen-Women' Case" or "The 'Men-Women' at Bow Street." The illustrated papers included vivid portraits of the two, both in and out of drag. (At the time of their trial, they appeared as well-dressed young men-about-town: Fanny had even grown whiskers, and Stella a faint mustache.) Public appetite for scandal in high places was whetted by claims that Stella had lived as the "wife" of an aristocratic young member of Parliament, carrying visiting cards that announced her as "Lady Arthur Clinton."

The case was vigorously contested; the defendants were represented by leading barristers of the day. They offered evidence that Boulton and Park were actors who took women's roles in both amateur and professional theatricals. The well-financed defense team called eminent professors of medicine to testify to the innocence of the men's bodily condition and to challenge "expert" testimony on the effects of repeated acts of sodomy. The uncertainty regarding the significance of Fanny's and Stella's female impersonations permitted even the most sober accounts to dwell on their appearance, capitalizing on the fascination displayed by the crowds who flocked to the Bow Street Magistrates' Court to see them. Police reports came to resemble society and fashion pages. Here is the usually somber *Times* on their first appearance in court: "When placed in the dock, Boulton wore a cherry-coloured evening dress trimmed with white lace; his arms were bare, and he had on bracelets. He wore a wig and a plaited chignon. Park's costume consisted of a dark green

Sodom on the Thames

satin dress, low-necked, trimmed in black lace, of which he also had a shawl around his shoulders. His hair was flaxened and in curls. He had on a pair of white kid gloves."[16] The *Daily Telegraph* reported a different look at their second hearing:

> On the last occasion, the prisoners Boulton and Park appeared in the dock in the evening dress which they wore at the theatre and considerable surprise was manifested at the successful "make-up." Yesterday they were attired in male dress. Both the prisoners had on fashionably-cut frockcoats and turn-down collars, the latter giving them a very youthful appearance. Boulton wore a sailor's scarf neck-tie and Park one which covered the front of the shirt. Their hair was roughly cut and therefore, rather altered the effeminate look they presented when possessing a more complete toilette than that which they were able to make at the House of Detention. Neither wore gloves.[17]

Not all of their audience appreciated the change in costume: "The Bow-street Police-court and its approaches were literally besieged by the public. . . . The prisoners appeared in male apparel on this occasion, much to the disappointment of the crowds assembled to see them." The *Times* offered a moral gloss, recalling earlier public disapproval: "The case excited unusual interest, probably owing to the notoriety acquired by certain young men who, for years past have been in the habit of visiting places of public resort in feminine attire, and who have been occasionally turned out or compelled to retire to avoid the consequences of the public indignation excited by their presence when detected."[18]

Public opinion was more ambivalent than the *Times* allowed. The popularity of the court proceedings gives the game away: a week later, "There was the usual rabble outside but ample provision had been made . . . to prevent the inconvenient crowding of the court. Nevertheless, the small area of the building was quite full, the audience including many persons of rank, besides many literary and theatrical celebrities."[19] The next week, the courtroom was again filled to capacity with crowds outside in the street: "Boulton and Park . . . appeared to be as cool and collected as on each former occasion, although looking somewhat the worse for their three weeks confinement in prison."[20] As more details emerged about the lives of the defendants and their friends, some in the audience gave voice to their enjoyment: "During the reading of the letters the audience in the body of the court appeared to be exceedingly amused, and the prisoners themselves smiled occasionally. Certain expressions of endearment addressed by one man to another, caused such an outburst of laughter that Mr. Poland [the prosecutor] begged that such unseemly demonstrations might be checked . . . but neither the admonition of the Bench nor the repeated remonstrance of . . . officers of the Court had any appreciable effect upon a certain portion of the public."[21] Remember that the "rabble" had been kept outside: this "portion" might have included "celebrities" and "persons of rank." In trying to stop Fanny's and Stella's public performances by arresting them, the authorities got more than they bargained for.

For over a month in the spring of 1870, the Bow Street Magistrates' Court offered one of London's most beguiling entertainments. The newspaper accounts, and those in the penny pamphlets that began to circulate, relied heavily on the details of court testimony. Each week brought new revelations to fuel speculation and fill the columns of the papers. Only the medical evidence was suppressed or seriously abbreviated in most reports. The final judgment of Boulton and Park would be deferred for a year until the trial at Queen's Bench, Westminster. The climax would be compressed into a week and a day of daily proceedings, but public interest would remain intense. These proceedings provide a treasure trove of material from which to reconstruct some Victorian "tales of the city."[22] The spectacle of Boulton's and Park's arrest and the drama within the courtroom reveal a social context of informal, sometimes intimate associations. The stories of the lives and loves of Stella, Fanny, and their friends range from romantic comedy to urbane satire to domestic drama bordering on tragedy. The episode cries out for theatrical treatment. Criminal trials are inherently dramatic in the procession of witnesses, the conflicting arguments of prosecution and defense counsel, and the ultimate resolution in the jury's verdict and judge's sentence if the accused is found guilty. The queer case of Mr. Boulton and Mr. Park unfolds in two acts, opening with protracted hearings at Bow Street in May–June 1870 and concluding with the full trial in May 1871. In the interval between the two, the press debated the meaning of the "extraordinary revelations" while both prosecution and defense weighed and revised their strategies. The legal rituals of testimony, cross-examination, and argument frame a series of fragmentary, overlapping, and competing disclosures. We glimpse the lives of the accused, their families, and their friends; witnesses for both sides; and the police and their agents as well.

2. "STELLA, STAR OF THE STRAND"

The hapless Mr. Mundell, arrested with Boulton and Park at the Strand Theatre, eventually appeared as a leading witness for the prosecution. He de-

Sodom on the Thames

1. "Stella, Star of the Strand," Ernest Boulton (1868)

scribes a distinctively urban scene while offering a closer look at the charms of Stella and Fanny. The former quite captured his interest:

> I knew the prisoner Boulton by the name of "Stella," no other name till I was in the Surrey Theatre. I made his acquaintance on the 22nd of April at that theatre, the two prisoners were there together in the dress circle. . . . I went there alone. I was principally in the stalls, my attention called to them, as being two women dressed in men's clothes, and I believed them to be women. They went together to an adjoining public house. I followed them, and they afterwards went back to their seats. . . . I followed them again. They said, I think you're following us. That was said in a joking manner. I said I think we are. They said nothing but returned to the dress circle, where they stood looking over. We got into conversation, after which I asked them if they would like to go behind the scenes.[23]

The play itself was eclipsed by the flirtatious socializing characteristic of the Victorian theater. Fanny and Stella in their balcony box became part of the show for Mundell in the orchestra seats below. The threesome entertained themselves so well during and after the intermissions that they made a date to return together to see what they had missed of the show. Mundell accompanied the pair across Waterloo Bridge: "As we were walking, I chaffed them, thinking they were women dressed in men's clothes, I told them, when they walked they had better swing their arms about a little more. We parted at the Strand end of Waterloo Bridge, they going toward the City. I went home."[24] They met again at the theater where, this time dressed in women's clothes, they handed him a letter: "The handwriting appeared to me like a woman's, the substance of the letter was that they were men, and I told them I did not believe it. They said it was quite true, we are men. I believed that they had written the letter as a joke." Joined by another man, the foursome went back to finish the play, then off to supper at the Globe Restaurant. Briefly alone with the object of his affection, Mundell sought an advantage: "I treated them as ladies. Stella/Boulton/ keeping me off whenever I made any advances. I put my arm around her back once, sure would have gone on, but the strange gentleman returned to the box, which prevented me. Boulton kept me off as much as he could."[25] The dance of proper names and pronouns underlines the witness's uncertainty about how to refer to his companions once police had disclosed their sex.

Mundell's flirtation with Stella culminated in the trip to the Strand Theatre. Earlier he had joined the pair at Park's rooms for a musical soiree. There he found them in men's clothes once again; his hosts played the piano and

Sodom on the Thames

talked about their theatrical performances. They agreed to go to the theater that evening, where Park had reserved a box for "Mrs. Graham." In the interim, the threesome visited friends in Chancery Lane, after which they all went shopping. Mundell insisted he had paid for nothing: "Nor did I give money to either of the prisoners." For the theater, his companions dressed as women: "I saw Park's dress was torn when in the box, a few stitches in the flounce. . . . There was nothing wrong in the box at the Strand, they behaved themselves as ladies."[26] Although hearing from another man that the pair were male, Mundell continued to resist: "I said, I had my doubts very much about one, but I was certain Boulton was a woman, and I was never taken in so in my life." Mundell avoided prosecution as a party to the conspiracy to commit sodomy, but he admitted that he had assumed Fanny and Stella were female prostitutes. Was that all there was to it? By his own account, he believed them to be cross-dressers, women disguised as men. Did he enjoy the ambiguities of their gender? Was his refusal to accept their disclosures a way of protecting himself while continuing to flirt with pleasure and danger? We cannot know, since his pursuit of Stella ended with the arrest of all three of them. In that denouement, Mundell portrayed himself as a perfect gentleman, oblivious to his own position, concerned only to assist the damsels in distress:

> One of the policemen at the theatre told me that he did not want the men, and that I might go off. I said I had done nothing wrong, but I did not like to leave them, as I had been with them all day, and I thought I could help them to get bail. I found myself in a cab on the way to Bow-street. I don't know how it was. (Laughter.)[27]

The arresting officers had their own versions of the episode. Police Superintendent James Jacob Thompson testified that he had arrived at the Strand at about ten o'clock that night, where he saw the prisoners in a private box dressed as women: "Boulton was pointed out to me as supposed to be the Duchess of Manchester."[28] (One historian describes the "real" duchess as "one of the great beauties of her time, [who] at receptions and balls . . . dazzled people by her stature, her clothes, and her gems.")[29] Officer William Chamberlain, who had followed Fanny and Stella to the theater from their rooms at 13 Wakefield Street, testified that "Park . . . went into the Ladies room and asked a female there to pin up a portion of the dress he was wearing which had come undone. The female did so, and Park gave her something for her trouble."[30] Eventually the attendant herself would be called to corroborate this violation, news of which created quite a stir in the newspapers. According to Chamberlain, "The prisoners last night told me they were men and were sorry for what they had done."[31] When another officer was asked whether they had said they were sorry, he could not recall, but said he doubted it, as the prisoners had appeared "very brave." Officer Frederick Kelly, who accompanied Boulton, Park, and Mundell in the van, gave a somewhat different picture of their attitude after the arrest. He testified that Park had said to him: "Look here, old fellow, it will do you no good to take us to the station, and if you will let us go, we will give you anything you may want." To which Boulton added: "Anything you require you may have. Only let us go." The stalwart Kelly was not deterred from his duty: "I said I would do nothing of the sort and took them to the station."[32] Mundell's doubts about his companions would be resolved, not by a "joking" note or sexual liaison, but by a police surgeon who attested in court to Boulton's and Park's biological sex and to other anatomical details that most papers chose not to print.

The police had Stella and Fanny under surveillance for over a year. Their observations were augmented by reports from theater managers and security personnel. After the arrest, many witnesses came forward with additional tales of the pair's promenades about the town; others, including former landladies and their servants, offered more domestic details of their lives. Some came forward with material evidence such as clothes, photographs, and letters. Among the first to testify were: the staff superintendent of the Alhambra Theatre; the former beadle of the Burlington Arcade; the coachman who had driven Fanny and Stella to the Oxford-Cambridge boat race; and the proprietor of the hotel where they had attended a fancy dress ball as well as two of the female guests. Reporters for the *Daily Telegraph*—perhaps with some help from the defense—quickly ferreted out the history of Boulton's and Park's careers as theatrical performers, noting that they "seem in their time to have acted many parts." A long article detailed their appearances in "drawing room entertainments" around southern England in 1869: at Romford, "they played under the distinguished patronage of Sir Thomas Barrett Lennard, Bart. and Lady Lennard." The piece described the programs in which the pair appeared and even quoted from reviews. Once, Boulton was listed as "Miss Ernestine Edwards" and Park as "Miss Mabel Foley"; more often, the two were identified by their own names. One critic found Boulton "very clever" in impersonating a woman: "It is very difficult for a spectator to realize he is a make up for the occasion. His song 'Fading Away' is exceedingly feminine." Another insisted, "There is nothing of the 'social monster' business connected with him," while praising his "natural gifts": "Looking at him with one's eyes

2. "A Lady in Disguise?" Ernest Boulton in male attire (1868)

both wide open, listening to his extraordinary voice, and criticizing however narrowly his wonderfully feminine manner and appearance, it is really very difficult for a moment to believe that he is not a really charming girl." Boulton's voice, "an imitation mezzo-soprano," consistently drew praise, receiving "thundering plaudits" and demands for encores. The paper noted that he had made his debut as Maria in "The Brigand" at the age of fourteen. Park's career was modest by comparison. Although Boulton's scheduled performance as Mrs. Chillington in "A Morning Call" once had to be postponed because he was ill, he eventually appeared opposite Lord Arthur Clinton as Sir Edward Ardent.

Even when not actually onstage, Fanny and Stella found theaters congenial settings for their performances. John Reeves from the Alhambra Theatre testified that he had seen them many times for over two years. Their first meeting ended with his throwing them out:

> My attention was first drawn to them two years ago when they were dressed as women. They were there together. I went to them and desired them to leave, as the public believed they were dressed as women. A person who was in their company and who I had often seen before, told me not to interfere, it was a mistake. I said it's no mistake with me. I believe they are men dressed as women and they'll have to leave. I called assistance then and we marched them out of the place and their friends followed them.[33]

Reeves reported that the pair had been "walking about as women looking over their shoulders as if enticing men." When they left, three or four men followed them. A few months later, they returned to a less friendly welcome. Reeves found them surrounded by a hostile group: "They were creating a disturbance, and persons believed them to be men."[34] Later they varied their theatergoing costume. They appeared dressed as men, but with their faces and necks painted and powdered: " Their shirt collars [were] much lower than they are now, their waistcoats were very open. They looked at people as they passed, and their manners were more feminine than masculine."[35] They did not behave like proper ladies: "I had heard them make noises with their lips, the same that I have heard made by females when passing gentlemen on the street."[36] The general impression was of streetwalkers, but with a difference: "I could not tell whether they were men or women. Sometimes I thought they were women, sometimes I thought they were men. Whenever I have seen them, their faces have been painted."[37] Once, they had taken a private box: "I saw people looking up at the boxes they were in, and saw that they were playing all sorts of frivolous games with each other. They were looking in front of the box, handing cigarettes backwards and forwards to each other and lighting them by gaslight."[38] When Reeves asked them to leave, they offered him a brandy and soda. He not only refused their offer but also saw that the guinea they had paid for the box was returned. Reeves had seen Boulton and Park at the Alhambra more than twenty times, but only twice in women's

Sodom on the Thames

clothes. He had also observed them on Regent Street, dressed as men with their faces painted.

Regent Street is not far from the Burlington Arcade on Piccadilly. One historian describes the stores in this early shopping mall as "dedicated to an aristocratic and upper-middle-class market. . . . Typically [they] remained quite small, rarely advertised, and spent little effort on window display."[39] Maintaining a select milieu required a private security staff working with police to exclude undesirable elements. This was not so easy to do, as George Smith, formerly the beadle in the Burlington Arcade, revealed. Testifying about his encounters with Boulton and Park, he admitted he had been fired for routinely accepting payment from female prostitutes to allow them to walk freely within the sanctuary. Smith, a former policeman, defended his conduct as good for business. He insisted that the shop owners themselves knew that "gay ladies" were among their best customers and adamantly denied that he later ejected women from whom he had accepted payment.[40] However, *Reynolds's* reported that Smith was "severely cross-examined" and "frequently rebuked for his flippancy." He acknowledged that he had volunteered to give evidence and "expected to be paid for his trouble." Conceding that he had accepted drinks from "the gay women who frequented the place," Smith asserted that "many of them he considered very respectable."[41] Fanny and Stella were another matter entirely:

> I went up to Boulton and said, "I have received several complaints about you. . . . I have seen enough of your conduct to consider you to be an improper person to be in the Arcade, you must leave at once. . . . Boulton said [to his companion and alleged coconspirator Cumming] "Take no notice of that fellow" in a feminine manner. . . . I forcibly took hold of Boulton and ejected him at the Piccadilly end. Cumming followed us down to the end of the Arcade and said something. I took hold of him saying, "You are as bad as the other. You leave the Arcade at once," and I put him out on to the pavement. There were a good many gentlemen present at the time and some of them hissed Boulton and Cumming. . . . I saw the prisoners Boulton and Cumming about a fortnight after this coming down the Arcade towards Piccadilly. I was in uniform and they saw me, and I went towards them. On seeing me, they directly rushed into a hosier's shop. . . . I stood at the door till they came out. I said to Boulton "I have cautioned you not to come here, you'll leave the Arcade at once." He said, "I shall go where I like." I replied, "You'll do nothing of the sort, you'll go out." He tried to pass me to go up the Arcade, and I again ejected him.[42]

What was the fuss about? Smith offered this account: "I noticed his face. It was painted very thickly with rouge and everything else on. He always caused such commotion, everybody was looking at him. I watched them and saw Boulton turn his head to two gentlemen who passed them, smile at them, and make a noise with his lips, the same as a woman would for inducement."[43] The crowning moment occurred when Boulton addressed the beadle as "Oh, you sweet little dear": "I made a note of that. It was about January or February 1869, when Boulton looked at the two gentlemen."[44] *Reynolds's* reported an outbreak of laughter in the courtroom at this point. (Today we might imagine Boulton thinking of himself as a street performer or queer activist.) In his testimony, Smith refused to answer questions about his current means of support. His acceptance of money from female prostitutes raised the suspicion that he had excluded Boulton, Park, and Cumming from the Arcade because they had tried to resist or charm him rather than offer a bribe.

London offered many opportunities for Fanny and Stella to show themselves off. In addition to theaters and shopping arcades, there were public festivities and private parties. The Oxford-Cambridge boat race gave them a chance to go out for a riverside picnic and to attend a fancy dress ball at a hotel in the Strand. Boulton and Park had hired a coach to take them to Hammersmith Bridge. By the time they got there, it was too crowded to get onto the bridge, so they had watched the race in the crowd along the bank. Henry Holland, who had driven the coach, patiently ferried a changing roster of holidaymakers around the city before and after the race. Park had appeared first as "Mrs. Parker," reporting that "her sister" was not yet ready. So off they had gone to get a hamper of food, stopping at a few public houses along the way. They had returned to collect Boulton later. After the race, they visited several more pubs and a pastry shop. Fanny and Stella generously provided food and drink for their driver. The arrangement worked so well that Holland was hired again later in the month. This time he had been told his employer was "Mrs. Graham"; he took the pair and their friends (including Mundell) to the Surrey Theatre and afterward to dinner at the Globe Restaurant. Holland claimed he had no idea that Boulton and Park were men, as they had always dressed as women. As for all those stops along the way, he stated that "they appeared sober when they went into the different public houses." Afterward the driver dropped Fanny and Stella at the Royal Exeter Hotel in the Strand, where Park discharged him. A gentleman called Amos Westrop Gibbings invited them to be his guests at the hotel and to attend a ball there the next evening.

Sodom on the Thames

Rumors had circulated from the beginning of the case that Fanny and Stella were part of a larger clique of cross-dressers: "It is more than suspected that there are others besides those in custody who have for some time past been engaged in personating females in London. In fact, it is stated that an association exists which numbers nearly thirty of these foolish if not unnatural young men, and that recently a ball was given at a well-known hotel in the Strand at which twelve of the party represented females and twelve of their companions the opposite sex."[45] Edward Nelson Haxell, landlord of the Royal Exeter Hotel (also known as Haxell's), testified that he had met the defendants when they appeared in early April as guests of Mr. Gibbings, "a gentleman of independent fortune" and "a very old customer" of his (Despite this accolade, Gibbings had only recently turned twenty-one.) He had paid for Boulton's room, which was on a separate floor from his own, introducing Stella to the proprietor as "the best amateur actress off the boards" who had come from Edinburgh especially for "a musical party." Although Haxell had seen him three or four times in women's clothes, Boulton was wearing men's clothes when he arrived. The proprietor had always known him to be a man. Gibbings and his friends had often gone out in a hired coach—Boulton and his host in women's attire, a Mr. Somerville "dressed always as a gentleman," and Park "sometimes as a lady, sometimes as a gentleman." Mr. Thomas, also "a gentleman of independent fortune," generally arrived in his own carriage dressed in women's clothes for an evening out with the others. On the day after the boat race, "there was an evening party with music at my own house." (At this point, the magistrate commented: "It strikes me that the evidence of this witness is as important as any that has been given." Boulton's attorney added without contradiction: "Yes, sir; in the interest of the defendants.")

The ball had been planned weeks in advance: "He wrote me and said he was coming up for a week's frolic. He is a most accomplished musician, and frequently gave musical parties. He afterwards said that, instead of having a musical party he thought he would make it a little fancy dress affair, and said, 'We shall come in drag,' which means men wearing women's costumes."[46] Here the magistrate interjected: "This is the first time the meaning of the word 'drag' has been given in evidence?" (*The Oxford English Dictionary* records the account of these proceedings in *Reynolds's* as the first usage of the word in this sense.)[47] The hotelier had sent invitations to twenty-five people, but forty-eight turned up. The party began at 9:30 p.m. and lasted until 3:30

3. *"Fanny," Frederick Park (1868)*

a.m., with supper "as nearly as possible at twelve o'clock." Gibbings paid for everything, including his guests' stay at the hotel. Boulton, Park, Cumming, Thomas, and Gibbings himself came in drag. Haxell mentioned one other man in women's clothes: when close questioning revealed he was named Peel, "in fact, I think he is connected to family of Peel," there was a "sensation" in the courtroom. All told, there had been thirteen at the ball dressed in women's clothes. Haxell believed seven of them were female: "Three were introduced to me, one young lady was with her father." The magistrate interrupted: "There was one old gentleman then?" To which the witness replied: "Yes, and only one." Although those in drag danced with other men dressed as gentlemen, everyone there knew of the impersonation: "I heard the observation round the room, How well the young fellows were acting! There was plenty of funning, but nothing coarse or improper." Haxell insisted on his authority as proprietor: "There was not the slightest impropriety. If there had been, I should have turned them all out."

Stella performed to great acclaim: "I heard Boulton sing, if I may say so, very charmingly. He sang 'Fading Away' three or four times with great éclat. I heard it said Boulton's was the most perfect female voice. I told the leader of the band it was Ernest Boulton, he said, 'It must be a lady.'" Haxell was familiar with Stella's career: "I had heard of him before, and spoken of as playing ladies' parts in good society. I believe I have seen some notices of his acting at Scarborough." (When the papers reported Haxell's mention that Boulton had played St. George's Hall, Langham-place, the owner wrote immediately to deny that any impropriety had occurred there.) Haxell had once warned Gibbings that he might get into trouble for parading in drag. However, he insisted that nothing sinister was afoot: "I was much surprised when I heard of this charge being made against them; and am now; but until convicted, I shall never believe it."[48] The only thing amiss at the ball was a dispute late in the evening about the entertainment: "Mr. Gibbings wanted to carry out the programme intact, but some gentlemen wanted more dancing and less singing, but Mr. Gibbings would not have it. So I said. 'Don't you think we had better wind up and clear out?' and he wound up and cleared out. (Laughter.)"[49] Haxell swore "on his oath" that "every gentleman at the ball knew that the young men in female attire were really men." At this point, the *Times* reported, "There was a most indecent manifestation of applause expressed by stomping and cheering, which the court had to reprimand."[50] The defense lawyer seemed to have been right in his judgment that the landlord's testimony could only help his case. The prosecution also called two women who had attended the fancy dress ball. Maria Cavendish more or less confirmed Haxell's account of the event. One newspaper described her as "a dashingly handsome woman attired in rich black."[51] She might even have given those in drag a run for their money. Her unprepossessing companion Agnes Earl seemed more confused about the whole thing, protesting in court that she wished never again to attend such a party.

Amos Westrop Gibbings himself came forward the following week to dispel any implication that his drag ball had been other than good clean fun. The young man created quite a stir when he appeared at Bow Street: "Some little amusement was caused by the very effeminate appearance he presented and the slightly affected manner in which he gave his evidence."[52] He calmly announced that he had often performed female parts in theatricals, usually for charity, enumerating his roles, including Lady Teazle in Sheridan's "The School for Scandal." Having seen Boulton perform at the Egyptian Hall (with Lord Arthur Clinton as the male lead), Gibbings invited him to be his special guest at the Royal Exeter Hotel. Before the ball, Gibbings had enjoyed supper with Boulton and Park, all three dressed as ladies. The party had turned out a grander affair than he had envisioned:

> It was to have been a very small party but it swelled to 45. There were many gentlemen but only myself, the two prisoners, Thomas, Cumming, and Peel were dressed as females. Several ladies were there, eight ladies. There was no impropriety that I saw in the room the whole night. There was no concealment as to the gentlemen who were dressed as ladies. . . . The servants and attendants knew all about it. The servants came to see us when we were dressed in the ball room.[53]

"Great laughter" greeted Gibbings's announcement that "in case of any insinuations I invited several *real* ladies"[54] (Perhaps some in the audience recalled the "dashingly handsome" Maria Cavendish from the previous week.) Gibbings admitted that "there was a squabble towards the end of the evening and I shut up everything."[55] Still it had been a social success for the host and his entourage: "We who were dressed as women at the Ball, danced with men. The prisoners also danced with men. . . . Nearly all the gentlemen who were at the ball called on the following afternoon."[56]

Gibbings almost stole the show from Fanny and Stella, who were not permitted under the law at the time to testify on their own behalf. He was quite forthcoming about his cross-dressing: "I went to several theatres during the week. I can't remember to which I went in female attire. Boulton went with me twice to Highbury Barn, a Bal Masqué, dressed as a man." Although manifestly unconventional in his style of life, the young man carefully drew his own lines of propriety: "I have gone about dressed as a woman in the day time in a carriage not more than three times. . . . On one occasion I was in a carriage which broke down in the Haymarket, and I was then compelled to walk down half the street, much against my will."[57] Since Haymarket was a notorious center of female prostitution, Gibbings was eager not to be mistaken for one of the "gay ladies": "I never went out in women's dress with the in-

Sodom on the Thames

tention of walking the streets. (Applause.)"[58] Unaware that Haxell had already initiated the court, he explained: "Going about in drag is a slang term for men going about in women's clothes."[59] Young Gibbings must have possessed commanding self-assurance, with the prerogatives of class redeeming his unorthodox dress and demeanor. His aristocratic bearing impressed audience, court, and reporter alike:

> His appearance in the witness box was regarded with intense curiosity and created quite a sensation in court. The young man stepped into the witness-box without any sign of diffidence, and gave his evidence with remarkable clearness and self-possession. His voice and manner were decidedly effeminate. He spoke in a slight lisp and with an air of simplicity and candour which impressed the court materially in his favour. He appeared to regard the modern pastime of "going about in drag" as perfectly harmless and repudiated with indignation the notion that he was being made the dupe of others, or that he was in any way implicated in the nefarious actions sought to be established by the prosecution.[60]

When Gibbings mentioned that he had returned from Calais to testify as soon as he heard of his friends' arrest, the magistrate Mr. Flowers commended him: "He had done quite right in stopping by those whom he believed to be suspected, and he had given his evidence very well."[61]

The proceedings at Bow Street focused the big city's bright lights on Fanny and Stella. There were sessions at least once a week for five weeks, with crowds in attendance and many column inches of newspaper coverage, reporting the proceedings as something of a spectacle. However discouraged they must have been by their arrest and incarceration, Boulton and Park flourished at center stage:

> [They] stepped lightly into the dock, and leant forward upon the rail for some time. The prisoners were both well-dressed. Boulton wears a dark cut-away coat, light trousers and dark tie. Park is not perhaps so smartly dressed. He has a dark coat also, dark trousers, and patent leather boots. The clothes of both have evidently been made by a fashionable tailor. The prisoners, especially Park, frequently communicated in notes written in pencil with their solicitor, Mr. Abrams.[62]

Park's note-taking is a reminder that in addition to playing supporting roles beside Stella on the boards, he had been a law student articled to a firm of solicitors. As criminal defendant in a celebrated case, he was able to combine his legal and acting skills. Not that the two are so easily separated: in the dock,

MEN IN PETTICOATS.

PRICE ONE PENNY.
Office : 5, Houghton Street, Strand.

4. The Ball at Haxell's Hotel. "Men in Petticoats" (1870)

he played the role of serious young professional. The prisoners, their lawyers, and the magistrate were not the only actors in this courtroom drama. The press assessed the audience as well:

> There was the same eagerness on the part of the public—not the public of Seven Dials but the fashionable public—to secure seats or standing room in the court to gaze on the prisoners and hear the filthy details related by the witnesses. Although the gratification of this peculiar taste involved the necessity of standing for five hours, and enduring an amount of suffering from the oppressive atmosphere which few persons care to undergo except on the rarest occasions, not one of the "distinguished visitors" showed the slightest disposition to leave or give up their places to any of the disappointed crowd outside; and at least one of them—a noble lord—surveyed the prisoners during the greater part of Friday through an opera glass. But perhaps the most notable, not to say the least creditable, feature of the whole affair was the unblushing freedom with which the privileged auditors manifested their sentiments, and especially their sympathy with, any revelations that appeared to tell in favour of the defendants. Their inclinations to "laugh" at disclosures which filled several people with disgust was repeatedly checked by officials of the court.[63]

Even the most censorious accounts needed public attention for their sermonizing, further advertising the show at the magistrate's court. Then as now, sex scandals sell papers. As the proceedings continued, one report noted: "The approaches to the court were, as on former occasions, thronged by an eager crowd, who sought to obtain admission, and it required a strong force of police to keep the way clear for persons engaged in business. The inside of the court was occupied by a large number of persons, including several actors."[64] The ambivalent response to the widespread coverage caused alarm among the more vigilant protectors of public morals. The source of their concern becomes apparent from this description in the *Times:* "A large portion of the crowd outside the Court cheered the prisoners as they were stepping into the van, while others booed and hissed at them. Boulton took off his hat, and both the prisoners bowed to the mob in return."[65] Fanny and Stella proved adept at playing to the crowds they attracted. Penny pamphlets, often simply reproducing stories from the newspapers, were rushed into print even before the preliminary proceedings had ended. One of them, with a picture on the cover of Fanny and Stella undressing at the police station, was entitled "The Lives of Boulton and Park. Extraordinary Revelations." The first page features yet another title (my favorite): "Stella, Star of the Strand."

The day after arresting Boulton, Park, and Mundell, the police returned to search the premises at 13 Wakefield Street, where Fanny and Stella had prepared for their evening at the theater. They confiscated photographs, personal correspondence, and a large quantity of women's clothes, which became material evidence and figured importantly in press accounts. The police followed incriminating letters all the way to Edinburgh, where they searched the lodgings of Louis Hurt, a surveyor with the post office, seizing his letters and photographs. They interrogated John Safford Fiske, the United States consul at Leith, going through his apartment until they found photographs and letters in a hatbox. They had refused to leave when he asked them, persuading him to hand over an album of additional photographs hidden in his fireplace. Fiske confessed that these pictures of Boulton in a variety of guises were "his weakness" and that he had written "foolish" notes. He insisted that he had "meant no harm" by them.[66] Eventually both Hurt and Fiske would be indicted as parties to the sodomitical conspiracy. The photos bolstered witnesses' accounts of Fanny's and Stella's appearances in drag. In the absence of any firsthand evidence, the letters would prove central to the prosecution's claim that the pair "solicited" others to join them in prohibited sexual practices. While the press applauded the diligence of the investigating officers, the Lord Chief Justice would eventually criticize the trip to Edinburgh (and the indictment of Hurt and Fiske) as an unauthorized excess of zeal.

Martha Stacey had rented rooms at 13 Wakefield Street to Boulton, Park, and various friends over a period of more than two years. They used the rooms primarily to prepare for their evenings out, rarely staying overnight: "They arrived dressed as men and left dressed as women."[67] Other lodgers knew of their cross-dressing and believed they were amateur actors. In a tactic they would use frequently, the prosecution closely questioned the landlady about the men's sleeping arrangements. She testified that each suite comprised a sitting room and a bedroom with a single bed. They had slept two to a bed. However, Boulton and Park had specifically requested two bedrooms, but she did not have them available. Mrs. Stacey repeatedly denied she had ever witnessed any impropriety and insisted that they had behaved like ordinary gentlemen, except for going out dressed as women. During April, Gibbings and Cumming had also stayed at the house. In fact, these two had broken open the apartment to retrieve the prisoners' masculine clothing and some jewelry after the police's initial search. An officer had testified that some items were removed between his first and second visits. Confronted with these allegations,

Gibbings responded with characteristic vigor: he paid for the rooms and had every right to take what belonged to him and his friends. He insisted that "the dresses we went about in were originally made for the stage." Gibbings vehemently denied any implication of ulterior motives:

I never had any other than an acting notion in putting on women's clothes. I could not entertain any other notion. I know that Mr. Cumming acted at Oxford female parts in the comedies. I have heard of him as a good actor. There were no insinuations against him or Thomas. If there had been they would not have been friends of mine. There has never been any insinuation of immorality against my character. I defy anyone to prove it. I certainly have not been engaged in any "horrible conspiracy."[68]

Questioned about money, Gibbings said he had offered to share expenses for the dressing rooms. With an eye to the soliciting charge, the prosecution tried to portray Stella as financially dependent on her acquaintances, but Gibbings would have none of it: "I have no knowledge of Boulton's means. He wished to pay when he stayed with me, but I would not let him."[69] In the end, Gibbings's immense self-assurance would carry the day: no charges were brought against him. However, he could not immunize his friends; Cumming and Thomas would be indicted as coconspirators. So too would William Somerville, whose only offense had been to accompany the drag belles to the ball in gentleman's clothes and to write mash notes to Stella.

The newspapers inventoried the confiscated paraphernalia in almost loving detail:

Amongst other things found were a silver-mounted gentleman's dressing-case, an elegantly fitted photograph album, bearing the initials of the prisoner Boulton, filled with portraits of young men, and a large wardrobe of female attire. There were between thirty and forty rich silk and other dresses, all of fashionable patterns and some elaborately trimmed with lace, furs, &c, a large ermine cloak, well stocked boxes containing ladies' gloves, more than a score of different wigs and head dresses, chiefly of the prevailing golden hue, some of them having plaited hair fall from twenty to thirty inches in length attached, a great number of girls' hats variously trimmed, ladies' white kid boots, Balmoral walking boots, richly embroidered, a large quantity of bizarre jewelry with some bracelets and necklaces of a better class, caps, feathers, &c.[70]

The *Daily Telegraph* reported frequent outbursts of laughter as the prosecutor read the list of items that had been seized.[71] From the outset, these items of very conspicuous consumption were linked to other indications of the young men's class status: "The cartes de visite found in Boulton's album were chiefly those of young men of apparent good breeding. In one group Boulton is found resting his hand upon the shoulder of a gentleman formerly remarkable in London for his love of fire-engines and in another both Boulton and Park make up a picture of which Lord Arthur Pelham Clinton forms the center" (see figure 5, below).[72] Their high-flying style of life may have been as fascinating to readers as the accusations of sexual impropriety: "The habits of these young men were not economical. It is known that within a few days they have filled private boxes at the Standard Theatre and the Surrey Theatre. Whilst being denuded of their feminine habiliments at the House of Detention, the voucher for a pit box at the Royal Italian Opera, Covent-garden, dropped from the folds of Boulton's elaborate costume."[73]

Not all the witnesses who came forward were motivated by public-spiritedness or moral outrage. Some had scores of their own to settle. Anne Empson, who had briefly rented rooms to Lord Arthur Clinton, recounted her suspicions about his living arrangements. More damagingly, she produced a cache of letters, photographs, and women's clothes, which she had seized as security for money owed her. Claiming that Clinton had failed to pay rent or to return money he had borrowed, the landlady displayed such obvious hostility that the newspapers commented on it. *Reynolds's* described her as "a lady of determined appearance, who eyed the prisoners with no friendly aspect." Although the letters she had confiscated would prove troublesome, her muddled testimony provided some comic relief:

> I let the dressing room floor to Lord Arthur Clinton. He lodged there a fortnight whilst he was there, Boulton came there and had mutton chops and bitter beer, pointing to the prisoner Park, that is the one, and that is the one I have seen dressed as a woman. I examined Lord Arthur's drawers, as I saw him go on tip-toes to let that person out, he assured me that that person was a woman. I found Boulton's shirts there. I saw women's clothes in a cupboard in the back dressing room, whilst Lord Arthur was there two boxes were brought, and the prisoners carried them upstairs. I saw Park only once at the Lodging, and I made him carry down a box. Park turned to me and I said, you have brought the boxes up and I will make you take them down, he turned round and said, I wish never to see your house again, and I replied, I'll take good care you don't. . . . Before Lord Arthur left he represented Park as his cousin, and the night he was at the lodgings in women's clothes he slept with Lord Arthur Clinton. Lord

Sodom on the Thames

Arthur left because he owed me money for rent. I advanced him ten sovereigns, and Boulton has part of it. I stopped Lord Arthur's clothes for the rent.[74]

At this point, the prosecutor declared to the audience: "It is no laughing matter, gentlemen. I hope you will keep order." Anne Empson claimed that Lord Arthur had fooled her by sneaking a woman into her house disguised as a man. She had gone to some trouble to accommodate the extra guest: "It was after I had purchased a bed for Lord Arthur's cousin that Boulton slept with Lord Arthur in the same bed, and I was surprised to see that the bed I had bought was not slept in." *Reynolds's* reported: "The witness here eyed the prisoners so sternly and defiantly that Boulton turned his head away contemptuously." The well-named defense lawyer was drawn into a contest of wits, which he may not have won:

> Mr. Straight here asked if she had been drinking. This she positively denied. He asked her if she was married. She replied "Certainly not."
> Mr. Straight: It might have been an advantage for you.
> Witness: Not if I had been married to Park, Boulton, or any of that lot. (Laughter.)[75]

Still Miss Empson's credibility was seriously undermined by her propensity to pronounce authoritatively on the defendants' conduct while continually confusing Boulton with Park, insisting that "the prisoner nearest to me [Park] who I call Bolton [*sic*] is the one who slept with Lord Arthur."[76]

The landlady from Louis Hurt's lodgings in Edinburgh testified about the living and sleeping arrangements when Boulton had visited. She also examined some of the more effusive letters the police had seized, identifying those signed "Louis" as being in Hurt's handwriting. (When they were first introduced in evidence, the magistrate and lawyers argued over whether the letters might have been written by a woman.) The prosecution wanted to establish that Boulton's visit had been very long, from October 1869 until April 1870, that Hurt had paid the rent, and that they had slept together. However, Mrs. Dickerson ("Dixon" in some accounts) undercut them by saying that Boulton had occupied a separate room, using Hurt's bedroom only when he was away. They had shared a bedroom only once, when Hurt had returned without notice and no other room was available. The landlady insisted that Boulton had always behaved like a gentleman. Although she had known he possessed women's clothes, she had never seen him wearing them. Hurt had always "behaved very well" and she believed him to be "related to a person in high position." As for the police, Superintendent Thompson "came down to my house and overhauled Mr. Hurt's things" while he was away from home. Thompson had told her she must come to London to testify.[77] As with Martha Stacey from Wakefield Street, the landlady provided testimony that proved to be a double-edged sword. Both women reported that the lodgers and their friends had been well-behaved and had kept women's clothes for theatrical performances. Their testimony about the police searches also raised questions for a middle-class public concerned for its privacy and still suspicious of the recently organized Metropolitan Police. Anne Empson's manifest hostility and considerable confusion made her an unreliable witness. The damage she did to the deadbeat aristocrat and his friends came from the letters she had confiscated. The prosecution now had a substantial collection of correspondence: "There were several distinct sets of letters. There were first the letters found at the lodgings of Boulton and Park. These were, of course, from other persons, and among them, were letters from Hurt and Fiske. There were letters also at their lodgings, to and from each other, and there were letters at Lord Arthur Clinton's lodgings from Boulton and Park."[78] The letters had enabled police to cast a wide net, resulting in the indictments of Lord Arthur, Fiske, Hurt, and Somerville. They would become highly contested terrain as the prosecution sought to prove what was in the minds of this group of friends charged with conspiracy to commit the felony of sodomy.

5. "HORRIBLE AND REVOLTING DISCLOSURES"

Despite their bravura in the spotlight, Fanny and Stella were subjected to a harrowing experience in May and early June 1871, transported between the house of detention and the magistrate's court, where the most intimate details of their lives were being aired. As the evidence against them accumulated, they began to show signs of strain. During the first court appearances, they had displayed high spirits: "The prisoners were then brought in. They were accommodated with seats in the dock and constantly exchanged remarks, generally in a laughing tone, upon the evidence, Park taking frequent notes, which he handed to his solicitor."[79] However, on May 21, the *Times* reported that the defendants "appeared to be as cool and collected as on each former occasion, although looking somewhat the worse for their three weeks confinement."[80] By the end of that week, *Reynolds's* was suggesting that the crowds outside the magistrate's court were in a more negative mood as well: "The prisoners as they got into the van were hooted by an immense crowd. The prisoners looked very crestfallen, especially during the first portion of the

Sodom on the Thames

evidence."[81] A week later, not even these accomplished performers could put on a happy face: "The prisoners looked much paler than before, and during the earlier part of the evidence, seemed greatly depressed."[82]

What accounted for this visible change in Boulton and Park? Incarceration certainly could not have been easy for any member of the middle classes, much less for Fanny and Stella. However, their darkening countenances also reflected the increasing seriousness of their situation as the evidence against them relentlessly accumulated. Their legal position would have appeared especially precarious, since court procedure did not permit any defense rebuttal until the prosecution had presented its case. Early on, the magistrate had signaled his inclination to release the defendants on bail pending trial. Having heard a parade of witnesses describing the public behavior of the cross-dressers, some letters expressing romantic sentiments, and testimony that they had sometimes shared beds with other men, Mr. Flowers remained unimpressed:

> Mr. Poland [the prosecutor] next submitted that the substance of the letters entitled him to ask that the prisoners be again remanded without bail. The letters must be taken with the other facts of the case. Here were four men proved to be going about in female attire, returning home together and sleeping two to a bed.
>
> Mr. Flowers hoped it was not suggested that such a fact was any proof of the horrible crime imputed to the prisoners. (Applause.) Still he thought he would be doing right in accepting bail for the prisoners.[83]

The prosecutor then suggested that one letter, tending to prove crimes of the utmost seriousness, should not be inflicted on the public: "A particular letter was then handed to the magistrate which he retired to read. It is said that the letter privately read by Mr. Flowers is of the most filthy and abominable nature."[84] The *Daily Telegraph* reported that the magistrate commented that "since reading the last letter, his opinion of the case had entirely changed." This announcement was met by "sensation" in the courtroom.[85] (Oddly, this letter would not appear again: all the epistolary evidence submitted at the trial had already been aired in the press reports a year earlier.) Although no doubt distressed by their continuing confinement, Boulton and Park were "greatly depressed" by "horrible and revolting disclosures" (as *Reynold's* headlined its story) from a different source. Two medical doctors who had examined them shortly after their arrest testified at the hearing. Members of the public who depended on the *Times, Pall Mall Gazette,* or most other papers for their news were deprived of the details, but *Reynolds's* published a fairly complete account. The *Daily Telegraph* reported: "Although much of the evidence was of a very revolting character, it was not observed that any of the public left court in consequence."[86] Still that paper offered its readers only very condensed summaries of the medical evidence.

Dr. James Thomas Paul, divisional surgeon to "E" division of the Metropolitan Police, had been asked to examine Boulton and Park "for the purpose of ascertaining their sex." He decided to pursue the matter further: "I wished to ascertain something more. That was of my own accord and my own idea." Paul's bright idea led him to examine the rear ends of the defendants as well as their genitals: "I do not in my practice ever remember to have seen such an appearance of the anus as those of the two prisoners presented."[87] *Reynolds's* provides this description:

> [I] told him to strip which he did. Both had on "tights," or drawers, over white stockings. Found that Boulton was a man. (Boulton smiled when this evidence was given.) Examined him closely, and found the anus much dilated, and the muscles readily opened. These appearances, and others were undoubtedly caused by the insertion of a foreign body. They were, he thought, attributable to the fact of his having frequent unnatural connexions—one insertion would not cause them. The other private parts of Boulton were, he considered, of an inordinate size, which was often occasioned by improper connexion.[88]

However he may have felt about the disclosure of his sex or the "inordinate size" of his "private parts," Boulton would not have smiled at the police surgeon's conclusions. As an apprentice lawyer assiduously taking notes, Park might well have recognized the worst. This evidence supported the most serious charge against them, namely, sodomy, which carried a sentence ranging from ten years to life imprisonment. The doctor claimed to have found a similar state of affairs in his case: "The rectum had much discoloration, probably caused by a recent syphilitic sore." Paul left no doubt as to the cause: "The foreign bodies he believed to be those belonging to other men." (The *Daily Telegraph* reported only that Boulton was dressed as a woman when examined and that "the further evidence of this witness tended distinctly to support the charge of felony.")[89]

The police surgeon appeared anxious to deny that his examination of two men had been excessive: "I did not use my hand with violence. I used both hands. I do not use the speculum in ordinary cases. I did not use it on this occasion. I could see without it."[90] The reference to the speculum would have reminded readers of procedures authorized for women suspected of being

Sodom on the Thames

common prostitutes under the Contagious Diseases Acts. During May 1870 the newspapers carried reports of demonstrations against the Contagious Diseases Acts beside their accounts of the hearings at Bow Street. Their letters columns included protests from women and working-class representatives against the indignities licensed by these laws. Questioned about the source of his authority, Paul replied: "I made the examination by order of the police." To which the redoubtable Mr. Straight replied: "If everybody did what the police tell them to do, we shall have some funny things done in the country before long."[91] Paul admitted that only his personal suspicions had led to such an extensive and probing examination: "[I] had the prisoners stripped naked, and laid across a stool to examine them, not only for the purpose of discovering their sex, but likewise from a belief that men so attired might commit unnatural offenses."[92] Paul's conclusions were buttressed by Richard Barnwell, who claimed he had recently treated Park as an outpatient at Charing Cross Hospital, administering an aggressive treatment for syphilis.[93] The evidence appeared devastating. Fanny and Stella might well have seemed "greatly depressed."

Press accounts of the medical evidence varied widely. *Reynolds's*, the only paper to publish the medical evidence in detail, recounted the following intervention: "A Mr. Collette, secretary to some society, asked his worship whether he could in any way influence the press not to publish the details of the case." (Earlier they had reported that Collette was present to "watch the case on behalf of the Society for the Suppression of Vice.")[94] No doubt the paper approved the magistrate's ruling: "Mr. Flowers thought he could not interfere. Secrecy in matters connected with the administration of justice was looked on with suspicion in this country."[95] Nevertheless, most newspapers exercised self-censorship, deeming the doctors' testimony unsuitable for their readers. For instance, the *Times* summarized Barnwell's evidence this way: "The witness here described the nature of the disease from which the defendant was suffering, the way in which it was communicated, and his mode of treating it." The *Times* did report the medical evidence offered by the defense in rebuttal. Perhaps the paper's editors felt that these conclusions would reinforce their readers' expectations about the venereal health of middle-class young men. Perhaps they simply believed they were less shocking.

The evidence of the defense medical experts at the magistrate's court undercut the prosecution's case and laid the groundwork for its eventual demolition at the trial. The defense attempted to rebut the testimony as expeditiously as possible. They would prove remarkably adept in answering this aspect of the prosecution case: medical experts undermined Paul's evidence in almost every regard, and diligent cross-examination would show that the patient whom Barnwell had treated for anal syphilis was unlikely to have been Park. Dr. LeGros Clark, fellow of the Royal College of Surgeons, examiner at the University of London, and for twenty-seven years surgeon at St. Thomas's Hospital, announced his conclusions after examining Park: "His body was in all respects healthy and natural. . . . There was no trace of venereal disease whatever. The skin and flesh were so clear and firm that he was certain the body was free from taint. Could not see anything to indicate the trace of disease or the presence of the syphilitic sores described. Perceived no unnatural extension, dilation or any symptom to indicate that unnatural intercourse had taken place." Similarly, as to Boulton, "there was nothing at all particular about his person . . . no unusual appearances anywhere. There was no dilation anywhere."[96] More generally, the defense expert challenged the prosecution's assumption that the commission of "unnatural acts" would result in manifest physical effects. LeGros Clark insisted that a medical examination could not determine whether a man had committed sodomy: "He would not expect to find any indication that would satisfy him of the fact, unless by communicated disease. Even disease so seated he should not consider unequivocal testimony of unnatural intercourse." *Reynolds's* reported that the audience burst into applause at the physician's announcement that "he believed the perpetration of unnatural crimes to be of so uncommon occurrence that no hospital surgeon would speak with certainty regarding them."[97] It is not clear whether the audience applauded the assertion that unnatural acts were rare or the exculpatory effects of the doctor's testimony.

The Boulton family physician testified that he had treated and eventually operated on Ernest for a fistula in 1868, which indicated his poor health at the time and made it unlikely that he had engaged in anal intercourse. William Henry Hughes testified that he was a friend of Boulton's father and had treated the young man in March 1868 for an abscess "resulting from natural causes." In February 1869, he and Dr. Taylor had operated successfully for a fistula but a scar was "still to be seen." He had again examined Boulton in May at the house of detention: "[He] found him in perfect natural condition. There was nothing to warrant the evidence of Dr. Paul that an unnatural offense had been repeatedly committed." On cross-examination he supported the judgment that a medical examination would not offer proof of sexual offenses.[98] Another witness, Dr. Harvey, testified about Park: "Every organ and part of his body was in a healthy state—no unusual elongation, enlargement or dilation. Did not notice the symptoms described by Drs. Barwell and Paul. There was no appearance of scars arising from syphilitic sores. If there had

Sodom on the Thames

been such sores, he thought some traces must have remained." He also gave Boulton a clean bill of health. "[He] found all of his organs thoroughly natural and his body healthy. There was no appearance leading in the least to the conclusion that any unnatural intercourse had taken place."[99]

By calling distinguished physicians and professors of medicine to refute the prosecution experts in magistrate's court, the defense hoped to eliminate the most serious charges from the indictment. They partially succeeded: the sodomy charges were dismissed, leaving the lesser charges of "conspiracy to commit the felony (of sodomy)," solicitation, and public indecency. Since there was nothing other than the testimony of Paul and Barnwell to show that any sexual acts had occurred, the defense would be unrelenting in its assault on the two at the trial. There it would succeed masterfully, with the prosecution practically conceding the demise of their medical evidence, and the Lord Chief Justice delivering the funeral sermon. The defense experts had much higher professional status than the police surgeon: they contradicted both his general views about the physical effects of sodomy and his particular findings about the condition of the defendants, whom they had also examined shortly after the arrest. The experts who examined Park found no indication whatever that he had suffered from, or been treated for, anal syphilis.

6. PORTRAIT OF A MARRIAGE

Among the most "extraordinary revelations" about Boulton and Park were allegations that Stella had lived as the "wife" of Lord Arthur Pelham Clinton, third son of the Duke of Newcastle and a Conservative member of Parliament. Landladies, servants, and fellow lodgers testified as to the behavior, language, demeanor, and dress of the couple as well as their sleeping arrangements. This intimate level of surveillance became increasingly important as the prosecution's medical case deteriorated and the defendants' letters proved difficult to decipher. However, the eyewitness testimony too was riddled with contradictions and would lend itself to high drama in the courtroom at Westminster. Ernest Boulton and Lord Arthur Clinton had not simply shared an apartment. One of the maids testified that they "represented themselves" as a married couple. Park's letters seemed to support the claim. He had written to Lord Arthur as "my sister's husband," referring to himself as "your affectionate sister-in-law" and signing "Fanny Winifred Park." In another letter, he referred to his friends' "matrimonial squabble." Boulton wrote Lord Arthur, demanding: "Send money, you wretch." A printer would testify he had received an order for a scroll bearing the name "Stella" and visiting cards in the name of "Lady Arthur Clinton." He had delivered the cards but had only sketched the monogram because, "I heard I should not be paid."[100] It was not only disputes about money that divided the couple. One very angry man came forward to complain that Boulton had deceived him into an extended flirtation, almost literally behind Lord Arthur's back.

Perhaps the most damaging testimony about the couple's intimate life came from Maria Duffin, who had worked as a maid at 36 Southampton Street, where they had lodged before their brief troubled stay with Anne Empson. Maria provided the juiciest and most provocative details, but they would be challenged by others who worked or lived on the premises. She claimed that she had been in service from July through November 1968 at Mrs. Peck's large house with another servant "to help me and Mrs. Peck" and someone else to do the cooking. Lord Arthur Clinton had lived there with Boulton while Park frequently visited, as had other men. Maria testified that Boulton wore women's clothes around the house, declared "herself" the wife of Lord Arthur, and shared a bed with him. She described the apartment as having one bedroom with a single bed and an adjacent dressing room in which there was another bed. When Park visited, he stayed for two or three days, using the bed in the dressing room. When Park was not there, Maria claimed that Boulton had slept with Lord Arthur rather than occupying the empty bed. There were other signs of intimacy between the two: "Lord Arthur spoke to Boulton more as a Lady than a man. He said 'my dear' sometimes, and I have heard him say 'my darling.'"[101] Despite the fact that she had seen Boulton "only once or twice dressed in gentleman's clothes," Maria had her suspicions. When she accused the lodger of being a man, "he would laugh, and show me his wedding ring keeper, and said, he was Lord Clinton's wife." (*Reynolds's* reported an outbreak of laughter in the courtroom at this.) Park usually visited in men's clothes but had gone out in the evening dressed as a woman. Boulton had spent most of his days lounging about in a dressing gown; Maria saw him "full dressed" only when he was going out. He had kept an array of women's clothes in a wardrobe in the bedroom he shared with Lord Arthur. When Boulton and Park were to go out dressed as ladies, a hairdresser visited in the morning to "clean" Boulton's hair, and "if he was going to an evening party or the theatre, the hairdresser used to come arrange the chignon and hair."[102] Lord Arthur had never dressed in women's clothes, but there were several other visitors who arrived dressed as gentlemen but went out as ladies. According to Maria, no "real" ladies had visited the couple. She strongly implied that her mother had urged her to leave Mrs. Peck's service after she described what went on there. However, the landlady, another maid, and a lodger came forward to contradict Maria's account of life in the house.

5. "Family Portrait," Lord Arthur Clinton (in chair), Frederick Park, and Ernest Boulton (on floor) (1868)

Some of the letters seized by Anne Empson seemed to confirm the house-maid's "portrait of a marriage." Superintendent Thompson, who interviewed Lord Arthur's former landlady, found himself with something of a windfall:

> She handed me over about 2,000 letters and papers. . . . There are two let-ters among them with the monogram "F.W.P." and one in the same hand-writing but on plain note-paper. One is addressed to Lord Clinton. They are respectively signed "Fanny Winifred Park," "Fan," and "Fanny." One of the letters contained a photograph of Boulton. I produce a letter signed "Stella Clinton." I also produce eleven letters in the same handwriting, some signed "Stella," some "Ernest Boulton," some "Ernest," and a twelfth signed "Stella," which appears to be in the same calligraphy, but rather more loosely written. These letters are addressed to Lord Arthur, and many of them sent through the post.[103]

The letters from Fanny and Stella to Lord Arthur display an intimacy that combines emotional exuberance with self-parodying overstatement:

> My Dearest Arthur, How very kind of you to think of me on my birth-day. . . . I require no remembrance of my sister's husband, as the many kindnesses he has bestowed upon me will make me remember him for many a year and the birthday present he is so kind as to promise me will only be one addition to the heap of little favours I already treasure up. So, many thanks for it, dear old man. I cannot echo your wish that I should live to be a hundred, though I should like to live to a green old age. Green, did I say? *Oh! ciel,* the amount of paint that will be required to hide that very unbecoming tint. My campish undertakings are not at present meet-ing with the success they deserve. Whatever I do seems to get me into hot water somewhere; but *n'importe,* what's the odds as long as you're *rappy?* Believe me, your affectionate sister-in-law, Once more with many, many thanks, Fanny Winifred Park[104]

(Fanny's use of "campish" antedates by decades the *Oxford English Dictionary's* first recorded use, in 1909, of "camp" in its contemporary queer meaning. It must have been unfamiliar: one newspaper reported it as "craw-fish.")[105] Soon afterward, in November 1868, when Boulton and Lord Arthur were living together at Southampton Street, Park worked to avoid getting in-volved in a domestic quarrel:

> My dearest Arthur,—You must really excuse me from interfering in mat-rimonial squabbles (for I am sure the present is no more than that); and

though I am, as you say, Stella's confidante in most things, that which you wish to know she keeps locked up in her own breast. My own opinion on the subject varies fifty times a day when I see you together. She may sometimes treat you brusquely; but, on the other hand, how she stands up for your dignity of position . . . I cannot really form an opinion on the subject. As to all the things she said to you the other night, she may have been tight, and did not know all she was saying; so that by the time you get my answer you will both be laughing over the whole affair, as Stella and I did when we quarreled and fought down here—don't you remember, when I slapped her face? Do not think me unkind, dear, as really I have told you all I know, and have not an opinion worth having to offer you. . . . Ever yours, Fan.

A third note from Park shows how easily he shared visits and household tasks with the couple:

My dearest Arthur,—I think I would rather you came in the middle of the week, as I fancy I am engaged on the Saturday (15th) in London, though I am not certain yet. If you came on Wednesday, and stayed until Saturday morning (if you could endure me so long), we could all go up together—that is, if I go. But please yourselves. I am always at home, and a fixture. I shall be glad to see you both at any time. Is the handle of my umbrella mended yet? If so, I wish you would kindly send it me, as the weather has turned so showery that I can't go out without a dread of my back hair coming out of curl. Let me hear from you at any time; I am always glad to do so. Ever your affectionate, Fanny

The letters from Boulton that survive are fewer and shorter. In part, he wrote less because he was living with Lord Arthur during the period covered by the letters the angry landlady had confiscated. Mostly, his voice, like his looks and manner, is reflected in other sources. This brief note—on a wine merchant's stationery—was introduced to prove both the impropriety of their relationship, as witnessed by the signature, and its pecuniary aspect:

My dearest Arthur,—I am just off to Chelmsford with Fanny, where I shall stay till Monday. We are going to a party tomorrow. Send me some money, wretch.
Stella Clinton

The next letter in evidence was signed "yours affectionately, Ernest": "My dear Arthur,—I shall be unable to come down on the 16th. Write at once, and if

6. "Sisters," Ernest Boulton and Frederick Park (1868)

you have any coin, I could do with a little." Boulton was not so hard up that he could not afford liquid refreshment: "My dear Arthur,—We were very drunk last night, and consequently I forgot to write, but I hasten to do so now." He concluded: "And now my dear, I must shut up, and remain affectionately yours, Stella." In a rather different tone, he wrote: "My dear Arthur,—I have waited for two hours for you, and do not like to be treated

Sodom on the Thames

with such rudeness—Yours, Ernest Boulton." In another letter he said: "I am consoling myself in your absence by getting screwed."[106] ("Screwed" here almost certainly meant "drunk.") Boulton's shifting signatures reflect the ongoing vicissitudes of his relation to his friend. Newspapers quoted extensively from the few letters that were entered into evidence. These passages would also figure importantly at the trial as the prosecution tried to prove the defendants harbored guilty desires. The conspiracy charges would depend on the jury's decision about whether they expressed youthful excesses of enthusiasm or the coded communication of criminal intentions. A verdict in the case would require answers to some complicated questions: What did these men really want? Did they intend to commit forbidden sexual acts? Did they expect payment in return? Did they parade about the town in search of clients? Was Stella being "kept" by Lord Arthur in exchange for sexual favors? What about all the other men who clustered "likes moths around a flame"? The letters contained the best clues as to what was really on their minds.

Despite her "marriage" to Clinton, Stella was entangled in a web of flirtatious correspondence. At least three additional suitors had sent her love letters. Unlike Mundell, who could claim some confusion, these men were under no illusion that the object of their desires was female. As a result, Boulton's friends from Edinburgh—U.S. consul John Safford Fiske and well-connected post office surveyor Louis Hurt—would also be indicted and tried as parties to the alleged conspiracy. A third, William Somerville of London, would be charged but would flee prosecution. Their letters were quoted extensively in the press and subject to critical scrutiny at the trial. One longer missive from Fiske to Boulton was particularly damaging to both. It began:

> My darling Ernie,
>
> I had a letter last night from Louis [Hurt] which was charming in every respect except the information that he is to be kept a week or so longer in the North. He tells me that you are living in drag. What a wonderful child it is! I have three minds to come to London and see your magnificence with my own eyes. Would you welcome me? Probably it is better I should stay at home and dream of you. But the thought of you—Lais and Antinous in one—is ravishing.[107]

When the prosecutor explained that "the term 'drag' was a slang phrase employed in certain circles to mean 'wearing women's clothes,'" the magistrate commented that he had always thought a "drag" was "a four-wheeled vehicle."[108] The reference to "Lais and Antinous" was more damaging: one was a fabled courtesan, the other, the young male favorite of the emperor Hadrian.

The love-struck Fiske imagines Stella as a gorgeous hermaphrodite, tarnishing the image a bit with implications of prostitution. The lawyers and magistrate debated whether the handwriting in the letter was that of a man or a woman, and whether "Louis" might be female.[109] *Reynolds's* reported that "the letter created a great deal of surprise and disgust in court, but Mr. Poland said he had others which went further."[110] Fiske's letter provided more than its share of scandalous material. The following passage displays a cynicism that undercuts its more sentimental effusiveness, shedding further light on the social milieu in which the men moved:

> Let me ask your advice. A young lady, whose family are friends of mine, is coming here. She is a charmingly dressed beautiful fool with £30,000 a year. I have reason to believe that if I go in for her, I can marry her. You know I never should care for her; but is the bait tempting enough for me to make this further sacrifice to respectability? Of course, after we were married I should do pretty much as I pleased. People don't mind what one does on £30,000 a year, and the lady wouldn't much mind, as she hasn't brains enough to trouble herself about much beyond her dresses, her carriage, etc. What shall I do?
>
> You see I keep on writing to you and expect some day an answer to some of my letters. In any case, with all the love in my heart,
>
> I am yours, etc.,
>
> JOHN[111]

We can only guess what "my darling Ernie" advised his American friend. As for Stella and Lord Arthur, for Fiske conventional marriage was closely linked to financial concerns. The historian Jonathan Ned Katz reports that Fiske never married but traveled in Europe, where he cultivated a series of romantic attachments to artistic young men. He settled in Italy and took occasional trips to the United States.[112]

The "marriage" of Stella and Lord Arthur had been stormy. Their "matrimonial squabbles" concerned not only recurrent worries about money but also matters of the heart. Stella's charms combined with an incurably flirtatious spirit to compound the difficulties. These went beyond the social whirl of drag balls and the literary excitements of amorous correspondence. When he hastened to testify about Boulton's deceptive feminine charms, Francis Kegan Cox also illuminated the couple's personal troubles. Cox had been introduced to them at a tavern near his business in the City by a mutual acquaintance, the solicitor W. H. Roberts (of whom more later). He had joined the three for lunch, attracted to Boulton despite the fact he was dressed in

7. *"Love Scene," Ernest Boulton with an an unknown admirer (1868)*

men's clothes: "I formed the opinion that he was a woman."[113] Boulton encouraged him: "Oh, you City birds have good fun in your offices, and have champagne." Rising quickly to the bait, Cox invited Boulton and Lord Arthur for drinks and continued flirtation: "I treated Boulton as a fascinating woman. Lord Arthur left the room we were in and went into an outer office. He appeared to be jealous." His companions quickly provided him with cause: "Whilst he was away, Boulton went on in a flirting manner with me, and I kissed him, she or it, at the time believing him to be a woman."[114] Cox's anger at his deception reduced him in court to a sputtering confusion of pronouns. *Reynolds's* reported that "here Boulton almost laughed outright."[115] At their first meeting, Stella had played her role to the hilt. Cox testified: "Shortly after, Boulton complained of being chilly. My partner whipped off the table cloth, wrapped Boulton's feet in it, and placed him in an armchair." *The Illustrated Police News* was so captivated by this scene that they had their artist portray it on the front page.[116] Still fascinated by Stella, Cox called on the couple a few days later. Boulton had "sung a few airs," after which "Boulton presented me with his photograph, secretly as far as Lord Arthur Clinton was concerned."[117] Although the lost portrait showed Boulton in men's clothes, Cox persisted in believing him a woman. When he afterward "heard something about his sex," Cox tracked Boulton to a restaurant in Covent Garden, where he was seated with his friends:

> I pointed out the three to the waiters and made a statement to them, the waiters. I went to the table where Boulton, Park and Lord Arthur Clinton were sitting. I said, "You damned set of infernal scoundrels, you ought to be kicked out of this" and remained some little time near the table. I used the language four or five times. They did nothing. Soon after I left.[118]

The Illustrated Police News depicts an agitated Cox denouncing a dinner party that ignores him with studied calm.[119] Cox was not one to let sleeping dogs lie: "I made a complaint about it to a great many people, amongst them an uncle of Lord Arthur Clinton."[120] On cross-examination, he admitted that Boulton had never said he was a woman, but that his hair, hands, feet, and "personal manners" had led the businessman astray: "They would not have been asked to champagne had I not believed him to be a woman. . . . I was not resisted by him when I kissed him."[121] At this point in Cox's testimony, "Boulton again smiled."[122]

Soon after Cox testified, W. H. Roberts appeared in court to protect his good name. *Reynolds's* reported the testimony:

> He conceived that his name having mentioned in connexion with such a case was prejudicial to him and he was therefore desirous of explaining to the court that he was by the merest chance present with the prisoner Boulton at the Guild-hall Coffee house on the day referred to. He [Mr. Roberts] was solicitor to Lord Arthur Clinton, conducting his bankruptcy case, and that was how—

8. *Francis Cox with Stella and friends: "A gentleman's delicate attentions to Boulton."*
Illustrated Police News, *May 1870.*

Mr. Flowers thought that any statement would be prejudicial and unfair to the defendants at the present time, and thought Mr. Roberts had better wait before making any statement.[123]

Roberts insisted he had "never acted for Boulton and Park."[124] Lord Arthur's bankruptcy reveals that his financial difficulties had passed beyond the point of occasional worry. When Boulton and Park made their first appearance at the Old Bailey, in a separate front-page story titled "Lord Arthur Clinton Again," *Reynolds's* reported that the aristocrat was being sued by a cab driver who had driven him for "upwards of six hours" and had not been paid. Apparently, the driver had been sent off to deliver a letter, and when he returned, the hard-up nobleman was nowhere to be found.[125] By the time of Boulton's arrest, the young member of Parliament seems to have receded from Stella's life. Boulton had gone alone to Edinburgh to recover from his surgery and remained for over six months. When he returned, it was to attend Amos Gibbings's ball. Asked about the nobleman, Gibbings had replied: "I know Lord

Arthur Clinton. There is a connexion between his family and mine, but it is very remote. . . . [He] was not at the ball." The magistrate intervened: "Neither will he be here as witness I take it." The defense counsel volunteered: "I should have thought that the Treasury would have done one thing or another—either put him in the box as a witness, or in the dock as a prisoner." To which the prosecutor protested: "It is not so easy to put people in the dock, sir." The defense implied that the son of a duke might receive special treatment: "It is easy to avoid doing so."[126]

The Treasury did not shirk its duty to prosecute: Lord Arthur was eventually indicted along with Boulton, Park, and five others. W. H. Roberts's last duty as Clinton's solicitor was to inform the authorities of his client's death and to forward his dying declaration of innocence. The *Times* published both letters in full. The unsigned last testament of Lord Arthur Pelham Clinton appeared under the heading, "MEN IN WOMEN'S ATTIRE." "Prostrate on a bed of sickness," Clinton declared he was guilty only of "the foolish continuance of the personation of theatrical characters, which arose from a simple frolic in which I permitted myself to become an actor."[127] He pledged to appear in court as soon as he was able, but it was not to be. Whatever his relations with Lord Arthur might have been, Boulton would face his trial without his friend. "Lady Stella Clinton" had become a widow.

7. "THE HERMAPHRODITE CLIQUE"

The hearings at Bow Street concluded on May 30, 1870, with the magistrate's decision to commit the case for trial on the conspiracy charges and to continue holding Boulton and Park without bail. The press began an extensive debate on the implications of the case. Given the large amount of prosecution evidence and the defense's preliminary rebuttal, there was plenty of room for speculation about its eventual outcome and social significance. Respect for the presumption of innocence required the papers to avoid conclusions about the specific charges against Boulton and Park. Instead, they treated the uncontested reports of their public behavior as symptoms of a broader social malaise. Fascinated and ostensibly repelled by the practice of "going about in drag," editorialists linked the scandal to London's metropolitan culture and its effects on the national character. They frequently emphasized the social class of the young men, expressing differing attitudes toward its significance. The flouting of norms of proper masculine conduct was an obvious theme, but the implication of "unnatural" sexual practices demanded more circumspect treatment. Most papers portrayed the case as dramatizing the conflict between traditional morality and urban life. They also considered the conduct of the police and more general policy and political questions regarding the legal regulation of social mores. Given Victorian constraints on the discussion of sex, the newspapers challenged one another as they debated the proper role of the press in reporting such affairs.

As the newspaper of record, the *Times* steered a middle course between the detailed coverage in the *Daily Telegraph* or the weekly *Reynolds's Newspaper* and the condensed summaries offered by the *Daily News* or the weekly *Pall Mall Gazette*. From early on, the *Times* deliberated on how much publicity the legal prosecution warranted. They considered the claim that prosecuting such offenses did more harm than good, "that a scandal caused by prolonging a process of this kind is a greater evil than the escape of the offenders themselves when once they have been exposed; for society will not fail to visit such breaches of decency with a reprobation which is in itself a sufficient punishment."[128] Public exposure of the miscreants subjected them to social condemnation, but too much detail might give people ideas. The *Times*'s assessment was deeply entangled with matters of social class:

> In the present day it is impossible to prevent such a case from being discussed by the public at large, and particularly by people who unite to a strong appetite for the morbid and the sensational a credulity beyond bounds concerning the malpractices of the classes above them. The extraordinary rumours which arise, and rapidly take form and consistence and become the belief of millions render it highly inexpedient that any scandal so serious and so public should be hushed up. The thing is never forgotten, and it is ten to one that some absurd romance comes into being which it is thenceforth impossible to refute.[129]

Publication not only generates social pressures that punish wrongdoers but also protects members of the upper classes from rumors based on unfounded accusations. No doubt readers of the *Times* would understand they were not included in the public that combined morbid sensationalism with credulous resentment. When the hearings had concluded, the *Times* considered the broader implications of "the most extraordinary case we can remember to have occurred in our time." What was so special about it? The editorial linked the "social misfortune" of the scandal to the class of the accused: "The charges made by the prosecution are such as are seldom advanced in this country, except against the lowest, the most ignorant, and the most degraded." The case exposed the existence "in English society" of "an association of young men," some of whom had been accused of "the most hateful immorality," while numerous others had joined them in relations "familiar and indelicate beyond expression." These facts alone provided cause "to be ashamed": "We have been accustomed to associate such offences with the sensuous civilization of antiquity, and with the barbarism or demoralization of certain races in our own day. But we were not prepared to even the suspicion of them attaching to youths of respectable family and position."[130] The evidence would surprise even those hardened enough to think they "had not much to learn of the wickedness of this world," such as criminal lawyers, police officers, or hospital physicians. The references to ancient civilizations and barbarous races suggested the "Greek vice" of sex between men. Such offenses in nineteenth-century England were supposed to be confined to the lower orders.

The public performances of these sons of the middle and upper classes might indicate no more than extravagant folly. Claiming ignorance as to "how 'drag' originated," the editorial acknowledged the evidence that "it has been the fancy of some empty-headed, effeminate young men to play female parts in amateur theatricals." In a curious reading of theater history, the *Times* suggested that such cross-dressing might have been a male variation on the practice of "pants roles" played by actresses in opera and drama. (Defense attorneys would later remind the jury that men played all the women's parts in Shakespeare's day, with boys specializing in heroine's roles. Women were not permitted on the stage until after the Restoration of 1660.) However, Boulton and Park, "the first of the set to act women's roles and go about in women's clothes," had gone "beyond the point of decency." Their offense was compounded by the fact that "they seem to have possessed considerable theatrical ability, and, no doubt, attracted curiousity and made many acquaintances." The unspoken fear is that Fanny and Stella might generate feelings stronger than curiosity and attachments more intimate than acquaintance-ship. Although the adoption of feminine names might have been a joking extension of theatrical practice, the *Times* declared it in "very miserable taste." Finally, in an apparent paradox that would prove central to the defense, the very publicity of their activities might show their innocence:

> But, whatever the relations between the prisoners and their friends, there can be no doubt that for more than a year they have carried on the practice of appearing in "drag" and, indeed, parading the town in it. Their conduct was so audacious that one can hardly imagine them to have been conscious of the scandalous nature of their acts, the interpretation that must be put upon them, and the danger they would inevitably run.[131]

Still, they ought to have known better, especially after being ejected so unceremoniously from theaters and shopping arcades, "though we would not

Sodom on the Thames

give implicit credence to all that is stated by such a class of witnesses as deposed to this part of the story." (Beadle Smith of the Burlington Arcade had certainly made an impression.) Like most other papers that condemned "the latest vile fashion,"[132] the *Times* worried that Fanny and Stella might have started a fad: "The most curious part of the story is the influence which these personations has on other young gentlemen of similar tastes." If the police had not arrested the pair, "There is no saying how far things might have gone in a year or two. 'Drag' might have become quite an institution, and open carriages might have displayed their disguised occupants, without suspicion, except to the initiated."[133]

The worst sign of this danger was the ball where more than thirty men accepted in good humor the appearance of at least six of them in drag. The editorialist underscored Gibbings's relative youth but accused him of "a folly which verges so clearly on criminality." His appearance in drag at the Oxford and Cambridge boat race exacerbated the offense. Admitting some uncertainty as to how far the law should regulate these social transgressions, the *Times* argued that the ball "ought not to escape the severest reprobation, even if no punishment were provided for it." But Fanny's and Stella's public promenades had made them "guilty of an outrage on propriety with which the law ought to deal." If current law proved inadequate, the legislature should act: "We must protest against any more sham women being allowed to parade their effeminacy in future under any pretence." The success of the impersonation makes it that much worse (although it complicates the imputation of unnatural desire):

> Men in chignons leering at other men from a brougham are bad enough, but the outrage is more intolerable when they presume to go to places of public entertainment like a theatre, frequented by ladies, and are enabled by their disguise to enter rooms reserved for women. We find it was the practice of several members of this epicene college to appear in public dressed with such care and success that it was almost impossible to recognize their sex.

The *Times* implicitly endorses vigilantism, though whether it is to protect the privacy of women or the innocence of men is unclear: "Should any one of them intrude himself among decent people again, it would be pardonable for any gentleman present to take the law into his own hands, and inflict on the offender a suitable castigation at once." The long editorial concludes with the wish for a speedy conclusion of the legal process. Despite the social benefits of the prosecution, "this disgusting case" had received far too much public attention: "There is nothing we would more willingly forget."[134]

The *Times* editorial provoked a storm of dissent from other newspapers. The *Daily Telegraph,* with a knowing air, urged a more forthright confrontation of sexual vice in the city, whereas *Reynolds's Newspaper* contested its assumptions about social class. The *Pall Mall Gazette* criticized the leading newspaper's role in promoting the scandal. Its editorial "Justice and Decency" argued that the authorities ought to pursue their investigation to the fullest extent but that newspapers ought to exercise restraint in publicizing the case. It was disingenuous to pretend that legal prosecution required the press to recount all the details. Similar offenses often received the briefest notice; preliminary hearings, as opposed to full trials, were rarely covered. The *Times* had a special responsibility since its financial position would not be jeopardized by restraint, whereas other papers depended for sales on public curiosity about just such matters. The *Pall Mall Gazette* urged avoidance of "any repetition of the filthy reports which on eight several mornings have been furnished to every London breakfast table." They expressed special concern for female readers:

> Most cases of this sort bear their character marked on their foreheads. No woman can be in any danger of reading about them unless she does so intentionally. But the heading "Men in Women's Clothes" need not . . . have served as an adequate warning of what was to follow; and a lady may have been left to make out the underlying filth for herself, or have had to be warned of its existence by some male relative.[135]

Intertwined themes of moral decay, class conflict, and national decline, aired by several papers, were most fully articulated in the radical republican *Reynolds's Newspaper:* "So rife are the crimes, vices, and insane follies in this nineteenth century of ours, that one may almost fancy that we were living far back in antiquity, in a barbarous age, and amidst barbarous surroundings." Their leading editorial titled "The Hermaphrodite Clique" finds the source of these threats to "Christianity and civilization" in distinctively urban forms of life, where "rank abundance breeds . . . sloth, and lust, and wantonness, and gluttonous excess." The worst dangers come from "the glaring infamies and the grave 'freaks' perpetrated by the aristocratic orders, and by people 'highly connected.'" A world-historical moral drama had been enacted in magistrate's court, where a "protracted and tedious examination" produced "revelations" creating "much horror": "They shed a glaring light upon dubious deeds, as well as give an insight into the wanton wiles in which certain 'fast' people in high life habitually indulge." Even if the practice of going about "in drag" turned out to be "an innocent freak," it still warranted "severe con-

Sodom on the Thames

demnation and punishment." However, the paper was skeptical: "Still, we own it hard to arrive at the conclusion that men who, in the garb of ladies, could lasciviously leer from their private box at gentlemen in the stalls, could possess aught but immoral intentions." Their unceremonious ejection from public places should have alerted them to the scandal they caused: "Yet they did not desist from their pet courses, until the arm of the law seized them in its vigorous clutch."[136] Their attorneys' failure of to persuade Mr. Flowers to set bail for Boulton and Park or to reduce the charges indicated the strength of the prosecution case: "No doubt the prisoners had influence and interest behind them. There was no lack of funds to engage counsel for their defense even when before a magistrate. Every exertion was made to clear their characters and wipe out the more heinous criminatory stain: but in vain, so far." Even if they were acquitted eventually, their arrest and trial would send a salutary message to "brainless spendthrifts": "The Gibbingses will have to contrive some other sort of amusement besides 'fancy' parties at London hotels, in which men appear in women's attire, and at which the 'gay' ladies of St. John's-wood disport themselves; nor will such eccentric young gentleman dare to go 'in drag' to a boat race in the full glare of day." A guilty verdict might invoke a full measure of Old Testament fury: "Why, the impression will be conveyed that this London of ours is as foul a sink of iniquity as were certain Jewish cities of old, which, for their flagrant wickedness, met with retributive destruction by fire from heaven." Of course, the most severely punished cities had been Sodom and Gomorrah, whose sins were not to be named. The sinners here are men of position "whose names were reluctantly disclosed by timorous witnesses." The writer cannot conceal a note of satisfaction: "It will strike the public mind with a thrill of horror to think that apparently refined and 'respectable' human beings may be more gross and devilish than untutored savages—and more brutish than the beasts that perish." The publicity alone has finished the "hermaphrodite clique": "But, whatever the verdict, we will be rid in future of androgynous adventurers."[137]

Immediately below this piece, in another editorial, entitled "Publicity Preferable to Secrecy—An Impudent Pharisee," *Reynolds's* defended its decision to publish the all the evidence. The writer rejected the position of Mr. Collette on behalf of the Society for the Suppression of Vice, arguing for a full airing of even the most delicate issues before the reading public. He quotes "one of the most respected members of parliament," who had opposed the expulsion of reporters from a recent debate in the House of Commons— about the Contagious Diseases Act. The MP had protested: "I believe there is ten thousand times more evil in attempting to carry on discussions of this character in secret than in public, and I hope and trust that we have not become so corrupt that we cannot bear to look in the face or name the vices around us." Every Englishman has the right to know what goes on in his nation's courts: "And this, in despite of the intrusive, impertinent interference of trumpery hole-and-corner associations." These comments were aimed at the prudery of a moral reform movement especially strong among nonconforming Protestants and reflected in the editorials of the *Pall Mall Gazette*.

Reynolds's took a few additional shots at the established church and newspaper of record, rejecting the *Times's* claim that sexual vice characterized the lower classes. It cited the defense expert with seventeen years' experience at a public hospital, who found such conduct very rare among his patients from "the working and poorer orders." If one had to locate "the perpetration of unnatural offences" in a particular "grade of society," "we should at once point to the episcopacy." In addition to the notorious case of the Lord Bishop of Clough, who had been "caught in the act of commiting an abominable crime with a private soldier," (!) the editorial mentioned two other recent cases involving similar charges, against a colonial bishop and a Scotch prelate: "These facts alone give the lie to the assertion that the humbler classes are more addicted to the commission of these execrable offences, which, at all events, seem prevalent amongst the prelacy."[138]

One paper adopted a more sophisticated attitude toward the urban scene. If the *Pall Mall Gazette* posed as a defender of female sensibilities, the *Daily Telegraph* explicitly addressed men of the world: "We are driven to write, if not boldly then intelligibly, on matters generally spoken of by police agents whispering to each other 'with bated breath' about these mysteries which they shrink from bringing before the courts." Knowledgeable city dwellers had long been aware of a sexual underworld at the heart of London: "The very places in the parks and in the public streets, the very cafes, refreshment houses, and assignation houses, which these people frequent, and the hours at which they are to be found there, are perfectly well known." Whose business was it if "a parcel of foolish and vicious young men should be found who delight in unsexing themselves"? The question remained whether Fanny's and Stella's "masquerade" hid "some dark and evil intent":

> What is it these young men have seen in such haunts as we have spoken
> of? Simply, practices concerning which no revelation need be made, but
> which have continued with impunity. You might have gone into the Hay-
> market lately—no doubt just now the thing is checked—and you might
> have witnessed the plying of a horrible trade. Whether these people were

Sodom on the Thames

in male or female attire, their errand was well known. Sometimes, rarely, one was caught, impressed, scourged if he overstepped limits.[139]

Behind the casual cross-dresser lies the image of the male prostitute. Provocatively, given ongoing debates about the Contagious Diseases Acts, the writer asserts that "what is ordinarily understood by the word 'prostitution' offers something like a guarantee—painful though it may be—against excesses which have lately been brought under the notice of the public." "Unnatural" vice flourishes in the shadow of the ordinary variety: "When, as opposed to being disseminated and scattered, vice is allowed to take up its quarters in any particular district, there will always be depths deeper than those which are apparent to the casual observer." London is characterized by the easy availability of commercial sex: "We allow nightly scandals in our streets as would not be tolerated in any other European capital. It should not be surprising that there should be a 'behind the scenes' even in these ugly theatres."[140]

Spectacular scandals sell papers. Penny pamphlets were rushed into print before the hearings had concluded. For the most part, they reproduced newspaper coverage of the testimony in magistrate's court. The cover of "Men in Petticoats" illustrated the ball at Haxell's Hotel: two couples with what appear to be women in fancy dress, a uniformed policeman at the door. The latter detail was artistic license, since the affair had been neither raided nor protected by the police (see figure 4, above). "The Lives of Boulton and Park. Extraordinary Revelations" features a drawing of "the toilet at the station" in which two uniformed policemen ogle one feminine figure in underwear, while another, still in her ball gown, looks on in horror with a third bobby, more stern than his fellows standing, behind "her" chair. The text begins with the ritual condemnation: "These misguided young men deserve the heaviest punishment which the law can possibly award." One act in particular reveals "the base and prurient natures which these misguided youths (for they are but little more) must possess":

> We refer to the entrance of Park into the retiring room, which is set apart
> for ladies at the Strand Theatre, where he had the unblushing impudence
> to apply to the female attendant to fasten up the gathers of his skirt, which
> he alleged had come unfastened. . . . What protection have those who are
> nearest and dearest to our hearts and hearths: these loved ones whom we
> recognize by the endearing titles of mother, sister, wife or daughter. Is it
> right, moral, or just, that their sacred privacy should thus be ruthlessly vi-
> olated. If every debauched roué can by assuming feminine garb enforce his

way with impunity into the chambers set apart for our countrywomen, then we call upon law and justice to aid us in exposing these outrages upon decency.[141]

Park's main offense was to jeopardize the privacy, and perhaps more, of the women of London. His feminine garb may have cloaked an aggressively masculine ambition to penetrate the secrets of the fairer sex.

The pamphlet concludes with the pervasive ambiguity surrounding the pair's gender: "These young men appear to be very unfortunate, for whenever they dressed in men's clothes they were always taken for women, and when they were attired in the dress of the fair sex they were always taken for men, under such circumstances what were they to do?"[142] The theatrical activities used by the defense to demonstrate the harmlessness of their cross-dressing are here numbered among the guilty pleasures of urban life. The pamphlet condemns as "ludicrous" the ways that press reviews portrayed their gender: in one account, the masculine identities of Boulton and Park are emphasized; in another, the former's disguise as "Miss Edwards" is not detected; while a third actually comments on nature's handiwork in crafting a man who can sing and act so much like "a really charming girl." The proliferation of possibilities is itself a source of alarm.

Fanny's and Stella's cross-dressing both fascinated and disturbed the popular imagination. The relatively new practice of publishing "letters to the editor" of newspapers allowed members of the public to air their views about the scandal. Under the heading "Private Theatricals," the *Times* printed three letters expressing concern about the fashion of "going about in drag." They focused on the practice of young men playing women's roles at school, especially at all-male "public" schools, where the elite in Victorian Britain sent their sons to be educated. The writer of the first letter published identifies himself as having had "several years' experience as boy and master of one of our most famous public schools." He argues that all the offenders had "been in the habit of acting female roles in performances." (There was no evidence that they had begun doing so at school: although the defendants were educated, the record offers no details about their schooling. Ernest Boulton started at home.) The casting of boys in female parts was a recent and extremely hazardous innovation:

> But the truth is, as those who know the inner details of public school life, that the danger which has culminated in so terrible a crisis, met with such an unparalleled exposure, in the case of Boulton and Park, is of a kind which, varying no doubt in degree in different schools, and under differ-

Sodom on the Thames

ent influences in the same school, is at once the darkest, the most insidious, and the most universal to which schools are liable.

Some students were particularly vulnerable and exposed: "The very quality of modesty in a boy exposed to such a risk increases his danger, for it makes consultation with friend or master upon such a subject impossible to him." The sometime master implicitly indicts any institution in which drag performances are permitted: "What, then, is to be said of a system which, under the sanction of authority, and with the most plausible pretence, deliberately selects young boys, who from circumstances are most exposed to the dangers alluded to, and places them in a position, which, however theoretically harmless, is likely to contain the germ of so fatal a mischief?" Although denying that he imputes bad motives to those who support the practice from an "honest, but to me unintelligible conviction of its utility and moral innocence," he intimates a more sinister prospect: "If any responsible person should be found to support it upon less worthy grounds, the sooner the millstone is hanged about the neck of this 'offender' of the 'little ones' the better for himself."[143] The very next day the *Times* published another letter endorsing these concerns on behalf of "many a man who has to deal with boys, either as father, or as tutor." The writer adds his own testimony:

> After being present at one of these school plays, after hearing the remarks made (in all innocence) on the boys selected for the female characters, and sometimes after reading the critiques on their acting in the newspapers, I believe that many besides the writer, who know the miseries which lurk behind the scenes of our great schools, must have felt a painful misgiving lest the devil should turn to his own purposes all this clever and graceful impersonation. But our head-masters have appeared to be blind to this danger. Surely, it is impossible now for them to ignore its existence, or to allow its continuance.[144]

The two letters relocate the threat posed by the "hermaphrodite clique" from the London underworld to elite same-sex institutions. Of the newspapers, only the *Pall Mall Gazette* had suggested such a link: "The existence of this conspiracy has been suspected for some time. It has looked on the universities as natural feeding ground." As a step in the right direction, the editorial applauded "the tardy prohibition at Oxford of theatrical performances in which women's parts are played by undergraduates."[145] In these contexts, theatrical performances do not provide an alibi but increase the danger.

The *Times* correspondence concludes with a defense of public schools. The writer assumes that the publicity about Stella and Fanny has already eliminated cross-dressing from school theatricals: "Your correspondent's attack . . . is therefore probably superfluous—a killing of the dead—and might be even mischievous, if left unanswered, in flaming public opinion against the schools where these performances have been permitted." To counter the image of vulnerable boys in the hands of well-meaning dupes and dubious offenders, the writer cites his school's "invariable practice" of obtaining the permission of the parents of the boys who were to perform. Signing himself "A TUTOR," this writer argues that, since "the imitative faculty" is strong in young people, "The careful acting of some of the best of our English dramas and a few judiciously selected farces was a legitimate indulgence of such proclivities, possibly even an instrument of education, and certainly a harmless recreation." Such supervised sublimation is superior to what boys might invent when left to their own devices. The image of the effeminate boy hovers in the background:

> Every possible precaution was taken by the masters, and by some also of the more influential among the boys, against the evils which we all alike dread. Farces were chosen where the female parts, if any, were of a burlesque character, for which effeminacy of appearance was no qualification. In the drama there was greater difficulty, but extreme care was always taken to exclude those boys from acting who, from peculiarities of character or other causes, were likely to be injuriously affected by it.

Stressing the extent of faculty supervision, the writer emphasizes his desire "to allay the anxiety which parents might naturally feel on reading such a letter, about their sons who had acted in school theatricals under their mother's sanction." The prosecution of Boulton and Park has dramatically changed the situation: "What might have been innocent and useful a year or two ago, has now become impracticable from its association with the grave disclosures of the last month."[146]

The extent to which the case carried the risk of contagion is further revealed by another, more specific set of letters to the papers. They reveal simple fear, or more diffuse anxiety, of being identified with Fanny, Stella, and their friends. Like the solicitor W. H. Roberts, who appeared in court to declare that only his limited professional interest had brought him near them, George F. Ball asserted: "I have never spoken to them [Boulton and Park] in my life. I have never seen them but once when I met them in the company of Lord Arthur Clinton for whom I was concerned during his bankruptcy."[147] B. R. Scheiber, who identified himself as a "homeopathic surgeon," took the

Sodom on the Thames

trouble to write that although it was reported that Anne Empson had lived at "42, Davies Street" when she had rented rooms to Clinton, he had lived at that address for several years, and neither Mrs. Empson nor the aristocrat and his friends had resided there.[148] In a longer letter, Wybert Reeve, manager of the Theatre Royal in Scarborough, explained why "The Morning Call" had not been presented there: "The second night of their entertainment Lord Arthur Clinton had the impertinence to introduce Ernest Boulton in female costume, and sit with him in a prominent place amongst the ladies and gentlemen assembled in the dress circle of my theatre." Although the offenders left with the crowd before the police arrived, Reeve had written informing Lord Arthur that he would be ejected "if he dares to repeat the offense." When Clinton nevertheless asked to stage the play, "I at once and decidedly refused."[149]

Not everyone was alarmed by news of "the hermaphrodite clique." I have found only one private response to the trial of Fanny and Stella, but it confirms the implication in the press coverage that the audience for the spectacle displayed a variety of attitudes. On first hearing of the case, the painter Simeon Solomon wrote from Venice to his friend Oscar Browning, then a master at Eton College: "What a joke this seems to be in the papers about men in women's clothes. I read a very funny account of it in the Times. The taste of such a thing is to say the least doubtful and I suppose they are a most disreputable set of young men."[150] The following year, Solomon got a closer look. After a day at the trial, he wrote to the poet Algernon Swinburne: "There were some very funny things said but nothing improper except the disgusting and silly medical evidence of which I heard but very little." Solomon reported: "I saw the writer of those highly effusive letters. He looks rather humdrum." After the morning session, the painter "was ravenous and went to the nearest restaurant," where he met the defendants and their lawyers: "Knowing the solicitor, I sat down with them, which as it was a public crowded room, I had no hesitation in doing. B —— n is very remarkable. He is not quite beautiful but supremely pretty, a perfect figure, manner and voice altogether. I was agreeably surprised at him." Despite the fear implied by his need to explain why he "didn't hesitate" to join them for a very public lunch, Solomon predicted: "Of course they will be acquitted."[151] Clearly, the trial meant different things to different people. Much of the drama derived from the publicity given to forms of life at odds with dominant social mores. We cannot say how large or small the minority may have been; its members also participated in the amorphous "general public." In fact, there were multiple audiences for the Boulton and Park trial, each with its own perspectives and interests. Not long afterward, Simeon Solomon would be arrested with a sixty-year-old workingman in a public lavatory and charged with sexual offenses. He pled guilty and received a sentence of six weeks in jail, followed by a period of supervision. Although his case did not receive newspaper publicity, the painter became persona non grata in the bohemian circle in which he had moved. His friend Swinburne dropped him completely.

8. THE IMPORTANCE OF BEING "ERNEST"

The appetite for news of the case did not abate with the conclusion of the hearings at magistrate's court. On June 12, 1870, the front page of *Reynolds's Newspaper* featured two separate stories on the matter. One announced the issuance of a summons for Lord Arthur Clinton on the complaint of an unpaid cab driver. The other was headlined: "Trial of Boulton and Park for the Commital of an Unnatural Offense: Warrants Issued for Lord Arthur Clinton and Others." The scene was the Central Criminal Court: "The aspect of the Old Bailey both within and without was of no ordinary nature. Nobody was allowed to pass within the building without permission, and all the morning men and even women were being turned back with civility and even firmness." The authorities made every effort to contain the carnival atmosphere that had prevailed at Bow Street:

> The interior of the court itself wore an air of unusual character. The bar was represented in great numbers, every idle possessor of a wig and gown within the building having discovered that he was "interested in the case." The arrangements for strangers were very carefully and cautiously made. The gallery was well filled, but not crowded and amongst the occupants of the seats near the barristers' benches were several well-known citizens.

Boulton and Park appeared unusually subdued: "Both had apparently dressed with great care, and they seemed to feel acutely the amount of curiousity that was manifested towards them. After taking a hurried and timid glance around the court, they edged away from each other, hung down their heads . . . and kept their eyes fixed on the counsel engaged in the case."[152] Louis Hurt appeared from Edinburgh to answer the charges and was granted bail. There was little to engage the audience: all parties consented to adjourn the trial for three weeks.

During the interval, defense attorneys were busy behind the scenes. On July 10, *Reynolds's* denounced "another judicial farce," reporting that the Lord Chief Justice had granted the defendants' motion to hear the case before a "special jury" of propertied gentlemen. The radical paper was outraged: "The affair of the 'Men in Petticoats' has completely collapsed. . . . A writ of certiorari removing the trial from the Central Criminal Court to that of Queen's Bench, is nothing more or less than a loophole offered to wealthy and influential parties to get out of the fangs of justice." The editorial cited other cases in which highly placed malefactors had been allowed to escape, including a "rich solicitor" accused of "bestiality with a soldier" who had got his case removed, been granted bail, and "bolted": "Many others have done this, and many others will do so again." Poor people facing charges like those against Boulton and Park were routinely tried at the Old Bailey. The paper rehearsed the evidence against them from the hearings and rhetorically asked whether any of it had been answered. (They do not mention the defense rebuttal of the prosecution's medical witnesses.) For *Reynolds's,* the cause of the retreat was obvious: "It is well known that the names of two peers of the realm and of a baronet have been associated with those of Boulton and Park although they have not been prominently before the public. We feel that some sinister influence has been at work to screen persons of high position from being placed in the same predicament . . . and hence the prison doors are thrown open."[153] Most papers treated the change of venue as a legal technicality. However, from the very beginning, the press had emphasized the social class and family backgrounds of the defendants. Virtually every story described Boulton as the son of a stockbroker or businessman and Park as the son of a judge. Mundell was a "gentleman" and the son of a barrister. When Fiske and Hurt were indicted, they were identified as, respectively, U.S. consul at Leith and surveyor with the post office. The unfortunate Lord Arthur Clinton was described as a member of Parliament and as the third son of the Duke of Newcastle. Without a doubt the financial position of the defendants' families enabled them to provide the young men with the legal talent and medical expertise that aggressively contested the prosecution. The government did not simply roll over in the face of such a challenge. Two of the highest legal officials—the attorney general and solicitor general—would appear at Queen's Bench to present the case against the "men in petticoats" and their friends. Nonetheless, shortly after the change of venue, Boulton and Park were finally released on bail. The fulminations of *Reynolds's* had proved accurate at least in that respect:

> We feel that some sinister influence has been at work to screen persons of high position from being placed in the same predicament as Boulton and Park; and hence the prison doors are thrown open; bail for ten times the required amount will be forthcoming; the trial, if ever it takes place at all,

will be postponed for months—no further exposures will take place—and so the farce is ended! It would have been more complete perhaps, if Lord Chief Justice Cockburn had stood upon his head, after granting certiorari, and before the final curtain fell on the first act of the comedy.[154]

The trial did take place, but not until May of the following year.

The scene at Queen's Bench was rather more dignified than Bow Street but no less widely publicized. The *Daily Telegraph* reported: "During the interval that has elapsed the investigation has given rise to disclosures—or, more correctly speaking, to rumours of disclosures—entirely unforeseen when the so-called female personators were brought before Mr. Flowers in their female attire. To judge from the crowd assembled in Westminster Hall at an early hour yesterday morning, there has been no falling off in the public interest in this twice-told tale."[155] The prosecution case was familiar. Once again, newspapers reported Mundell's ill-fated flirtation and the attempts to discipline the cross-dressers in their visits to theaters and the Burlington Arcade. Francis Kegan Cox, who had felt so betrayed by the discovery of Stella's sex, had died in the interim and was represented by his widow, who identified his signature on a sworn deposition. The prosecution relied heavily on the medical evidence, which fell apart in the course of the trial, and on a detailed examination of the letters and living arrangements of the group. The sense of déjà vu is most dramatically conveyed by the *Daily Telegraph,* in a story that echoed the themes of social respectability and street life:

> Yesterday for the first time in its history, the Court of Queen's Bench has been turned into an old clothes' shop. In the purlieus of London, more especially in the streets round and about Leicester Square, you may find scores of shabby-genteel shops devoted to the sale or hire of second-hand ladies wearing apparel. In their windows you see the ghosts of rich silks. . . .
>
> In the glare of gaslight you might fancy that at such places as these you might attire yourself—assuming you to be a purchaser of female attire—in the height of fashion and elegance—and the class of customers who most frequent these marts of soil finery are not as a rule particular.
>
> But if you are a philosopher of the streets and peer into the windows of which we speak in the broad glare of daylight, there are few more melancholy spectacles than the repositories of fineness which has lived its day. It seemed yesterday as if the out casts of one of these Monmouth-street establishments had been scattered over the Court. . . . All the paraphernalia of the "girl of the period dress" was turned out ruthlessly upon the floor.

Sodom on the Thames

Whether the articles thus displayed were "quite a lady's" costume may be doubted.

Boulton's and Park's status remained central to the trial. Were they respectable young men with an extravagant sense of fun, decked out in discarded finery? Or were they male prostitutes disguised as streetwalkers?

The attorney general opened the case by emphasizing the social position of each defendant. For him, their very respectability required condemnation of their outrageous behavior. At best, Boulton, Park, and their friends had challenged norms of masculine demeanor and public propriety. At worst, they had conspired to commit the most despised sexual offenses and to solicit others to join them. The defense argued that the group had displayed nothing more than the exuberance of youth accustomed to a privileged freedom. The families of Boulton and Park came forward to reinforce their portrayal as high-spirited performers who had carried a prank too far. Stella's and Fanny's career in drag was linked to their playing women's roles in theatricals. Their promenades about the West End were portrayed as harmless "larks" or "frolics" testing how far their impersonations could be carried. The feminine names they had adopted were taken from roles they had played. Even the romantic effusions in their letters were presented as a special hazard of the theatrical milieu. The "marriage" between Stella and Lord Arthur Clinton had been a playful extension of their onstage performances as man and wife. The friendships within the group had been family affairs, including visits to parental homes. The prosecution seems to have decided that Gibbings's ball at Haxell's Hotel was too hot to handle, while the defense made every effort to situate the accused within circles of domestic and professional respectability.[156] Although Judge Alexander Park made a brief appearance, the leading witness for the defense turned out—perhaps not so surprisingly—to be Mrs. Mary Ann Sarah Boulton, mother of Ernest aka "Stella, star of the Strand." She attested to her son's habit of playing dress-up games from early childhood and to the theatrical career he had shared with Park and Clinton. A fellow actor also testified about their work as performers. Prosecution witnesses who were called to prove the charges of cross-dressing were interrogated by the defense to elicit details that supported these claims. The photographer who had taken pictures of Boulton and Park in drag, together with Lord Arthur in masculine dress, testified that the poses were taken from a play in which the three had appeared to great local acclaim (see figures 1–3, 5–7, above).

Alexander Park testified briefly and with evident discomfort at finding himself a defense witness for his son rather than presiding officer in the courtroom. The papers had repeatedly informed the public of Frederick Park's background. This early report differs from most only in that it reaches back a generation: "Park is the son of Mr. Park, the Master of the Court of Common Pleas, and the grandson of the late Judge Park."[157] The judge confirmed that his son followed the family tradition, having been articled to "a gentleman at Chelmsford" to be trained as a solicitor. Frederick had received a "normal allowance" of £160 a year; however, "he spent a great deal more." Park's father had provided his son with a total of about £2500 pounds, or £500 a year since 1866, when he first went to Chelmsford. Frederick had brought Ernest Boulton to the family house on a week's visit, but Mr. Park could not remember when it had occurred: "It made no impression." Perhaps out of deference to the witness's status, or to avoid further embarrassment to a colleague, the attorney general, invited to cross-examine, replied: "I have nothing to ask Mr. Park."[158] The defendant's father had testified primarily to refute the charge of solicitation. The prosecution had repeatedly implied that both young men were hard up for cash: they had become accustomed to an expensive style of life and so had taken to the streets as prostitutes. If the judge had not quite vouched for the character of his son, he did appear as the grudging source of an ample income and the embodiment of respectable authority.

Mrs. Boulton faced a more complicated task in portraying her son and his friends as a perfectly normal collection of middle-class young men possessed by a passion for theater. Her husband, a stockbroker, was away on business at the Cape of Good Hope at the time of the trial. Ernest was the older of her two sons. He had displayed an "extraordinary taste for acting female parts" from early on in his life: "Before he could well speak he was fond of dressing up."[159] His earliest triumph had been to escape detection when he had served supper to his own grandmother disguised as a maid: "My Mama did not recognize him in the least. She said, after he went out of the room, 'I wonder that having sons you have so flippant a girl about you.'"[160] The family had encouraged Ernest by organizing "private theatricals at which we all performed."[161] As he grew older, he had taken the show on the road, performing at other private homes in the neighborhood and at the Egyptian Hall in Greenwich.

Ernest's friendship with Lord Arthur Clinton had been a family affair as well. Mrs. Boulton and her son had first met him at the house of a mutual friend, another stockbroker. They quickly discovered that Lord Arthur shared Ernest's taste for theatricals, and the young member of Parliament had participated in one of the family performances. Lord Arthur had been a guest at the Boulton house, sometimes sleeping over. When Ernest came of age in De-

Sodom on the Thames

cember 1868, Lord Arthur wrote his friends offering to send down "any little thing for the supper if Ernest would like him to do so." Mrs. Boulton had instructed her son to decline: "My answer to my son when he told me of having received the letter [was] 'Then write and tell Lord Arthur that it would not do for you to name such a thing to your mother or she would be offended.' Those were my words. Everything was provided."[162] Lord Arthur, she said, had sent a case of champagne "as a birthday present for my son." Mrs. Boulton produced letters from Lord Arthur, including this reply: "Please accept my sincere thanks for your most kind invitation which I accept with the greatest pleasure, especially as it is to celebrate the coming of age of your son Ernest for whom I entertain the most sincere regard."[163]

Still, there had been confusion and some tension about the birthday supper: "When I was dressing for the evening on my son's birthday, two persons arrived from Birch's and said they had been desired by Lord Arthur Clinton to provide a supper and my words were these, 'I feel assured that Lord Arthur means this kindly but it is a mistake.' Then they went away."[164] The misunderstanding led Lord Arthur to make amends: "I fear from a note received from Ernest I offended and caused annoyance to you on Friday last. If so, pray let me offer my sincerest apologies, etc., etc."[165] One newspaper had earlier noted that "these letters showed that the mother was aware of the acquaintance between her son and Lord Arthur. Reference was made to presents by Lord Arthur to the family, and to the son, for entertainments at her house." The defense made every effort to include the young nobleman within Ernest's family circle. The spirit of Mrs. Boulton's testimony is reflected in a note her son had written to Lord Arthur: "Mamma sends her kindest love, and hopes to see you tomorrow."[166]

Relations between Ernest's family and his aristocratic friend were generally congenial. Mr. and Mrs. Boulton joined them twice when Lord Arthur reserved a box at the theater. They "took refreshments with him first" in the drawing room at Southampton Street. Asked if Ernest had worn men's clothes, she replied: "Oh yes, he never dressed in any other way with me." The Lord Chief Justice intervened with the obvious question: "Was your son living with him at that time?" To which she answered: "He was on a visit to him."[167] These arrangements had been "entirely" with Mrs. Boulton's approval. Her twenty-one-year-old son was a model of filial obedience: "He has been a most dutiful and affectionate son. The only fault he ever had was a love of admiration which has been fed by the gross flattery of some very foolish people."[168] Asked whether he had her permission for his out-of-town visits, she asserted: "He never went anywhere without it."[169]

Mrs. Boulton had followed Ernest's theatrical endeavors closely. At the Egyptian Hall, he took the female lead while Lord Arthur took "the gentleman's part": the two friends had played husband and wife. Although neither she nor her husband had attended this charity performance, she had seen the program for "The Morning Call," which identified the female lead as "Ernest Boulton." The successful benefit had launched Ernest on a series of performances as women in different plays and venues. He and Lord Arthur had appeared together again at Scarborough; Boulton went on tour in 1869 with Mr. Davitt playing the male leads. The dutiful son had sent his proud mother programs from all his performances. She had witnessed one triumph personally: "I went to see him once at Brentwood where he acted for a charity—a school. I believe he carried the audience quite by storm and was quite a success. . . . Everyone in the hall wanted to be introduced to him."[170] Another time, when Park had appeared under the stage name "Mr. Vivien Grey," "bouquets were thrown upon the stage. . . . It was something wonderful."[171] Ernest had musical talent as well: he could play the piano and sing, with "a very good soprano voice."[172] In April 1869, he had given a recital billed as "Laura with Song—Mr. Ernest Boulton." Photographers frequently took pictures of her son in various roles: "He always sent me one of each."[173] Mrs. Boulton knew he had the nickname "Stella" among his friends.[174] Despite Ernest's enthusiasm and apparent success, Mrs. Boulton had reservations about life in the theater: "I was always rather opposed to his acting, but at the same time, I did not forbid it. I would rather he would have done anything else, but he always had such a penchant for it that I was almost compelled to give it my sanction."[175] For members of the upper middle class, acting was not quite a respectable profession. Mrs. Boulton inadvertently revealed this attitude in characterizing Davitt: "He was a gentleman who intends, I believe, to make a profession of acting eventually, but at the time I first knew him, he was a gentleman."[176]

Mrs. Boulton portrayed the group of cross-dressers and their admirers as a cozy domestic circle of young male friends. Only some of them had appeared onstage, mostly as amateurs. Park and Boulton had visited each other's family homes as well. Not only that: "He came and nursed my son through an illness."[177] Ernest's health had become an ongoing concern. He lost his job as a bank clerk in the City: "He was consumptive and had a bad cough, and they found he was so constantly absent that they said they could not keep him on that account. My husband had lost three brothers about the same age from consumption, and of course, we were very conscious and were glad for him to give up his situation on that account." Mrs. Boulton had known Louis

Sodom on the Thames

Hurt also and approved her son's trip with him to Scotland and Wales to recover from his illness: "We were very glad of the chance for him to go away with a friend that we esteemed."[178] Hurt had visited the Boultons at home, spending several evenings with the family. Not only had her meeting with Hurt built confidence in their friendship, but her son routinely shared his letters with her. She regarded Hurt as "a very intimate friend of his,"[179] acknowledging that the letters were couched in "very intimate terms of attachment."[180]

Questioned about the expenses for Ernest's trip, Mrs. Boulton revealed that money had been in short supply. Her husband had provided their son with "some money": "I do not remember exactly what it was; but, whatever he required, he always had from me."[181] Ernest's mother appeared uncertain whether her son had received a fixed allowance and admitted sending him small amounts while he was away. The family had been through hard times financially but, she said: "I never allowed any cloud to fall upon my children. I always supplied them with everything they required whatever troubles we have had, I have always sheltered them from everything."[182] The Lord Chief Justice intervened to ask who had provided the dresses worn in theatrical performances. Mrs. Boulton vacillated: Ernest and his friends had "provided amongst themselves" but she had paid for at least one dress, and Park's father for another. She believed others had been paid for with receipts from the performances. Asked if her son had been "passionately fond" of theatricals, she answered: "It has been the aim of my son's life." Mrs. Boulton reasserted that she had known her son's friends and had been continually aware of his movements, approving the repeated extension of his stay with Hurt in Scotland. Further, she denied that he had ever occupied "lodgings" of his own in London. He had been "on a visit" to Lord Arthur and had stayed with Park at Chelmsford and in London. Specifically asked about the rooms at 13 Wakefield Street, she replied, "They never stayed there. I believed they merely dressed there if I recollect rightly, but I do not know anything about that."[183]

The attorney general cross-examined Mrs. Boulton about her family's financial situation. She admitted that her husband had been unsuccessful in business, suffering "great reverses." However, she insisted that these losses had not affected her sons: "But I have always had what I wanted from my own family as far as pocket money went, and that I always appropriated to the comforts of my children." Ernest always had enough to maintain him: "My family has always given my son a great deal of money."[184] Pressed as to whether Lord Arthur Clinton had helped out, Mrs. Boulton asserted that he had been in charge of their performing endeavors: "Well, I know they took money for theatricals, and he received that, I suppose. . . . I believe Lord Arthur received it all but I do not know how they managed that at all. When they were at Scarborough he took it all, but then I believe he paid all the expenses."[185] When the Lord Chief Justice asked whether they had performed "for the purpose of making a profit," she replied: "I really do not know my Lord. I enquired very little into it. I knew they did take money, and I supposed they kept it. My son was a visitor at Lord Arthur's at the time, and I did not enquire anything about it."[186] Mrs. Boulton admitted that Ernest had borrowed money from Hurt, but she seemed surprised that he should have been expected to pay for his stay with him in Scotland: "He was a visitor there." The relations of host and guest were reciprocal: Hurt had visited the Boultons "for many nights at a time and a fortnight once."[187] The devoted mother did not waver in her portrayal of Ernest as a flawed but respectable figure: "He has been a dutiful and affectionate son. The only fault he ever had was a love of admiration which has been fed by the gross flattery of some very foolish people."

The defense offered Mrs. Boulton's portrait of an extended family circle as an alternative to the rather different domestic picture of Lord Arthur and "Lady Stella" Clinton provided by Maria Duffin. The housemaid's detailed and damaging testimony about life at 36 Southampton Street was contradicted in almost every particular by the landlady, Mrs. Peck, who had come forward after reading about her former servant's testimony in the newspapers. She also testified at the trial, supported by her sister and a lodger who had become her brother-in-law. Mrs. Peck explained that Maria had worked at 36 Southampton Street for only one month and that Lord Arthur and Boulton had been away "on a theatrical expedition" for about half that time. The landlady insisted that both men had behaved as gentlemen, as had their visitors Park, Thomas, and Cummings. She had heard that Boulton and Park dressed "in female attire" for a "theatrical entertainment" but had never seen them in costume. Mrs. Peck confirmed Maria's evidence that there were only two beds but added that there was a couch in the sitting room. Neither she nor the servants entered the rooms after the men "had retired to rest," so she could not say where they had actually slept. She insisted that both beds had been regularly occupied. As far as Mrs. Peck was concerned, "All the time Mr. Boulton lodged with me, he conducted himself as a gentleman, and any conversation I heard was always proper. I never heard any terms of endearment used by either of them."[188]

Cross-examination revealed that the landlady had earlier declared her suspicion that Boulton, Park, and some of their visitors were women disguised

Sodom on the Thames

as men. She admitted that she had found them effeminate, but denied that they wore powder or scent or that she had ever seen a hairdresser on the premises. Mrs. Peck expected Lord Arthur to pay since she had rented the rooms to him. Bills were made out in his name, and "Boulton never paid me anything." The landlady had neither heard Boulton referred to as "Stella" nor seen visiting cards announcing "Lady Stella Clinton." Mrs. Peck's sister and her husband, Arthur Gladwell, an art dealer who had occupied the second floor of the house, buttressed the landlady's account. Boulton had always dressed as a man, except once when Gladwell had been invited down to see the party before they went out for the evening—Lord Arthur dressed as a gentleman, Boulton and Park as ladies. He recalled that they were going to the West End to perform in a theatrical entertainment: whereas Boulton had been "made up to represent a young woman," Park appeared "more matronly."[189] The art dealer's visit to their rooms had been unusual; more often, he greeted them only in passing on the stairs. However, their door was usually open, and he could hear them talking. Gladwell maintained that "had there been anything coarse in it I must have heard it but I never did." He had heard Boulton playing the piano almost daily. In sum, "I knew them as gentlemen and never expected anything to the contrary."[190]

The conflicting stories of Maria Duffin and Mrs. Peck focused attention on Eliza Clark, who had been in service at 36 Southampton Street from May 1868 to April 1869. Her testimony at magistrate's court had supported the landlady's version. However, when the case came to trial, Eliza was nowhere to be found. Defense attorneys sent out investigators to find their missing witness. The attorneys had already begun their closing arguments when Boulton's attorney interrupted to announce: "Gentlemen, a telegram has been handed to me which I will read to you. 'Have served Eliza Clark. No train until tomorrow Sunday afternoon. Shall bring her with me.'"[191] Only matters of the utmost importance would have justified delaying the conclusion of the trial. As the Lord Chief Justice emphasized, her evidence was necessary to resolve the disparate accounts of the domestic lives of Ernest Boulton and Lord Arthur Clinton.

When Eliza finally arrived, she testified that Maria had worked there for only a month and that she was the housemaid: "Duffin did the kitchen work, and her services were confined downstairs." Importantly, it was Eliza's duty "to tidy the beds and to do up the rooms."[192] She recalled Park's having visited overnight only once: "At all times the bed in the dressing room was used, independent of the night that Mr. Park slept there."[193] Only once had Boulton worn women's clothes: "I understood they were going to a private amateur performance."[194] Park, also in drag, had accompanied him in a cab: "That was the only occasion I saw Boulton and Park in female costume." Thomas and Cummings appeared occasionally, always dressed as men. Eliza was clear that she "never saw anything indecent about his clothes," nor did she ever hear "any obscenity" in the conversation among Boulton, Park, and Lord Arthur: "I never heard Lord Arthur address Mr. Boulton as my dear or my darling, but they addressed each other as men to each other."[195] Acknowledging some ambiguity about Boulton's appearance, Eliza turned Maria's suspicion on its head: she "used to accuse him of being a female," and he "used to pass it off as being a joke."[196] On cross-examination, Eliza admitted that she had once thought Boulton might be a woman disguised as a man, although he always had been addressed as "Ernest" in her presence. Boulton's musical performance had aroused her suspicion: "His voice was like a lady's."[197] Her doubts had been resolved by a visit from Mr. and Mrs. Boulton: "I believed he was a woman until his father and mother came."[198] Eliza admitted that she had not been completely convinced. Moreover, her testimony confirmed some aspects of Maria Duffin's evidence: she recalled the hairdresser coming once or twice a week and seeing both Boulton and Park with powder on their faces. Indeed, it emerged that Eliza had once believed Park to be a woman as well.

The letters of Louis Hurt reinforce Mrs. Boulton's picture of respectable friendships while underlining Ernest's weaknesses. In contrast to his friend Fiske's enthusiasm, he disapproves of Stella's going about in drag. He is also impatient with Boulton's cavalier treatment of his bills. Hurt seems very much concerned to maintain appearances. He has been so charmed by Ernest that he wants him to meet his mother, but not before straightening him up a bit:

> My mother goes to Boulogne on the 22nd of this month, and I must manage if possible to be there with her. I have told her I can be there on the 16th of May if she can send me some money before that. Will this be too early for you. I am not altogether sorry that you should meet her. Will you promise not shave your moustache from this time until we meet for any consideration whatever? I beg you will promise this.[199]

Hurt regrets the news of Ernest's cross-dressing, pleading that his friend conform to standards of proper masculinity:

> I am rather sorry to hear of your going about in "drag" so much—partly, I confess, for a selfish reason. I know the moustache has no chance while this sort of thing goes on. You have now less than a month to grow it, for my mother has arranged to stay at Boulogne until the 21st so as to meet

Sodom on the Thames

me. . . . I have told my mother you are coming, but have not yet had time to receive her answer. I have thought it well to tell her that you are very effeminate, but I hope that you will do your best to appear as manly as you can—at any rate in the face. I, therefore, again beg of you to let your moustache grow at once.[200]

Money also plays a part in the exchange between the two, becoming a lever in the campaign against drag: "I hope you ain't hard up. I can't send any money for a week or two; next month I will you send you some, both for pocket and clothes, so you can order the latter at once. Of course I would [not] pay any drag bills except the one at Edinburgh. If you haven't paid this, let me know about this and other bills."[201] Hurt tempers his affection with a note of criticism: "What bills have you left in Edinburgh? I wish you would make an attempt to pay some other earlier bills. I should be very glad to help you. I should like you to have a little more principle than I fear you do as to paying debts." Still, he signs, "Your loving, Louis."[202] As for the mustache, the proposed visit to Boulogne in May did not materialize: by then, Boulton was accommodated at her Majesty's pleasure in the house of detention while his letters were being aired at Bow Street and in the London newspapers.

The ambiguity surrounding Ernest's sex was a continuing source of trouble to Hurt. After the long visit of recuperation in Scotland, he got into trouble with his employers because of reports he had been traveling on official visits for the post office in the company of a woman. He explained repeatedly that Boulton was, and was known to be, a man. Hurt turned to Lord Arthur Clinton for help, believing that a letter from the nobleman and MP attesting to Ernest's sex and to his friendship with Hurt's traveling companion might make an impression on his supervisors. Lord Arthur readily complied. After the arrest of Fanny and Stella, Hurt took a leave of absence (perhaps to avoid being fired) and hurried to London to follow the case. He met with Boulton's lawyers and tried to talk with prosecutors to vouch for the defendants. Hurt was completely taken up with concern for his friends and increasing anxiety about his personal position. Walking the streets of the capital, he could not escape the situation: "I have just seen a crowd standing around Boulton and Park's photographs in a shop."[203] Sensing danger, he warned Fiske, who remained in Edinburgh: "I have seen a copy of the suppressed letter, which as I have telegraphed to you, contains your full name and address. There is nothing indecent in it, of course, but it is in the most high flown language. After this letter, I cannot understand why your rooms have not been searched. Perhaps it is because you have been consul."[204] Hurt went to Bow Street for a glimpse of his dear friend: "Yesterday I was in court and rather regretted going when I saw how pale and worn poor little Ernie looked."[205] After the magistrate committed the case for trial, he urged Fiske to come help: "It is possible I shall be called as a witness for the defense, and I advise you to go to London at once in case you should be required. I really think, that for your own sake as well as for Ernest's, you should go and explain, if called as a witness, what utter nonsense your letters were. At any rate, send an explanation of your letters and a full statement of your acquaintance with him."[206] Fiske's diplomatic status did not qualify him for immunity. Neither he nor Hurt was able to help "poor little Ernie," since they ended up standing trial beside him. By indicting Fiske and Hurt, the prosecution not only put them at risk but also silenced their efforts to defend their friend. That burden fell to Mrs. Boulton and Judge Park; sympathetic landladies, housemaids, and fellow lodgers; medical experts; and, primarily, the barristers who were well paid to speak for the four men in the dock.

9. THE CLASH OF INTERPRETATIONS

The queer case of Mr. Boulton and Mr. Park had become such a high-profile matter that the prosecution was conducted by the attorney general. Each of the accused was represented by counsel drawn from the top rank of Victorian trial lawyers. Since dozens of witnesses had appeared to present evidence, the proliferation of information required interpretation if the jury was to reach a final decision. Each barrister gave two long speeches outlining his view of the case. The attorney general was obliged to make an opening statement and to speak again after the defense evidence. Defense counsel spoke on behalf of their clients at the conclusion of the prosecution case and again after their own witnesses had testified. Finally, the Lord Chief Justice gave instructions to the jury on the relevant law and offered his own commentary on the evidence. The "special jury" of propertied gentlemen had the job of resolving this clash of interpretations. As the voluminous publicity reveals, the trial of Stella, Fanny, and their admirers was fraught with contested issues touching on gender, sexuality, social class, and urban culture. The lawyers' rhetoric occasionally suggests that the fate of the nation might hang on the verdict. At the same time, each defense counsel oddly reflects the character of his individual client. Since the defendants were barred from testifying on their behalf, their attorneys were licensed to speak for them.

The law court is not insulated from the greater world. The attorney general opens his case by referring to the widespread publicity surrounding the "revelations in the police court" that led to "a popular apprehension . . . that

Sodom on the Thames

a crime held in peculiar detestation in this country had been committed." As the defendants were four "gentlemen . . . well educated and well connected," the prosecutor acknowledges that all "might experience a sensation of relief" if this "apprehension" were unfounded. Anticipating character evidence on behalf of the accused men, he summarizes their social background and employment histories. Still the prosecutor's task is to demonstrate that the "most searching investigation" by the Home Office showed that serious crimes had been committed. His summary of the indictment outlines what he had to prove:

> The defendants and other persons mentioned in the indictment, and also I regret to say, other persons whose names have not yet been discovered, associated together, spoke and wrote to each other, in such a manner as to indicate that relations subsisted between them such as are only permissible between men and women; that by sometimes dressing in female costume, sometimes in male costume, with a studied air of effeminacy, powdering their necks, painting their faces, by amatory airs and gestures, they endeavored to excite each others' passions and to make themselves objects of desire to persons of their own class. That they slept together, that they lived together upon the terms of man and wife, or I should more properly say of lover and mistress, that they addressed each other in terms of endearment, such as men only address to women, and that they wrote to each other in the language of love, sometimes in that of violent passion, in short . . . they conspired for the purpose of the commission of unnatural offenses.[207]

The attorney general emphasizes the difficulty of finding direct evidence, since sexual offenses are likely to be committed in private and the participants to be equally guilty. Witnesses with circumstantial evidence may be reluctant to come forward, fearing guilt by association. The public promenades of Boulton and Park remain central to the case. Since playing women's parts in theatricals is perfectly legal, the prosecutor concedes that an occasional foray offstage might be excused as a "lark" or "frolic." However, going about in drag "appears to have been the main occupation and business of their lives . . . adopted with such a persistence as leads to success in the profession." Both sides invoke professionalism as an explanation of Fanny's and Stella's cross-dressing. The jury has to decide whether their profession is acting or prostitution. The attorney general argues that their feminine display invites other men to pursue them as objects of desire.

The case is dominated by questions of sex, money, and class. The prosecution must prove that Boulton's and Park's very public conduct had the goal of sexual intimacy. The attorney general uses the private living arrangements of the accused to establish the point. Sharing beds becomes a major issue, as he turns the social position of the defendants against them: "Among the poorer classes, as we all know, such a habit is not very uncommon, and perhaps it was not very uncommon among our own class some 50 or 60 years ago." The prosecutor confidently assumes that the jury shares his social assumptions: "It does seem exceedingly strange that a gentleman in Mr. Hurt's position accustomed to all the comforts and luxuries of life, and well acquainted with the ways of the highest classes in this country should sleep in the same bed with another gentleman."[208] Money also comes into play: "Having plenty of funds to purchase silks, satins and velvets it seems strange they could not afford two beds."[209]

The attorney general argues that Boulton slept with Park at 13 Wakefield Street, with Hurt in Edinburgh, and with Lord Arthur Clinton at Southampton Street and elsewhere. His friends paid the bills: "Boulton was kept by Lord Arthur Clinton."[210] The men's letters show the amorous feelings they shared and document Boulton's demands for cash: "He had no resources and no occupation. . . . He is constantly asking for money."[211] The prosecutor has trouble tracking Stella's relationships. He argues that Boulton went from Lord Arthur's bed in London to Edinburgh, "where Mr. Hurt always paid his expenses and supplied him with money."[212] But Fiske's letters provide the best evidence of "violent passion": "Mr. Fisk [sic] was in point of fact in love with Boulton."[213] These extravagant effusions border on impropriety. Reading Fiske's comparison of Stella with "Lais and Antinous in one," the prosecutor interjects: "Combining the attributes of male and female prostitutes, that is ravishing." About the signature "With all the love in my heart," he comments, "Why this is the language of Corydon to Alexis," assuming the jury will recognize his allusion to Virgil's homoerotic pastoral.[214] To decide the case, the jury needs answers to some complicated questions: What did these men really want? Did they intend to commit forbidden sexual acts? Did they expect payment in return? Did they parade about the town in search of clients? Was Stella being "kept" by Lord Arthur in exchange for sexual favors? What about all the other men who hovered "like moths about a flame"?

Both the prosecution and defense attorneys imply that the verdict will reflect on "the state of England" if not quite of Western civilization. The attorney general defends his medical evidence with an odd nationalism: "Fortunately there is very little learning or knowledge upon this subject in this country; there are other countries in which I am told learned treatises are written as to the appearances to be expected in such cases."[215] He concludes by urging the jury not to shrink from their patriotic duty: "You will do what in you lies to stop this plague which if allowed to spread without check or hindrance might lead to a severe contamination of the national morals."[216] Boulton's attorney responds by commenting on the police surgeon's attempt to buttress his discredited testimony with foreign expertise, "having strengthened himself with the newfound treasures of French literature upon the subject—which, thank God is still foreign to the libraries of British surgeons."[217] He concludes his appeal for Ernest's acquittal by inverting the prosecutor's patriotism: "Pronounce by your verdict that they libel the morality and character of this country who say that that plague exists."[218] His enthusiasm carries him to heights of rhetoric: "Your verdict will establish that the moral atmosphere of England is not yet tainted with the impurities of continental cities, and that free as we are from our island position, we are insulated from the crimes to which you have heard allusion . . . that London is not cursed with the sins of Sodom, or Westminster with the vices of Gomorrah."[219]

Boulton's and Park's attorneys turn their clients' public "outrages" into a defense against the much more serious conspiracy charges. They outdo the prosecution in condemning "improper" and "unjustifiable" "acts of extravagance and folly." However, they argue that potential sexual offenders would avoid calling attention to themselves. Fanny's and Stella's display refutes the implication "that they were contemplating something over which the pall of darkness was to be drawn—something which was to be drawn away from the public light—which was to be indulgence of some secret horrible crime that men would shrink from suggesting even a trace or a suspicion of their intention." More positively, the lawyers stressed their clients' youth and their artistic milieu. Excesses of behavior and expression grew naturally from "a community of tastes and love for the theatricals, fondness for music, and other attractions of that kind."[220] In this context the young men found "charm" in each other's company and "familiarity" grew up among them. Mrs. Boulton testified that the intimate ties among Ernest and his friends were part of the family circle. His parents had encouraged his taste for performance and his friendships. Lord Arthur Clinton had shared these enthusiasms. References to their "marriage" were "banter" that took off from their performance as a couple in "The Morning Call." The women's clothing displayed in court was professionally required. Trying to fool people about their sex was Fanny's and Stella's "stupid lark," "feckless" youth out "for a laugh."[221] Boulton's talents had placed him at the center of the group: "[He] had a charm in his manner, an ability in performing the various parts to which he gave his attention which was naturally calculated to win the frank affection and the esteem of his friends, and to draw from them many of those high flown expressions which you find in these letters."[222] The "extravagant" and "theatrical" language of his admirers fed the "passion for admiration" that had become almost "second nature" to him.[223]

While condemning Boulton's "foolish vanity," his lawyer sets out to demolish claims that Stella had been a streetwalker or a kept woman. Lord Arthur Clinton was "a notorious insolvent," hardly "an apt subject for professional practice of this kind." The deadbeat aristocrat's correspondence showed "rather a disposition to make love and to dally with the fair sex in the natural way than an inclination to be guilty of this horrible crime."[224] Boulton's other admirers were well-off, but not in a position to offer more than occasional assistance. Stella's casual acquaintances had not been paying clients. Mundell had "paid for nothing"; Cox, for champagne only. Boulton did not behave like "these professional—shall I say—sodomites": "The profession was not bringing in very large profits apparently. If it was trade, it was an uncommonly beggarly one."[225]

The extensive surveillance to which they were subjected would have unearthed proof of sexual misconduct if there had been any. The testimony that they had solicited in the Burlington Arcade was incredible: "Will you accept in its entirety the evidence of that ex-beadle, ex-policeman, ex-railway servant and extra-ordinary witness?"[226] Despite their professional hermeneutics of suspicion, the police had found nothing beyond the public displays of Fanny and Stella:

> Of all men they are men whose every practice and career in the detection of crime makes them quick to detect the scent of guilt: A policeman's eye and his very vision becomes intensified in the pursuit of crime—his ear becomes rapid and quick in detecting words or expressions in favor of guilt— looks cannot escape him—acts in public cannot escape him and believe me if the police have their eye on a particular character or if it be their duty to ransack London and Westminster for the purpose of obtaining evidence of acts of criminality the London and Metropolitan police may at all events receive the credit to produce, if it is to be the foundation for suspicion, something like evidence in favor of the conclusion to which they ask you to come.[227]

Even with the assistance of theater managers, landladies, and housemaids, the prosecution found not one instance of Boulton's engaging a stranger in conversation, much less going off with him or taking him home.

Sodom on the Thames

Park's counsel develops the claim that Boulton and Park had immersed themselves in the culture of the theater. The legal scholar reminds his jury of "what we have read," that at earlier periods of history, all the female parts were taken by men and that "it never was suggested that these male actors who personated female characters were guilty of any unnatural conduct." Rather, "they prided themselves upon this performance of female parts and were petted for it."[228] Fanny and Stella had been celebrated and invited in costume to the homes of admiring spectators. The lawyer underlines "how openly it was all done." Park's counsel appeals to the jury as men of the world: "Great familiarity is bred upon the stage. Actors and actresses probably have a more thoroughly familiar life with each other . . . than any other class of people, and there is bred an intimacy which I believe is unknown in other portions of society; but you gentlemen must know that this is so and must not judge this young man by the circle of Society in which you yourselves move. You must take a broad glance and see what other men and women do before you judge them."[229]

Their crossing the border between stage and street in the West End was "absolute idiocy," but it did not make them male prostitutes. The most offensive of Park's follies undercuts the prosecution's case: "But, gentlemen, does a man go into the Ladies Retiring Room for the purpose of committing the detestable crime charged here, or soliciting it, or inviting anyone to commit it?"[230] The physical evidence too points toward the performing life. Whereas the jury had greeted the display of clothes with a "thrill of horror," the lawyer put it in its place: "These dresses are theatrical wardrobes, neither more nor less." As for the makeup: "There is paint—there is powder—all this is theatrical. It is theatrical and—I must use the word plainly—not sodomitical."[231] The jokes among the group are explained by their theatrical experience: "Off the stage, [Boulton and Park] treated each other still as females, going by female names and having, as it were, female relations towards each other—there is no doubt they did it."[232] The sisterly relations between the two rebut the implication of unnatural practices (see figure 6, above). The only man with whom Park was proved to have shared a bed was Boulton: "It is charged in reference to them that they leant their persons to others of the defendants, but it is hardly suggested . . . that they indulged with each other in the practice of this dreadful crime."[233] Their shared femininity apparently ruled out sexual intercourse.

Since Hurt and Fiske had not been part of the crowd following Fanny and Stella around the West End, their attorneys' main task was to rebut the apparent implications of their clients' letters. Both men seemed smitten by Boulton, so Stella shines bright in their lawyers' speeches. The police expedition to Edinburgh had yielded some photographs and ambiguous information about sleeping arrangements, but also raised questions about whether the investigators had gone too far. Since Hurt and Fiske were men of evident character and respectability, their lawyers underlined the damage already done to their reputations. Hurt's attorney claims: "A man who has a charge of this sort made against him never regains his position. It may be proved to be false— it may be proved to be unfounded—but when he goes into the world he is pointed out as the man who has been charged with it and there are too many who will believe he has been guilty of it."[234] He insists on the conventional character of Hurt's "intimate friendship": it was perfectly natural for him to reciprocate the hospitality of Mr. and Mrs. Boulton by inviting Ernest to Scotland to recuperate. Hurt's letters had urged Boulton to give up going about in drag, to start paying his bills, grow a mustache, and assume the responsibilities of a gentleman. His innocence of "the most filthy vice" is proved by his plans to introduce "the man with whom he has been living to his mother" and to travel with her in Europe.[235] Still the attorney has some explaining to do:

> Well, but he calls him "Stella." What a horrible offense. Gentlemen, I cannot call Mr. Louis Hurt to tell you how the name originated, nor can I call Mr. Boulton, but at Scarborough in Essex, all over the country wherever this young man assumed female characters, you heard of him as being the star of the evening.[236]

Some of his friends used the nickname "even in the presence of his mother— who never resented it." Boulton's effeminacy made him a "curiousity," exciting admiration and comment wherever he appeared. There are quite respectable contexts where beautiful young men are given women's names: "There are none of us who have passed through a public school who have not known at least half a dozen boys who have always been called by female names and laughed at and treated as girls." While most men outgrow this kind of "chaff," Boulton became "enamored" with ambiguous performances: "He was constantly playing, and his greatest amusement in life seems to have consisted, first of all in going out in men's clothes pretending to be a woman and going out at other times in women's clothes, acting the part and character."[237]

Ernest's "folly" did not prevent him from being a "most agreeable companion": "He had great powers of amusing; he had wonderful powers of mimicry." How attractive such a "cheerful companion" would be in Scotland's "dull country quarters"! Boulton was much better company than "some long-headed Scotchman who would be speaking of subjects above his head."[238] The lengthy stay offered Ernest a rest while providing his host with a welcome taste of the city. Lord Arthur Clinton had consented to the visit, which would have been unlikely if Boulton were sexually intimate with either of them. The attorney offers elaborate proof that Boulton had never shared a bed with Hurt. The extravagance of some of Hurt's letters, departing from his generally sober style, express the enthusiasm of youthful friendship: "Undoubtedly they were exceedingly fond of one another, talking together more as boys than as young men would, making a noise with their piano, and singing and taking part in theatricals whenever they got a chance."[239] The only complaint from Hurt's landlady about Ernest's visit had been that they played secular music on the Sabbath![240] On hearing of his friend's arrest, Hurt had rushed to London, attending magistrate's court and trying to explain "those letters which may have been a great deal too foolish and warm in their expression."[241] He had written Fiske urging him to admit "what utter nonsense" his own letters were. When Hurt writes of "poor little Ernie," his lawyer comments: "You will see he treats him almost as a boy still."[242] Hurt's responsible behavior is incompatible with Hurt's guilt.

Fiske's letters are the most extravagant of the lot, but his lawyer emphasizes that his client had met Boulton only a couple of times in Edinburgh. He too had come voluntarily to London: "This young man who is a foreigner, an American with no duties here but his official duties [at Leith], might have taken the first Cunard steamer to America."[243] Still, Stella had made quite an impression. Fiske's "high-flown language" is a kind of "mock adoration," which Hurt had described accurately as "utter nonsense." Other witnesses, including Mundell and Cox, had been charmed by Stella's impersonation: "It seems to have followed in the most natural way that everybody who became at all intimate with this young man addressed him in accordance with the character he had assumed, that of a pretty woman admired by all who came into contact with her." His letters were those "which Mr. Fiske would address to a young fellow whom he liked and who was habitually addressed as a young and pretty woman."[244] He had addressed "this dainty youth, or pleasing boy" as one might write "a very young brother who is still a child."[245]

Fiske's lawyer argues that the romantic intensity of his client's prose precludes sexual vice. The attorney works hard to explain Fiske's classical allusions:

Whatever may have been the case with a Pagan, and we know from classical literature that this abominable sentiment has been clothed by classical authors in language not wanting in grace and feeling, and even in sentiment, but in modern times for any man to suppose it possible that that kind of attachment which must subsist between two persons who have this horrible and guilty relation can be coupled with any other state of mind than one of gross sensuality, and one of self-abasement; or that anything resembling the poetry and sentiment which attaches to the tenderness of feeling between a man and woman is . . . to anybody who considers what way the human mind and the human conscience are constituted inconceivable.

Hadrian's favorite, Antinous, represents neither "unnatural vices" nor prostitution but rather "manly beauty," as attested "in every gallery of Europe." Lais is the "type" of female beauty along with Aspasia and Cleopatra: "I am afraid none of them would be able to bear the moral criticism of my friend the Attorney-General."[246]

In Victorian England, sodomy is incompatible with sentiment: "It is inconceivable that two Christians in the nineteenth century, having towards each other the relations that are imputed to these young men, should express their mutual attachment in language savoring of sentiment, refinement or respect."[247] The lawyer even argued that Fiske's extravagant language might be a national trait: "Not only is Mr. Fisk a young man, but he is an American, and our trans-Atlantic cousins whose home is in the setting sun, use language more figurative and warm, and far more colored than is usual with us."[248] Fiske's letters reveal excesses of literary culture rather than any propensity to sexual vice: "Is this the way that persons committing unnatural crimes express themselves when writing to the object of them? Is it by far fetched similes and metaphors drawn from classical learning that such things are spoken of?"[249]

Linguistic arguments do not carry the day. The Lord Chief Justice demurs: "There are American productions in the first ranks of literature, but I do not know that they use a different language from what we do." In his turn, the attorney general comments: "I will not libel the Americans by supposing they are in the habit of addressing each other in this way."[250] He also rejects the claim that sentimental language precludes unnatural vice. Distinguishing "the language of friendship" from "the language of love," he rules out the "intimate friendship" invoked by the defense.[251] When the language of "passionate love" is addressed by a man to another man, it becomes the language of "lust."[252] The letters to Stella from her admirers reveal "guilty desire."[253] The allusion to "Lais and Antinous in one" offers the key to Boulton's and Park's variations in dress: "Sometimes a male prostitute, sometimes a female."[254]

The judge in a criminal trial gets the last word before the case goes to the jury. His task is to explain the applicable law and, in British courts, to comment on the evidence presented at trial. The Lord Chief Justice has strong convictions about both these matters. His charge to the jury takes much of the final afternoon. From the beginning he criticizes the conspiracy prosecution, explaining that it places defendants at a double disadvantage. One may be prejudiced by evidence against a codefendant that has no bearing on the other defendant's actions, while being deprived of potentially helpful testimony from those charged along with him. Hurt and Fiske had been eager to testify in Boulton's and Park's defense until they found themselves in the dock beside them.[255] The judge emphasizes that the offenses against "public decency" relating to Fanny's and Stella's cross-dressing are not before the jury. They had to decide the charges of conspiracy to commit "the felonious and odious act" of sodomy and to induce others to do so. This involves two distinct questions: whether members of the group planned to have sex with each other and whether they tried to get others to have sex with them. As to the former, "private" intentions might be deduced from their correspondence or domestic behavior; the latter turned on their public conduct. The jury had to decide whether evidence of their personal relations showed that they "have combined together to commit the offense of sodomy among themselves."[256] Similarly, they had to decide whether their public conduct was an invitation to third parties to join them in prohibited sexual practices. However "repulsive," "offensive," and "objectionable," their cross-dressing alone does not prove them guilty of conspiracy to solicit.

The Lord Chief Justice vehemently condemns Boulton's and Park's transvestism: "Where it is done even for frolic, even for the amusement of the individual at the expense of public decency, it ought to be subject to the most severe and summary punishment."[257] (He proposes the treadmill and flogging for repeat offenders.) However, this behavior may not be a solicitation of sexual intimacy. Although their repeated conflicts with security personnel and their attempt to bribe an arresting officer show consciousness of guilt, this does not necessarily imply they are guilty of the more serious charges. Cross-dressing itself was an offense against public decency. What inferences may be drawn from "men unsexing themselves . . . adopting the garb and appearance of women, painting and powdering themselves, and tricking themselves out in tawdry tinsel finery, assuming not only the appearance of women to whose sex they do not belong, but of fallen women of the lowest description, what in euphemistic language are called gay women but what you and I should call prostitutes of the street"?[258] The pair's theatrical activities provide a "satisfactory" explanation for how they had come to possess and wear women's clothes. The judge practically endorses Mrs. Boulton's theory of her son's development: "He got to be inspired with that feminine vanity which we do not always object to in the female but which is repulsive in the man."[259] Ernest's extravagance "gratified a marked and a vitiated taste and a feeling of vanity in finding themselves addressed and made much of and explored."[260]

Although Fanny's and Stella's conduct had been "as extraordinary as one ever heard of in almost all the extraordinary scandals that from time to time have arisen," the Lord Chief Justice nevertheless finds the evidence "wanting in proof of the purpose which is alleged in this indictment."[261] The extensive surveillance by police and security personnel failed to detect any attempt to solicit strangers. On the one occasion when an officer observed a tipsy encounter, "they parted with those gentlemen and went home. They did not take them to their home."[262] Even the most hostile witness had not offered conclusive evidence: "I daresay that if they had taken the precaution of offering a suitable gratuity to that guardian of the public morals in the Burlington Arcade, Mr. Smith, they might not have been so forcibly dealt with, but it seems they did not take that step, and therefore Mr. Smith, the austere guardian of the public morals when he is not paid for being the contrary, very properly excluded them."[263] Expressing outrage at Stella's and Fanny's affront to "public decency," the judge clears them of conspiracy against "public morals." Their teasing exhibitions were indefensible but did not amount to "solicitation."

The Lord Chief Justice's summary of the conspiracy case inclined toward the defense. Repeatedly adverting to the social position of the accused, he appeared to accept their interpretation of the group's conduct and relationships: "Mrs. Boulton I have no doubt very naturally thought that it would grace the private theatricals which she from time to time had at her own house if she had amongst her performers a man of the distinguished rank of Lord Arthur Clinton."[264] The judge is more disturbed by familiarity across differences of age and class than by any implication of sexual impropriety. Fanny's letters to her "brother-in-law" posed a problem: "'My dearest Arthur,' addressed to a man considerably older than he, . . . a man of much higher rank than himself . . . the word 'wretch' is stranger still."[265] The debate about classical allusions in the defendants' correspondence provoked a spirited defense of Greek love:

> We know that love of this description has been associated with the name
> and with memory of the greatest philosopher of antiquity, but the learned,
> the wise, and the good in every age have come to the belief that the senti-
> ment which undoubtedly Socrates entertained for the youths with whom

Sodom on the Thames

he delighted to associate, was one of a spiritual and ethereal character in which no sensual desire was mixed. . . . There was nothing beyond that which was purely spiritual and had nothing to do with gross and degrading sensuality, that the soul of that great philosopher who in all his aspirations loved beauty in its purity and virtue in its holiness was never contaminated and soiled by the sensuality of gross and unnatural and loathsome lust.[266]

The judge's detailed examination of the medical evidence left no doubt that he found it without probative value. He refused to lend judicial authority to the prosecution's zeal. The Lord Chief Justice criticized the police surgeon for undertaking an intrusive and unauthorized physical examination; the police, for traveling beyond their jurisdiction to Scotland in search of evidence and wrongdoers; and the legal authorities, for charging a conspiracy.

In the end, the jury took less than an hour to acquit the defendants. In the spirit of earlier coverage, one paper reported the climax under the headline "The Female Impersonators": "They did not display their light-coloured kidgloves, as on former days, and the familiar bouquet was dispensed with. Boulton fainted upon the verdict being returned, and upon his recovery, the prisoners left the court with their friends."[267] Who were these friends unembarrassed to show their solidarity with the notorious pair? Why did the crowd cheer? Were they convinced of the innocence of the young men? Or were they complicit in a successful subversion of legal authority?

10. FANTASY ECHOES

"You remember the Boulton and Park scandal court case? Well; I was present at the ball given at Haxell's Hotel in the Strand," announces John Saul in *The Sins of the Cities of the Plain, or Confessions of a Mary-ann*. He has just asserted: "The extent to which sodomy is carried on in London between gentlemen and young fellows is little dreamed of by the outside public." Perhaps to protect the actual landlord while opening the way to further titillation packaged as historical truth, he claims: "No doubt the proprietor was quite innocent of what our fun really was; but there were two or three dressing rooms into which the company might retire at pleasure."[268] The novel goes on to describe in extensive and explicit detail multiple couplings during the orgy concluding the evening's entertainment. What would the fastidious Mr. Gibbings have said? Was this the cause of Agnes Earl's distress? Of the altercation that led Gibbings to end the party prematurely? Or have we stumbled onto the source of its success despite those mishaps?

Boulton and Park must be among the few historical individuals to become major figures in a pornographic novel. Privately printed in London in 1881, the book opens with the narrator's account of his encounter with John Saul of Lisle Street, the eponymous "Mary-ann," whom he met in Leicester Square. The succeeding chapters purport to be based on Saul's account of his life. During the Cleveland Street affair of 1889–1890, a man by that name came forward to give statements to police and to testify in court (see part 3, below). On the witness stand he described himself as a "professional sodomite." There is more than a passing resemblance between John Saul, the person represented in official papers and press accounts, and the character by that name in the novel. Although these *Confessions* should not be taken as an accurate depiction of anyone's "real life," the work maps a Victorian sexual underworld not so different from the spaces traversed by Ernest Boulton and Frederick Park.[269] It resonates in a different key with the suspicions voiced in the press about what went on "behind the scenes" of their public performance.

The book's publication just ten years after the trial demonstrates the existence of an audience willing to pay well for an imaginative elaboration of the possibilities conjured by the pair.[270] Fanny and Stella move through a domain where social reality and erotic fantasy intersect. The trial testimony did not touch on actual sexual conduct, except for the highly problematic and ultimately rejected medical evidence. The jury had been asked to infer illicit sex from the defendants' public behavior and the expressions of affection in the letters of Stella's admirer. In the end they chose not to make that leap of faith. Most newspapers, which abbreviated the medical evidence or omitted it entirely, left readers to fill in the details from their own imaginations. There can be little doubt, however, that many who observed and interacted with Fanny and Stella had sex on their minds. The pair is immortalized in a limerick:

> There was an old person of Sark
> Who buggered a pig in the dark
> The swine in surprise
> Murmured: "God blast your eyes,
> Do you take me for Boulton and Park?"[271]

The Sins of the Cities of the Plain goes much further in developing fantasmatic possibilities evoked by images of the cross-dressers. The narrative both capitalizes on the ambiguities surrounding their sex and gender and purports to expose the "truth" about their sexual activities.

The pornographic fiction does depart from the historical record. Whereas Gibbings had testified that Clinton did not attend his party, the novel reports that Boulton "was superbly got up as a beautiful lady and Lord Arthur was very spooney upon her."[272] Saul follows the couple to one of the dressing rooms where he spies through the keyhole on their lovemaking: "Quietly kneeling down I put my eye to the hole, and found I had a famous view of all that was going on in the next room. It put me in mind of the two youths which Fanny Hill relates to have seen through a peephole at a roadside inn."[273] The literary reference should increase suspicion about the historical accuracy of the tale. Boulton is called "Laura," not "Stella." Her drag name and costume is conjoined with a male organ that commands the attention of both her lover and the randy spy: "His lordship quickly opened Laura's thighs, and putting his hand into her drawers, soon brought to light as manly a weapon as any lady could desire to see."[274] Lord Arthur performs fellatio on his partner with great enthusiasm before anally penetrating her. Saul leaves his post before the climax. Later he meets the couple together with Park, who is called "Selina," not "Fanny." At this point the Mary-ann reveals that he too was in drag: he is introduced by the proprietor as "Miss Eveline."[275] The sexual enterprise of the guests at the drag ball is not restricted to encounters behind closed doors: "Soon after the lights were turned out and a general lark in the dark took place. I do not for a moment believe there was one real female in the room, for I groped ever so many of them, and always found a nice little cock under their petticoats."[276] At the end of the evening, Eveline goes off with Laura and Selina to their flat, where "I believe the people of the house thought that we were gay ladies," that is, female prostitutes.[277] Of course, a threesome is in the offing: "'Now Eveline, Selina and I want a bit of fun with you all alone by ourselves. It will be real love; not the mercenary, paid love we give our customers. I have grown quite fond of you, and Selina won't be jealous. She will assist to make me happy.'"[278]

For John Saul, "Mary-ann" and "professional sodomite," Boulton and Park are fellow prostitutes; in *The Sins of the Cities of the Plain*, they all take pleasure in their work. First, Boulton regales his friends with a tale of seduction in which the inversions of sex, gender, and desire multiply at a dizzying rate. For those who followed the case, the story recalls the anxieties generated by Park's entry into the ladies' room at the Strand Theatre. The object of Boulton's desire is a woman—"Miss Bruce," a milliner whom "Laura" had enticed to her rooms with promises to buy her a new dress. Laura offers her guest pleasure without the risks that accompany sex with men. She "blushingly" explains that she suffered from "a malformation, something like the male instrument." After rounds of mutual oral sex, the transvestite manages to engage in vaginal intercourse with the milliner, who had been gulled by the assurance that she was not being penetrated by a penis.[279] Laura concludes: "She will be very lucky if she does not get a big belly!"[280] Excited by the tale, Selina and Eveline join her in an orgy that includes mutual masturbation, birching, and anal sex during which Saul penetrates Park while himself being penetrated by Boulton.

The Sins of the Cities of the Plain begins with a scene of urban cruising in a locale not far from the alleyway where Symonds was accosted by the young grenadier: "The writer of these notes was walking through Leicester Square one sunny afternoon last November, when his attention was particularly taken by an effeminate, but very good-looking young fellow, who was walking in front of him, looking in shop-windows from time to time, and now and then looking around as if to attract my attention."[281] Despite the attribution of effeminacy, the bulge in the fork of his trousers seems the main attraction: "Evidently he was favoured by nature by a very extraordinary development of the male appendage." The conjunction of apparently contradictory marks of gender should not surprise the student of Boulton and Park, or the admirer of Stella and Fanny. In this case, the narrator follows the ambiguous object of his desire into a picture shop, where he makes his move. Soon they are off in a cab to his chambers.[282] After a sustained bout of sexual athletics, the narrator, "Mr. Cambon," offers to pay Saul to write the story of his life. However, this account of the text's genesis ends on a note that should give further pause to the historian in search of verisimilitude: "At each visit we had a delicious turn at bottom-fucking, but as the recital of the same kind of thing over and over again is likely to pall upon my readers, I shall omit a repetition of our numerous orgies of lust, all very similar to the foregoing, and content myself by a simple recital of his adventures."[283] Like a campy latter-day Scheherazade, Saul must entertain his patron (and *his* readers) with tales of erotic adventure so diverse and imaginative that their prurient interest will not pale. He emphasizes the mixing of aristocratic and middle-class clients of apparent respectability with male prostitutes who may be got up in full feminine drag or military uniform—some in both. (What might Symonds have made of that?) This material is unlikely to reflect social practice, but it does illuminate the erotic imagination of Victorian gentlemen seeking alternatives to a more domestic sexual regime. The police are nowhere in sight.

But the historical Boulton and Park were arrested and prosecuted. Their trial continually crossed and confounded conventional lines between private and public. The prosecution argued vigorously that the pair's cross-dressing, flirtatious interactions, and epistolary effusions manifested unnatural desires

Sodom on the Thames

and a propensity to sexual vice. The defense contended that the very publicity of the offensive conduct was proof of its innocence: no one engaged in the pursuit of criminal pleasures would call so much attention to himself. Contestations of meaning entered a plurality of intermediate zones: households, clubs, parties, restaurants, theaters, streets, and arcades. The home itself is shown to be a site of discipline and surveillance. Landladies and servants testified to the details of daily life. Police entered domestic spaces, searching flats and confiscating clothes, photographs, and personal correspondence. Ironically, the only act of anal penetration proved in this case of alleged sodomitical conspiracy was performed by the police surgeon. To rebut the charges, Boulton and Park introduced their own personal revelations. Park's father testified about his finances while Boulton's mother offered a portrait of her son's childhood. Physicians testified about the condition of the defendants' most intimate bodily spaces. Fanny and Stella got themselves into trouble because they had flouted social norms regarding the proper boundaries between public display and private desire. The effort to police their activities culminated in the licensing of acts of medical sodomy and the staging of a public spectacle beyond their wildest dreams.

PART TWO ❦ LOVE STORIES

1. SCHOOLS FOR SCANDAL

West of London along the Thames lies Eton College, perhaps the premier "public" school in England. In 1872, William Johnson, one of its most distinguished teachers, resigned his post under a cloud of suspicion. Rumor had it that his love for his pupils had got him into trouble, but they rallied around to help him through difficult times. Friendships between the teacher and his students, and among the students themselves, lasted for the rest of their lives. These lives were marked by the continuing importance of love between men. Scandals at school did not often make the newspapers. Troublesome boys were subject to local discipline or were expelled to meet with further punishment from their families if they went too far. Errant masters were urged to resign quietly or were simply dismissed if they did not see the error of their ways. The English public school (though private in the American sense) occupied a central role in educating the male offspring of prominent and aspiring families throughout the nineteenth century. Boys were sent off very early in their lives, often at seven or eight years old, and remained with their fellows until they went off to all-male universities or the army.

Thomas Arnold, headmaster of Rugby, had become a nationally celebrated figure for the reforms he introduced, emphasizing the school's role in forming not only the minds but also the character and sensibilities of the young. The boys were taught by men and lived together in houses over which their teachers presided with the assistance of matrons, who saw that they were properly fed, clothed, and nursed when ill. The houses themselves were organized with older boys serving as prefects and heads of house accountable to the headmaster for maintaining public spirit and proper discipline. The boys were placed in strict hierarchies, the younger ones serving as "fags," virtual servants, to their elders. Corporal punishment in the form of flogging could be administered by teachers or older boys. Sports, clubs, and other activities were seen as integral to the boys' education. Often "games" overshadowed classroom instruction in the collective life and shared ethos of the school. Debates about the proper curriculum and organization of public schools took on national importance, since so many elite families sent their boys there to be prepared for places "serving" their country. Statesmen, soldiers, clergymen, and scholars of the future often began their careers in these schools. Their teachers and masters were celebrated for shaping the leaders of the future, many of whom excelled even as boys. Life at school was a formative experience for the elite of the British Empire.

School days exerted a powerful hold on the imagination. Here is a lyrical moment from Benjamin Disraeli's *Coningsby,* written in 1844 by the future prime minister, who had been educated privately at home:

At school, friendship is a passion. It entrances the being; it tears the soul. All loves of afterlife can never bring its rapture, or its wretchedness; no bliss so absorbing, no pangs of jealousy or despair so crushing and so keen! What tenderness and what devotion; what illimitable confidence; what infinite revelations of inmost thoughts; what ecstatic present and romantic future; what bitter estrangements and melting reconciliations; what scenes of wild recrimination, agitating explanations, passionate correspondence; what insane sensitiveness, and what frantic sensibility; what earthquakes of the heart, and whirlwinds of the soul are confined in that simple phrase of schoolboy's friendships.[1]

Yet the removal of young boys from their families and their isolation in almost exclusively masculine company for crucial years in their development had effects beyond those intended by the men in charge and their supporters in society at large. (The letters to the *Times* in the wake of the Boulton and Park case debating the dangers of cross-dressing in theatrical performances offer a glimpse of the anxieties that all-male schools could provoke.) Headmasters and teachers exercised considerable power over their charges, while the concentration of so many unruly young males in closed settings escaped the most intensive efforts at discipline and surveillance. Public schools could become sites of brutal bullying, erotic turmoil, and potential scandal.

Such scenes could become the subject of a fantasy rather different from Disraeli's. In *The Sins of the Cities of the Plain*, the narrator, "John Saul," provides a vivid picture of his brief stay "at a boarding-school near Colchester when ten years old." On his first night in the dormitory, sharing a bed with "a senior named Freeman," he repeats the practice of mutual masturbation already learned from a cousin at home and is initiated into the joys of anal sex when encouraged to penetrate the older boy. The next morning, Freeman proudly introduces him to the other six boys in the dorm, asking Jack to display the instrument of the previous night's pleasure: "They all crowded 'round to handle and admire what they called a wonder for such a little'un."[2] The boys draw lots to see who will be first to penetrate our hero, and the orgy that follows culminates in a daisy chain: "Looking 'round to see all that was going on, I found my lover also has one in his bottom, and the whole of them soon formed a perfect string in action, each one in the bottom in front of him, forming a fleshy chain of eight links." When they climax in unison, "I almost fainted from excessive emotion."[3] The narrator provides only a cursory glance at the nights that followed, reporting that they frequently "changed place and partners" and sometimes switched from anal to oral intercourse. John Saul's school days play only a small role in his fictional erotic autobiography. The brief chapter concludes with the news of his father's death, which led his mother to bring him home because she could no longer afford the fees: "As it turned out, this prevented my constitution being ruined for life by such early precocity; besides, it was all found out and the school broken up soon afterwards."[4]

Toward the end of the book, the narrator offers the school stories of another character whose adventures included sex with a junior teacher as well

Sodom on the Thames

as his fellow pupils. In an appendix, "The Same Old Story: Arses Preferred to Cunts," we are told that "the prevalence of sodomy amongst schoolboys is little suspected of being so general as it really is."[5] This claim is supported by "the master of a large academy where it appears the scholars have learnt something much more interesting than Latin and Greek." The suspicious schoolmaster spends several nights spying on the boys' nocturnal orgies until he is driven to seek medical help: "It nearly drove me wild. If I don't stop it they will draw me into their practices, and I can't resist the temptations my peepholes afford; so what is to be done I don't know. Besides, my school would be ruined if it were found out."[6] The realities of life at school must have fallen somewhere between Disraeli's romance of boys' friendship and Saul's fantasy of group sex. Outside the restricted domain of pornography, Victorian society was so discomfited by sexual matters that trouble of this sort tended to be handled informally, if at all. Johnson was not the first master to steal quietly from the scene, nor would he be the last.

Dr. Charles John Vaughan, a student and admirer of Arnold at Rugby, served as headmaster at Harrow from 1844 until he retired precipitously in 1859. After that, he occupied the relatively obscure position of vicar of Doncaster. In 1864, he first accepted and then declined Prime Minister Lord Palmerston's offer of the bishopric of Rochester. Eventually, he took on the more visible and prestigious church posts of Master of the Temple in 1869 and dean of Landalff in 1879. When he died in 1897, Vaughan left instructions that his papers be destroyed and no biography written. The fullest account of the circumstances surrounding his departure from Harrow is offered in John Addington Symonds's *Memoirs,* written in 1889–1893 but not published until 1984. During his school days at Harrow, Symonds had keenly disapproved of the sexual antics of other boys, while recognizing the direction of his own desires. He was shocked to hear from fellow student Alfred Pretor that he had been having a "love affair" with Vaughan: "I soon found that the boy was not lying, because he showed me a series of passionate letters written to him by our headmaster."[7]

Symonds was profoundly disturbed by this revelation, touching as it did his own struggles with his attraction to other males in the context of a stern upbringing and rigorous personal morality. His discovery also troubled continuing relations with his teacher:

> I used to take essays and verses at intervals to Vaughan in the study, which was the scene of his clandestine pleasures. . . . On these occasions, my young brain underwent an indescribable fermentation. I remember once

that, while studying Greek iambics, he began to stroke my right leg from the knee to the thigh. This insignificant caress, of which I should have thought nothing two months earlier, and which probably meant nothing, seemed then disagreeably suggestive.[8]

He did not tell anyone else what he had learned until after he left Harrow to study at Balliol College, Oxford. There he confided the story to John Conington, a Latin scholar who became his friend and who urged Symonds to inform his father, a distinguished physician. Symonds was able to substantiate his accusation with a letter from Vaughan to Pretor that he had saved, and with his own contemporary diaries. His father used the threat of public exposure to compel the headmaster's resignation from Harrow and his eventual refusal of a bishopric. The youth who had confided his affair to Symonds never spoke to the other man again.[9] We have only Symonds's account of the events leading to his exposure of Vaughan. Apparently he saved the incriminating letters between the headmaster and student but had them destroyed at his death.

Young Symonds's ambivalence about his intense feelings for other men and his own relationship to Vaughan complicate his account of this affair. The chapter of the *Memoirs* in which he discusses it begins with a surprisingly candid description of boys' life at school:

> Every boy of good looks had a female name, and was recognized either as a public prostitute or as some bigger fellow's "bitch." Bitch was the word in common usage to indicate a boy who yielded his person to a lover. The talk in the dormitories and the studies was incredibly obscene. Here and there one could not avoid seeing acts of onanism, mutual masturbation, the sports of naked boys in bed together. There was no refinement, no sentiment, no passion; nothing but animal lust in these occurrences.[10]

Still Symonds concedes that the headmaster's "passionate letters" to his student were a "love affair." His own feelings with Vaughan in the study reveal the ease with which an "insignificant caress" might become a sign of "clandestine pleasure." One cannot tell what Symonds knew, or believed, about actual practices between Vaughan and Pretor. Equally important, Symonds did not find in his own schoolboy friendships any of the "refinement," "sentiment," or "passion" for which he had longed. He did not develop such attachments until later, with a chorister at Bristol where his family lived and with fellow students at Oxford. For much of his life Symonds would negotiate internal conflicts between demanding moral standards and powerful sexual urges.

Sodom on the Thames

Three years after William Johnson resigned from Eton, Oscar Browning was fired by the headmaster. Browning had been a student and then a colleague of Johnson's. Both had become students and fellows of Kings College, Cambridge, where they were members of the elite Cambridge Conversacione Society, known as the Apostles. Each left Eton under a cloud in the 1870s amid suspicions he had behaved improperly with students. Although the two had much in common, they differed greatly in personal style and in their handling of similar crises in their lives and careers. The story of Johnson and his friends will take up the balance of this part of the book. First a brief sketch of Oscar Browning.

A charismatic, flamboyant, and contentious character, Browning was known to his contemporaries and to posterity as "OB." Unlike Johnson, he had become master of one of the residential houses, presiding over an institution known for the relative amenity of its life. OB's mother and sister helped run the place, which offered better food than most and boasted evenings of music and conversation attended by representatives of the larger world as well as by students and teachers from other houses. Browning and Johnson were both committed to including modern topics in the curriculum, and OB cultivated the aesthetic interests of his students as well. He too developed close personal ties with the boys, and sometimes with their families. Browning seems to have been an irritating colleague who often found himself in situations of conflict, both personal and ideological. One of these led him to clash with F. W. Hornby, the school's headmaster. Hornby was opposed to curricular innovation and emphasized that athletics built school spirit and boys' characters. Browning made no secret of his contempt for the headmaster and his views. He self-consciously promoted an alternative ethos, surrounding himself with young men drawn to more intellectual and aesthetic pursuits: "Boys will always admire the body, and it is the duty of the schoolmaster to make them admire the mind."[11] OB eagerly went beyond the boundaries of his own house to seek out promising (and attractive) young men. (In one of his letters, he defended this practice as analogous to that of a coach always on the lookout for athletic talent.) Browning's ongoing conflict with Hornby reached a crisis when another master complained that OB had "poached" on his territory by cultivating a friendship with one of his pupils, George Nathaniel Curzon. (Lord Curzon would become viceroy of India.) In a fraught interview, Hornby came close to making slanderous charges regarding OB's interest: "I hear that Wooley-Dodd has a good-looking pupil." The headmaster forbade any further contact with the young man at school. The youth was angered and disappointed by the loss of his older friend's company:

"I wrote a very long letter on Saturday evening to my father who I am sure takes a right view of the case, asking him at once to call upon [Hornby] to revoke his unjust decision; he cannot know how much harm he is doing by separating you from me."[12] Curzon's father, Lord Scarborough, supported his son, writing to OB:

> I am fully aware of your warm feelings + keen desire that he should grow up a manly, pure minded lad—+ though it is possible your notice of him may have tended to annoy his tutor—I give you full credit for acting from the purest motives + I do not wish the kindly relations between you + my boy to fall through. I quite believe that you were instrumental in rescuing George from companions of more than doubtful repute, + that your sole desire + object has been to elevate his character.[13]

With Scarborough's support, Browning avoided outright disobedience but signaled his defiance of the headmaster by traveling in Europe with the young man during the school vacation.

In 1875, Hornby sacked Browning for having enrolled more than the authorized number of students in his house without having obtained prior permission. OB had violated the rules, but he had easily received retroactive approval in the past. Browning was outraged by Hornby's action, and few observers at the time doubted that the reason given for his dismissal was a pretext. Powerful friends, often devoted parents of OB's admiring pupils, rallied to his defense. Questions were asked in Parliament, editorials appeared in the *Times,* and the governing board of Eton debated the matter. In the end, Browning lost. The board was not prepared to fire Hornby over this matter and declined to undercut the headmaster's authority. Whatever might have been said in society, no question of sexual impropriety was raised in public.

After leaving Eton, OB defiantly took up his life fellowship at Kings College, where he became a major Cambridge figure—and somewhat notorious "character"—for many decades. Browning effectively promoted the study of modern history at the university, though he was repeatedly disappointed in his ambition to be appointed professor. He energetically organized all sorts of activities, from political discussion groups to musical salons. OB ran unsuccessfully for Parliament as a Liberal and helped to establish institutes for workingmen's education and teacher training. Throughout his life, Browning maintained a wide and various acquaintance. Notoriously snobbish, he traveled to India at Curzon's invitation after he had become viceroy and jockeyed unsuccessfully to become tutor to Prince Albert Victor, older son of the Prince of Wales, when he studied at Cambridge. At the same time, he be-

Sodom on the Thames

· friended and assisted numerous young working-class men, who expressed their affection and gratitude in hundreds of letters now collected in the archive at Kings College.

2. INVENTIONS OF LOVE

I'll borrow life and not grow old;
And nightingales and trees .
Shall keep me, though the veins be cold,
As young as Sophocles.

And when I may no longer live,
They'll say, who know the truth,
He gave whate'er he had to give
To Freedom and to Youth.[14]

Not surprisingly, the author of the above lines was a schoolteacher, indeed one of the most celebrated tutors of young men in mid-nineteenth-century England. In another poem, "Heraclitus," William Johnson focuses on the loss of a dear young friend rather than on the vocation of pedagogy:

They told me, Heraclitus, they told me you were dead,
They brought me bitter news to hear and bitter tears to shed.
I wept, as I remembered, how often you and I
Had tired the sun with talking and sent him down the sky.[15]

In 1862, as an assistant master at Eton, he addressed these words to his fifteen-year-old student Lord Dalmeny, later Lord Rosebery:

My dear Dalmeny,
    What is the matter?
    Wood says you are not coming here any more, because I cut you.
    I don't agree to that.
    You cut me for four days.
    You came here on Thursday night and I was very polite, only Mr. Day's presence prevented any ordinary conversation.
    On Friday night I made reasonable overtures, stomaching my pride, which is not less than yours: only reason convinces me it must be subdued, or else I shall lose more than I can afford to lose in this dearth of sympathy.
    Why could you not be civil enough to come in on Saturday, or today; I have been in the whole of both days.[16]

To the contemporary reader, the plaint of the disappointed lover is hard to miss. After his sudden resignation in 1872, the author of these words would change his name to William Johnson Cory. The school continued to use the texts he had compiled for teaching Latin, but removed his name from the title page. Cory's poetry, steeped in classical rhyme schemes and allusion, continued to enjoy a limited but enthusiastic readership.

As Johnson, he had taught at Eton from the 1850s until 1872, exerting an extraordinary influence on generations of students. Many remained in touch with him throughout distinguished careers in public life and the professions. He had written textbooks; published *Ionica,* a volume of his own verse in 1859; and contributed to debates about public school curriculum and pedagogy. His best-known work may have been the Eton boating song. Although committed to classical education and inspired by ancient Greek models, Cory included modern history and current events in his teaching, urging students to develop their own critical capacities. He insisted on the centrality of personal ties between teachers and pupils in nurturing the young. Although fiercely demanding of his students, Cory criticized disciplinary models that established too great a distance between teacher and taught. He argued that learning was facilitated by ongoing conversation of the young with their teachers and with each other. Cory took great joy in the process. Both his classroom and lodgings became favored places for students to gather and talk. He defended a pedagogy grounded in personal relationships similar to that promoted by John Henry Newman in the Oxford tutorial system. Self-consciously committed to training future leaders, he numbered among his former students members of Parliament, cabinet ministers, and several prime ministers. Cory remained friends with Lord Rosebery throughout his life, though he did not live to see his favored pupil become prime minister.

Cory had been completely engaged with his work and was celebrated as an exemplary public school teacher. He impressed generations of students as a vivid, sometimes comical character and as an inspiring, demanding instructor. "He was tall, extremely short-sighted, indeed almost blind, with a high-pitched voice as if shouting in a very high wind," said one former pupil. "Nothing he taught could ever for a moment while he taught it, be dull," wrote Herbert Paul: "That he was teaching 'dead languages' never occurred either to him or his pupils. It was the living voice that came to us."[17] Another of Cory's students complained that he was "versed in the vocabulary of contempt" but proclaimed him "the most remarkable man I ever knew or am likely to know." The historian G. W. Prothero described Cory as "the most brilliant Eton tutor of his day"; Arthur Coleridge, a fellow teacher, called him "the wisest master who has ever been at Eton."[18] Yet some of his contemporaries judged him temperamentally ill-suited to the task of teaching boys.[19] Eton master Arthur C. Benson judged that "he was apt to make favorites. . . . He forfeited a wider influence by his reputation for partiality, and by his obvious susceptibility to grace of manner and unaffected courtesy."[20] After his resignation, Cory retired to Halsdon, a house belonging to his family, where he was joined for a while by one former student and visited by others.

In 1858, Cory had anonymously published *Ionica,* a collection of verse addressed to a young man, since identified as a former student, Charles Wood, later Lord Halifax.[21] The historian Timothy d'Arch Smith provides an account of its publication:

> His own two small books were issued in a strange way at the eccentric author's whim and expense. Ionica "was made up in a fortnight spent in solitude at Pangbourne on the Thames, August 1850, and was published secretly at the cost of £40 paid in advance." The second part, simply called Ionica II (1877) was privately printed without capital letters or punctuation, at Cambridge University Press. The two volumes were reprinted in one, bound in the pale blue of the Eton colours, in 1890 (dated 1891); and this is the edition—supplemented by a second edition and a de luxe issue in large paper published the following year—which circulated among the Uranians and became well-known, together with Benson's edition.[22]

One of the places Cory's verse had circulated was Balliol College, Oxford. As early as February 1859, John Addington Symonds, in his first year as an undergraduate, wrote his sister Charlotte: "I suppose you have not any of you read some poems called Ionica: they are making a stir in Oxford, both on account of their true poetry & the curious personal history involved. The author is an Eton Master, & I had all the enigmatical facts expounded to me."[23] *Ionica* had quickly made an impact within the small world of elite schools and universities, provoking speculation about its author. A later admirer of the book was Simeon Solomon, whose interest Cory noted in his journal of 1868: "Browning says that Solomon, a young painter, wishes to give me one of his drawings as a compliment for printed rhymes. I said I should be glad to have it. But it has not come yet: perhaps my vanity was flattered in vain."[24] (Solomon would lunch with Boulton and Park during their trial in 1871, meeting disgrace not long afterward after being arrested for having sex with another man in a public toilet.)

Cory's book mattered a great deal to Symonds. In 1889, he wrote his daughter Madge: "I wonder what you think of 'Ionica.' I used to dote upon that book when I was a lad at Oxford. But the best things in it (those written about Eton) are morbidly sentimental. The art of the verse is fine."[25] At about this time, he had begun work on the *Memoirs*, where he offers a fuller explanation of what *Ionica* had meant to him as a young man. He was given a copy by John Conington, the Oxford don who had persuaded him to tell his father about the affair between his classmate and the headmaster of Harrow:

> Conington was scrupulously moral and cautious. Yet he sympathized with romantic attachments for boys. In this winter he gave me Ionica; and I learned the love story of its author William Johnson (now Cory) the Eton master, and the pretty faced Charlie Wood (now Lord Halifax) of Ch. Ch. [Christ Church] who had been his pupil. That volume of verse, trifling as it may appear to casual readers, went straight to my heart and inflamed my imagination. It joined on in a singular manner to my recent experiences at Harrow, and helped to form a dream world of unhealthy fancies about love. I went so far as to write a letter to William Johnson, exposing the state of my feelings and asking his advice. The letter, addressed to O.D.Y. at the Union, duly came. It was a long epistle on paiderastia in modern times, defending it and laying down the principle that affection between people of the same sex is no less natural and rational than the ordinary passionate relations. Under Johnson's frank exposition of this unconventional morality there lay a wistful yearning sadness—the note of disappointment and forced abstention. I have never found this note absent in lovers of my sort and Johnson's, unless the men have cast prudence to the winds and staked their all on cynicism.[26]

What did it mean to be a "lover of my sort and Johnson's"? From early on, Symonds referred to the kind of love he shared with Cory as *"l'amour de l'impossible."* He also called it "Arcadian," but his explanation of that terms undercuts its conventional associations: "Heaven forgive that innocent euphemism! I took it from an oracle from Herodotus that attracted my attention by its great strength and beauty: . . . ['You ask me for Arkadia; a great request you make of me. I will not grant it.']"[27] Cory shared and helped to shape Symonds's unconventional understanding of love between men. Both adopted and transformed the model of ancient Greek pederasty, which placed the ties between older and younger men at the heart of civic education. Symonds combined this ideal with celebrations of Renaissance *sprezzatura* and democratic camaraderie, while Cory tapped veins of sentiment from classical pastoral elegy and English romantic poetry. The Eton master introduced

Sodom on the Thames

generations of students to modes of feeling and forms of friendship inspired by this heady brew.

3. "THE FAERY REALM OF BOYHOOD"

When Johnson resigned in 1872, Simeon Solomon wrote Algernon Swinburne: "Have you heard that Johnson has left and changed his name to Cory? It is creating quite a sensation at Eton."[28] Old Etonian Reginald Brett left Cambridge to help his former teacher move to the cottage at Halsdon, where he would live for the next few years. Known to his circle as "Regy," Brett withdrew temporarily from Trinity College to stay with his friend for several months during this difficult transition. Cory, affectionately known as "Tute" (short for "Tutor"), had been the center of student life for a small group of his favorites. They not only studied with him but also spent their free time together in his classroom, called "the Cabin," and his lodgings, "the Trap" (for "Mousetrap"). Some of them, including Regy and Charles Williamson, known as "Chat" (for "Chatterbox"), would continue their friendships with one another and with Tute past their school days. They exchanged letters and visits over many years. Brett, the son of a successful barrister and judge, would launch a political career, serving briefly in Parliament, working actively behind the scenes in Liberal Party politics, and becoming a high-level civil servant in the Ministry of Works, which made him a close adviser and confidant to several generations of the royal family. On his father's death, he became the second Viscount Esher.

The disgraced schoolmaster would soon marry, become a father, and eventually set up house in London. After a period of youthful wanderlust, Regy also got married and fathered four children, becoming an increasingly powerful figure behind the scenes of British politics. Chat would distress his friends, especially Cory, by converting to Roman Catholicism, and would interrupt his intimate relationship with Regy by joining the Oratorian order. None of these men simply conformed to conventions of Victorian respectability and masculinity. Regy maintained a series of romantic attachments to much younger men over many years. Chat's spiritual yearnings were not easily satisfied: after a time, he distanced himself from his order, settling in Sicily with a succession of young Italians who served as houseboys and intimate companions. Cory continued to long for youths lost long ago. Through these differences and difficulties, the three men remained friends so long as they lived. Their shared time at Eton became a touchstone for negotiating the vicissitudes of later life. After Cory died in 1892, Regy and Chat exchanged and reread letters and journals, revisiting the history they shared.

In January 1892, Regy writes Chat: "I found yesterday a journal of Tute's given me years ago . . . on an occasion when he believed himself to be dying. Will you read it? and I send it by this post for the purpose. It is of an interesting time."[29] After Cory's death later that year Regy is drawn into discussions with other old Etonians and current masters about publishing selections from his teacher's letters and journals. Regy worries about editorial intervention:

> My difficulty about Tute's letters is that Canon Furse *insists* on editing any volume which may be published. In a letter which I have seen, he deplores the "sentiment" in Tute, and I have no doubt would use the scissors freely. A bowdlerized edition of Tute's letters I could not stand. Nor would a false picture of the writer, which such editing would necessarily present, give me the smallest pleasure.[30]

Less than a week later, Regy decides to "keep aloof" from the project. He offers to copy his own letters from Cory and to circulate them among their friends. "I have no desire to read what he wrote to others. He said to me all that I wish to know from him, and in the way I wished to hear it." He suggests that Cory's letters to their friend "Howdy" (Howard Sturgis) were so indiscreet they should not even be submitted to Furse, a Johnson family connection, for vetting.[31] (The author of *Tim,* a schoolboy novel fraught with homoerotic sentiment, Sturgis lived openly with a young man known to their friends as "the Babe.") Regy becomes quite possessive of the material, emphasizing its significance for him and Chat: "Our journal, I feel confident, would never be exhibited if ever it gets into the Canon's clutches. I think— as Tute gave it to me on an occasion when he imagined himself near death, he probably intended me to keep it." And keep it he did.

Cory's journal covers the period from mid-July to early November 1868, when the author was forty-five years old. It opens with an extended meditation on the question "Did I regret being a lone man?" He imagines himself in a marriage portrayed in comic, self-deprecatory, and perhaps misogynist terms. A milquetoast in the grip of a powerful and pious lady, he envisions persistent nagging about the demands of the world and his failures to meet them adequately. He would resist both her high ambitions for him and her repeated invocations of divine providence. The satire gives way to an almost lyrical digression:

> The will of God. How can I tell what it is? I only *take* it: I take it in bed with fever on me as on that rather distressing Friday July 10 of which no

Sodom on the Thames

record shall stain this peaceful book. I take it, with an even mind, when breeze and caressing wave welcome me and the sky cuts itself with my beloved —— without a shirt. . . . When it seems easy to own myself part of the blind helpless creation. When will is not in abeyance but just active enough to give me the pleasure of consent.[32]

Cory's fantasy is an odd mix of sense and sentiment. He compares a potential spouse to students he has known:

Would it have been selfish had I wished for the presence of a girlish lady whom I could love like an Eton boy or a Cambridge young man with the difference that she would have no home but such as I could give her: if she were sunny enough to delight me, I should, as mankind reckons, be too old for her. Yet at what the world would call the right age, I was really too young, too silly, too clumsy: besides being far too poor. Let the world go its own way to Jericho—though frail and gray, I am as sunny in heart as any of the ball givers. If I were not, how could that lad aged 16, glowing with life and joyousness *make* me his friend of his own will.[33]

This feeling of boyish friendship results from a letter the "lad" dictated to his sister. The teacher copies passages into his journal: "Nothing gives me greater pleasure than coming with you anywhere if I am allowed. . . . This summer half has been my happiness at Eton, and it has all been owing to you: you have made me different from what I have ever been."[34] The student's effusiveness offers Cory a world of sentimental attachments: "I have seen young lovers interlacing like honeysuckle rose and jasmine, romantic chivalrous friendships forming under my eye, to which I am almost admitted as a partner."[35] Tute escapes from an imaginary hectoring marriage into a remembered bower of boyish bliss.

Cory writes Regy, his pupil at the time, vividly portraying these "chivalrous friendships." He dotes on his current favorite: "Elliot goes on Wed: for nine wks, I shall miss him and be the worse for it. . . . Other good lads will come but different in kind. Does it not give you a new notion of boyhood to have known him."[36] Elliot is the very model of Eton manliness, while Regy displays more ambiguous qualities:

. . . the peerless virtue of Elliot. *He* commands himself, denies himself, lives methodically, and yet so that you can hardly say he is working for himself; it is so much for a common cause, for the honor of the rowing eight and of the shooting eleven. That he should have been able this summer to bend from his Spartan severity and touch with part of his character the

Athenian group of playful lounging loving boys is to me surprising. *Your* life is more like what the books tell one of a Provençal troubadour than anything I have seen; sweet and pretty as it is, I doubt whether there is enough backbone to it: perhaps you wanted a little more training for "lower eights" and would have been the better for a "house four." But you showered blessings and comforts on my loneliness, and I thank you.[37]

Elliot's "Spartan severity" contrasts with "the Athenian group of playful lounging loving boys," providing a salutary lesson for the "Provençal troubadour." Tute manifestly enjoys all these youthful paradigms, urging Regy to visit: "You shall come and murmur to me histories of your Eton life. . . . I never yet knew anybody like you with so much 'effusion' and power of making yourself known to people: other people are as sweet in heart, but have no conduit leading from heart to face at all hours."[38] In the same month that he meditates on his unmarried state in his journal, Tute writes Regy, comparing his situation with that of his pupils' parents: "The wonder to me is how people ever part with their children unless they be horrors." Teachers reap the benefit of parents' work: "People labouriously mould and sweeten *for us* boys whose best qualities and best efforts *we* see and the parents do not see."[39] Tute indulges the "sentiment" that so put off Canon Furse and which Regy would continue to cherish: "I must go to bed. I long to dream of Elliot. I adore him more every week." His letter concludes: "I love you dearly and faithfully."[40] Cory shares a world of sentimental attachments with Regy. In fact, he presides lovingly over a circle of young men, entangled with each in changing constellations of feeling.

Although intensely emotional and erotically charged, these relations are neither exclusive nor especially private: "Fortescue's face, beautified, comes back to me continually out here, more the photog. than the real flesh. And one night I dreamt I was at Therapeia where Elliot is. We don't agree, you and I. I love *him* so much more than 'your Charlie' [Chat], dear and delicious as *he* is."[41] In 1868, Tute is especially enamored of the triangle composed of Elliot, Chat, and Regy himself. His letters reveal some degree of self-consciousness about attaching so much importance to feelings and their expression. Cory refers approvingly to a lady who had recently befriended Regy: "She is like me a true lover of youth and beauty, and thinks the sentimental part of life as *real* as the jotting in the ruts of business."[42] Although the "true lover of youth and beauty" evokes Hellenic models (and Keats's "On a Grecian Urn"), Tute identifies himself with a woman and with the feminine cultivation of sentiment, in contrast to the masculine world of business.

Sodom on the Thames

However, he cautions his young friend about the risks of unfettered expression: "With the Griff you should be careful: he is given to what I tell him is excess in talk, to want of reticence. He talks of things that had better be passed over, and just now he is morbidly sentimental by reason of his exile from young people's society." Cory links "excess in talk" to letter writing: "Be somewhat reserved in writing to the little Master [Chat again]. He used to show his Mother all his letters, including yours."[43] The world of romantic sentiments among boys and their tutors must be protected from exposure to parental eyes, which might not understand or approve what they see. Moreover, some boys remain more attached to family than to school friends: "I remember Mouse Wood being vexed at getting letters he could not show; whether Chat is vexed or not I don't know. He goes upon a rule of destroying all letters."[44]

Tute displays an almost voyeuristic interest in his pupils' involvements with one another. Letters are a frequent medium of this exchange, sometimes destroyed but sometimes shared. The boys circulate letters among themselves and to their teacher as well:

I have had a very odd, rather pretty subject to think about: a lad sent me to read a secret valued letter from another lad, who defends the character of a third whom he says plainly he loves: his own old mate: "if he is not good, then I can't be good" is the spirit of it: the apologist has changed lately, at least he says and thinks he has changed and out of generosity or "chivalry" clings to his friend so as to put his neck in the same halter.[45]

For Cory the letters are not only expressions of present feeling but also mementos for the future. He is keenly aware of the transient nature of the boys' passions. Chat refuses to play the game, "always destroying every letter," but first shows some of them to Tute. Cory regrets the loss: "Woe for wasteful boyhood, that destroys what it should keep to fill up the retrospect . . . when he will wish to have something that brings back the fragrance of the early friendship."[46] The teacher's position is increasingly complicated, as he writes some of these letters while a guest of Chat's family. Cory reports to Regy on their friend's parents: "His Mother feels very sadly that he is getting estranged and 'hardened.' They were such perfect friends. Even now though they never kiss each other before us, they are more nearly allied than any mother and son I ever knew." In his journal, he writes: "She is now clouded with anxiety: 'if he cannot get through a public school, how can he be fit for the Guards'. . . . She mourns over his no longer showing her all the letters he receives."[47] Cory is almost a double agent, enjoying the family's confidence while looking after Regy's interests: "I wish her to think of you as a good friend for her boy, not to be afraid of your petting him as she is now I guess: you would admire her if you saw her." (Years later, in the margins of the typescript of this letter, an ambivalent Regy would write: "She is really a very silly little woman but quite *excellent*.") Chat's family and friends are anxious about his future: "His Father, who has a great dread of 'bad women' rejoices in his fondness for ladies, and wishes him to marry at 21." Tute concludes: "He is really a most affectionate father and rather spoony about the boy."[48] Cory's interest has its "spoony" or sentimental side too: "I wish also they would not put on the dinner table two candlesticks in a line between me and the boy."[49] He is uncertain whether Chat reciprocates his feelings: "With a courteous lively lad it is not easy to understand how far one is understood."[50] Cory wants mutuality rather than simple acceptance of his own affection: "When I came in the boy came and sat an hour with me in my bedroom without his jacket, warming himself on a stool, and talking simple old stuff about school which was fresh to me by virtue of his fresh manner. He read a page or two at the beginning of this volume."[51] The volume begins with the already-quoted reflections on being unmarried and the consolations of boyish friendship. Chat is fourteen when Tute shares his journal with him.

The sentimental side of Cory's relation to his students does not preclude a more worldly ambition. He displays continuing interest in his pupils' development after Eton:

> I have had . . . a long clever friendly [letter] from my old pupil Lord Rosebery who still calls himself Joab: he is going to reside at Dalmeny in the winter reading for his degree and wishes me to come and stay with him that he may talk history and politics: this is very delightful to me. When he was thirteen I delighted in his cleverness taste wit and friendliness: our friendship was in abeyance a year or two and he comes to me now quite of his own accord. His wit is quite original and remarkable: his handwriting quite beautiful. He has not chosen his political creed yet. I thought he meant to do without one.[52]

After another letter from Rosebery, he mentions a figure from Plato: "A pretty day. It brought me one letter from Edinburgh full of youthfulness and worthy of a Phaedrus."[53] Cory implicitly compares himself with Phaedrus's older friend—Socrates. By continuing his dialogue with former students in positions of public responsibility, Cory vicariously enters the world of affairs. Rosebery would culminate his political career as foreign minister and would spend a brief troubled time as prime minister in 1894–1895.

Sodom on the Thames

9. *"Socrates and His Agathodaemon [Guardian spirit]," Simeon Solomon (1865)*

Cory's connections with former students are not his only contact with a wider world. The wistful passions of Eton masters for their students seem very distant from the public performances of Fanny, Stella, and their admirers in London's West End. However, Cory enjoys his trips to the city: "The great delight in London, which I took fully this last Monday, is listening to the Guards' at 11. ——— [illegible] and I walking with them towards their barracks: no girl has a steadier 'scarlet fever' than I."[54] On another visit, he notes, "[I] met Baby Doyle who used to be a pretty Queens Page, is now a not-pretty guardsman, but talked with some intelligence about his travels in the East."[55] Symonds met his "young grenadier" not far from the guardsmen's barracks near Leicester Square in 1865. Perhaps Cory is unaware how readily some of these guards might treat his "scarlet fever" in exchange for money or gifts.

Occasionally Tute also shows a more knowing and urbane side in his letters to Regy: "Warre [another Eton master] and I dined last night at the Rifle Brigade Mess and were received with great cordiality, particularly by an old pupil of mine. But after we were gone one subaltern said to the others 'Doesn't it make your bottom smart to see these fellows.'" This is Cory's only reference to the widespread use of flogging as a punishment for misbehavior at school. His publications on pedagogy suggest that he would be critical of the practice. The story of his visit to London takes a surprising turn: "One of these subs was an old fag of Warre and an Irishman. Dick Thompson told me that he was at a ball and his partner said to him, 'Whom do you consider the prettiest girl in the room?' to which he replied with his hand on his heart 'Your humble servant.'"[56] As in *The Sins of the Cities of the Plain,* handsome soldiers (and Eton pupils?) may be easily transformed into feminine beauties. Cory's circle at Eton flourished in the late 1860s at about the time Boulton and Park began their nocturnal promenades. The trial of Fanny and Stella would not completely destroy the practice of military cross-dressing. In 1875, Regy writes in his journal: "Eugene [his younger brother] came to London this morning and told us of his fancy dress ball at Sandhurst, half the young men dressed as girls, and the others in character."[57] (Sandhurst is the royal military academy where future officers were trained.)

Cory's moments of worldliness are easily eclipsed by a commitment to sentiment rooted in his love of English romantic poetry:

We are the sons of Wordsworth; and after a quarter of a century which has fed us with highly spiced dainties, here we are back with the unlearned prophet of Nature, back to our moonlight and mountain shadows, and the healing touch of Nature. It is wonderful that we should, without forcing

Sodom on the Thames

ourselves or learning or imitating, take from Wordsworth by inheritance, as we take tastes from our parents . . . that yielding of ourselves to running water and to still clouds, which seems to predispose us for the recognition of delicate simplicities in child or peasant, and tunes us for the street or schoolroom.[58]

For him, the scene of romance is more likely to be the schoolroom than the countryside or city street. Wordsworth missed out on Tute's poetic inspiration: "I suppose he never saw anyone at all like the Chatterbox: he left me the faery realm of boyhood to explore."[59] The boy has become Cory's muse and ideal reader: "Perhaps the most noticeable pleasure is that Chatterbox has been reading and talking about my 4th form verse book . . . asking me to give him a book of these verses: this is a most gratifying bit of reviewing."[60] When Browning tells him that Solomon wants to give him a drawing as thanks for his published poetry, Cory admits: "This is rather soothing to a stillborn author but I shall take care not to make much of it."[61] When the gift does not materialize, Cory consoles himself with his audience of pupils: "It is odd, one's having a little set of readers. I am not sure that I care for these unknown readers so much as for boys who take pleasure in my Latin verse books."[62] One cannot help wondering how much Cory knows about the "unknown" readers such as Solomon and Symonds, whom he rejects in favor of the boys at Eton.

Although mostly caught up in observing the tangled web of attachments among his students, Cory occasionally gives way to memory. An invitation to visit a fellow undergraduate from his Cambridge days almost involuntarily returns him to his own youth:

Of those honest well-spent years I have hardly a trace or a relic: some are dead, some gone to the Pope, many serve the world: no one cares much for me: I did not make strong friendships then, as other young men do: partly because of poverty, chiefly because of mental perplexity, and the fear of other men's opinions . . . but the thistledom of sentiment hung about me all the time, luckily. . . . Men would have liked me then in the undergraduate days if I had let them.[63]

Uninvited, images of past comrades appear in his dreams: "I dreamt of Bauerstock, who is dead, who was a rustically pretty pinkfaced boy 27 years ago: what made me dream of him: I have hardly even remembered him since we were boys."[64] Johnson was forty-five when he wrote these words; he would have been eighteen when last he knew the other boy.

In 1868 at Eton, Chat and Regy occupy center stage: "It was good to see them together again. Yet there was a little cloud of shyness between them, just perceptible."[65] The two boys are musical. Regy plays piano and Chat sings: "I shall get him ['my singing boy'] I hope to bring me other musical boys."[66] Tute locates Chat in a spiral of schoolboy attachments present and past: "I gave him to read the letter of his old friend, now lost to him, the Dalmeny [Rosebery] that was once so fond of him: he read it; perhaps with a sigh. . . . I fear the child is spoilt. Yet what a treat it is to have him wanting me."[67]

Although always couched in the most self-deprecating terms, there is something almost teasing in the way that Tute plays one boy against another. Cory recounts his pleasure in being invited by a fellow teacher to cultivate a shy boy who has no mother. Inviting the youth for breakfast, he wonders: "Why should not a man of Senatorial age give way sometimes to an impulse. Why should we live with 'calculated kindness'. . . . It must surprise and puzzle a boy to find that one likes him across such a gulf: but what harm." Still he continues to obsess about Chat: "Is it possible that he should like me for my own sake?"[68] In late October, they go for a walk together to Windsor: "We shopped rapidly together and were friends. He is within two days of his fifteenth birthday. Being greatly and laughingly reproached for something he had said he replied just now 'It's only the bumptiousness of fourteen, it will soon wear off.'"[69] A few days later: "The little master came to his fifteenth birthday and I did verses, remote from him, about Socrates and Phaedrus."[70] But perhaps not so remote. If Cory remains the Socratic teacher, Chat now gets his chance to play Phaedrus.

The shifting attachments among Chat, Elliot, and Regy are played out in the Cabin and the Trap: "The three enjoyed each others delightful company in a new and pretty way. One of them, who has the gift of utterance, tells me since how happy he was: and I looking on was deeply content. This is something like a place to live in now. One of these young people likes me as he likes his schoolfellows, just in the same way: which is odd."[71] The friends use letters to keep in touch during holidays and after the students leave Eton for university and the world beyond. On New Year's Eve 1868, Tute reports to Regy:

I wrote to Chatter yesterday; don't cease to adore him, he is so much wiser and kinder than he was. I wish he was as fond of you as he ought to be: but he is attached to you and you might love him as much as Bickersteth. I think of Elliot incessantly: he will be in the Egean by this time perhaps; he must be sighing in his Spartan way for you and Chatter. How wonder-

Sodom on the Thames

ful he has been since September, getting gradually more and more tender and sweet, till he became a walking Elysium.[72]

The pattern of relations—between Regy and Chat, Tute and Elliot—is complicated. Does Cory play down his feelings for Chat out of deference to Regy? He situates himself a bit outside the now-triangulated relationship of Regy, Chat, and Elliot, acknowledging his special attraction to Elliot and introducing another beloved of Regy. (Ernest Bickersteth, known as "Ivy" and "Beak," will play an increasingly important role in the group after Elliot leaves for Oxford.) The connections among these figures are multiple, overlapping, and fluid. Cory sums up school life during the past year but also indulges in some moralizing: "My *domestic* party at breakfast was a new kind of comfort, and the loves of Elliot and Chatter at night were the loveliest I ever imagined. Poetical and rapturous affection *without passion* is what you display and if you can keep it up you will be happy: but *passion,* disturbing the reason, turns sweet to sour." His distinction between affection and passion is conventional but may not be shared by his students. What does Regy make of a "poetical and rapturous affection" emphatically "without passion"? Is Cory referring to Regy in particular? to all of the boys? Where does he situate himself? Does he conceal his true sentiments? Cory treads a fine line—or vacillates uncertainly—between desiring and identifying with the boys who are so large a part of his life.

Elliot's departure for Balliol College, Oxford, crystallizes Cory's feelings and transforms the pattern of relations among the boys. Tute writes to Regy: "I have not written down and wish I had, the dear events of your last day at Eton . . . your last kissing of Elliot, his statuesque attitude in the chair with his arm around you, sitting still to be kissed and cherished. I wonder whether I shall see him again in one of these delicious moods."[73] Later in the same letter: "If Elliot does leave must he not come back and stay at the Trap as soon as his vacation begins, and lie abed every morning till you and Chatter come and kiss his heavenly eyes open." Tute allows himself the occasional kiss as well: "Elliot was ill last Sunday: thought he was going to faint. I nursed him on Monday, and kissed his feet which were very hot, but he is silent, dreadfully shut up." Tute notices his "reserve" with the adults who nurse him: "I think he has actually been pining for and craving for boys, particularly two who need not be named. But he would die sooner than own it in talk, and I don't allude to it. All his long dormant passion is burning now, I fancy. Did you notice how eager he was for Chat that last night when you were together?"[74] Tute's attachment to Elliot feeds on the paragon's interaction with the other boys. He refers almost casually to overcoming the young man's "sin-gular shyness" to make his room a refuge for Elliot from "Satyrs & Priapes." The "faery realm of boyhood" generally excludes its more aggressive and physical aspects. This reference to "Satyrs and Priapes" evokes the "animal lust" with "no refinement, no sentiment," that Symonds observed during his school days at Harrow. Cory has saved Elliot from such coarseness and in-troduced him to a more affectionate milieu:

> Slowly he got used to us. I daresay there was much even there that he shrunk from: but I used to treat him respectfully as a student, and I had the sense to sympathize with his steering. Hundreds of times he must have been vexed and bored by me: but I loved him all along and more and more, till now he is my glory and delight and sweet pain. Let us make a religion of remembering him and longing for him. I envy you being kissed by him. If I were dying like Nelson I would ask him to kiss me. I kissed his dear foot last Tuesday in the grass at . . . a good little spot where I found "for-get-me-not" growing just where he landed and gave it to Chat to wear: I wonder what they said to each other that evening: twice I left them by themselves . . . folded in each other's arms on the sofa. We can't measure affections, but it is probable that his love for Chat is as strong and sweet as any that a lad of 18 ever felt since the world began: yet it will be the morn-ing star to the dawn of his love for some happy enviable woman.[75]

Perhaps Cory's enthusiastic portrayal of Elliot and Chat stirred some envy in Regy. Long afterward he would write in the margin: "He married a woman who looks to me very dull."

Where does Brett figure in the cult of Elliot? Tute writes him: "I rejoice that I helped him, not a bit too soon to be sweetly intimate with you. Per-haps he could not have had that sweet sisterly friendship at all had he not had my rooms for his home."[76] Earlier, Cory wrote of his pleasant surprise that Elliot had enjoyed "the Athenian group of playful loving lounging boys" who spent time at the Trap. Now he contends that they—he and his student friends—offered Elliot "a romance of affection and a family life that were un-known at school." In writing of Elliot's departure, Tute evokes a sentiment charged with rapture: "I can at any moment see him leaning towards you and yielding himself to your ardent, melting, entrancing fondness—or with his other exquisite look drawing Chat to him and drinking up his infantine charms with a glistening eye and caressing hand."[77] When Cory inserts him-self emphatically into the picture, it is in an abject posture: "Now that I have

Sodom on the Thames

ceased to be his teacher I would be his humble retainer, sec'y or valet. I have loved other Eton boys, but none was so *great* as he, so devoted to the public good, so exalted above me."[78] At the conclusion of this long letter, Tute considers the attractions of women with a somewhat different twist from his earlier imagining of Elliot's marriage: "I see ladies whom I like: but I really cannot see any charm in them which Elliot has not. I see in him indescribable charms which they have not."[79] Cory's lament for Elliot finally positions Regy closer to the ideal beloved and farther from his loving teacher: "Some day, not long hence, you will be so steeped in love for a woman as not to comprehend the old affection for boys. Meanwhile come to me and be friendly, for though old, I am just like a boy in feeling."[80] Elliot's departure has awakened in Tute a more rapturous affection for Regy: "I passed by your castle yesterday at no great distance and remembered your dear self whether mind or body, eyes or lips or voice or cheeks, whatever it was, something dear and sweet and rare, and all the more precious since Elliot is gone so far away."[81] Soon Regy too will leave Eton, and after him, Chat as well.

Tute continues to mediate the relations among his young friends. During the summer of 1869 he again visits the Williamson home. He writes to Regy of anxieties about Chat that he appears to share: "There is much fear of his growing up a butterfly. He is very quick in picking up what he hears people talk about, but this will not prevent his being superficial. Reading gives a young popular man some deliberate thoughtfulness and independence in listening: a man who has neglected books seems to intelligent women empty and slight and soon gets stale."[82] Tute worries about Chat's matrimonial prospects while continuing to obsess about Elliot. He complains that "Chat disappoints me by never mentioning Elliot," but delights that the youth welcomes the offer of "an Elliot locket with an inscription."[83] Cory seems to praise Elliott at the expense of Regy's favorite: "Mrs. W. says she wonders at Elliot's attachment to Chat: 'if he was not my own boy I should feel he was not the sort of character to admire.' She laments his selfishness."[84] By Christmas, Tute has returned to his earlier enchantment with Chat, and Regy appears on the verge of displacing his rival Elliot. Cory writes Brett: "[Chat] actually reproached me once for naming you as it gave him such pain to feel you were gone. I have known a great deal of fondness lately, but I have heard no one speak so passionately."[85] The circle at the Trap and Cabin now includes "Buttons," Arthur Lyttleton, later bishop of Southampton, and "Ivy" aka "Beak," Ernest Bickersteth, first mentioned a year before. In Regy's absence, Tute presides over another ménage à trois:

You will be wofully jealous of Buttons; he and Chat played tennis the last morning, and it was pretty to look on. . . . Chat is deeply enamored of him but I suppose it will pass off: however it was very desirable that they should break the ice as they sit together so much at work in the Cabin, and they both are so peculiarly intimate with Ivy. He seems to wish them to be good friends.[86]

With Elliot at Oxford, Tute's fluctuating affections focus on Ivy. He seems an almost inaccessible object of longing and potential loss: "I wish he would tell me his lovetale as you do. But he is lost, never indeed belonged to me in any way. I think of him habitually with great sorrow, partly because I cannot see him or nurse him: partly because I fear he will die & leave the world with one less object of true romantic affection."[87] (Years afterward, Esher would write in the margin: "He died 3 years later.") As always, Cory situates his own feelings and those of his favored pupils within the general climate and character of the school. He worries a bit, listing the academic difficulties of several of his favorites, including Chat, Ivy, and Regy himself: "It seems as if being in love at Eton was fatal to school work." One student is said to have failed French, "possibly because his head was haunted with sentimental thoughts of Chat and Ivy." Despite this, love remains at the heart of the Eton experience, at least for some: "How little the wiseacres know that this sentiment is actually part of the staple of life at school." Cory embraces this attitude, implicitly taking credit for fostering that special spirit: "Lady Winchelsea once wrote to me that she liked me because I was the only person she knew who habitually considered sentiment as a serious part of life. Which is in short taking a Keats or Wordsworth view of the world." These general reflections conclude with his current favorite: "I shall write rhymes about Ivy mysterious and inaccessible creature."[88]

4. ETON RENAISSANCE

"You very rightly describe our time at Eton as the
culminating point of the Renaissance there."
—Regy to Chat, January 24, 1893

Regy Brett's contemporary journals and later correspondence provide a counterpoint to Cory's account of the "faerie realm of boyhood" at Eton. Beside the fervent and somewhat voyeuristic pedagogue, we hear the voice of a favored student who had been much caught up in the "romantic chivalrous friendships" so dear to his teacher. His surviving journals begin in 1870. Not yet eighteen and still at Eton, he adopts an almost elegiac tone in writing

Sodom on the Thames

about another boy: "He and Ivy are linked for ever in my recollection, shadowed by the stronger images of Chat, and he is with me now; and with him near me the last days of boyhood are floating away." In April 1870, Regy and Chat spend a holiday together with Cory at Halsdon. Regy reviews his important friendships, lamenting the passage of time: "So many new friendships opened this half: to be dropped and lost forever." Cory's house offers a pastoral setting where Regy's love flourishes:

> In the evening Chat and I slipped out of the window and walked to the end of the hill: a gorgeous moon overhead, and warm as in July. . . . We had one long kiss under the moon-shadows. We have stood lip to lip under the woodland and by the murmuring Torridge. I have kissed him in every room in Halsdon. Five days of free and unencumbered love. Our rooms are opposite and he wanders in and out quite easily and simply. Today we strolled down to the river, through the oak copse. His arms were round my waist. He was dressed most sweetly in flannel shirt, wading trousers, a bright tie and my Victory cap. I carried a plaid and the basket. I put up his rod and arranged his flies, then he fished and I read on the bank. Every fish he hooked I jumped down to land for him. So for three hours.[89]

Chat reciprocates his feelings: "It is a delicious life, so easy and quiet, canvas shoes, and flannel shirts, and astrakhan caps and flannel coats. Chat has thrown himself into our rapturous love and Halsdon is Elysium to me."[90] Chat exemplifies "a true genius of a certain type": "The most silvery laugh, the fairest face, and the blithest heart and sweetest mind in Strathearn." However, Cory has invited the whole group of his student friends. Regy's spring idyll is complicated by the arrival of Elliot, apple of their teacher's eye: "Our positions are curious with respect to Chat." At Eton too, relations among the three have been complex:

> Returning Chat got on the box seat with me and drove, making me put my arm around him to keep him warm and hold him on. After supper at the Trap Elliot and I lay together on the long sofa. He put his dear strong arms around me & his face against mine. Chat, not very well, sat near the fire. . . . W.J. in the big red chair close to our sofa. We kept on calling for Chat, & finally he was lifted on to us, nestling between Elliot and me. My arms were round him, & Elliot's were round him and me. Chat liked our both breathing in his ears.[91]

At Halsdon, some rivalry appears within the triangle, as Regy quietly celebrates his victory. His focus is strictly on Chat:

After dinner he is lying on the sofa, Elliot talking to him; he is here in the room while I write this; my head has just left his shoulder, my lips his hair, my hand from clasping his: so we have been lying, and so the last evening is passing, the last forever in these relations, in the free love of so many days. Chat and I said good-bye faintly enough in his room: he rushed up to his window as we drove off, remaining there until we were out of sight. Our lips met for the last time at the foot of his bed, and so I saw the last of him I love best.[92]

This delicate parting will prove the first of many in a friendship that endures throughout their lives. We do not hear much from Elliot himself. He is reflected in the admiring gaze of Tute and the slightly green-eyed perspective of Regy. However, some years later, Brett finds a letter from Elliot to his teacher, which he copies into his own journal. We are back at school in the Eton renaissance, as Elliot worries whether he has been "a great baby" by crying when he bid his tutor farewell for the summer: "I really could not help it: he was very kind; he gave me a book." He frets about the future of his friendship with the beloved boy at the center of their circle: "Chat hardly said good-bye; he was in such a hurry to go. I wonder if he'll speak to me next half, and remember me at all in a year. What do you think he and Brett would like to have? Only don't find out by asking them." At that time, Tute himself was totally in thrall to Elliot, remarking in *his* journal that this was the "only voluntary letter he ever wrote" to him before taking flight to Oxford:

> I have seen him this year, as I never saw any other person, openly and unreservedly loving his two boy friends and enjoying their love, in truth we have all four lived together in such intimacy and joyousness as never was described or thought possible: he has been the central object, the greatest of us. . . . At 10 . . . I left them: sorrowful even to tears was I, with rejoicing that they could be once more together to take leave of their boyhood. The little one says he will try to be like Elliot. It must do him good to have such a wish.

Cory concludes by referring to letters from both Regy and Chat that he had received at the same time and which gave their own accounts of the multiple partings, Regy in "a very tender and mournful letter." Cory continues to cherish his role as intermediary among the boys. A letter from Chat arrived the same day as Elliot's: "I sent the best of it's little sentences on to the dear lad who wonders whether 'he'll speak to me' and now as I write this, I hope he is reading on board ship my comforting assurances about the little darling."[93]

Sodom on the Thames

Although Elliot leaves for Oxford in 1869 and Regy for Cambridge in 1870, the "circle of warm loving lounging boys" around Cory stay in touch. In the spring of 1871, Regy and Chat return to Halsdon, where each room has been christened with an esoteric name, such as Zoar, Wellington, Mr. Pitt, and Bellew.[94] This time Ernest Bickersteth accompanies them. Known as "Beak" and "Ivy," he has become a favorite of Cory's: "Beak and WJ [Cory] went out to see the moon. They returned and we are in Zoar. Chat is young as ever: bright as ever, clever and brilliant. Gay, original, perfectly, rapturously lovely. . . . His eyes are pools of life to me. Beak is the Ivy of yore: more manly; but bright, fresh and young still."[95] Regy detects some of the feeling that moves his teacher, but his focus remains on Chat: "WJ is kind, thoughtful, but un peu exigeant. Chat is the world: l'âme et la vie." Last year's triangle has been replaced by a more comfortable foursome:

> Chat and I, arm in arm, found daffodils and anemone, violets and primroses without end. . . . Went up and lounged. Chat's feet were washed in Bellew: he lay on the sofa in his peignoir. Beak and I bathed in Torrington. Joined Chat, who was carried to bed amidst uproarious mirth. Beak went to bed, WJ read to him. I took Chrysie [a cat] to Chat.[96]

While Chat wades, Regy goes off with Cory to get a towel: "I found Chat at the same spot: he paddled in the stream: and I pulled off the wet socks: wiped his pretty feet dry and reclothed them." The pair take long walks together alone or with the others. Chat and Regy carve their names in a windowsill. Regy enumerates his beloved's virtues: "Chat is gloriously sweet. In body and mind. His dear little feet in transparent silk: his great waving sea of hair; and brilliant pools of wit and cleverness. The brilliance of his mind surpasses everything: the beauty of his person eclipses the most extravagant ideal." Minor differences only add spice to the mix: "Chat and I made up a tiff on Saturday and on Sunday walked together through the copses talking of old times. . . . How adorable has Chat been. I cannot write about him."[97] When he returns to London to accompany his father on the judicial circuit, Regy continues to obsess: "I feel quite unable to write to Chat: the thoughts won't even come, much less the words. . . . Chat again. Chat everywhere. I think of him ever: dream of him sleeping and waking. Would I could tell the story of our friendship."[98] When the words do come, they are a short elegy:

> Our brother Friendships we deplore
> And loves of youth that are no more.
> No after friendships e'er can raise

The endearments of our early days
And ne'er the heart such fondness prove
As when we first began to love.[99]

Regy had just turned nineteen when he wrote this lament for lost youth. In less than a year, Cory would resign from Eton in disgrace, and Regy would help him take up permanent residence at Halsdon.

5. *ET IN ARCADIA EGO*

Although their ongoing friendship adapts to Regy's departure to Cambridge in 1870 and Chat's to Oxford the next year, their Eton "renaissance" comes to a more precipitate and dramatic end. In late March 1872, again at Halsdon, Regy writes: "Eton much the same as ever; just recovering from a scandal, about a boy . . . who has been sent away with four admirers. The ushers look at one coldly. They cannot shake off the feeling that all old Etonians must necessarily endanger the discipline of the school."[100] Regy finds his former tutor Arthur Ainger "very gloomy" about life in general and Eton boys in particular. Another student friend is in trouble because one of the masters opened "a foolishly written, affectionate note" written to another boy. The school's governing body has sent a warning to the entire choir, and one of its leaders has departed in disgrace. The circles of sentiment that Cory celebrated as a staple of school life have suddenly become suspect.

On April 9, Regy records without elaboration: "Tute talked to me all the morning. He has resigned his Eton appointment and has offered to take me on here [at Halsdon] until June."[101] Five days later, that offer appears more as a plea for help: "I am to stay with Tute and give up my Cambridge term. Tomorrow I go to town and Eton to arrange Tute's affairs."[102] Before the end of the month, Regy removes Cory's last belongings from the school where he had taught for twenty-six years: "Tuesday I went down to Eton where I picked up Tute's valuables, said good bye to the Trap and Cabin: played the Addio on the piano, saw Rich Merrick and Tom Brown."[103] Tute's circle remains loyal to their teacher. No longer at Eton where the Cabin and the Trap were home to their youthful amours, Regy and his friends continue to enjoy the pastoral delights of Halsdon: "Chat has been with us since Tuesday convalescing from an indisposition evidently the result of the whirls of Oxford life. He looks pale, but is as gay and bizarre as ever." Tute shares Regy's "ecstasy" at Chat's arrival: "They are out together at this moment arranging flowers, setting improvements, and perfectly happy. Chat is far more engaging than ever he was."[104]

Sodom on the Thames

10. *"The Bathers," Frederick Walker (1867). "All the brightness and glory of youth was there." Reginald Brett in his journal, August 1876.*

Provoked by a letter from his younger brother Eugen, now at Eton, Regy meditates on the vicissitudes of time: "At Eton all was bright and fair, a free and outspoken truth-before-everything kind of life, with liberty carefully restricted, but encouraged. At Cambridge, less heartiness, less openness, although maybe a little more freedom of action." He imagines life beyond university as he has glimpsed it traveling with his father: "In the world you are your own master, free to go where you will, do what you will, but fettered with social chains heavy to bear, impossible to break. Later on professional ties bind you down more closely than ever school discipline did. Intercourse is shallow and heartless between man and man, friendships rare, intimacy impossible." As Regy approaches twenty, the future seems to offer only a progressive narrowing of the spirit and attenuation of the ties between men. He would later write in the margins beside this entry: "I have not found this to be the case." Meanwhile, as the feared eclipse of love approaches, Regy finds Chat a continuing delight: "Chat lights up the whole place by his mirth and playfulness."[105] The next day, "Chat is very joyous, singing about the house, quite in his old way." When Tute goes to bed early feeling sick, the pair stay up for billiards. Sometimes Regy plays piano. After Chat leaves, Regy mourns the loss of this "jewel in the house": "The place is a desert without him."[106]

Left to their own devices, Regy and Cory return to Plato. Perhaps Cory finds special consolation in resuming the old pedagogical relationship. Regy records, "This morning we did some 'Apology' after Chat's departure, and I translated the glorious chapters about death." This return to the practices of a halcyon past will soon be interrupted. Death intrudes without warning and more intimately than as a theme of Socratic reflection.

The events of 1872 cast a dark shadow over the lives of these three friends for many years to come. Cory's disgrace becomes entangled with the death of Bickersteth later that summer. It is impossible to say precisely what led to Tute's resignation. Regy's journals do not go into detail. Regy seems to have deliberately destroyed the evidence. No letters to Chat during this period survive. The first volume of letters from Cory ends with April 1870; the second begins in August 1872. In the flyleaf of that second volume, Esher would write some time later: "All the letters between 1870 and 1872 were not kept."[107] However, in his letters to Chat after Tute's death, Regy revisits the crisis of 1872:

> Arthur Benson said that he knew everything about Tute. As Oscar Browning was his informant he probably does—and—as you say—he has stood the shock. Still I am altogether your way of thinking about the letters. I am no judge of how they would shock an outsider. . . . I care for those up to 1870 very much—and I tolerate those for another few months—but roughly speaking between 1870–72 the madness—hysteria—of love was excessive.[108]

It was not the first time that he had protected his former teacher by destroying incriminating evidence. The letters still in his possession in 1892 had survived an earlier culling: "I have gotten together some letters written by him in '68 and '69, and a few later ones—up to 1872—rescued from the holocaust made at that time."[109] We cannot know what Tute actually may have said or done during this "madness," but we must imagine an intensity of feeling and expression exceeding any in the letters that Regy had so carefully typed, bound, and preserved.

Beak's death comes to haunt the friends. When Regy left Halsdon to join his father in London and on the judicial circuit, Tute undertook a trip to Europe in the hope that the scandal would be forgotten when he returned. Chat and Beak accompanied him. In Baden in late July, Beak came down with a fever and chill; the doctors advised rest. Within a few days the youth was dead. He was the delicate Ivy about whom Cory had worried three years before. Tute and Chat were shattered. Regy records his own distress and his efforts to protect his friend's memory:

> I started at 10 for Cambridge where I arrived about 4, took some letters from Beak's rooms, which would have pained his relatives. . . . I cannot think of that restless boy lying at peace forever. I cannot write and I can think of nothing but him. . . . Death in another, a beloved and beautiful friend, has all the bitterness assigned to it by one who knew what friendship was! . . . At Eton, he was the only one in connection with whom an early death was mentioned.[110]

In the margins, Esher would later write that his attempt to find and destroy the letters had failed: "I hurried there for that purpose—but alas! A fruitless visit."

Regy exchanges letters with Chat, who is plunged into a spiritual crisis that will eventually lead him to convert to Roman Catholicism and take holy orders. Cory is restrained in expressing his own feelings but preoccupied with the effects of Beak's death on the younger man: "I think he is sure now to be either a clergyman or one of those laymen who live with the clergy, etc., at least for some years, till he marries. We talk of these things with calculating confidence, but how can we reckon on his living long enough to marry?"[111] Cory's attachment to Chat intensifies along with his anxiety: "I have written three long grave sad letters wise letters to Chat. He does not answer them and yesterday I was tormented with the fears of a break off, though resigned to the inevitable gradual parting which in fact began at Baden, yet I can't in my present bruised state bear to lose him suddenly."[112] In the absence of Chat's testimony, Regy's journals offer some sense of the impact of Beak's sudden death on his contemporaries. Regy's immersion in Platonic philosophy and elegiac poetry has not prepared him for the real thing. Deeply disturbed, he records in detail his dream on learning of Beak's death:

> I dreamed a fearful dream Wed night. I was at Lambton Castle on a Sunday. Lord Durham was very strict and we had services in the Hall. Jacko, methought, was next to me, and suggested during the Litany that we should have a rat hunt after. Just then the organ broke in with a tune that haunted me ever since. Prayers over we started through a pouring rain, Freddy leading, then Jacko and I. A fear kept tearing me that Lord Durham watched us through the windows, where I could constantly see his eyes. . . . The rain coming on fiercely, Fred and I ran back, and as we passed along the shrubbery he said, "Father's watching us" so we turned and bolted into the hall, where I ensconced myself in a cupboard like our old one in Princes Terrace near Violet's room. I drew the curtains and became aware of someone next me, who proved to be Beak. I seized him in my arms and kissed his cheek, which was icy cold. It was his dead body.[113]

The shared loss draws the surviving friends together but with some strain. About a year later, Regy writes: "Ivy has not faded away. Chat remains ever interesting, ever fascinating. At Oxford in June I found him surrounded with friends very foreign to what I had ever thought possible."[114] After a later, more troubled visit with Chat: "Does he find me strange? But after all what can I expect? . . . My Cambridge life is very pleasant and there is nothing but one recollection to embitter it. I wonder that the very stones do not weep for him, for our Adonais. My heart breaks when I think of him. Chat told me the other day the story of his death, the terror of it, the trouble of it. How all labour fell upon him, and how terribly those few days scarred his life."[115] During the ensuing years, Cory would write often about tensions with Chat, sometimes in a mood of complaint. It is possible that the older man somehow failed his friend at a dark time. As the final entry to this volume of his journal, Regy writes: "It records the greatest sorrow that hitherto has touched my life."

The image of Beak presides over Tute's abiding sense of grief and loss. In October, he reports that he has changed his name to Cory and resigned his fellowship at Kings. His account of these decisions seems less than candid; he presents them as matters of practical calculation. Regarding his change of name, he writes: "I did just as my solicitors bade me. It is a saving of time in writing." As to the fellowship, "I can make up to 1,000 a year without it, and I cannot see that I have any right to take £200 or £300 more from the Founder's alms. Please to say this for me in case anyone deigns to notice the

Sodom on the Thames

little event."[116] The unnamed, doomed Beak figures in his most intense expressions of feeling: "When I wake in the dusk here his voice comes to me; the memory of him is the chief thing that remains in me. I wonder Cambridge does not miss him, his unique incomparable ardour and gallantry: he should have been in some heroic campaign . . . to be honoured by warriors. I am ashamed to outlive him."[117] The echoes of classical elegy here are unmistakable. Did the early death of Beak enable Cory to cherish him in a way that approaching maturity prevented with his other young friends? Almost two years after Beak's death, Cory writes to Regy about the difficulties of grieving lost friends without the consolations of traditional faith. Ancient exemplars are much on his mind: "Perhaps there will be some day people of our sensibility who will be relieved of our aching doubts about reunion with beloved persons. Seneca, Pliny, Quintillian, perhaps Cicero, may have felt as we feel about losing people. I can't tell. Quintillian's lament for his son is about what I feel."[118]

The conjunction of Beak's actual death and poetic conventions raises deeper questions about the interplay of desire, longing, and loss in Cory's feelings for young men. In sentimental terms, the lover of boys inevitably confronts the loss of beloved objects as they grow into men. Even when erotic attachment to a youth becomes friendship between adults, the attractions of "boyishness" fade. A month after his meditation on mourning, Cory writes Regy about Chat: "Fix your time and bring the beloved auburn hair lad with you. I dare say he will be happy here with you and it warms my tepid soul to think of seeing him again even if he is no longer a loveable boy."[119] He repeatedly asks to hear about Regy's younger friends: "I want to hear of Sir Reginald and Bertram Buxton, not of those middle aged vain men. Youth is the one charming thing. Youth that hopes, youth that listens, youth that becomes fragrant in the rapid germination and decay of ideas and impressions, like the oak trees in Siberian springs."[120] Cory finds consolation in new generations of the young despite his exile from Eton.

6. AFTER THE FALL

Even in involuntary retirement, Tute maintains his connections with a large number of young men, most of them former students. Romantic friendships and ongoing instruction continue to intersect: "Primrose [Rosebery] says he is coming to me on Saturday, he used to say he was indebted to me for being happy at Eton, and he certainly has been grateful and faithful."[121] A long letter to Regy about a boy named Graham is fraught with anxiety about interference with private correspondence and the dangers of parental intervention.

Cory's troubles at Eton may well have resulted from the interception of one of his letters by a disapproving parent. There is no hard evidence, but Cory's tone supports such a view. He displays an odd combination of apprehension and near recklessness:

> I have a most unhappy and embarrassing letter from Graham, which I enclose. Please to burn it as soon as read. It makes me very uneasy. Can you help me by writing to him, of course write a letter that anyone may read and enclose a note. You see I am afraid of getting him into a worse quarrel by writing to him, it is clear that I must not communicate with him at present and yet I can't bear to leave his letters unanswered. I wish to urge him once for all to be a good son and quite patient, and it strikes me that if you wrote . . . you could forward my last sad note. It makes me ache to look at his worn passionate overeager face now framed in a pretty Viennese frame and to feel that this is the house that he loves and that he is banished from it: deeply pitying his sick fretful disappointed and perplexed father.[122]

It is tempting to see this letter as the "smoking gun" that resolves the mystery of Cory's disgrace. However, there were so many boys, so many letters, so many parents. One can infer only that something very like this constellation of indiscreet letters, mutual attraction, emotional excess, and parental disapproval was at work. Certainly, Cory betrays the sense of danger with which he now lives: "In writing to him of course you must not in any way allude to me or to this house. . . . Do be kind to him as well as prudent. But if you can't write to him burn my note and let me know only if it is burnt."[123]

The feared breach with Chat has been avoided: "On the 6th Dec. comes Chat, to read Greek with me, he is quite glad to come, bless him."[124] The admirable Elliot also visits. At Halsdon during vacations, Cory reestablishes the pedagogical connection: "Elliot reads Livy very steadily and listens to my interminable discourses on economy and politics etc. etc. I practice on him and use very correct language." Chat's interests now run to architecture and church history, but Cory's response extends beyond the lessons: "[He]was extremely sweet, gay, sage, cozy. Much more affectionate to me than he used to be, and not at all gloomy. He made me call him in the morning and often come to take his candle and sitting by his bedside in Bellew was perhaps my nearest approach to what I lost and what I have imagined."[125] Cory adopts a more and more elegiac tone about Bickersteth, whom he hesitates even to name: "No one will replace that birdlike impetuous tragic darling whom I lost, most cruelly. I bless the good German maid who wept for him."[126] Still he invests emotionally in a number of young men.

Sodom on the Thames

In April 1873, he resigns himself to increasing distance from Chat as he moves closer to Roman Catholicism: "I do not love him less for his being the admirer and votary of good men whose friend I cannot be myself, as long as I may hold the hem of his raiment I am content." In the same letter Cory expresses his longing and affection for other young men, including two who would also die young, according to Esher's later annotation. He concludes: "It is so hard for a young person to remember an old one."[127]

Cory's references to Chat are increasingly vexed. The young man's turn to Rome embitters his former teacher: "I suppose the priests allow you to see Chat because they think you convertible and an heir presumptive, whereas I am not worth fishing for. It is sickening to think that all you say has to be reported to those sneaks in Confession: beware of them."[128] Elsewhere he writes: "Popery always destroys poetry. Englishmen who write good verse as Anglo Catholics cease to write good verse as Roman Catholics." Verse sent by a former pupil who has converted "is a very pale imitation of 'Lycidas' and 'Adonais.'"[129] (Note the comparison with elegies for lost friends by Milton and Shelley.) Cory offers Regy "relics of Chat," reporting that "two of his many portraits are dethroned and put away." The teacher has saved not only letters but also school exercises, "happy traces of that blossoming mind."[130]

When Regy responds positively, Cory modifies the offer: "As to relics, I may not send letters. He would think it wrong but I can send an exercise or two and half a dozen photographs." Cory seems to have recalled Chat's aversion to having his letters circulate. Instead he offers Regy, apparently for the first time, a full account of his grievance against Chat, in a chronicle of hurt feelings and wounded pride. Cory's enumeration of the objects marking his ties to Chat—letters, exercises, photos, gifts, money, locks of hair—amount almost to a catalog of fetishes:

His offense is that he parted in the spring of 1876 in a letter which did not contain a single touch either of kindness or of nature, and this as the sudden ending of a most affectionate pathetic correspondence. . . .

When he was at Folkestone he flung himself on my charity and I was his support when neither parents nor proselyte makers were ready to rescue him from destitution.

Imagine his sending back the gold necklace I then (at his request) gave him, sending it back without one word. I feel after this, that if he inherits Lawers [his family's estate] I have a right to . . . remind him that he had £50 at the same time as the necklace. . . .

I will look up the things to send you. I shall in any case keep two or three of the prettier photographs; my visitors rather like them to look. I cannot find either the big enlarged photograph or the painted one; probably given away since they remained unframed. I keep some letters and a copy of verse. . . . I keep also a pebble, size of a big pea, which he picked up at Scarborough July 1871, and of course I keep the locket which contains his hair, the hair of one who was faithful unto death to me, nor do I wish to part the two.[131]

By the conclusion, Chat has been unfavorably compared to Beak, whose early death immunizes him against charges of betrayal.

During Tute's increasing estrangement from Chat, the friendship between the two younger men undergoes its own less dramatic vicissitudes. In his journal for February 12, 1875, Regy notes gravely: "This morning Chat wrote to me that on Monday last . . . he was received into the Roman Communion at the Jesuit Church in Farm Street."[132] He expresses hope that this turn of events will not disrupt their relationship, but he also has some anxiety: "There are so many links that bind me to him that there is no danger of a snap or separation. I hope and pray this is so."[133] The intensity of their shared history continues to haunt him: "I dreamed that Chat was reconciled to Tute, and that we were together again at Halsdon: with only a shadow of Ivy and the past about us." He is not easily reassured: "I fear Chat is in retreat, as I get no answer to my letter. He is not strong enough to stand such asceticism."[134] Regy devotes that Easter to remembrance: "My offerings to friends have been sent. There is no one forgotten, to whom I could have written. Elliot I remember with tears. Tomorrow I hope once in the day, if it is but for a moment, they will remember our lost joys."[135] Two weeks later he commemorates an anniversary: "This day five yrs ago Chat and I went to Halsdon for the first time. I hoped to get there again today, but am foiled."[136] Chat remains at the center of Regy's emotional landscape. His conversion consummated, Chat now contemplates the priesthood. He will eventually join the Oratory, an order established in England by John Henry Newman, himself a distinguished convert and Prince of the Church. Newman had also been a founder of the Oxford tutorial system that Cory's pedagogy at Eton so much resembled.

The two young friends continue to exchange their deepest thoughts as Chat prepares to leave the social world they have shared. Regy visits him at Oxford, where "we talked of him and his plans, and he read me some of his poetry, and I quoted him some verses." As Chat sleeps in the other room, Regy meditates on their friendship in quasi-religious terms: "Near to him,

Sodom on the Thames

one of those dearest to me on earth, I feel that immortality, such I can imagine it: free from temptation, free from anxiety: calmly living, feeling those we love calmly about one: knowing we are beloved in return. Perhaps, there is, for some, a heaven of that kind." For a time, they have achieved a calm not always apparent in the tempest of their earlier passions. Browsing among Chat's books, Regy finds two mementos of their love:

> I had put this book away not intending to write any more tonight: But I have just taken up two volumes with a tragic interest for me inscribed in their title pages. One is an early collection of Tennyson's poems and in the fly leaf written in a boyish hand "Charlie Williamson" Feb 14 1868, "A gift". I remember how with trembling hands and aching heart, recorded in my old journal in the foolish scrappy manner, I laid that book on the table in the room in which I had nursed him when he suffered from a wounded foot. I dared not put my name in it: I dared not let him see me put it down; and I crept away, and never knew if he knew the giver. The other volume is a "Keats" unnoticed by me to this day. In another hand, small and fine is written Chat's name, and the date "April 7 1870". What does that not recall? The eve of my last day at Eton. And this was the leaving book, or rather the wreath placed on the shrine of our affections by a loving careful hand. Perhaps we are better friends now than then, this lad and I: but oh! The passionate weeping of that last evening: the tightening of heart, the misery of leaving the trees and fields when the next morning came.[137]

Perhaps inevitably, he is reminded of the loss that intervened: "Between that past and now, is fixed a tragedy, awful, firm, hideous in some of its bearings, and the peace of these latter days seems difficult to imagine."[138] Eton remains the scene of Regy's emotional awakening. When a younger friend is about to leave the school, Regy spells out its continuing hold on him: "Eton was the first sorrow that left an impression, not faded yet, and which bids fair to remain indelible for some time to come. It is not a morbid feeling of regret, nor any foolish wish to be back again, foolish from the mere hopelessness of the thing, but merely a dull sense of something which was once part of my life having passed away, and that nothing worth having has taken its place."[139] The school is not simply the site of early education and budding romance but stands for an ethos that may not survive in the adult world. First among its charms, he mentions "fearlessness of tongue," which boys lose on leaving school and never find again: "Clever and beautiful women of the world have it: but men never." The second charm is an excitement in entertaining and examining ideas for their own sake, allowing them quickly to grow and decay:

"And this charm can be watched slowly fading through university life, until it is lost in convictions and fixed."

Regy's own erotic travels are as important as Chat's spiritual journey in shaping their ongoing friendship. He remains attracted to those who display the qualities that so captured his imagination at school. In his first romantic attachment after leaving Eton, Regy finds himself playing an almost peda-gogical role. On circuit with his father in August 1874, Regy meets Ernlé Johnson, then fifteen and still at school.[140] Music mediates their first en-counter one evening, when Regy plays Bach and Ernlé sings, accompanied by his younger brother. Regy later comments that the youth's singing reminded him of Chat. Mutually attracted, the pair begin a friendship that will endure for years. (Regy would eventually collect the boy's letter between 1875 and 1882 and would have them typed and bound as "A Schoolboy's Letters.") In his journals, Regy records an increasing preoccupation with Ernlé. They meet at Malvern, the boy's school, and in London. Regy's intense feelings become entangled with his own schoolboy romance and with memories of Bicker-steth: "Ernlé's fair hair haunts me, and his voice, modulated as it is almost with a theme. It is curious that he should be living in a world which could not retain our Ivy. He is as pure and simple as Ivy was when he used to stand under the moonlight in the open window of my dame's passage in 1868."[141] Almost twenty-three and a postgraduate at Cambridge, Regy introduces the youth to the ideal of civic virtue: "I try to make him a patriot: and to bring him up, young as he is, with a fixed love of England and of freedom."[142] His praise of Ernlé tends to reflect his own success as a teacher: "He has learned, young as he is, to love Italy, to glory in her liberties, and to hope for Greece. Is there another boy in England aged 16 who cares for those two things."[143] Mixing pedagogical, paternal, and romantic interests, Regy begins to sounds a bit like Cory:

> I did not sleep well last night. Thoughts of Ernlé, of his health and the pre-cariousness of his life, it's certain hardships, torments me. It requires a faith in Mill's "individual initiative" that is the necessity of encouragement of individual growth to bring out great things in youth sustained and fresh. I am not in a fit state to write to him. Besides I think it is better to give him a rest. We have corresponded and met so much of late. Again a day passes without my having written to Chat.[144]

Ernlé does not completely displace Chat. In a turbulent mood fraught with bad dreams and vague fears, Regy takes refuge in friendship: "The only hap-piness has been in writing letters to Chat and Ernlé."

Regy's life is not totally taken up with new romance and memories of love and loss. He rereads *Middlemarch, The Mill on the Floss,* and *Tom Brown's Schooldays,* "the latter with some tears."[145] During his time at Cambridge, Regy had met George Eliot twice. He was much impressed by her talk, which was "like the best parts of her books, the parts where she analyzes without dissecting, the parts out of which compilers get her 'wise, witty, and tender' sayings. Her presence would be one of the glories of life were it not for her amusing vain mountebank of a husband. . . . I suppose it is an event to have spent the day in her company."[146] His reading often informs his personal reflections and relationships. Yet Regy is an indifferent student at Cambridge and flirts with following his father into the law. His ongoing passion will prove to be politics and administration. However, he continues to read voraciously, including both English and French literature, and to write poetry of his own, publishing some while circulating others only to friends. He uses his journals to record and analyze his intense feelings and attachments.

Regy articulates a sense of being divided within himself similar to the experience reported by Symonds: "Perhaps everyone has felt the presence of two distinctly differing natures one sometimes standing in a neutral and critical attitude towards the other: perhaps everyone perceives this; for we are all apt to think ourselves singular and marked in those respects which are the common conditions of the existence of us all."[147] These generalities may have been linked to a growing awareness that his close attachments to younger men fall outside social norms now that he has left school. For the first time, he recognizes a need for discretion, even secrecy. In the same week he records his internal self-division, he writes; "I pray Ernlé to keep our friendship dark from the world which contaminates and destroys. Let us live in the world as though we were not of the world, and so shall we keep our lives fresh and unwithered."[148] The religious language cannot disguise his fear that exposure may destroy the friendship. Regy sees his ironic awareness of a disparity between public appearance and personal attitude reflected in an actor's performance: "He seems . . . to look on himself and his sorrow in much the same way as I look on an ordinary actor playing a tragic and rather forced part. He mocks, and he mocks at himself."[149] On New Year's Eve 1875, Regy reflects that "the last memories of the year are kept" for Ernlé: "It is essentially his year, just as 1869 was Chat's year, and 1867 Coney's year, and 1868 Elliot's year, and 1870 Ivy's year." He charts his personal history through a succession of intimate attachments. In this catalog of loves, Ernlé is the first since Eton. However, the greater difference in age and the absence of a shared school experience leads Regy to sound more like his old teacher:

This year has given me a new friend. He thinks he has learnt something from me. Perhaps he has got a few bookthoughts, which must have come to him sooner or later. But I have got from him a higher love. And my life is marked with his influence exerted unconsciously like the mark of moving water on mountains, or the wind in the trees. I can record some new impressions, a little knowledge: but after all linger more affectionately over past sensations than over thoughts.[150]

Like Cory before him, Regy chooses warm sentiment over cool rationality and embraces a present affection resonant with memories of past loves.

As Regy works to incorporate his Eton experience into a reluctant encounter with maturity, Cory confronts the need to build a new sense of self and find his vocation in involuntary retirement. During his "exile," Tute does not simply preserve old associations and habits, he expresses some enthusiasm for change: "Is it unreasonable to wish to start again in a new line? I wish to be a Dalton man and a Torrington man. I am told I am going to made a J.P., which is rather premature."[151] At Halsdon, he takes on the responsibilities of a country gentleman. Not surprisingly, he takes a special interest in the local talent: "We have a deaf teacher here, he teaches Louisa and Fred. He says he has a good pupil in John Gayden, a graceful boy of 14, who gave evidence beautifully last petty sessions and interested me. I . . . hope to know John G.—he is pupil teacher in the school."[152] Cory asks Regy to help find work for one boy: "There is a very fine lad Charles Lyne, aged 13, who wants a place in a gentleman's house; please to look out for him. He is idling in the village now and will soon be a loafer or rowdy, unless employed."[153] In a later encounter, Cory reveals the complex mix of parental and erotic sentiments that animate him. Visiting a household with many children, he notices the brightest among them, a boy of 15, who seems "very cold, very shy," much eclipsed by a more personable older brother. Cory is clearly drawn to the youth: "I thought I had not a chance of knowing the shy one." One day the boy develops a boil that requires immediate treatment but no one is available to take him to the distant doctor. Tute seizes the moment:

I offered to go with the boy: to my surprise he came from his bed where he had been lying in pain and just showed himself in case I was ready. He was in too much pain to talk, but he said something now and then in a gentle way . . . whilst the Doctor lanced him the stupid man did not put him into a chair and he was faint from the pain. Therefore when we went back he was glad enough to take my arm and for once, after years, I was a helper to a boy in pain. And when it is a shy proud intellectual boy, this is a very taking luxury. . . . I liked my two miles walk with the faint sufferer better than anything that came with laughter or smiles. That is all. I shall never see the lad again nor hear from him, hardly of him.[154]

Cory invests extraordinary feeling in this brief encounter, yet it leaves him with a renewed sense of loss.

He also resumes his pedagogical commitments in visits with old friends like Elliot: "I found my notions crystallizing as I dropt them into his sound mind; I formulated several bits of politics offhand, new to myself; this is the great privilege I have still. What I used to enjoy as a teacher, the sudden originating of things whilst talking; to do this is the one thing that compensates for great privations."[155] Cory remains engaged with his former students' erotic prospects: "I am sorry that Rosebery is still addicted to badinage; let him fall in love."[156] As for Elliot, who will eventually become minister to Greece: "It is rather dismal his going away again in May, and I hope he will fall in love next summer; he is only half-alive but he will bud like my bay or plane."[157] (Years later, in the margin of this letter, Esher would write: "Did he ever bloom, poor dear?") In March 1876, Cory writes Regy: "It is so odd, your seeming to be in need of someone to be fond of. I always imagine you have a necklace of sweet souls, male and female, hanging on you; not a day without an embrace and a sensation. . . . I always imagine you at night in a transport of love and by day in a flush of political zeal."[158]

7. HAPPY ENDINGS?

In fact, at just about this time, in September 1876, Regy struggles to come to terms with Chat's imminent departure and change of life. Recognizing his deep ambivalence about his friend's decision, he reflects on the diverse character of love. At twenty-four, Regy finds his complex entanglements with other men more important than almost anything else in his life. Chat remains his great passion:

> Chat is here. He goes to the Oratory in a week. In St. Francis or St. Bernard we call it saintly or divine, and blame the young man who would not sell all his goods and follow Christ. In a friend we call it weakness or superstition. So are actions judged by their fruits, and differently classed only according to their nearness to or remoteness from us. Different people love with different degrees of intensity. Love may be altogether different in kind as well as in degree, if I understand the poets. A mother may love after one fashion, a lover after another. I know of a love that combines the passionate devotion and persistent fervour of one, with the forgiving tenderness

and self sacrifice of the other. The sort of love rhymed about by the an-
cients—and idealized by the noblest Greeks. Something like it, during ten
years, I have felt. I courted for a year. For a second year I worshipped. Then
came three years of passion, intensified by marvelous aids from books and
music. Then a breakage of hopes until I floated into smooth waters. After
next Tuesday we shall be nothing more to each other, except in my dreams.
Still for the week he is with me. His room opens into mine. We can talk
each other to sleep, and I can hear him breathing through the night. And
this is meorum finis amorum.[159]

A few months later, Howard Sturgis, another old Etonian and former student of Cory's, writes Regy from London with a glimpse of the new model:
"The other day going down Piccadilly in a handsom [sic], I saw a beautiful
face that seemed familiar surmounting a queer muslin collar & long black
garment: it was Chat looking more lovely than I ever remember to have seen
him since he was quite small. I did not recognize him till I got past: I was so
sorry."[160] Regy consoles himself by deepening his friendship with Lord
George Binning, who had been at Eton five years earlier. Regy's account of
Binning's school days displays a darker side of that experience:

> His cleverness, a good voice, and an odd only half conscious ironical man-
> ner won him several distant admirers among the ushers. Dark eyes, a clear
> skin, many friends among the boys. He retains still his youthful appear-
> ance and the indescribable charm that I find in boys who have been
> beloved at school. But the physical effects of his Eton life were bad. Per-
> fect recklessness, overstraining at games, contempt for exposure, and un-
> controlled desires have left him in a state in which long life is almost
> impossible.[161]

Binning has paid a high price for his youthful excesses. To Regy, he is already
a broken man, with failing health and little prospect for a long life. He doubts
his new friend's protest that his love for Eton is so strong that he would do it
all again given the chance: "Still at the bottom of his heart, brave as he is, I
doubt whether in moments of intense pain, he thinks the game worth the candle. . . . His high spirits are subdued now, and only rarely flash out. He speaks
to me very freely, saying affecting things in a half tender, half mocking manner."[162] When Binning visits Regy at Cambridge, the older boy takes an almost maternal role, insisting on a quiet life, intimate conversation, early
bedtime. Binning seems to recognize and appreciate the concern: "What
strange whim induced you to take up the 'shy, gruff, hunted looking animal'

(your description) you found and by what strange process you have transformed it into a 'fairly decent member of society' (your description again) I will not conjure. . . . You have done more for me down here than I can set down on paper."[163] Their time together exemplifies that combination of devotion and fervour that Regy defined as the Greek ideal in his meditation on love several weeks earlier, but Eton remains the imaginary scene: "He has fascinated me to an absurd extent. I could hardly be more in love with him, were we still under the limes at Eton."[164] However, Binning himself turns away from school and looks in a different direction: "You must get married, Regy. . . . You need some tie—you are too much of a rover—than a faithful one, I am bound to say, in some instances." However, his prognosis is not encouraging: "Of course you will get bored by your wife unless she is very model indeed—in about 6 months, but that can't be helped."[165]

Writing to Regy at about this time, Cory again refers teasingly to his friend's polymorphous erotic interests: "I have lately read again Balzac's Sarrazine. The revolution in a man's feelings caused by discovering the sex of Zambinella is perhaps what you would not have undergone in similar circumstances."[166] (In that story the beautiful singer turns out to be male.) Although the awkward syntax suggests some degree of discomfort, Cory goes on to declare: "It is very odd, at the end of life, to find myself liked by all sorts of females. Everything of the kind I score as a compensation for losses."[167] Regy himself seems preoccupied by the darker aspects of erotic friendship. On New Year's Eve 1876, referring to Plato, he asks himself: "What do you think of the line quoted in the Phaedrus: 'As wolves love lambs, so lovers love their loves.' . . . Remember always friendship should be for the advantage of both, and the injury of neither." Not long afterward, Regy refers to Cory's former pupil and colleague Oscar Browning, who had taken up his fellowship at Kings College, Cambridge, after being sacked at Eton in 1875: "OB's weak points are numerous and obvious, but he really has an abundant flow of the milk of human kindness and is courageous in his friendships. . . . [He] is the only person I know who could really help Graham. He would understand and sympathize with the boy who is passing through the most perilous stage of a stormy youth."[168] It was Graham who so provoked Cory's concern immediately after his retirement, when communication between the teacher and his former student was forbidden by the boy's father. Tute has again been much on Regy's mind. At about this time, he finds himself rereading Cory's journal from 1868. Regy revisits the Eton renaissance as he faces Chat's departure for the Oratorians and negotiates his own complex relations with Ernlé, Binning, and others.

Somewhat surprisingly, Cory moves further away from the masculine ideal of Eton love. Although he teased Regy a few months earlier about the polymorphous character of the younger man's desires, Tute embraces marriage before his former student does. In June 1877, he reports with pleasure: "I make at least two new friends every week amongst young people of the female persuasion from 10 upwards."[169] Rather precipitously, less than two weeks later, Cory declares "the sweet astonishment" of discovering that he is loved: "I had a true love letter to-day from a girl of twenty. . . . It is an absurd thing. Anyone would scoff. It is as if Miranda had fallen in love with Gonzalo or Alfonso instead of Ferdinand; she has been kept at school till the last year & since then 'suppressed' by mother and sisters, her word."[170] Cory declares that this is only the second time in his life that a person has been "really fond" of him. Who, among all those whom the schoolmaster loved with such enthusiasm, was the first? Cory's biographer reports that the discovery of Rosa Caroline Guille "seemed a sort of repairing of the dreadful loss at Baden." In a letter to a friend, Cory compares Rosa with the lost Beak in terms of "entrain, chaleur, abandon, only with a different kind of voice: in the morning soft and demure in the carriage telling us her school experiences; it is the sort of voice and manner that bewitches one in comedy." He concludes with a turn to tormented introspection: "I write all this because I want to talk to myself and to make out whether my notions are clear and reasonable. I am void of 'passion' anyhow; *sentiment,* and that, too, subdued by the consciousness of being double-natured."[171] Cory's reference to himself as "double-natured" echoes Symonds's "divided self," torn between powerful desires and relentless moralizing, and Regy's reflections on the ironic split between actor and observer. It also recalls Cory's own recurrent ambivalence about masculinity. These doubts do not prevent him, with the support of his brother, from responding to the young woman's interest. On December 14, 1877, Regy writes: "I have heard startling news from Halsdon, but I dare not write what it is: for fear of the matter falling through."[172]

When they marry, Cory is fifty-six; Rosa, twenty. Writing to Regy, Tute still has doubts about his forthcoming marriage. He focuses on the effects he will have on his young bride: "It is certainly a very wild eccentric business; if I had no such authority as my Brother's to lean on I could not let the girl do anything so reckless. I cannot trust my own judgment. I reason it out and come back to the conclusion that I ought never to have indulged the wish and yet that I am not going to do her any permanent harm."[173] Cory's fears recall his reflections on being single ten years before: "I am not at all sure that I wished for any companion at all. Do I now? Yes, but not at the

Sodom on the Thames

price of an indissoluble bond, nor at the price of another innocent person's happiness or freedom."[174] Despite his marriage, Cory continues to revisit old attachments. Writing from Madeira where he and his bride have settled, he begs to hear about Elliot: "I ache for want of knowing about him: his absence and silence always pain me and his letters always put me at arm's length." He welcomes news of Chat: "Is it credible that he can still think kindly of me. I should not be dangerous to him."[175] In the fall, in a missive marked *Private*, he writes: "I am sure I have a perfect wife; at first I found her mind too forgetful, as well as empty, but she grows apace here in understanding."[176] The ambiguous judgments of the schoolmaster are replaced by happier news six months later: "Don't bother yourself about me. I am the most contented of men, and quite youthful and gay."[177] Cory does not share with Regy the further vicissitudes of his married life. Let that door close with this report: "I have been married a year now and on reflection I think mine one of the most curiously romantic marriages ever heard of in the bourgeoisie: it was a mutual rescue."[178]

In the meantime, Regy increasingly adopts the posture of a teacher and admirer of youth. It is almost ironic, but not surprising in the smallish world these men inhabit, that in August 1877 he befriends George N. Curzon, "who last Tuesday ceased to be one of the cleverest and most engaging boys at Eton."[179] Curzon is the young man whose friendship got Oscar Browning into such trouble with the Eton headmaster. Regy writes the youth of his visit to OB: "He praised you, as you may guess. Your verdict upon him is probably the right one, but I felt more than ever that my nature is not responsive to his touch. Perhaps I could give a reason for this, but there is not much need, He is a good friend to you, and I can imagine a faithful one."[180] Now Regy delights in the prospect of becoming a mentor to the young man:

> In recommending George Curzon Mill's books, I tell him that they will help him to be temperate in thought and guide his impulses. Perhaps they will help him to beware of cheap successes, easily earned praise and such forms of flattery. I tell him not to mind my recommending him books now and then. It appears almost a solemn duty, as well as a pleasure to offer to those I am fond of, books which have been of service to me; just as if they were friends who had been useful and pleasant and whose company I had no wish to monopolize.[181]

At twenty-six, he already sees himself as a maker of men and keen observer of the world of affairs: "As you may suppose, we are very busy in town: this evening I have been dining with the chiefs of the Liberal party and heard a

11. *"The Bride, Bridegroom, and Sad Love," Simeon Solomon (1865)*

juicy talk over things in general. Their reflection that men are more easily governed by their passions than their intellect, is not a wholly satisfactory one to come away with."[182] Future statesmen abound among the old Etonians. Not long after meeting Curzon, Regy develops his acquaintance with Cory's old favorite, Lord Rosebery; it will soon blossom into friendship. The Liberal politician has recently married a Rothschild: "Certainly Rosebery is very agreeable, witty, reasonable, and well informed. His wife is ugly, and people are angry with him for marrying so much money. They are both ambitious. She is susceptible to flattery. So is he."[183] The great and the good figure importantly in the pattern of male erotic relations in which Regy is entangled. But he also admires the "mad, bad, and dangerous to know." In his journal, he invokes Byron to vindicate his faith in romantic friendships among men: "At school he loved and was beloved passionately. He records in verse the little quarrels, the reconciliations, the jealousies I remember so well. His friends were Delaware and Clare. At Cambridge he fell in love with a chorister, Eddlestone, about whom he wrote some good verses." In affirming his Byronic affinities, Regy implicitly acknowledges the risk of social disapproval as well as a broader, more positive political context. He also registers the elegiac note that sounds whenever he refers to school days:

> The memories of his friendships all through his life seem to have been stored in the best part of his mind. Owing to a stupid prejudice, this side of his character would not be dwelt on, and it just redeems his whole nature. It underlines his love of Athens and of liberty. He was very far from being a virtuous man, but what virtue he had sprang from this refined sense of the beauty of friendship.[184]

Regy enlists not only Byron but also Dumas and Disraeli in support of male friendship:

> In L'Affaire Clemenceau which I am reading again (I read it ten years ago and formed too high an opinion of the book) there is a curious corroboration of all that has been written about schoolboy friendships. Dumas says of French boys what Dizzy says of Etonians in Conigsby, and what is known to every public schoolboy to be simple fact. He dwells on the erotic and sentimental sides of this attachment, at an age when boys long for affection outside the domestic circle irrespective of sex. His allusions to paederastia are curious.[185]

Maintaining these relationships in adulthood is not so easy as commemorating them in novels or poetry. Chat visits Regy before he returns to his third year with the Oratorians. The new distance between them causes tension. Their efforts at reconciliation lead them to recognize an old asymmetry:

> He says we are absurdly shy with each other, considering our friendship is of ten years' growth. In talking we found the reason. There is no difficulty when we speak about him, but neither I like to confess to him, nor can he bring himself to ask me about myself. It is because for years we have been accustomed to talk about him. I have always questioned and examined him about his own soul, whereas he would not have cared to know about me, and I never could bring myself to try and create in him an interest. He seems to regret it. So do I.[186]

Perhaps his discomfort with this discovery leads Regy to some hesitation in his pursuit of Curzon: "Our friendship is young still, and can hardly be called more than an experiment yet. It is very advisable then to clear as much ground of tangle as we can, and to stand as full face to face as possible. There will be fewer deceptions in that way between us, and he may tire of me less soon."[187]

Although Regy explores the vicissitudes of his new friendship with Curzon in his journals, the pattern of his intimate life would be more significantly transformed by another new acquaintance. He spent the summer of 1877 sharing a house at Brayfield, a few miles up the Thames from Eton, with Howard Sturgis's older brother Julian, also an old Etonian. The pair socialize with the family of Mme van de Weyer, an American cousin of Sturgis who had married a Belgian diplomat. Regy spends time with her youngest daughter, Eleanor, known as "Nellie." When Cory first heard of the plan to take a house with Julian, he wrote with some skepticism: "How mean, and absurd, and indiscreet and muggy: all weeds, midges, gudgeons, shandygaff and spoonery of the stalest kind."[188] Later Esher would write in the margins of the typescript of this letter: "Yet it was this that led to my knowing Nellie, and to all the subsequent turn of my life."[189]

On September 24, 1879, Regy and Nell would marry. Although Regy records few details of their courtship in his journals and letters, he remains in touch with her over the next two years. Apparently he had already made an impression when he first met Nellie in Pisa two years earlier, when she was thirteen. In some diary notes, she had written: "Mr. Brett sends word that I shake hands in a most unbecoming fashion; that is neither pretty nor taking. This is very likely. I have never studied the becoming, which he apparently does to a very great extent, both in himself and others. . . . He wishes to improve himself and everybody: he is quite right." Almost prophetically, the girl concluded: "The greatest praise a husband of mine could give me would be

Sodom on the Thames

to say that he did not feel in the least tied down; or any more encumbered than when he was a bachelor."[190] Like Cory, Regy has doubts about what kind of husband he will make. He takes some pains to warn his future wife:

> Why you have thrown yourself away upon one who is the converse of you in all things remains a mystery. Very sincerely I feel quite unworthy of you, and I think you must be a kind of St. Theresa, a reforming soul. Some day, like [George Eliot's] Romola, you will find me out and you will hate me. Are you prepared for this?[191]

More positively, he informs her: "It astonishes me I can write to you so easily and in this strain. You are the only girl with whom in writing I have felt on equal terms."[192] However, he concludes on a darker note: "Do not, I ask you, start thinking too well of me, for I dread the disenchantment."[193] Nellie van de Weyer was not to be deterred. She married Regy and would remain with him until the end of his life, bearing and raising their four children. Brett's biographer reports that she carried this letter with her until it literally fell to pieces in 1935, five years after Esher's death.[194]

On hearing of Regy's decision to marry, Cory offers advice, urging his pupil always to let his wife have the last word and to have a bank account of her own. He goes on at great length about the need not to interrupt or differ with her in public, despite his recognition that "it is very trying for a man who is cleverer than his wife to have to listen to her feeble and exaggerated aphorisms." Since Cory has not met Nellie, these remarks probably reflect his own first year of marriage with Rosa. However, he tries to finish on a more upbeat note: "Marriage without mutual respect must be painful without respectful *affection* and reserved confidence. It must be oppressive but not intolerable. I dare say your Flamande will be reasonable and even-minded. . . . If you have anything like the sweet humility and tenderness in your wife that I have in mine you will be fortunate."[195] As the wedding date approaches, Cory responds more directly to Regy's own doubts: "I am very glad to hear from you and sorry that you are going to be married so phlegmatically. Doody [Howard Sturgis] gave me a description of Nel—and was very hopeful about her—"[196] Regy's experience of marriage quickly proves more positive than these grim prognoses: "A month ago this day Nell and I were married! She says she is quite happy now, no longer doubtful."[197] Regy reads Eliot's *Romola* aloud to his bride; they have already finished *Silas Marner* and *Daniel Deronda*. They discuss in detail the heroine of the latter novel, to whom Regy attributes that "fearlessness of tongue" he previously admired in boys at school: "The proudest and noblest natures sometimes see their way to confess where those less sure of themselves would hesitate. Gwendolyn was too proud and had suffered too acutely to fear breaking the ordinary so-called rules (for they cannot accurately be called rules) of social intercourse between fashionably bred people."[198] To Curzon he writes: "It does not appear strange to me, this fact of being married, which is odd. Somehow I find no difficulty in reconciling it with my habits of thought, and anticipate none when it ultimately comes to my habits of life. Then I have married a very clever child who fairly well understands me. You must like her when you know her."[199] Earlier he had observed: "I think it will all go straight and that I shall not be *very* much changed by marriage."[200] Regy even tries to reassure an apparently anxious Chat: "On All Saints' Day Charlie wrote to me from the Oratory. He not the least of the Saints. Although, I tell him, I cannot answer for the future, I shall try hard to be kind and thoughtful with Nell. Hitherto our life has been smooth."[201]

The marriages of Cory and Brett may seem an accommodation to dominant mores that brings an end to the homoerotic exuberance of their Eton renaissance. Chat remains the odd man out, though his passions must have been constrained somewhat by the vows of celibacy required by the Oratory. However, all these stories resist such conventional "happy endings." Perhaps Cory comes closest to a kind of conformity, but even he remains a nonconformist by late Victorian mores. The passions that moved him so powerfully as a teacher at Eton are not completely stilled in later life. Cory and his wife would return eventually to England and, again with help from Regy, settle in Hampstead. Here he resumes his vocation, but with a difference: "The really astonishing thing about my poor life is that in old age I take such delight and even pride in the visible results of the most blessed of changes, the modern education of English girls."[202] As Oxford and Cambridge open colleges for women, even granting them university degrees, Cory prepares them by teaching Greek and Latin. His strongest feelings are inspired still by the interchange between teacher and pupil, whatever the gender. In a letter to Rosa Paul, a former student, he writes: "The twenty-seven years of converse with the ruder sex gave me no such listeners or speakers as I get from the gentler sex in these last years. The two undying evergreen languages have been for me made beautiful by this aftergrowth of girlhood."[203] Cory's description of his interaction with his new pupils suggests a mutuality not always present at Eton:

It is easy, and perhaps common enough, even vulgarly so, for old men to pet girls and by flattery to keep them about their haunts. But here I am administering not sensational but critical instruction to young women from fifteen to thirty, all of them far more completely educated than I was myself, and I am by teaching actually becoming a much better scholar than I was at forty.[204]

Cory would spend his remaining years married to Rosa, raising their son, and teaching young women with the energy and commitment he had previously reserved for boys. As these boys grew into men, many of them remained devoted to their former teacher. Regy would correspond with Tute for the rest of the older man's life.

8. DANCE TO THE MUSIC OF TIME

When Cory dies in 1892, his friends and former pupils again revisit the scene of their youth: "I found yesterday a journal of Tute's given me years ago . . . on an occasion when he believed himself to be dying. Will you read it? And I send it to you by this post for the purpose. . . . Tell me what you think. It is of an interesting time. I think it is the latest of all his journals."[205] The remembrance of their former teacher brings back earlier experiences of loss: "Your mention of Beak induced me to look up old journals and letters in which his death, and many forgotten incidents recorded around it, are recorded. You can see them when you wish."[206]

As the project of publishing a selection from Cory's journals and correspondence proceeds, Regy becomes increasingly alienated. He and Chat conduct their own, less conventional reminiscence, recovering experiences of love, longing, and loss. At the same time, each of them enacts his own variations on the theme of school friendships. Over forty years old at the time of Cory's death, married and the father of four children, Regy is also involved in a romantic attachment to Edward Seymour, or "Teddie," then a fifteen-year-old student. At Eton of course. As for Chat, he has separated from his order and is living in Italy—with a houseboy and intimate companion named Salvatore. As they confront the death of their friend and former teacher and come to terms with middle age, both friends are caught up in romantic attachments to younger men. Outside the school setting, each invents his own form of erotic friendship. Regy suggests the complexity of these ties:

> These last few days—since my boy came here on Thursday—have been significantly happy ones. You can imagine the pleasure of having him quite to myself all day. He breakfasts in bed—after I have generally found him asleep—and then gets up slowly. Uses my dressing sink—and has my big bath. We spend the day in my room among books, photographs, and letters. He has seen all your books full of Greece and Spain, and nearly all the beauties which you recently sent me. One curious thing, which shows how

your taste has remained boyish in these matters, differing from that of every older person I know, is that Teddie admires the picture of Salvatore more than any of the others. He thought it "beautiful" and said "he looks so nice." He knows nothing about him, and it was an unaided choice.[207]

The two men send photographs as well as letters back and forth between them, not only of their special friends but also of beauties that they have noticed. Regy comments with some frequency on those he receives from Chat in Italy and less often on those he sends. These are mostly pictures of boys or young men. Since Chat's stay in Sicily overlaps with the time that Baron von Gloeden lived there, that amateur photographer's famous portraits of scantily clad youths in peasant dress and archaic poses provide a clue to what the two friends admire. Writing about Teddie, Regy uses the language of love and delights in the proximity of the young man; he even shares with him the photos of Italian and other boys.

He entertains the youth at home with his wife and family; Teddie visits with the approval of his parents and of the Eton authorities. Regy's love for Teddie has important paternal and pedagogical aspects, but it is also intensely erotic. The sentiments and practices of love between them are not easily translated into contemporary terms. We must try to let the participants speak for themselves. Brett increasingly devotes his journals to political and professional matters, using his correspondence with Chat for more personal matters. Writing about Teddie, Regy remains attentive to his special relationship with Chat. He sometimes teases his old boyfriend: "So many years after—I am well nigh giving you cause for a retrospective jealousy."[208] Once again relationships are triangulated, this time with Regy at the apex between Teddie and Chat. When Chat takes up with Salvatore and others, the vectors of feeling proliferate. Present ties reverberate with earlier passions, attachments, and losses. As the two middle-aged men compare notes on their connections with men much younger than themselves, they return to their teacher and friend Cory as a point of comparison and source of complex lessons.

A long letter to Chat in February 1892 provides an interesting glimpse of Regy and Teddie. Brett shares Cory's habit of idealizing his young friends: "His taste is wonderfully good and he picks out all the best things." His attitude toward the young man combines the concerns of a parent and those of a teacher. Their time together is often devoted to mundane aspects of education: "In the afternoon he reads geography, in which he has to be examined, and I hear his lesson when learnt. After dinner we read, or talk French! Of course, I talk to him by the hour. . . . One day he wanted to know all about

Sodom on the Thames

Khartoum and Gordon's death." Brett had been friends with the controversial General Gordon and served as parliamentary private secretary to Lord Hartington, who was at the War Office during the siege of Khartoum in 1885. Happy to talk endlessly about such worldly matters with his young comrade, Regy performs more intimate tasks as well: "Then about 10 he goes to bed and at 11, I go up and sit on his bed till he is asleep. This sometimes is for a long time—as his wakefulness is abnormal. That is a sketch of the average day." Regy celebrates the emotional qualities of the connection: "No ebullition of temper. No naughtiness. Wonderful sweetness. Perfect gentleness to me. Caressing manner at times. Absolute and adorable intimacy altogether without reserves or secrets. I suppose it is the culminating point of a perfect passion tempered by the most enchanting romance." After commenting on the danger of Chat's retrospective jealousy, Regy credits his boyhood love with his own erotic awakening: "Think but for you—and all the old time with you—none of these later emotions would have fallen to my lot."[209]

Brett, not having followed Cory or OB in returning to teach at Eton, adapts the ancient Athenian model of "noble pederasty," in which men introduce their younger friends to the responsibilities of citizenship. (This practice was the subject of Cory's letter to an admiring young Symonds in 1859.) During the summer of 1892, Regy completes a book that he hopes to dedicate to Teddie. He asks for Chat's help in finding a title that is "short, suggestive, unboring." The subject of this work reveals the seriousness of his Hellenic ideal: "The idea is that the book should help a young lad to comprehend the *origins* of modern constitutional government in England." The dedication is not an afterthought to more general aims: "It is written for Teddie. I care very little if no one else reads it."[210] Regy is not completely confident that he will be understood. He worries that publicizing his interest in Teddie exceeds the conventions of pedagogy and patronage, asking Chat: "Do you approve the dedication to Teddie, or do you think his initials ought to be left out, and the secret more closely kept."[211] Regy admits to some reservations about the unfolding relationship, developing a variation on the Greek theme as Zeus and Ganymede hover in the background: "He is unlike what you and I were at his age. His quickness, the audacity of his mind, are delicious; but he is a young barbarian in knowledge. . . . Although it sounds conceited I now step down into his arena very much as the Olympian deities were wont to do. This affords a pleasant diversion in his life of conflict and sensation. But I should shrink from the experiment of love."[212] If it is not love that binds him to Teddie, then what is it? Something like the "poetical and rapturous affection" emphatically "without passion" that Cory praised in Regy's youth? Despite his efforts to normalize their relationship, Regy knows that their intense connection is unconventional:

> Talk never flags a moment—and I cannot think that he is bored. But then he is not so easily bored as you were in the old days: and I try very hard to interest and amuse him. His mind expands like a rose. Anyhow he will not be the worse for having known me. He said once that he often compares his Eton life with that of his contemporaries, and wonders how they can stand the lack of interests and excitement which I give him. So if this was not a mood, but a permanent feeling, I am satisfied. The disparity of age only now and then strikes me. In your Tutor's [Cory's] mind, it was a constantly recurring thought. When Teddie is with me—either riding or in London—I forget that such a gulph of time full of experience of life divides us. Of course at Eton it strikes me oftener: but by no means constantly. Is not this curious?[213]

Like Cory too, Regy expresses his sentiments in poetry filled with classical allusions, and shares it with the youth: "He went up to his rooms about 10 and an hour later I followed him. He was reading through my book of verses, and putting his name against those he liked. . . . Imagine the charm of questions asked, and observation made, by him under such circumstances."[214] Regy performs as mother and nurse as well as pedagogue: "Since I wrote last, almost daily I have been in Eton. Teddie has been laid up. . . . No one was allowed to see him, except me. I sat with him, and read books to him. . . . You may imagine that I have had nothing to complain of."[215] He is even more pleased when he is allowed to take Teddie back with him to recuperate: "Talk about bringing home a bride . . ." Whatever his desires and fantasies, Regy's ambition requires that the youth grow up to marry and take his place in the Victorian establishment. Teddie's graduation from Eton that summer provokes some reflection on his future: "*I never resent the advancing years, nor the love of women. Neither have stepped between me and those I have cared for. I can conceive neither coming between him and me. His is not the sort of nature which women will dominate.*"[216] It is not clear who the lovers of youth who fear "the advancing years" and "the love of women" may be.

Regy uses his letters to choreograph an odd dance among Chat, Teddie, and himself. The priest's vows insulate him against conventional pressures to marry. Nevertheless, Regy reassures his old friend in the face of some criticism:

> Yes, I know that hopelessly banal view of the thoughtless "miss" that marriage is the one solution for all troubles of the soul. It may be that one

doesn't know oneself, but we know each other fairly well, and I have no fears. I should have thought that even the most commonplace of female cousins could have recognized the uncommonplace in *you*. . . . Of course women think themselves so attractive that the priesthood is a kind of treachery to the sex! If they only knew.[217]

More than simple recollection is at work in Regy's repeated references to the resemblances between Chat and his current amour:

Later, when he was in bed, I sent him to sleep by combing his hair with my hand—something he adores. Two things he has in common with you in old days,—the love of having his hair brushed through, and his joy in his own physical beauties. I remember this so well in you. He loves himself with all the ardour of Narcissus. How true to life is all the old mythology: for I imagine this self-love (simple and physical) is commonly true of youth, where there is any beauty or grace.[218]

Relations among the three play out metaphorically in references to the bedroom at Brett's home where his old friend has stayed over the years. Urging Chat to come and stay even while the Bretts are away, Regy writes: "Your home is here ready for you. Your room is unchanged save for a photograph of Teddie which I have hung near the bed. I sit in the room, but no one else has used it."[219] Several months later, when Regy brings Teddie home to nurse, he places the boy in the same bedroom:

Now he has gone up to bed, and is lying in your rooms, among all our pictures and books and relics of old days. No one has or should have your rooms, but in his case there is no desecration, and you can think of his fair head resting on your pillow with the beautiful photograph of the Olympian Hermes above him. It seems a bringing together of all my youth and maturity: the loves of my boyhood and full manhood: the romance of a lifetime. I could not let the day close altogether without writing to you of so strange an event: one to which I have not dared look forward; which has come in that unexpected way in which sometimes the keenest delights come to us.[220]

The room is both a shrine to Regy's past and a setting for his present love, with some tension between the two. Only a week or so after being installed, the youth asserts his own claims: "Teddie insists that the room shall be repapered! So of course it must be. I don't suppose you will mind."[221] Teddie is not simply a passive partner in awe of his powerful friend and patron. Regy often seems at the mercy of his beloved:

Yesterday I was to have gone to Twickenham (?) to see Lady Stafford but that monster of a boy telegraphed on Tuesday to say he would be at Lincoln yesterday—so of course I threw over the Duchess. We had a happy day together. He is genuinely glad to see me, I know. He says he wonders whether "some day he will hate me" as he can "never feel indifferent" to me. I don't think it follows that he will like me less than he does now. It is such a curious blending of love and friendship.[222]

Teddie himself has his say in a handwritten note enclosed by Regy to Chat. He expresses a boyish desire combined with the expectation that it will be fulfilled without question. In a childish hand, referring to himself in the third person and signing it "RB," he writes: "Teddie is very anxious to have a fetish and it is to take the form of a very small gold medal. . . . Choice of a subject is left to you: it *must* be blessed by the Pope and he says it may also be blessed by you, provided that your blessing is warranted not to counteract that of the Holy Father!!!!!!! Will you please see that this commission is duly executed as soon as possible—"[223] The very next day, Regy follows up: "You will have been amused by that monkey's letter. Get him what he wants. Send it to me, as I want to give it to him, although the gift will have passed through your hands. I want a *gold* medal if possible."[224]

Chat is not amused. The relationship between Teddie and Regy clearly strains the bond between the two men. When Chat finally meets Teddie on a trip to England in winter 1893, he is not impressed. A frustrated Regy tries to convince his old friend of the virtues of the new. Chat exacts revenge by comparing Teddie to one of their less attractive schoolmates: "What a horrid idea of yours that likeness of T's photo to Loulou. I wish you would destroy it. I send you another, which hitherto I have always carried with me. You shall have one of the larger ones as well. But please destroy the Loulouesque image."[225] (Loulou is Lewis Harcourt, son of the Liberal politician Sir William Harcourt and a fellow old Etonian, of unprepossessing appearance and suspect character.) Regy's later reply to Chat acknowledges explicit criticism from his old friend: "I am sorry you cannot stand the combination of Teddie and me except at a distance! It makes me feel tactless."[226] Writing again the next day, he returns to the unfortunate picture: "I send you the other photo taken at the same time. Please destroy the one in your possession."[227] A few days later, Regy is still protesting: "You misjudge him and me. And your hypersensitive faculties deprive us of a great deal of pleasure. He likes you, and of course is not flattered by your aloofness."[228] It is a difficult time for the old friends, as Chat remains reluctant to embrace Regy's new friend. Regy reveals

Sodom on the Thames

how high the stakes may be: "It was amusing to see Teddie for the first time among these familiar faces. Like taking a bride home."[229] As Chat continues to withhold his blessing, Regy writes in some torment: "You gave me some pain. I like *you* (of all people in the world) to be altogether sympathetic, and to feel for my joys and sorrows, and not to laugh in your sleeve, and turn your head away."[230] Nelly Brett tries to mediate:

> You think me "preoccupied." So Nelly says. Why? Do I show it much? I think there is nothing so different in me *this* year from last. The difference is in *you*. Possibly your changing moods have not had so sympathetic a listener: but then they have not been so truly communicated. . . . I never varied in my wish to know *all* that frames in your mind—that you are wishing to tell. Perhaps I did say rather more to you—than formerly—of *my* inner feelings. Perhaps I thought you were more interested than you really were? But I am certain that there is no change in me. Constantly I think of you, and of all that your life has been, of the curious developments of the past three years, and of what the future holds in store for you. Here I have longed to have you to walk with and to talk to.[231]

Regy pleads for Chat's acceptance, insisting that he has remained loyal to his friend through many passionate attachments to others. He has simply been more forthcoming about Teddie: "Don't drift away from me. I am not unfaithful—and if a passion has absorbed rather more of me than usual—it is not so much the fact—as that you have been in the secret—which makes an apparent difference." He hopes that sharing his feelings will bind the two more closely: "My life has been one long sequence of absorbing passions. Hitherto you know it vaguely. Quite lately you have been in touch with one of them. That is all. I have hoped it would interest you as much as though it were medieval and Italian! Perhaps it does?"[232] Almost a year later, Regy still has not convinced Chat to welcome Teddie. Again he recruits his wife to the cause: "They have become very great friends, and there is no effort now on her part to put up with *my* intimacy. Do you grasp this? You know the measure of her adaptability. Well, it is more than complete in this case. I thought you should know this!"[233] By this time, Teddie has gone off to Cambridge, but Regy manages to maintain the connection: "He travels always now without luggage—and has a pied à terre fully mounted here and in London. So you see *my* arrangements are at least as good as yours with Salo."[234]

Chat has not exactly been celibate or without his own passionate attachments during the rift over Teddie. On New Year's Day 1893, Regy sends his greetings not only to Chat but also to Salvatore. Soon after, he advises his friend on how to treat the younger man after some trouble:

> Only be kind to the little chap, even in his shortcomings. It is sweet—a luxury—no doubt to be angry and forgive, but one can never be sure of not inflicting a wound which will not heal. Your old nature was to give pain to those who loved you, and you never realized what sorrow you inflicted upon your victims, I am inclined to plead for Salvatore—whichever his offenses—which *must* be trivial. Want of straightforwardness does not seem to me a very formidable crime in one so sweet. Of course affection so strong as yours magnifies little crimes into great ones.[235]

Regy responds to a photograph of the boy: "You should have dressed Sal as Mercury, with a little winged hat and a Thyrsus. Has he changed since those photographs of him were taken. His age and Teddie's are counted by the same number of years: but what a difference in size; and I suppose in knowledge of this complicated planet."[236] He takes pride and vicarious delight in Chat's stay at Amalfi, comparing his friend to Byron at Venice and Shelley at Genoa.[237] Chat continues to travel, despite his domestic arrangements: "Yes, I know all about Venice, and your delight in the place—gloriously unique—does not surprise." He finds young men there as well, developing a taste for gondoliers not shared by Regy: "That Augusto (not Antonio) should be found *does* surprise me. It seemed to me, from what I remember of gondoliers, that he should not be a noticeable person. As a rule, they are so plain and uninteresting."[238] The mercurial energies of his youth have become restlessness in the mature Chat:

> Your moods change so quickly. After all some passing whim, or some small unnoticed event, will determine it; and then we shall see what the effect of local colouring will produce upon your romance. As you know, I have no views, or wishes, except that you should keep up "appearances." It is a low view, but I like mystery, and I hate scandal. So do you, for the matter of that, although you do suffer from fits of bravado occasionally.[239]

Regy worries that Chat may become reckless as well. Salvatore provides a kind of anchor. When the youth dies suddenly, Regy tries to console his friend in elegiac language reminiscent of their old teacher: "Perhaps it is better thus—for after the sweets of such a friendship, life might have held some hard realities for him. You will now have memories which will never fail in their charm, and *perfect* romance."[240] Expressing a desire to hear more about the boy's final moments, he immediately asks about his potential replacement: "I should like to hear about your last talks with him: also what Marco writes when he answers your letter."[241] Marco's place is soon well established. Regy probes the character and publicity of their relationship: "You go to Wales with your mother? Is that so? And does Marco go with you? I wonder whether you are wise to bring him. However, it is not the canons of wisdom which determine such issues. Personally I think celibacy for two months or so would lend keenness hereafter to the return to Venice."[242] Perhaps Regy worries that his friend will fail to "keep up appearances." He is not himself eager to experience separation: "Teddie is back at Cambridge and comes over here on Saturdays, much as he used to do. . . . He is still wonderfully sweet and dear to me."[243] A year later, as the men approach fifty, Regy offers reassurance: "Dearest, we needn't look too far ahead. As long as you and Marco exist comfortably, nothing else matters."[244]

Chat's attraction to Venice and to young Italian men is shared by Symonds, though there is no evidence that the two men met or corresponded. Nonetheless, Regy and Chat avidly read the published work of the older man, especially his studies of Italy. It is not clear that their curiosity about Symonds's private life was ever satisfied. If it had been, they might have learned about his long-standing relationship with Angelo Fusato. Symonds frequently traveled to Italy to pursue both research and erotic adventure. In Venice he befriended Angelo, who worked as a gondolier but was also willing to offer more personal services in exchange for money or gifts. Symonds was conscious of the risks of exploitation in such relationships, working to established ongoing friendships often colored by financial patronage. Initially he employed Angelo as a gondolier. After they became lovers, he took the young man along with him on trips to London, where his presence embarrassed Symonds's more timid friends. Eventually he persuaded the Italian to settle down and marry the mother of Angelo's children; Symonds employed the wife as his housekeeper and supported the family for many years. He devotes an entire chapter of his *Memoirs* to this friendship. Of their first meeting, he writes: "This love at first sight . . . was an affair not merely of desire and instinct but also of imagination. He took hold of me by a hundred subtle threads of feeling, in which the powerful and radiant manhood of the splendid animal was intertwined with sentiments for Venice, a keen delight in the landscape of the lagoons, and something penetrative and pathetic in the man."[245] Did similar feelings govern Chat's attraction to his somewhat younger Italian amours?

During the years after Cory's death, as Regy and Chat negotiate their ongoing friendship and their amours with Teddie and Salo, they return time and again to their days at Eton and their memories of Tute. He appears frequently as touchstone, exemplar, and cautionary tale. The other figure often invoked as the pair try to make sense together of their lives and loves is Symonds. During the early 1890s, they read his work enthusiastically, wonder about his personal life, and almost make him an imaginary interlocutor. There is no evidence that they knew of the exchange between the young Symonds and their teacher, which occurred when they were very young. However, the two older figures share a space in their conversation, especially when it is devoted to love between men. Symonds would die in 1893, before the publication of *Sexual Inversion,* his collaboration with Havelock Ellis, which appeared in 1897. The book was then withdrawn under threat of prosecution. *Memoirs,* which would have interested Regy and Chat enormously, would not be published until 1984. Instead, the two men read and comment on Symonds's historical and literary work. Cory's presence is mediated by the journals and letters to which his former students often return, as they distance themselves from the publication project and engender their own remembrance. The material that captivates them most powerfully has to do with their teacher's intense attachment to his pupils, including them. The exchanges between Tute and Regy, beginning in Regy's school days, were extraordinarily intimate, and Cory mentioned as early as 1868 that he had shown his journal to the fourteen-year-old Chat.

In the midst of his romance with Teddie, rife with comparisons between the boy and Chat, Regy stresses the distance between him and his young friend. He emphasizes that Teddie is much less knowledgeable and sophisticated than he and Chat had been at the same age. In an extravagant allusion, Regy compares his relation to Teddie to that between Zeus and Ganymede, worrying that the boy may be dizzied by the heights to which the man has taken him: "Someone—I cannot remember who it was—wrote some very apposite verses upon a Ganymede lamenting in Olympus the simple pleasures of the Earth."[246] When he steps back from his enthusiasm and pauses to reflect, Regy recognizes the need to honor the difference between them. He invokes Cory's salutary example: "I remember so well how careful Tute used to be not to attempt to absorb too much of your life or mine. This was the main secret of his influence and success."[247] In the letter that includes this direct reference to his own situation, Regy insists that Tute means more to the two former boyfriends than to others involved in posthumously publishing his work. Canon Furse, the relative who had taken charge, is a source of special contempt, treated as generally priggish and probably hostile to love between men. A select group among masters and old Etonians share a more intimate knowledge of Cory and a greater sympathy for his concerns: "All my letters—and I have numbers of them—can be copied, and you can read them at your leisure. So can Tutor [Ainger] and Arthur Benson, and anyone else who is worthy."[248]

Regy is fascinated by Chat's expatriation to Italy and looks to Symonds as a guide: "I was absorbed all the morning in Symonds' Life of Michelangelo. This is a book really well done. Written obviously for the purpose of walking—oh, so nimbly—over the forbidden ground of the friendships with Thomas Cavalieri and others. It is perfectly managed."[249] In addition to the biographical study and "de-bowdlerized" translation of Michelangelo's sonnets, Symonds published a multivolume history of the Italian Renaissance, which the friends undertake to read. Regy is less impressed with a more literary study circulating at the same time: "Let me know how Symonds gets on? Also whether I should repurchase Pater's Renaissance. I sold my copy years ago. It was not a book I cared much about."[250] Three weeks later, he accepts Chat's description of the friends' time at Eton "as the culminating point of the Renaissance there." In the same letter, after deploring Tute's "defection from perfect taste," he mentions that he has sent Chat a copy of Symonds's *In the Key of Blue*. This collection of essays includes a protracted meditation on a photograph of a young Italian—"and very sweet it is."[251] Regy also thanks Chat for sending photographs and brings Cory into the frame: "The photographs are perfectly lovely. . . . I now want to look through them all with you and tell you which I prefer. Imagine how Tute—in his best days, which I take to be 1868, would have enjoyed these pictures. They illustrate all his, and our love of beauty—before the folly of passion had dominated him—for I am not sure that even I was ever overwhelmed to that extent."[252] A week later Regy mentions Symonds in a slightly censorious tone that does not disguise his fascination: "You are right about Symonds. He is extraordinarily audacious. It is hardly credible that such things should be printed and excite no comment. I am told that his character has suffered a little of late years by the audacity of his behaviour. Have you heard anything about him?"[253]

As Regy works his way through Cory's letters and journal, sending some to Chat and sharing them with other friends, he brings together their former teacher and the admired man of letters: "I am no judge of how they would strike an outsider. Of course Symonds would delight in them."[254] Reading the letters again forces Regy and Chat to reassess Tute's disgrace and the conduct that led to it. The circle of survivors is divided between those who know something about it and those who remain in the dark. Symonds, remote from these individuals and events, is vicariously embraced within the circle of those who would understand. Cory's "deflection from perfect taste" now appears to Regy as an excessive "madness—hysteria—of love." This characterization and the question to which it leads suggest that Chat has mentioned Symonds's *A Problem in Modern Ethics:* "How is that volume of Symonds to be got. Would he give it to a sympathetic acquaintance?"[255] The volume was published privately and anonymously in 1891; there were only fifty copies in circulation. It is the first work in English to present and criticize the work of the Continental sexologists who first articulated conceptions of homosexuality as a medical rather than a moral matter. Symonds keeps turning up in the friends' correspondence, though sometimes the context is unclear: "It was curious running into Symonds' tracks."[256] On another occasion, Regy has upset a mutual friend by showing him a "curious piece of diary"—it is not clear whose—but he refuses to destroy it: "It amused me. It is so perfectly renaissance and half-truth, half-irony which would have been relished then, and by Symonds in later days!"[257]

Regy combines personal reminiscence with a concern for posterity. He collects and preserves letters from Chat as well as from Cory: "Your two volumes of letters bound in blue morocco are now in the room and look very smart. I fear the 3rd volume cannot be bound up at present: or I should have to get a locked cabinet for them!"[258] Apparently these letters contain more erotic candor than would be acceptable to the uninitiated. However, Regy is equally intrigued by his friend's spiritual journey: "I have just finished reading your letters from 1868–1875 to the beginning of the year in February of which you became a Catholic. This piece of autobiography will interest you—whether the subsequent portions do or not. The letters from Eton are very outspoken and full of things which it will now amuse you to recall. They were wild times those! Heavens—what alternations of pleasure and pain for me!"[259] Regy imagines future readers whose passion differs from his own: "Your letters are the greatest pleasure to me, and the journal which they make is as good as St. Augustine. How thrilling they would appear to Catholics some centuries hence."[260] However, Chat's love life is also a theme of the letters: "What a curious autobiography they will present to some generations hence. I cannot imagine a more exciting literary find! . . . Does M[arco] know that he is glorified for posterity?"[261] When the selection from Cory's letters and journals finally appears in 1897, edited not by Canon Furse but by Eton master Francis Warre Cornish, Regy and Chat share their distress:

I agree with you about the letters and journals. Shocking lapses. Cornish knew too much or not enough. To edit the journals required one quite ignorant of the tragedies, or with full knowledge, and the courage which full knowledge engenders. It is painful to see the dégringolade after 1872. This came of two events in his life—both humiliating to the character—exposure and marriage. The whole tone of his mind underwent a change henceforth. Flashes of the old WJ cropped up now and again: but the prisonhouse shade was about him always.[262]

Regy proposes that Chat go over the material still in Regy's hands. He urges Chat to undertake "a biographical sketch . . . from the viewpoint of the Academy" and offers to help: "*You* might perhaps do it—if you would. I am sure it would enormously interest you, if you would take it in hand this autumn. We could talk it over—for I know exactly how it should be done. What would you say?"[263] The publication brings the old friends together as they try to salvage the memory of the Tute they knew. It even results in a visit from Regy's old rival: "Elliot came to see me a few days ago. Not so dry as usual and quite pathetic about old times."[264] Chat resists all these proposals for future publication. Regy himself eventually undertakes the task of composing a proper memorial for their teacher. Cory's biographer Faith Compton Mackenzie describes *Ionicus,* which Esher published in 1923, as based on "a steadfast affection which did not end with William's death. The biography is proof of that. . . . It is the appreciation of a character loved and understood through a communication of minds that was constant and intense."[265] Although Regy would live until 1930, he had charged Chat already in 1897 to attend to posterity: "Will you remember that should 'anything ever happen to me' . . . all my papers, letters, etc are to be examined personally by you—rubbish etc destroyed and the rest sealed up and handed over to Nellie for Oliver [his older son] to see later on."[266] Brett's papers, the Esher archive housed at Churchill College, Cambridge, are voluminous. Chat, however, always reluctant to have his letters circulate, removed them from the collection. On the day of his old friend's death, he wrote to Regy's younger son: "My dearest Maurice, my love for your father was inexpressible. You know that, but though you know part, it is only a small part of what he was to me, and what he did for me all through my life. I won't say more. It is not the moment, but you will understand."[267]

PART THREE ❧ WEST END SCANDALS

DRAMATIS PERSONAE

Journalists
Henry Labouchere, *editor,* Truth; *Radical member of Parliament*
W. T. Stead, *editor,* Pall Mall Gazette
Ernest Parke, *editor,* North London Press

Politicians
Sir Charles Dilke, *Liberal member of Parliament*
Charles Stewart Parnell, *Irish Nationalist member of Parliament*
Lord Salisbury, *Conservative prime minister*

Civilians
Lord Euston, *heir to the Duke of Grafton*
Lord Arthur Somerset, *aka Podge, son of the Duke of Beaufort*
Lord Henry Somerset, *brother of Lord Arthur*
Lady Blanche Waterford, *sister of Arthur and Henry*
Prince Albert Victor, *aka Prince Eddie, grandson of Queen Victoria*

The Cleveland Street staff
Charles Hammond, *proprietor*
Harry Newlove, *recruiter*
G. D. Veck, *recruiter*
John Saul, *"professional sodomite"*
Charles Swinscow, *telegraph delivery boy first interrogated by police*
Algernon Edward Allies, *special friend of Lord Arthur Somerset*

1. SCANDALOUS POLITICS

In the flyleaf of his journals for the years 1886–1890, Regy Brett would later write: "All politics—mainly the Home Rule imbroglio. Then the disastrous year 1890 with the scandals that overwhelmed poor P. the Baring smash the fate of Parnell." His entry of November 5, 1890, reveals a more personal aspect of the scandals: "From June 1889 onwards, certain events in connection with a great sorrow to a personal friend and his unfortunate family, occupied nearly all my time. They ended disastrously for all concerned in the closing months of last year. The worry of them was maintained through the first half of the present year."[1] "Poor P." was a reference to Regy's friend "Podge," equerry to the Prince of Wales and one of the younger sons of the Duke of Beaufort. Podge's troubles so occupied his friends that Brett would eventually gather the correspondence he had received and have it bound in a leather volume, which he called "The Case of Lord Arthur Somerset." Regy had become involved in the matter through his friendship with Lord Arthur. However, to the broader public, the "West End scandals" in which Somerset was implicated appeared to be the last in a series of episodes in the late 1880s in which allegations of sexual impropriety against highly placed individuals became entangled with the politics of social class and moral purity. These events included: the Dublin Castle affair of 1884; "The Maiden Tribute of Modern Babylon" in 1885; the Crawford divorce of 1886, in which Sir Charles Dilke was named as corespondent; and the O'Shea divorce of 1890, in which the Irish leader Charles Stewart Parnell was implicated.

The main focus of this part of the book is on the "West End scandals," also known as the "Cleveland Street affair," and the men who got caught up in them. However, I will situate these tales within the broader social contexts in which they were framed in press accounts and political debate. Only Dublin Castle and Cleveland Street involved sex between men. However, changes in the criminal law and in public morality targeted heterosexual conduct as well. These all combined to set the stage for Oscar Wilde's trials in 1895. In the West End scandals, police discovered that telegraph delivery boys from the postal service had been moonlighting at a male brothel at 19 Cleveland Street, patronized by well-connected and highly placed gentlemen. The affair led to speculation that members of the royal family itself might be involved. Delays in prosecution by the Conservative government enabled Charles Hammond, the proprietor of the house, and Lord Arthur Somerset, one of those rumored to be among the clientele, to abscond to Europe before they could be apprehended. Criticism in the radical press and in Parliament led to widespread debate about moral standards, law enforcement, and equal justice. The Cleveland Street affair was the first scandal alleging homosexual conduct after the passage of the Labouchere Amendment to the Criminal Law Amendment Act of 1885, which had banned "gross indecency" between men. (Wilde would be convicted of violating its provisions and sentenced to two years' imprisonment "with hard labour.")

Although the West End scandals filled the papers from the fall of 1889 through the winter of 1890, the story had begun quietly on July 4, 1899, during the investigation of some petty thefts in the central post office. Questioning a telegraph messenger boy named Charles Swinscow about his spending more money than his salary ought to allow, Police Constable Luke Hanks learned that several young men employed by the post office picked up extra money working as male prostitutes at 19 Cleveland Street. They were paid four shillings a session for engaging in "indecent acts" with adult males from the middle and upper classes. Swinscow revealed that he and the others had been recruited by Harry Newlove, a former messenger boy employed as a clerk in the post office. (It is hard to imagine that even Dickens could come up with better names for the figures in this affair.) Swinscow admitted that before coming to Cleveland Street, he had engaged in sexual acts with Newlove (and others) in the lavatory at the central post office. Hanks's investigation led him to George Alma Wright and Ernest Thickbroom (!), who told similar stories of sexual play with fellow youths, leading to proposals that they earn extra income by making themselves available to the customers at Cleveland Street. Statements by the telegraph boys are quite matter-of-fact about their willingness to perform sexual acts with older men in exchange for ready cash. Newlove admitted that he had had sex with clients at Cleveland Street and recruited colleagues from the postal service. In the end, only Newlove and an associate named G. D. Veck were arrested and charged in the affair. (Veck was yet another former post office employee who went about in clerical garb, lived at Cleveland Street, and had helped recruit boys whose favors he also enjoyed.)

Hardly the stuff of major scandal, but rather more was going on than met the public eye. As W. T. Stead commented in the *Pall Mall Gazette,* the presence of the director of public prosecutions at the arraignment of Veck and Newlove implied a larger context:

> The question . . . Stephenson will have to answer is whether two noble Lords and other notable persons in society who were accused by witnesses of having been principals in the crime for which the man Veck was committed to trial are to be allowed to escape scot free. There has been too much of this kind of thing in the past. The wretched agents are run in and sent to penal servitude: the lords and gentlemen who employ them swagger at large and are even welcomed as valuable allies of the administration of the day.[2]

The crusading editor echoes the attitude of Newlove himself. "I think it very hard that I should get into trouble while men in high position are allowed to walk about free," he said to the police just before naming, among his clients: Lord Arthur Somerset, son of the Duke of Beaufort; the Earl of Euston, heir to the Duke of Grafton; and other less well-known figures from the nobility,

Sodom on the Thames

military, and professional classes. After arresting Newlove, Chief Inspector Frederick Abberline, already notorious for his unsuccessful efforts to track down Jack the Ripper, followed the leads to Cleveland Street, where he found that the proprietor, Charles Hammond, had already fled. Abberline also sent two of the messenger boys with a police constable to identify Somerset at his club in Piccadilly and at the Hyde Park barracks in Knightsbridge, where the Royal Horse Guards were quartered. When Veck was arrested, letters from a youth named Algernon Allies were discovered. They referred to a "Mr. Brown" who had provided him with ongoing financial assistance. Allies eventually admitted that his benefactor was Lord Arthur Somerset, who had paid him for ongoing sexual favors. In November 1887, *Vanity Fair* had characterized Lord Arthur this way (see also figure 14):

> He is now Extra Equerry to the Prince of Wales and as such has the control of the Marlborough House stables, for which his knowledge of and affection for horses well fits him. He hunts much with his father's hounds, he is the best of sons, a true Somerset, a gentleman, a good sportsman, good natured, and of much solid sense. He is favorably regarded by the fair sex, and his irreverent brother officers long ago nicknamed him Podge.[3]

Evidence that Podge had been a frequent visitor to Cleveland Street brought the West End scandals perilously close to the royal family. Stead's editorial publicized gossip that had been circulating in diverse London circles for some weeks. As in the Boulton and Park case, the arrest of some visible players generated suspicion that others higher up on the social scale were being protected. This time it was not only sons of dukes who might be involved. The highest officials in the country expressed concern about who might be touched by disclosures at a public trial. Hamilton Cuffe, assistant to the director of public prosecutions, wrote to his chief: "I am told . . . that Newton [attorney for Somerset] has boasted that if we go on a very distinguished person will be involved (P.A.V.). I don't mean to say that for one instant I credit it—but in such a case as this one never knows what may be said, be concocted, or be true —"[4] "P.A.V." refers to Prince Albert Victor, older son of the Prince of Wales. As heir presumptive, "Prince Eddy," as he was called, was second in line to Queen Victoria's throne.

Rumors of sex in high places have always been grist for the mills of speculation—the higher the place, the kinkier the sex, the more productive the mills. (No one with a memory of the Monica Lewinsky affair needs reminding of this fact.) The official files on the Cleveland Street affair were closed to the public until 1976. When they were opened, scholars quickly produced two books on the subject.[5] In the wake of an earlier White House scandal arising from a burglary at the Watergate Apartments, the authors were keen to find evidence of a governmental cover-up in late Victorian Britain.[6] Although differing in their emphases, these works elaborately document a complex round of policy discussions involving the Home Secretary, chief of police, attorney general, director of public prosecutions, Lord Chancellor, and even the prime minister. The Prince of Wales himself intervened through two courtiers. By the time Lord Arthur Somerset was indicted in November, after resigning from his regiment and his post in the Prince of Wales's household, he had taken off for France. Throughout the fall, the radical papers made allegations of unequal justice and implied the existence of a far-reaching conspiracy to protect aristocratic malefactors. Under the headline "The Painful Society Scandal," *The Echo* observed: "It is singular that while the accomplices could be captured the principals were allowed to escape."[7] Radical MP and journalist Henry Labouchere, known as "Labby," mounted a relentless campaign in his newspaper *Truth,* accusing the Home Office of "impeding the police and warning high-born criminals to get out of the jurisdiction of the British courts."[8] When the affair was no longer being litigated, he presented the case against the Tory administration in the House of Commons. Labby was suspended from Parliament for a week for insisting he did not believe the explanations offered by Prime Minister Lord Salisbury (see figure 12, below).

The Cleveland Street scandal led to three separate legal proceedings. Veck and Newlove quickly pled guilty to "gross indecency" and received relatively light sentences: the older Veck got nine months at hard labor, the nineteen-year-old Newlove, four months. The other trials were not prosecutions for sexual wrongdoing. The attorney Arthur Newton and his associates, who had acted on behalf of the absent Somerset and had been paid by the Duke of Beaufort, were accused of obstructing justice by offering to finance the emigration and resettlement of the telegraph delivery boys before they could testify in court. The solicitor pled guilty, while the charges against his subordinates were dismissed. To the surprise of all the attorneys involved, an angry judge sentenced Newton to six weeks in jail and refused to recommend lenient treatment. The only proceeding to go to trial was the libel case brought by Lord Euston against Ernest Parke, editor of the *North London Press.* The radical newspaperman had published an editorial condemning the special treatment of prominent persons and claiming that the administration had allowed Lord Arthur to flee to France and Euston to Peru. Although he had been named to the police, Lord Euston had not left the country and subsequently took legal action to vindicate his name. At Parke's trial, a man called

Sodom on the Thames

"John Saul," identifying himself as a "professional sodomite," testified that Euston had indeed been a client at Cleveland Street. (Recall that "John Saul" is the name of the hero and alleged narrator of *The Sins of the Cities of the Plain, or Confessions of a Mary-ann,* published in 1881.) Nevertheless, the jury convicted the editor, and Judge Henry Hawkins sentenced him to one year in prison. The most severe legal punishment in the case was imposed on a journalist who had sought to expose the affair rather than on anyone engaged in "gross indecency" between men.

This outcome reflects widespread attitudes about the dangers of publicity such as those championed by the Society for the Suppression of Vice and debated in the newspapers during the Boulton and Park prosecution. Even the highest legal officials asked whether it might not be better to allow the guilty to go free rather than expose sexual indecencies to public scrutiny. However, the legal situation had changed somewhat since Fanny, Stella, and their friends had been tried for "conspiracy to commit the felony" of sodomy. Perhaps the primary force behind these changes had been a controversial exposé of child prostitution published by the *Pall Mall Gazette.* Considering whether to pursue the Cleveland Street affair, Lord Halsbury, the Lord Chancellor, had written in his official capacity to Cuffe at the Department of Public Prosecutions:

> The punishments already inflicted seem to me very inadequate and are likely to do more harm than good. If as is alleged in the papers, the social position of some of the parties will make a great sensation this will give very wide publicity and consequently will spread very extensively written matter of the most revolting and mischievous kind, the spread of which I am satisfied will produce enormous evil. If a successful prosecution could be reasonably looked for, and if the sentence could be penal servitude for life, or something which by its terrible severity would strike terror into such wretches as the keeper of such a house or his adult customers; I should take a different view, but . . . the only offence alleged is the new misdemeanor and at present I very much doubt the success of a prosecution.[9]

The recipient of this judgment from the chief legal officer of the kingdom commented: "If identification by respectable witnesses is a condition [of prosecution] . . . it comes to saying there shall be no prosecution. People do not do these things in the presence of persons of respectability as a rule."[10] The "new misdemeanor" of "gross indecency" had been defined by clause 11 of the Criminal Law Amendment Act of 1885:

Any male person who, in public or private, commits, or is a party to the commission by any male person of, any act of gross indecency with another male person, shall be guilty of a misdemeanor and being convicted thereof shall be liable at the discretion of the court to be imprisoned for any term not exceeding two years, with or without hard labour.

The act had been passed largely in response to the public furor generated by "The Maiden Tribute of Modern Babylon," with its graphic revelations about poor girls being sold into prostitution. Stead had organized a "Secret Commission" to investigate child prostitution and the "white slave trade" in London.

For four days in early July 1885, the *Pall Mall Gazette* devoted itself almost entirely to exposing in lurid detail sexual crimes in which middle- and upper-class men preyed on vulnerable girls from the working classes. When the news dealer W. H. Smith refused to sell the paper, volunteers appeared to hawk it on the streets. These issues sold so well that Stead published them as a separate pamphlet. As much concerned with moral reform as with sensational journalism, Stead recruited assistance from the clergy, the Salvation Army, and Josephine Butler, a feminist campaigner against the Contagious Diseases Acts. The historian Judith Walkowitz has described the public response to "The Maiden Tribute" as a "moral panic" whose effects far exceeded the intentions of the reformers. Agitation for greater legal protection of poor girls culminated in a demonstration in Hyde Park that drew a crowd estimated at 250,000. Stead presented a series of lurid and melodramatic tales in which unbridled male lust was satisfied by sacrificing young virgins. The narratives were organized around the analogy suggested by the title. The original "tribute" had been exacted from Athens by the Cretan Minotaur: seven boys and seven girls sent every nine years to be ravished in the labyrinth, until Theseus joined them and slew the monster. Stead did not hesitate to mix his metaphors of corruption: "modern Babylon" demanded far more numerous and frequent sacrifices of the young. Its denizens include a "London Minotaur," a "wealthy man whose whole life is dedicated to the satisfaction of lust": "During my investigations in the subterranean realm I was constantly coming across his name." The journalist tracked this figure into "the upper world," where he discovered that the man "actually boasts that he has ruined 2,000 women 'in his time.'"[11] These "women" were paid to consent, but in large measure they were very poor girls, innocents of thirteen or fourteen.

The major reform enacted by the Criminal Law Amendment Act was to raise the age of consent for girls from thirteen to sixteen. Stead had also em-

Sodom on the Thames

phasized the "traffic in women" by which poor children from the country, often from Ireland, were abducted into a life of prostitution, in London or abroad. To prove that his allegations were grounded in social reality, Stead had actually arranged the purchase of a girl of thirteen for five pounds. He told how, through a procuress, "Lily" had been bought from her mother and transported to Belgium. (There she was entrusted to the care of the Salvation Army rather than immured in a brothel.) Stead's zeal took him outside the law. He had neglected to secure the consent of the father and found himself on trial for committing the very offense he had sought to expose. As it turned out, Stead was convicted of abducting Eliza Armstrong, the girl's real name, and sentenced to three months in prison. He emerged a hero and for the rest of his life ceremoniously dressed in his prison uniform on the anniversary of his release.[12]

Although the tribute sent by Athens to the ancient Minotaur had included both boys and girls, all the sacrifices chronicled in "The Maiden Tribute" were female. The fervor for reform mobilized by Stead's revelations was directed at ameliorating the condition of poor young women. The villains in the piece were wealthy men driven by lust to abuse innocent girls vulnerable to exploitation because of their age and poverty. The fault lines that emerged in the ensuing debates were those of gender, social class, and sexual morality. In addition to getting into legal trouble, Stead was denounced by defenders of rank and privilege, who believed he was invoking moral purity to limit personal liberty. (Foremost among these was George Cavendish Bentinck, a Tory MP denounced to the police as a client at Cleveland Street. He would be neither prosecuted nor mentioned in the press.) Regy Brett, who had formed a friendship with Stead based on their shared support of General Gordon at Khartoum and their enthusiasm for the British Empire, was also concerned. He wrote to remind Stead that in "The Maiden Tribute" he had distinguished between "vice" and "crime" and argued that the law should govern only the latter. Consenting adults should be allowed to make their own decisions where personal morality was concerned. In fact, Stead had been emphatic in his declaration of "Liberty for Vice, Repression for Crime":

Sexual immorality, however evil it may be in itself or in its consequences, must be dealt with not by the policeman but by the teacher, so long as the persons contracting are of full age, are perfectly free agents, and in their sin are guilty of no outrage on public morals. Let us by all means apply the sacred principles of free trade to trade in vice and regulate the relations of the sexes by the haggling of the market and the liberty of private contract.

Whatever may be my belief as to the reality and the importance of a transcendental theory of purity in the relations between men and women, that is an affair for the moralist, not the legislator. So far from demanding any increased power for the police, I would rather incline to say to the police, "hands off," where they interfered arbitrarily with the ordinary operations of the market of vice.[13]

Brett wrote to Stead after reading the series the editor had sent him. He declared he had found nothing in it offensive, "when once the necessity for plain speaking is admitted."[14] At the same time, he wanted to hold the journalist to his declared intent to go after crime, not vice. Regy praised Stead for refusing to make public the names of even the worst offenders, such as the "London Minotaur." However, he insisted that it was unfair to protect "one of the worst offenders of the criminal kind" while "introducing the name of the Prince of Wales into Thursday's leader as if he were a degree worse or at any rate as bad a criminal as the 'Minotaur' in question. Yet I understood from you that he was not a 'criminal' in the sense of your primary definition."[15]

Regy may have been motivated by the courtier's instinct to defend his patron, but he had identified a slippage in the class politics mobilized by moral purity campaigns. They created the impression "that these crimes were peculiar to 'Princes of the Blood and prominent public men.'" In contrast, Stead's investigation had shown that "the offenders were nearly all obscure persons, with money no doubt, but even of no influence or importance whatever in public affairs or even in our social system."[16] Brett opposed "setting class against class" and "fixing upon a small body of men, a stigma perhaps undeserved by them, and certainly shared by the mass of their countrymen of all classes of the community." This small group, of course, is the aristocracy, increasingly distinguished from a rising middle and professional class whose claims to power derived from merit and industry rather than birth. Although the middling classes of nonconformist religious conviction were often the base of the moral purity movement, the chief villain in "The Maiden Tribute" was a self-made man: "The Minotaur himself is a man, as you are perfectly well aware, of no education or position, whose power of mischief depends upon the accident of wealth having been accumulated in hands unfit to use it."[17] At this time, Regy Brett was completing what would be his only term as a Liberal member of Parliament. He complained to Stead: "I was sorry to hear in the H[ouse] of C[ommons] that Labouchere tells people that you came across the tracks of Mr. Gladstone in the course of your exposures. He also has told people the name of the 'Minotaur.' I tell you this privately in order that you

Sodom on the Thames

may beware of him as a confidant, if you by chance mentioned these things to him in confidence."[18] A later comment suggests the deeper disagreements between Brett and the moral purity campaigners: "[Stead] gave me two letters from Josephine Butler to read. They show that craze for chastity which in the XIXth century is a Fetish whatever uses it may have had in the XIth century."[19] The difficulties of reconciling moral norms and individual liberty intersected with issues of social class and party loyalty to complicate the politics of a movement to protect poor and vulnerable girls from sexual exploitation.

To this volatile mix Labouchere added male homosexual activity. The ban on "gross indecency" between men, in public or in private, with no reference to the age of the parties, was included without debate in the Criminal Law Amendment Act that raised the age of consent for females to sixteen and imposed more serious penalties on those who benefited from prostitution. Labby's aim in proposing the amendment remains unclear. The journalist Frank Harris, friend to neither moral purity nor same-sex desire, later claimed it was an effort to sabotage the entire bill:

> Mr. Labouchere, the Radical member, inflamed, it is said, with a desire to make the law ridiculous, gravely proposed that the section be extended to apply to people of the same sex who indulged in familiarities or indecencies. The Puritan faction had no logical objection to this extension and it became the law of the land. It was by virtue of this piece of legislative wisdom, which is without a model and without a copy in the law of any other civilized country, that Oscar Wilde was arrested and thrown into prison.[20]

This view is hard to square with Labouchere's role in publicizing the Cleveland Street scandal in his journal *Truth* and in the House of Commons. The uncertainty about the legislative intent and factual basis for regulating sexual behavior was not accidental. The interdiction on public discussion of such matters extended to parliamentary deliberations. Labouchere's explanation when he offered the amendment was brief and somewhat vague:

> At present any person on whom an assault of the kind here dealt with was committed must be under the age of 13, and the object with which he had brought forward this clause was to make the law applicable to any person, whether under the age of 13 or over that age. He did not think it necessary to discuss the proposal at any length as he understood Her Majesty's Government were willing to accept it.[21]

The only parliamentarians who addressed the issue asked whether it was appropriate to include it in a general bill bearing on female prostitution and suggested raising the proposed punishment from one year in prison to two. Without discussion, the question was answered in the affirmative, and the suggestion incorporated into the bill. During the furor over "The Maiden Tribute," only *Reynolds's* raised the issue of male victims of "offenses which, if less harmful in their immediate physical effects, have yet a horrible degrading influence on childhood and manhood." Ever mindful of the abuses of privilege, the radical paper noted that whereas the "sated voluptuaries" of the metropolis are not "called to account," at "every country assize, there are sure to be several ignorant rustics charged with kindred offenses."[22] However, the comment implied that it was not a question of law reform but of enforcement. In fact, charges of "attempted sodomy" and "indecent assault" were available to protect all boys and men from unwanted sexual attention. The Consent of Young Persons Act of 1880 had deprived adults charged with abusing children under thirteen of the defense that the children had consented. (Scholars have demonstrated that previous case law had established the age at twelve for girls, fourteen for boys.)[23] However, rather than specifically protecting the young, Labouchere's amendment effectively criminalized all sexual contact among males regardless of their age.

Although eclipsed by "The Maiden Tribute," the Dublin Castle scandals must have figured in the background. Just a year before, in early July 1884, the London papers had been filled with news of a libel trial that pitted prominent figures in the British administration against Irish nationalists who had accused them in print of sexual irregularities. The episode had begun when William O'Brien, an MP and editor of the journal *United Ireland,* published an unsigned article demanding that "the life and adventures, and what is known as the 'private character' of various Crown employees in Ireland" be "laid bare to the universe."[24] The piece named Inspector James Ellis French, head of the Criminal Investigation Department at Dublin Castle, the headquarters of the English government in Ireland. French brought a libel action claiming five thousand pounds of damages against O'Brien as editor. When the police who had leaked the information refused to help for fear of losing their jobs, O'Brien consulted Sir George Lewis, a leading London solicitor who specialized in handling sensitive cases involving prominent people. As he would do again when called on by the Marquess of Queensberry in 1895, Lewis recommended hiring a private detective. The investigator came to Dublin where, as O'Brien would later recall, he quickly uncovered "a criminal conspiracy which for its extent and atrocity, almost staggered belief. It included men of all ranks, classes, professions, and outlawries, from aristocrats of the highest fashion to outcasts in the most loathsome dens."[25] The "aristocratic" conspirators included Gustavus Augustus Cornwall, secretary of the general post office in Ireland, and Captain Martin Kirwan of the Royal Dublin Fusiliers. O'Brien named these men in a speech in Parliament together with Crown Solicitor Bolton, French's superior, whom he accused of covering up evidence to protect his subordinate. Although the speech was protected by parliamentary privilege, in reproducing it in *United Ireland* a copy editor had added the caption "A Precious Trio," which was enough to make O'Brien liable for the accusation. He now faced libel actions from Cornwall, Bolton, and French amounting to seven thousand pounds. When the first case came to trial in July, it received daily coverage in the London papers, including the august *Times*.[26] Cornwall, sixty-two at the time, testified after his brother-in-law, a baronet, had attested to his good character. O'Brien later recalled: "A man of imposing stature, of a dignity that did not deign to argue and of an iron nerve, he delivered his answers with a majesty that seemed to fascinate the court . . . and he left the witness stand without a break in the superb chain of his perjuries."[27] It almost worked. After a period of high anxiety for O'Brien, during which his witnesses debated whether or not to appear, three men came forward, at considerable risk of incriminating themselves, to testify about their own sexual misconduct with Cornwall. The witnesses were "a man of independent means," "a young bank clerk," and "a shipping employee." The jury found in O'Brien's favor and imposed costs on Cornwall. Bolton lost his action as well. (French had withdrawn his case because of financial difficulties.) The Irish Nationalist camp celebrated the victory of their champions and the vindication of charges of corruption at the center of English power.

In the meantime, police arrested Cornwall, French, Kirwan, and seven others, who would be indicted for sodomy and "conspiracy to commit buggery." The grand jury that heard the witnesses presented an unusual resolution to the presiding judge, Baron Dowse: "In the interest of public morality, we most respectfully suggest that Your Lordship should prevent and forbid the publication of any part of the evidence in the felony cases which have just come before us, and if possible, make a ruling that any such publication be a contempt of court."[28] The judge did not issue that order but instead commended the resolution to "the discretion and Christian forbearance of the Press." That did the trick. The historian H. Montgomery Hyde writes: "Consequently in the ensuing trials none of the evidence was published either in the Irish or the English newspapers, and as all the court records were destroyed in the Irish civil war, it is impossible to state the allegations in any detail."[29] As might be imagined, the case depended almost completely on witnesses who themselves had been involved in the alleged offenses and who had received promises of leniency in exchange for their testimony. Juries were reluctant to convict, but the authorities were relentless in their prosecution. Cornwall and Kirwan were tried together for conspiracy: the first trial ended in a hung jury; in the second, both men were acquitted. French was not so fortunate: twice the trial ended in a hung jury; at the third trial, the jury convicted him. The judge sentenced him to two years' imprisonment. One of the other defendants who pled guilty got twenty years of penal servitude. The Dublin Castle affair reveals what a powerful weapon charges of sexual impropriety could become when mobilized in a larger political conflict. Hyde concludes: "The widespread belief that homosexual 'vice' was rampant in official circles in Ireland did much to discredit Gladstone's Liberal Administration at this time." When Earl Spencer, who had been Lord-Lieutenant of Ireland, stepped down after the Liberal electoral defeat the following year, "a Dublin wit" suggested that Queen Victoria should elevate him to a new position—"Duke of Sodom and Gomorrah."[30] Accusations of immorality could be potent weapons, but they were also double-edged swords. In late 1890, revelations of the Nationalist leader Charles Stewart Parnell's affair with a colleague's wife would deal a mortal blow to the cause of Irish home rule.

The Dublin Castle affair may well have influenced Labouchere's decision to add clause 11 to the Criminal Law Amendment Act in 1885. One fact Hyde was able to unearth from conversation with men who remembered the trials was that the accused men had frequented "a house in Golden Lane near the Liffey, apparently a male brothel."[31] When Labby took the floor on February 28, 1890, to challenge the government's handling of the Cleveland Street scandal, he offered a retrospective account of his aims. He combined a sense of urgency in the face of social decline with the linguistic delicacy and indeterminacy that marked official Victorian discussions of sex: "There is no doubt that of late years a certain offence—I will not give it a name—has become more rife than it ever was before."[32] Labouchere claimed that "the case was pretty well proved": "Therefore, in 1885, Parliament armed the guardians of public morality with full powers to deal with this offence. . . . They expressed their desire that it should be stamped out; and, presumably, it was intended that the law should be used equally against high and low."[33] Labouchere expressed concern for the national reputation while recognizing the urban context of the offenses: "In no other city in the world are such abominations openly carried on. Parliament has done its best to put down houses of ill-fame, but compared with this place a house of ill-fame is respectable."[34] The only details he mentioned, from police observations at 19 Cleveland Street in 1889, referred to two soldiers—a Life Guardsman and a Royal Artillery-man—seen meeting and going off with "gentlemen." The offense alleged to have been on the increase could be the sexual exploitation of the young, whether girls or boys, or the corruption of those in government service. Labouchere never specified. The confusion is compounded by his character-ization of the legal situation. He argued that the "offence" had previously been hard to prove, and that similar offenses were not prohibited at all, which may mean he intended to expand the scope of the sodomy laws beyond anal intercourse. (Even so, the crimes of "attempted sodomy" and "indecent as-sault" covered most homosexual activity.) In contrast, he claimed that his model was French law, but sodomy had been *decriminalized* by the Napo-leonic Code of 1815. The only same-sex behaviors that remained subject to criminal penalties in France were those involving force, the abuse of minors, or public display. Further evidence of the unreliability of Labouchere's 1890 account of his amendment is his assertion that he had originally proposed a penalty of up to seven years' imprisonment, which had been reduced by Par-liament: in fact, he had proposed a one-year maximum that had been in-creased to two.

The press coverage of the West End scandals also emphasized the heinous character of unspecified underlying sexual offenses, while linking hostility to-ward the aristocracy to suspicion of deviant desires and practices. When the story first broke in the fall, the radical papers joined the Cleveland Street af-fair with another tale of sexual misconduct involving a highly placed figure. One extended headline read "'Our Old Nobility': Charges of Infamous Con-duct Against Peers. The Earl of Galloway Examined before the Sheriff—No-blemen Concerned in an Unspeakably Gross Case in the West End Are Allowed to Escape While Their Panders are Mildly Punished."[35] Lord Gal-loway was the brother-in-law of Conservative Prime Minister Lord Salisbury. The paper reported that he had been observed "committing indecencies upon a little girl upon a wall." When a witness had interrupted the pair, the girl was "pale and trembling" but the man indignantly asked: "Do you know who I am?" The witness could indeed identify the noble lord, and the case was re-ferred from the police to the procurator-fiscal to the sheriff. It turned out that there had been a previous case "where the Lord had taken liberties with a girl of sixteen." The *North London Press* printed the details of Galloway's career, in-cluding his service as an MP, as Lord High Commissioner of the General As-sembly of the Church of Scotland, and as president of his local Conservative Association. The paper concluded with Lord Galloway's London address.[36] *Reynolds's* also covered the two stories with a series of lurid subheadings:

12. *"Modest Assurance,"* *Henry Labouchere,* Vanity Fair, *1874*

"Horrible Charges Against Peer. Lord Salisbury's Brother-in-Law Before the Procurator Fiscal. Aristocratic Doings in London. Charges of Abominable Crimes Against Peers and Officers. Confessions of the Alleged Paramours. The Inaction of the Police. The Heir of a Duke Implicated."[37] The details of the Galloway story were reprinted from the *Scottish Leader,* the leading liberal journal in Scotland, while the account of Cleveland Street came from Parke's *North London Press.* One detail reinforced the national resonance of the Cleveland Street case: "The Queens Cavalry Participated. Not only telegraph messengers but soldiers of the Household Cavalry were regular frequenters of the house."[38] *Reynolds's* quoted at length Parke's editorial entitled "One Law for the Rich, Another for the Poor":

> We are constantly assured . . . that in this country all are equal before the law. There is no distinction of persons, rich and poor are treated alike, equal measure is meted out to peer and peasant, millionaire and pauper. No statement could be wider of the truth, and these incidents serve to demonstrate the absurdity of the contention; serve to show that there *is* one law for the rich and another for the poor. . . . What would have happened if he had been an ordinary dock laborer rather than Earl of Galloway—a warrant would have been issued for his arrest.[39]

These two episodes proved grist for the mill of the radical papers, combining the sexual exploitation of working-class children by titled malefactors with the implication of official inaction. The stories promised to awaken the energies mobilized by "The Maiden Tribute" five years earlier.

Despite Galloway's links to Lord Salisbury, it was the Cleveland Street story that proved to have legs. Perhaps events in Scotland were too far away to excite the metropolitan press for long, or the hints of a connection with the royal family trumped the involvement of a prime minister. Perhaps the revelations of yet more sexual opportunities in the heart of the West End tantalized the London readership. Ernest Parke embarked on a relentless crusade in the *North London Press* that would land him in jail for a year. His urgent advocacy emphasized not only equality before the law but also national honor: "A minister at Hackney had been condemned to penal servitude for life; with . . . no hope of a mitigation of his dreadful doom. Yet there was no trace in his case, as there is in this, of a foul and widespread plot to poison the morals of the community, and make the name of England a hissing and a reproach in Europe."[40] The editorial concluded on an almost apocalyptic note: "If half of what we know, and are learning from day to day, comes out in a court of law, there has been accumulating under our feet a store of moral dynamite sufficient to wreck the good name of the nation."[41] The sexual peccadilloes of the clients at Cleveland Street were blown up into the moral equivalent of the Gunpowder Plot. Labouchere pressed the case vigorously in *Truth,* but was careful to direct his fire at the government, not the royal family: "I have seen it stated in the foreign newspapers that the Prince of Wales used his influence to hush up the affair. . . . The Prince urged that there should be a full and public investigation, and that no effort should be spared to bring the guilty to account. . . . As the head of society he is determined that, so far as he is concerned, the malpractices shall be stamped out and the guilty punished."[42] Touched by the rumors concerning his elder son and vulnerable to accusations of libertinism, the heir to the throne worked hard to distance himself from the house on Cleveland Street. The West End scandals had become vehicles for the aggressive assertion of a middle-class morality seeking to define the national character. As in Stead's earlier campaign, an ethos of respectability was used to condemn both upper-class decadence and lower-class brutishness.

The drive for moral reform had played an increasingly important role in radical politics throughout the 1880s, opening rifts within the Liberal Party.[43] What Frank Harris labeled "forces of religious prudishness and nonconformity" held public figures accountable to puritanical standards in the conduct of their private lives. In 1886 Stead led the campaign against Sir Charles Dilke, an up-and-coming Liberal leader, declaring that "any one who was unfaithful to his wife was not fit to sit in the House of Commons."[44] In a widely publicized divorce case, the wife of Donald Crawford, Liberal MP, denied to her husband that she had had an affair with one man, only to confess to a clandestine relationship with Dilke. Many observers believed she was trying to protect her true lover, and there was no evidence to support her claims about the Liberal politician. Crawford got his divorce but the action against Dilke was dismissed. On his lawyer's advice, the Liberal politician had declined to testify, since the judge had already declared he had no charges to answer. The anomalous legal outcome—that Mrs. Crawford had committed adultery with Dilke, but he had not done so with her—failed to satisfy the moral reformers. Public attention was riveted on the details of Mrs. Crawford's story, particularly her description of a threesome with Dilke and a housemaid in which he had allegedly introduced her to "every French vice." The recognized leader of the radical wing of his party, Dilke was excluded from Gladstone's cabinet because of the pending divorce case. Before the next election in July 1886 he would face a second trial in the Crawford case.

Involved as he was with the Liberal Party, briefly as an MP and consistently as a behind-the-scenes player, Regy Brett managed to maintain his contacts across the spectrum of opinion without compromising his own tolerant stance. When Stead completed the prison sentence to which his zeal for "The Maiden Tribute" had led, Regy wrote: "I am not sure whether to congratulate you upon your release; but I congratulate myself and others who have missed you sadly."[45] Yet, when the Crawford divorce first became news, he urged Dilke to go abroad for a short time for his health: "There is nothing to be ashamed for in illness. Look at Lord Melbourne. . . . You will see he was completely knocked up by an unfounded charge of a similar nature." Later he seems to have changed his mind about the circumstances, writing in the margin by his copy of this letter: "This was the beginning of the Dilke scandal. The facts were not then known."[46] About a week later, Brett met with Lord Rosebery, then the Liberal foreign minister, and recorded this memorandum in his journals:

> R. said that as a friend of Crawford and Dilke, he had carefully abstained from taking any part in the dispute. He had not communicated on the subject either with one or the other, and he did not read the case. Like the rest of the world, he seems to have no doubt that the story is true. And he evidently thinks Dilke has no chance of ever reestablishing his position.[47]

Given the complexities of English divorce law at the time, an official called the "Queen's Proctor" could intervene before a judgment became final. The result in this case was a second trial in July 1886, at which both Mrs. Crawford and Dilke testified. The jury did not set aside the divorce, which many now took to be a condemnation of the Liberal MP. He, his family, and friends continued to maintain his innocence. However, at the general election that month, Dilke was defeated in Chelsea after eighteen years of service, the Liberal Party lost its majority, and the Conservative Lord Salisbury became prime minister.

When in 1892 Dilke again ran for Parliament, this time in the constituency of the Forest of Dean, Stead resumed his campaign against him. Replying to the draft of a piece the journalist had sent him, Regy did not mince words: "I don't like the *subject* and although the sketch is brilliantly clever, it is full of things which to me are odious, and hard and unforgiving, etc, etc. You know that from your point of view so much is justifiable that is altogether impossible from mine. The whole struggle with Dilke is distasteful to me."[48] Brett emphasized his own reluctance to judge Dilke and the right of the voters to decide for themselves: "Why on earth should they not have him. You, as a propagandist have a right to say they shall not. You have been defeated so far."

Dilke was elected and would remain in Parliament until his death in 1911, though he never again held a leadership position in the Liberal Party. In his criticism of the journalist's campaign, Regy suggested that Stead's high moral tone had not been the most effective weapon in swaying public opinion: "Ridicule and contempt would do more to carry your point than the loftiest invective."[49]

Late in 1890, as the Cleveland Street affair faded from public attention, revelations of Charles Stewart Parnell's affair with the wife of a fellow MP would expose him to both moral condemnation and public ridicule, bringing down the Irish leader after forged evidence linking him to terrorist activities had failed.[50] Parnell had been the head of the Irish Home Rule Party in the House of Commons, and president of the Irish Land League, which championed the return of land from absentee landlords to poor tenants. The league had developed the tactic of "boycotting" those who took over the land of tenants evicted for nonpayment of rent. Parnell himself had been imprisoned on suspicion of being behind a series of terrorist attacks, but no evidence had been forthcoming. Earlier in 1889, the *Times* had published what purported to be letters from him endorsing plans to use violence; however, a parliamentary inquiry proved the letters were forgeries. Parnell's popularity among supporters of home rule had earned him the title "The Uncrowned King of Ireland." His most important political achievement had been to persuade Liberal Prime Minister William Gladstone to adopt his cause.

When William O'Shea, fellow Irish Nationalist MP, named Parnell correspondent in the divorce action against his wife, Katie, this alliance was placed in jeopardy. The ensuing trial resulted in disgrace for the Irish leader, the dissolution of the Nationalist/Liberal alliance, and the end of hopes for Irish home rule. Apparently Parnell and Katie O'Shea had been lovers for almost ten years, almost certainly with the reluctant acquiescence of her husband. He himself seems to have had numerous extramarital affairs, while his wife regularly welcomed Parnell to her cottage and eventually shared a house with him in Brighton. Katie bore three children to the bachelor Parnell, although legally they were registered as O'Shea's children. When the divorce came to trial in November 1890, the couple did not appear to contest it despite the fact that Katie had submitted a counterpetition accusing her husband of committing adultery and of condoning her affair. Willie O'Shea easily won the case. The evidence that most caught the public eye came from the cook at a house where Katie had stayed in Brighton in late 1883 and where Parnell had been a frequent visitor. She reported that once, when Parnell was staying there, O'Shea had arrived unexpectedly. No sooner had the husband been admitted to the house than the doorbell rang to reveal Parnell on the doorstep asking to see O'Shea. Asked how the Irish leader had managed this feat, the cook replied that he had climbed down the rope ladder used as a fire escape from the upper floor.

As with Mrs. Crawford's charges of "French vice," this story was frequently repeated in the press and among the public. However, whereas many came to regard Dilke as innocent of the charges against him, there was little question that Parnell and Katie O'Shea had been lovers. Indeed she was the love of the Irish leader's life. The exposure of their affair led to a crisis in the leadership of the Nationalist Party. Gladstone, ever sensitive to pressure from the moral purity wing of the Liberal Party, repudiated Parnell and demanded that the Irish do likewise. Although Parnell fought vigorously to retain his position, in the end he was defeated, and the cause of home rule with him. Caught between the moralism of the Protestant reformers in England and that of the Roman Catholic bishops in Ireland, Parnell didn't have a chance.[51] One of Regy Brett's friends wrote him: "Parnell's *amours* were undignified, but not nearly so discreditable as some of mine! But he has been exposed, so must pay the penalty in this most hypocritical and *virtuous* land."[52]

The evidence in the O'Shea divorce case initially appealed to Regy's sense of the ridiculous: "It is trying to think of the Leader of the Irish People flying from the avenging O'Shea down a fire escape. The relentless detail of the Divorce Court is too severe a test to apply to a politician under 40 years of age. The evidence leaves it clear why Mr. Parnell looked always so extremely delicate."[53] However, his sympathies remained with the Irish leader and his cause. Stead published a pamphlet, "The Discrowned King," while unionist Liberal politicians celebrated the defeat of home rule:

> The excitement in the lobbies has been unprecedented. Harcourt [Liberal MP] says the Irish are raging against Parnell. But in spite of them all, if he is a strong man, he will stick to his guns. Mr. Gladstone has, under pressure, written a letter which is to be published, the net effect of which is to say "You must choose between me and Parnell." Harcourt says "Well whatever now happens we shall have got rid of that cursed Home Rule." This is wild talk, but it shows how right Parnell is to mistrust English parties and politicians.[54]

As public support grew for Gladstone's repudiation of Parnell, it became clear that Parnell faced a losing fight. Brett remained steadfast: "These men ignore that they violate the essence of Home Rule. They wish to dictate to Irishmen whom they shall employ as their leader. What greater interference with liberty. At the meeting of Irish members yesterday, Parnell was cold and silent. One of them said afterwards—'He treated us as if *we* all had committed adultery with *his* wife.'"[55] Brett deplored the political ramifications of the scandal: "If Parnell goes, the Irish party is broken up. All the work is to begin again. Can the Liberal Party be trusted to do it? Very doubtful."[56] He did not hesitate to identify religious and national prejudice as a factor in the Parnell scandal: "The nonconformists generally—the Presbyterians particularly—were originally very difficult to gain over to [home rule]. They feared the Irish character, and looked especially to their co-religionists in the north of Ireland. Now they will say 'we were justified in our fears and never again trust the Irish.'"[57] Whatever gains the nationalist cause might have realized from the Dublin Castle affair in 1884, the fall of Parnell was a devastating setback. The Irish leader was destroyed by the scandal. Although he was able to marry the divorced Katie O'Shea in June, his health was destroyed. "The Uncrowned King of Ireland" died on October 6, 1891.

Sex and politics proved a volatile mixture. No politician, party, or cause was immune to the effects of scandalous politics. Public response to Mrs. Crawford's allegations seriously damaged Sir Charles Dilke's career as a radical leader and permanently derailed his ascent to the leadership of the Liberal Party. Radical journalists and politicians used revelations about the male brothel at 19 Cleveland Street and its habitués to discredit the Conservative government headed by Lord Salisbury. The O'Shea divorce not only destroyed Parnell but also set back the movement for Irish home rule and further divided the Liberal Party. Accusations of any kind of sexual irregularity could be political dynamite during the final decades of the nineteenth century in England.

2. WHO'S AFRAID OF JOHN SAUL?

What about the specifically *homosexual* component of the West End scandals? The crime of "gross indecency" perpetuated the legacy of sodomy, "the crime not fit to be named among Christians," in its legislative indeterminacy. The prohibition of sodomitical acts applied to behavior between men and women and men and animals as well as between men. Sodomy had been made a capital offense by the "Buggery Act" of Henry VIII in 1533. The death penalty remained on the books until 1861! This fact partially explains the tendency of juries to acquit in sodomy cases and of judges to require proof that was difficult to find. Carrying forward prohibitions of the canon law, the Buggery Act forbade conduct that defeated the procreative possibilities of sexual intercourse. However, judicial interpretation restricted the crime of sodomy to

Sodom on the Thames

anal intercourse and required proof of penetration. (In 1781, judges began to demand evidence of "emission of seed," but this requirement was overturned.) Since both parties to the act were equally guilty regardless of the role they had played, firsthand evidence would inculpate virtually anyone in a position to know the details. Convictions for sodomy were rare. More frequently, persons were prosecuted for "attempted sodomy" or "indecent assault," which were easier to prove and carried a less draconian punishment.[58] (Recall that Fanny, Stella, and their friends had been tried for "conspiracy to commit the felony" of sodomy.)

After Parliament repealed the death sentence, life imprisonment could be imposed at the discretion of the court. Convictions for any of these crimes might lead to exposure in the pillory where, as with the "Vere Street coterie," offenders were subjected to verbal and physical abuse, including assaults with garbage and offal that could result in serious injury, mutilation, or death.[59] These laws had a chilling effect out of all proportion to their actual enforcement and worked to reinforce and legitimate informal sanctions, from ostracism by "society" to mob violence against men believed to engage in unorthodox sexual activities.[60] The ban on gross indecency prescribed lower penalties but appeared to increase the range of prohibited activities, effectively defining all erotic conduct *between men* as criminal. In principle and sometimes in practice, the Criminal Law Amendment Act intensified social control over female prostitutes and men who had sex with other men.[61]

In the Cleveland Street affair, "gross indecency" between men was inflected differently in the lives of the telegraph boys, their aristocratic clients, and the "professional sodomite" John Saul. The legal proceedings, press coverage, and political debate about the "West End scandals" include few signs of Foucault's "new species" of sexual invert as defined in Continental sexology.[62] Nowhere in the newspaper accounts or official documents are there references to medicine or psychiatry. Traditional moral condemnations of sodomy gained political force by combining with a powerful republican discourse that emphasized aristocratic corruption and contested the alliance between governmental power and social status. Stead editorialized: "The wretched agents are run in and sent to penal servitude: the lords and gentlemen who employ them swagger at large and are even welcomed as valuable allies of the administration of the day."[63] Labouchere sounded a revolutionary note: "Very possibly our Government of the classes is of the opinion that the revelations which would ensue were the criminals put on trial, would deal a blow to the reign of the classes, and to the social influence of the aristocracy."[64] The radical press portrayed powerful clients exploiting working-class

13. *"The House on Cleveland Street,"* Illustrated Police News, *January 1890. Notice the "Piccadilly Vulture," lower left.*

youths eager to improve their lot. The fact that the boys had been employed in government service reinforced the note of national alarm: the police asked each of them whether he had worn his uniform while performing indecent acts for pay.

Parliamentary debate focused on reports that soldiers had frequented 19 Cleveland Street. The young men themselves were exempted from the attribution of an invidious sexuality by their age and class.[65] One trade union spokesman even suggested that gross indecency was congenital to the upper classes but could only be acquired temporarily by sons of the workers: "Bringing up our boys as we have to do, we should not submit to a state of things which might end in their temptation, for their tempters are men of position and wealth. Working men are free from the taint, and for gold laid down our boys might be tempted to this fall."[66] Despite the emphasis on their youth and respectability, the evidence in the police files shows the telegraph boys were hardly sexual innocents. Two of the three who made statements admitted that they had "behaved indecently" with Newlove (himself nineteen) in the lavatory at the post office *before* he recruited them for Cleveland Street. George Wright describes acts that amount to an attempt at sodomy under the law. Although at first he admits only that Newlove attempted to sodomize him, toward the end of his statement, in response to an assertion by Newlove, he admits that he had done the same in return. No one publicly suggested that these boys should have been prosecuted for "gross indecency," much

Sodom on the Thames

less "attempted sodomy." Both their acts and their character were insulated against condemnation by their representation as diligent sons of the working class eager for a leg up in the economic struggle and vulnerable to corruption as randy young males. The following exchange between defense attorney and prosecutor when Newlove pled guilty displays the legalistic and moralizing scrutiny of adolescent sexual activity:

> [Newlove] does admit that he did take them to this house, knowing what might happen to them. On the other hand, the three boys had admitted that they had all indulged in indecent practices before Newlove approached them. . . .
> "In justice to the boys," Poland broke in here, "I wish to say that they had played with other boys but had not committed these acts."
> "They said they had done such acts with boys before but not with men," Matthews retorted. "That goes to the degree."[67]

Note the different implications drawn from emphasizing the acts performed as opposed to the age of the sexual partners. To mark such practices *between* young men as seriously deviant was a risky undertaking in a society where they were quite often segregated in same-sex settings such as boarding schools, army barracks, navy ships, and universities. Recall the anxious letters to the editor about amateur theatricals in boys' schools provoked by the Boulton and Park case, not to mention the complex erotic relations among Cory's students at Eton. However, most of these young men were approaching twenty at the time of the scandal; only one was in his midteens. As employees of the post office, they contributed another element of forbidden desire: Symonds's encounter with the grenadier reveals how fascinating young men in uniform could be to other men. One scholar suggests that telegraph delivery boys were particular favorites, quoting a turn-of-the-century writer who described them as "the aristocracy of the messenger world."[68]

If the telegraph delivery boys were unlikely representatives of an emergent homosexual species, what about their clients? Despite their escape from legal punishment, they suffered opprobrium for their sexual activities. However, they may have been stigmatized for their abuse of power and exploitation of lower-class youth as much as for their choice of members of their own sex. The press never defined the precise character of their vicious propensities. Their offense was exacerbated by the fact that such things were forced on the public in the first place. To provide a bill of particulars would only compound the damage. Saul had told the police details of his contact with Lord Euston that the newspapers refused to print: "He is not an actual sodomite. He likes to play with you and then 'spend' on your belly." The messengers reveal a similar reluctance on the part of some clients to engage in anal penetration. Here specific sexual practices appear to make one an "actual sodomite."[69]

However, sodomy could also be linked to a conception of *character*, if not of identity. The "sodomite" was a figure of excess who posed a danger of corruption to those around him. Charges of sodomy were inflected by social contexts beyond theological proscriptions on nonprocreative sex.[70] In the Middle Ages, the Church accused unorthodox sects of "unnatural" sexual practices. Later, Catholics accused Protestants, and Protestants, Catholic priests. Some historians argue that the Buggery Act was first passed as part of Henry VIII's campaign against the monasteries. As national feeling grew in the early modern period, deviant sexualities were attributed to foreign vice: Germans accused Florentines; English, the French. In the Dublin Castle affair, Irish nationalists accused English administrators. Acts of sodomy could betray a spirit of revolt and tendencies toward heresy and treason. Excessive desire could lead to the abuse of power. The most notorious sodomite of earlier times, Lord Castlehaven, had been executed in 1631 for buggering both his household servants and his wife. He exemplified the sodomite's willingness to use anyone at his disposal to obtain sexual satisfaction.[71]

Although Stead's lurid exposé in "The Maiden Tribute" had detailed the mistreatment of girls, the target of campaigners for moral purity was unbridled male lust. The dominance of such images helps explain Symonds's relentless efforts to establish an ethical defense of male same-sex desire. Nevertheless, by 1891 Symonds had become worldly enough to condone the Cleveland Street establishment, though his defense took a peculiarly democratic turn. He reports a conversation about the affair with a British steamship officer in Venice: "[He] volunteered the opinion that it was absurd to disqualify by law passions which seemed so harmless & instinctive, although he added that his own (I suspect very free) self-indulgences were in the opposite direction. The way of thinking among the proletariate, honest artizans, peasants, etc, in Italy and Switzerland—where alone I have fraternized with the people—is all in favour of free trade."[72] What Symonds saw as "free trade" looked like exploitation in the English radical press. Still the acceptance of a "free trade in vice" but not in crime had figured importantly in the introduction to "The Maiden Tribute." Very little effort was made in the public debate occasioned by the "West End scandals" to make distinctions that had seemed important to both Stead and Regy Brett five years earlier. John Stuart Mill had helped shaped Brett's thought about the reach of government; Brett frequently recommended Mill's work to his protégés. Mill's influential essay *On*

Sodom on the Thames

Liberty had been published in 1859. Its argument informed the public prosecutor's distinction (in correspondence with colleagues) between what adult men might do together in private, in contrast to sexual exploitation of the young and underprivileged. However, no voice was raised in public to defend the liberty or privacy of the clients at Cleveland Street. Same-sex desire was assimilated to child abuse and class domination in the same way that some opponents of lesbian and gay rights today identify homosexuality with pedophilia.

The necessary distinctions were certainly available in 1890, but there was no political interest in articulating them. George Bernard Shaw saw some of this very clearly. Early in the emerging scandal, on November 26, 1889, he wrote to Labouchere's journal *Truth,* insisting on the difference between the abuse of minors and the consensual activities of adults: "We may presently be saddled with the moral responsibility for monstrously severe punishments inflicted not only on persons who have corrupted children, but on others whose conduct, however nasty and ridiculous, has been perfectly within their admitted rights as individuals."[73] Shaw insistently defended a "liberal" perspective that was eclipsed by the intersection of class, party, morality, and sex in the controversy. His argument was not free of the prejudices of his time and class, but he distinguished such social attitudes from their enforcement by criminal law: "To a fully occupied person in normal health . . . the subject of the threatened prosecutions is so expressly disagreeable as to appear unnatural. But everybody does not find it so." Shaw was willing to state facts that were obscured by the treatment of the West End scandals in the press. He emphasized that a minority of people, both men and women, had been moved by same-sex desires throughout history, and that many others, when deprived of sexual contact with the opposite sex, turned to their own for satisfaction. Alone among the responses to the West End scandals, Shaw's recognized an issue of human rights:

> I appeal now to the champions of individual rights . . . to join me in a protest against a law by which two adult men can be sentenced to twenty years penal servitude for a private act, freely consented to and desired by both which concerns themselves alone. There is absolutely no justification for the law except the old theological one of making the secular arm the instrument of God's vengeance.[74]

Shaw conflates the penalties for sodomy, which had not been charged in the Cleveland Street affair, and those for gross indecency. However, his point of principle remains: English law seriously penalized same-sex activities between men even when committed in private by consenting adults. The crime of "gross indecency" *supplemented* the sodomy laws; it did not replace them. Insisting that the protection of children "is quite on a different footing," Shaw characterizes the laws against same-sex activity between adults as "the evil of our relic of Inquisition law" and condemned as "moral cowardice" the failure of the press and others directly to address the issue. His analysis of social attitudes reflects the complexity of Victorian England: the general interdiction of candid discussion of sexual matters coexisted with considerable tolerance in some reaches of "society." Indeed, Shaw claimed that while ostracism was often a response to revelations of sexual vice, society remained open to people widely known to prefer partners and practices prohibited by law so long as they remained discreet. As we shall see, he underestimated the forces of moral purity and the hypocrisy of a society that tolerated deviance only so long as it remained secret. Although liberal arguments would finally carry the day when the Wolfenden Committee Report of 1957 recommended decriminalizing private consensual acts between adult men, they were not aired in 1889. The editor of *Truth* chose not to publish Shaw's letter. "Gross indecency" between men remained a crime in England until 1967, when Parliament exempted sexual activity between two men so long as it occurred in private.

As the West End scandals developed, the telegraph boys continued to be cast as victims. Press accounts and public agitation capitalized on the fervor to combat the sexual exploitation of children that had animated Stead's "Maiden Tribute" and led to the passage of the Criminal Law Amendment Act in the first place. This, despite the fact that most of the young men were about twenty. The illustrated London papers featured drawings on their front pages showing the lads as handsome, clean-cut, and respectable. Political opposition to upper-class corruption and moral condemnation of the sexual exploitation of children relieved the younger men from any imputation of irregular sexuality. The director of public prosecutions summed up his reasons for proceeding with the affair in these terms:

> Whatever may be said, and much may be said—as to the public policy of allowing *private* persons—being full-grown men—to indulge their unnatural tastes—in private—or in such a way as not to come to public knowledge—in my judgement; the circumstances of this case demand the intervention of those whose *duty* it is to enforce the law and protect the children of respectable parents taken into the service of the public as these unfortunate boys have been, from being made the victims of the unnatural lusts

Sodom on the Thames

of full-grown men—and no consideration of public scandal—owing to the position in society or sympathy with the family of the offender should militate against this *paramount duty*.[75]

The only thing that distinguishes this argument from that of the editorials in the radical press is the radicals' emphasis on the privileged status of the corrupting adult males. Labouchere, editorializing in *Truth*, provides the missing point: "It would be really too monstrous if crimes which, when committed by poor ignorant men, lead to sentences of penal servitude were to be done with impunity by those whom the Tory government delights to honor."[76] The clients at Cleveland Street were defined not primarily as men who desired their own sex, but rather as "privileged" sodomites. Lord Arthur Somerset and Lord Euston were initially paired in the press, joined as much by their noble blood as by charges of sexual irregularity. Each of them was juxtaposed to a specific victim. Regy Brett's friend Somerset was portrayed as the corrupter of the messenger boys and caricatured as "my Lord Gomorrah." (In fact, the most telling evidence against him had come, not from them, but reluctantly from a youth with whom he had formed an ongoing relationship.) Euston was more fortunate; his accuser was John Saul.

The most dramatic court proceeding in the Cleveland Street affair was the trial of *Euston v. Parke*, the libel action initiated by the aristocrat against the editor of the *North London Press*. On November 18, 1889, that paper ran the headline "The West-End Scandals: Names of Some of the Distinguished Criminals Who Have Escaped." The text declared:
The men to whom we thus referred were

> THE EARL OF EUSTON,
> eldest son of the Duke of Grafton, and
> LORD H. ARTHUR C. SOMERSET,
> a younger son of the Duke of Beaufort.

The former, we believe, has departed for Peru; the latter, having resigned his commission and his office of Assistant Equerry to the Prince of Wales, has gone too. These men have been allowed to leave the country and thus defeat the ends of justice because their prosecution would disclose the fact that a far more distinguished and more highly placed personage than themselves was inculpated in their disgusting crimes. The criminals in this case are to be numbered by the score.[77]

Unfortunately for editor Ernest Parke, Lord Euston was very far from Peru, at home in London. While Lord Arthur Somerset followed the case from

France, safe from prosecution, Euston confronted his accuser in court. Lord Euston was the oldest son and heir of the Duke of Grafton. He had been mentioned first by Newlove after his arrest, along with Somerset and others as a patron of the house at 19 Cleveland Street.[78] At his interview with Scotland Yard in August, John Saul, though confused about his family status, made a similar charge: "The young Duke of Grafton, I mean the brother to the present Duke, was a constant visitor at Hammond's. He is a tall, fine looking man with a fair moustache." In his memoirs, Frank Harris offered this description: "He was a big, well-made fellow of perhaps thirty, some six feet in height and decidedly manly looking, the last person in the world to be suspected of any abnormal propensities."[79] However, Euston was not exactly a model of rectitude and respectability. His marriage to chorus girl Kate Cook had ended after seven years. During the divorce proceedings in 1884, it emerged that Kate was married to someone else when she had wed Euston. The noble lord escaped prosecution for bigamy only because Kate's husband himself already had a wife when he married her. Clearly Euston moved in fast company. However, immediately on learning of the article in the *North London Press,* he consulted the solicitor George Lewis (who had advised O'Brien in the Dublin Castle case) and decided to initiate a libel action, in which he was represented by Sir Charles Russell, Queen's Counsel and Liberal MP, a once and future attorney general who would end his legal career as Lord Chief Justice. Parke's attorney was Frank Lockwood, also a QC and Liberal MP, who would become solicitor general in 1894 and would prosecute Oscar Wilde in his second criminal trial. After Euston's formal denial, Lockwood presented the evidence in support of the editor's plea of justification—that the charges were true and that it was in the public interest to reveal them. A number of witnesses were called to say they had seen Euston arriving or leaving the brothel on various dates. However, the main witness for the defense was John Saul. In rebuttal, Lord Euston took the stand to deny the allegations of sexual impropriety, though he admitted he had once visited 19 Cleveland Street. The press and public were attracted not only by the contest between two of England's leading barristers but also by the highly charged courtroom encounter between Lord Euston and the man who appeared to accuse him of indecent acts.

John Saul's statement to the police spelled out particulars of his contact with Euston: "He is not an actual sodomite. He likes to play with you and then 'spend' on your belly." The newspapers did not print anything so explicit as this. Despite their uniform reticence in reporting the details he offered, the press played up the drama of the self-confessed "professional sodomite" who

Sodom on the Thames

was accusing Lord Euston to his face. We get a vivid sense of Saul's personality from the newspaper reports. Although doubly contained—by the formal constraints of acting as a witness in a criminal trial and by the press's dramatization of the scene—Saul emerges as an irrepressible figure. He displays a high theatricality, making the most of his day in court; a gentle and generous responsiveness to the police and the defendant; a touch of irony; an occasional flair of anger and self-pity; and, sometimes, a note of sadness. The reporter for the *Star* was impressed: "Dramatic indeed was the situation when this young man, asked whether he recognized anyone in court as having been to Hammond's house, pointed to Lord Euston, and in his effeminate voice, said distinctly 'Yes, that one. I took him there myself.' It seemed minutes before another question was asked. So intense was the thrill which this declaration excited." And that was certainly no accident. The description of Saul's coup de théâtre betrays the ambivalence of the observer; not even "his effeminate voice" could undermine the powerful effect of his dramatic pointing and distinct articulation. The response to Saul here is reminiscent of the reception of Amos Westrop Gibbings's testimony in the Boulton and Park case; however, whereas Gibbings's performance was buttressed by his privileged status, Saul lived on the fringes of London's underworld. His description of life in the house was almost genteel: "During the time I was there I remember many persons visiting the house, and many I brought myself." This note is struck again, evoking a laugh from the onlookers, who have to be chastened by the judge, when Saul describes bringing Euston to Cleveland Street: "Letting him in with my latchkey, I was not long in there, in the back parlor or reception room, before Hammond came and knocked, and asked if we wanted any champagne or drinks of any sort, which he was in the habit of doing."[80] Readers of the *Star* were deprived of the climax, making do with reactions to the inappropriate laughter:

> Mr. Lockwood addressing his lordship expressed the hope that his task would not be made more difficult by such expressions of feeling. The whole thing was too horrible.
>
> The Judge said such levity was brutal and disgusting, and he trusted it would not occur again.
>
> *After saying what we cannot report,* witness said Lord Euston gave him a sovereign leaving it on the chest of drawers. (my italics)

Saul was Lockwood's witness. He could not permit laughter in the courtroom to undermine Saul's credibility. But there are multiple displacements at work here. The expressions are overdetermined: "The whole thing was only too horrible." What was "brutal and disgusting"? Laughter in the courtroom? The acts Saul described? Or was it his effrontery in testifying at all?

I have skipped over an important moment in Saul's direct testimony. Its importance was underlined by both the judge and the press. Note again the displacement from act to word: "The brutal callousness with which this witness told his story both shocked and revolted the court." The paper did not quote the judge, who must have said something, but presented the response as a matter of fact, implicitly endorsing it. What was so "brutal," "shocking," and "revolting?" "I picked him up," he said, "just as I might have picked any other gentleman up." And how was that? Earlier, Saul had testified:

> "Where did you meet this person?—In Piccadilly, between Albany-courtyard and Sackville-street, near the Yorkshire Grey. He laughed at me, and I winked at him. He turned sharply into Sackville-street.
> The Judge: Who did?—The Duke, as we used to call him.
> Mr. Lockwood: Go on and tell what happened?—The Duke, as we called him, came after me, and asked where I was going. I said, "Home," and he said, "What sort is your place?" "Very comfortable," I replied. He said, "Is it very quiet there?" I said, "Yes, it was," and then we had a hansom cab there. We got out at Middlesex Hospital, and I took the gentleman to Cleveland-street.[81]

The "brutal callousness" of this tale certainly earns it a place in any history of the art of cruising. It is also the only glimpse we get of Euston as anything more than a tall icon of the aristocracy with a fair mustache. The initial encounter is irresistible: "He laughed at me, and I winked at him."

Of course, Lord Euston had a different tale to tell. Taking the stand after the defense had presented its case for justification, he denied he had ever seen Saul or heard of the other witnesses against him. Here is his story:

> I recollect being in Piccadilly last May or June and having handed to me a card bearing the words—"C. Hammond, 19 Cleveland Street, *Poses Plastiques*." I put the card in my pocket and read it when I got home. About a week afterwards I drove up in a hansom to this place. . . . I went alone and got there about eleven. I rang the bell and the door was opened by a man of medium height, clean shaven except for a dark moustache, and with hair that is getting thin on the top. . . . He took me into the first room on the right of the passage. He asked me for a sovereign, which I gave him, and then I asked when the *poses plastiques* were going to take place. He said, "There's nothing of that sort here," and then stated the real character of the

Sodom on the Thames

house. I asked him what he meant by saying such a thing as that to me, and told him that if he did not let me out I should knock him down. He opened the door and let me out, and I went away. At that time I did not mention it to anyone; but later on I mentioned it to some friends of mine.[82]

Poses plastiques were a kind of female strip show with artistic pretensions. Although generally sympathetic to Euston, Labouchere in *Truth* could not resist commenting on "the astounding folly of going—a man of middle-age, and experienced in the ways of the world—to see an exhibition that was advertised by cards and suspiciously at midnight by an unknown man in Piccadilly."[83] The editors of the radical *Reynolds's Newspaper* were more skeptical: "He told a somewhat cock-and-bull story about receiving a card as he was walking in Piccadilly, indicating where a display of naked females was on view. It seems odd that a person like Hammond should allow tickets, indicating where a criminal exhibition was on view, to be indiscriminately distributed in public thoroughfares, where, amongst others, the passengers might comprise plain-clothes detectives."[84]

Mr. Justice Hawkins expressed no doubts at all about Lord Euston's account. Nor did he disguise his hostility to John Saul. The *Standard* of January 17, 1890, reported the following from the judge's summary of the evidence for the jury:

As to the witness Saul, a more melancholy spectacle he could not imagine. Was Saul's story true? Lord Euston said it was as foul a perjury as a man could commit. Of course directly they could have only the oath of Lord Euston against the oath of that man. It was necessary to speak out, and they would have to ask themselves which oath they preferred—the oath of the man who, according to his own account, if he spoke the truth, was liable to be prosecuted, or the oath of the Prosecutor [Lord Euston]. So far he marveled that no one suggested that the man should be prosecuted.

Hawkins argued against crediting Saul's claim that he had come forward to the police prior to the libel action. The judge implied both that Saul had lied about the interview having occurred at all and that the police had failed to corroborate his story. One cannot be surprised that a judge should side with the heir to a dukedom rather than a "professional sodomite." But his vehemence in dealing with Saul reveals unusual hostility and contempt: he repeatedly referred to him as "that creature." Consider the asymmetry in his discussion of the witnesses' credibility: Saul should not be believed because, if he were telling the truth, he would have admitted to breaking the law;

whereas Lord Euston should be credited because his denials establish his innocence. But Saul had testified against his own interest, whereas Euston's evidence had been self-serving. If he had admitted the allegations against him, he would have been subject not only to penal servitude but also to social disgrace. He had a lot to lose. The law usually regards this as a powerful motive to lie. Of course, Euston's oath was that of a noble lord.

The jury believed him. They found Ernest Parke "guilty of libel without justification." Hawkins sentenced the journalist to a year's imprisonment, claiming that "a more atrocious libel than that of which you have been guilty has never been published by any man."[85] The judge also urged the public prosecutor to take action against Saul for perjuring himself to perpetuate the libel against Euston. *Truth* took up the cry, arguing that leniency would be yet another example of unequal treatment. Its editorial compared Saul's situation to that of a poor woman who was sentenced to twenty-two years in prison for stealing provisions worth ten shillings: "To say that a poor woman was justly punished in this cruel fashion for the pettiest of larceny, and that a wretch like Saul is to be allowed to swear away the honour and good name of a person with impunity . . . is an insult to law and justice."[86] A week later, when it became clear that Saul would not be prosecuted, Labouchere wrote: "A more scandalous decision never was taken. A jury has declared that the 'creature' committed one of the most horrible perjuries on record—a perjury for which the longest sentence permitted by law could not be sufficient. An eminent judge has endorsed this opinion of the jury. And the Public Prosecutor takes no action!"[87] Labby's concern for equal justice was reduced to seeking the imprisonment of a "Mary-ann" who had dared accuse a noble lord. Generally the press welcomed the verdict and celebrated the imprisonment of their fellow journalist. Dissenting voices were few. Not surprisingly, *Reynolds's* commented on the ease with which both judge and jury had bought Euston's "cock-and-bull story" and dismissed Parke's defense:

> The evidence of the witnesses who testified to having seen him several times was ridiculed by [Euston's attorney] as being that of persons of a very low grade of life. Surely he did not expect that the Archbishop of Canterbury would appear in the box and testify to having met the Earl coming to or from that den of infamy.
>
> Saul is unquestionably a filthy, loathsome, detestable beast, but he has evidently played no inconsiderable part in the abominable orgies of Cleveland Street. Judge Hawkins seems to us to have committed a grave error . . . when he evidently intended the jury to believe that Lord Euston's state-

ment of how he got there and what transpired when there, although utterly and entirely unsubstantiated, was a plain unvarnished truthful statement.[88]

The editorial concluded: "As the judge and jury have exculpated and whitewashed the future Duke, it is to be hoped his ardour for witnessing exhibitions of nude females will be somewhat cooled by recent circumstances." Labouchere allowed himself to express some skepticism about Euston's story: "Morality aside, a man of any common sense, would as soon have gone alone to a thieves' kitchen on the invitation of an anonymous tout of the thieves."[89] The press's response to the intersection of class privilege and allegations of sexual irregularity displays the complexity of Victorian attitudes. These accounts displace their animus against deviant sexuality onto the bearers of the bad news, a tendency already evident in the press and judicial attitudes toward Saul. While Saul had been a self-admitted "professional sodomite" who seemed to delight in discomfiting his audience, Parke was a crusading journalist. Frank Harris, who had raised a dissenting voice in his *Fortnightly Review*, later wrote: "Ernest Parke was a convinced Radical and a man of high character, yet he was sentenced to a year's imprisonment for reproducing, so he told me, a police inspector's statement, and one which in any case did Lord Euston no harm at all. Yet no one in London expostulated or thought of criticizing the judge, though it seemed to me a harsh and vindictive sentence only possible in England." For Harris, there was no doubt that the verdict and sentence were designed to protect the aristocracy: "If Lord Euston had been Mr. Euston of Clerkenwell, his libeller would have been given a small fine."[90]

It is not surprising that conservative papers welcomed the verdict and sentence as a vindication of a sound social order more threatened by muckraking journalists than by highly placed malefactors, but they were not alone. The *Daily Telegraph* declared: "The condemnation of Parke to imprisonment for twelve calendar months prevents for that time, and perhaps for all future time, a foul-mouthed slanderer from inflicting any further injury on society and poisoning the very air we breathe."[91] The *Saturday Review* condemned Parke in terms that apply to all those engaged in purveying the news for profit: "Mr. Parke's profession . . . is to minister to a foul taste with fouler lies; and he deserves as much mercy as a polecat. Nay, he deserves much less; for, after all, the polecat did not choose his peculiarities, does not stink or murder for notoriety or lucre, and, above all, does not pretend that its practices are 'for the public benefit.'"[92]

The "West End scandals" were not publicized solely by the radical press and popular broadsheets but were featured in most newspapers of the day once the story broke. The Tory *St. Stephen's Review* was one of the few that expressed sympathy for the editor, claiming that he "did no more than thousands of gossips about town were doing every day. Each one of these gossips is as worthy of punishment as Mr. Parke. He had the misfortune to put his on paper, so he gets a year's imprisonment; the others go free and continue their observations."[93] The rhetoric condemning Parke contains a strong undercurrent of violence. Thus, in the *People* we find: "Lord Euston has earned the gratitude of society for enabling the law to stamp upon a miscreant who, if he had his deserts, would be whipped at the cart's tail from one end of London to another."[94] Such public outrage had been expressed in the past through licensed attacks on sexual offenders displayed in the pillory. The violent approval of the editor's imprisonment crosses class and party lines. The *Labour Elector*, published by the dockers' union, whose strike Parke had supported the year before, treated the nobleman as a victim of injustice with a right to defend his injured honor:

> If Lord Euston had gone to the office and there and then twisted the little wretch's neck nobody would have blamed him. We are not, as a rule, in favour of Lynch Law, but there are undoubtedly cases in which it is permissible, and this was one. Penal servitude for life or for a lengthened period of years might have met the justice of the case; but twelve months' imprisonment, without hard labour, is little better than mockery.[95]

This passage resonates with unconscious and ironic echoes of other comments on the affair. The Lord Chancellor himself had mentioned the inadequacy of the sentences imposed for "gross indecency" as a justification for dropping the case, given the harm that might come from publicizing the offenses. Strikingly, the paper implicitly endorses Euston's self-reported threat to knock Hammond down if he did not permit the lord to leave the premises immediately. The outrage generated by reports of the male brothel was now directed against those who had accused pillars of Victorian society of patronizing the place. Had popular hatred of sexual deviance so colored class indignation that it contributed to a whitewash of the powerful and privileged? Many in all walks of life preferred to believe that radical journalists had fabricated the charges to gain political advantage or sell papers rather than think that the sons of dukes had paid for sex with young men. One interested party, Lady Blanche Waterford, sister of Lord Arthur Somerset, wrote privately: "So *thankful* poor Lord Euston has won his trial, and only *wish* it were poor Arthur. However, it is a mercy that somebody is made happy."[96]

Sodom on the Thames

Saul described himself in court as a "professional sodomite." His social status and personal identity were quite different from those of the telegraph delivery boys or their clients. He was the only witness sexually involved in the affair to appear in court, testify against a noble lord, and be scrutinized by jury, judge, press, and public. Like the messengers, Saul admitted to working as a male prostitute, but his contacts with men amounted to more than an opportunistic aberration from a life of working-class normalcy. Indeed, Saul seems to have fallen outside the structure of class relations in Victorian England. He exemplifies an urban underclass tied to crime, vice, and especially sex. Indeed Saul actually inhabited the underworld only glimpsed in the publicity surrounding the prosecution of Boulton and Park. He had come to London from Dublin, but we hear little of home or family, just one reference to sending money to his mother. (It is tempting to believe that attitudes toward Saul were affected by his Irish origins, but the only hint I have found is one reference to his speaking with a "foreign" accent. Most papers described his speech as "effeminate.") Apparently he had some contact with the circle around Dublin Castle. One paper reported: "In 1884 he offered to give evidence with regard to the Dublin scandal, but the story was too old. It was not true that he was told that his evidence would not be received on oath because of his disreputable character."[97]

In London, he moved around a West End neighborhood where male and female prostitutes, pornography, sex paraphernalia, and casual cruising among men are still on offer today. In his statement to the police, Saul recited a proliferation of addresses, most between Soho and Leicester Squares, not far from the alley where Symonds had met the young grenadier. Saul and Hammond "earned our livelihood as sodomites." They had lived together in a succession of households that also included a number of female prostitutes, one of whom Hammond married, and at least one "spooney boy," who also procured for him. This world resembles that depicted in *The Sins of the Cities of the Plain,* though it is unlikely that its inhabitants performed so prodigiously. Saul's prostitution located him in an underclass, but he advertised closer connections with the aristocracy than those available to the respectable middle classes. In court, he bragged of his intimacy with nobility: "We always called him the Duke." One name mentioned by Saul in his interview does not surface elsewhere in the police reports, court proceedings, or popular press—that of George Cavendish Bentinck, "who frequently visited the home and had to do with boys." One scholar describes Bentinck as an "ultra-Tory" member of Parliament who had been a "hard-line opponent" of the Criminal Law Amendment Act of 1885.[98]

Saul's contact with the upper crust had not improved his material circumstances; he lived always on the edge of poverty and destitution. Rather plaintively Saul admitted: "I am still a professional 'Mary-ann.' I have lost my character and cannot get on otherwise. I occasionally do odd jobs for different gay people." The Criminal Law Amendment Act had targeted female prostitutes—"gay women"—and "gross indecency between men"—the defining activities of those who were to become "gay men." Saul's history provides a site where the two converge. He named a number of fellow "Mary-anns," including a cross-dresser called "lively Poll." Others plied a rougher trade. Saul described an acquaintance who offered sex to set up robberies: "Clifton takes gentlemen home to his room where by arrangement two or three men are secreted under his bed, and just as they are performing, the men suddenly come out and bounce money out of them by threats."[99] Not just formal prohibition, but social circumstance, gender nonconformity, and predatory practices placed "professional sodomites" outside the law—heightening the distance between them and their clients. When the Labouchere Amendment was passed, one commentator called it "the Blackmailer's Charter."

John Saul became an object of fascination and repulsion in the reports of Parke's libel trial. He refused simply to play the role assigned to him. He remembered Euston's return to Cleveland Street because it had coincided with his own grievance against Hammond: "I complained . . . of his allowing boys in good position in the Post Office to be in the house while I had to go and walk the streets for what is in my face and that is my shame." The *Star* remarked: "Saying which the witness turned away from the court, with a somewhat theatrical gesture." Saul's resentment of the telegraph boys underlines the difference between men who occasionally prostituted themselves to supplement their income (like soldiers and uniformed messengers) and the "professional sodomite" who occupied a more precarious social and economic position.[100] The theatrical anger may mask an underlying sadness. I have not been able to determine John Saul's age. Each of the telegraph boys recited his—it ranged from fifteen to nineteen—in the police reports. Saul did not, nor is it mentioned elsewhere. His connection with Hammond began in 1879, and he admitted to having been arrested in Dublin in 1875. I am afraid that John Saul was no longer young, at least for a "Mary-ann." He supported himself by walking the streets for "what is in my face," cleaning the quarters of female prostitutes, and occasionally working at a theater.[101] (See the "Piccadilly Vulture" in figure 13.)

These few sad notes should be set beside the virulent attacks directed at Saul by both the court and the press after Parke's conviction for libel. Some-

Sodom on the Thames

thing very like homophobia was at work when anger occasioned by accusations of aristocratic license was so easily redirected at the whistle-blowers, especially at the outrageous but powerless and poor John Saul. His performance on the witness stand mobilized deep-seated fears and unleashed violent hostility. Who's afraid of John Saul? And why? He may have represented something new on the social scene: a figure of abjection who refuses his status, a flamboyant queer. The responses to Saul reveal how much he discomfited his respectable audience. Remember that by the time of their trial, Fanny and Stella were got up as respectable scions of the middle class. Unlike them, Saul got to speak for himself. Faced with the majesty of law and society, he refused to be ashamed:

> And were you hunted out by the police?—No, they have never interfered. They have always been kind to me.
>
> Do you mean they have deliberately shut their eyes to your infamous practices?—They have had to shut their eyes to more than me.

He defended himself with campy defiance, undaunted by judge, lawyers, jury, press, and public. Does John Saul represent the emergence of the modern homosexual who accepts himself as defined by his sexual activities but refuses the shame attached to same-sex desire? Does he embody a queer sensibility existing outside the norms of middle-class respectability? Or does his offensiveness result from his flaunting of sexuality as such? Because Saul was a "professional sodomite," his personal identity and sexual activities were closely linked. Although his effeminacy did not extend to cross-dressing, he had more in common with the "gay ladies," full-time female prostitutes, than with his clients or with part-time male prostitutes such as the telegraph boys. The complexity of late Victorian responses to prostitution suggests that the proclamation of any form of sexualized identity may have provoked an intense reaction. Even the scandal-peddling press tiptoed around the details of Saul's testimony; the representation of sexual activities remained deliberately vague. Saul's main offense may have been to insist on the subject at all.[102]

3. DID "MY LORD GOMORRAH" SMILE?

My Lord Gomorrah sat in his chair
Sipping his costly wine;
He was safe in France, that's called the fair;
In a city some call "Boo-line"
He poked the blaze and he warmed his toes,
And, as the sparks from the logs arose,

He laid one finger beside his nose—
And my Lord Gomorrah smiled.

He thought of the wretched, vulgar tools
Of his faederastian joys [*sic*],
How they lay in prison, poor scapegoat fools!
Raw, cash-corrupted boys!
While he and his "pals" the "office" got
From a "friend at Court," and were off like a shot,
Out of reach of Law, Justice, and "that—rot—"
And my Lord Gomorrah smiled.

He thought of the editor clapped in a cell,
And the Bow Street Bail refused,
While he and his "chappies" got off quite well,
Though a "leg-bail" was all that they used.
And my Lord Gomorrah has cause to thank
His stars for the privilege of rank;
His luxurious couch he preferred to a plank—
So my Lord Gomorrah smiled.

He smiled to think of the law's delay
When the criminals were great;
He smiled to think of its swifter way
When it fixed a humbler fate.
And as he remembered the trashy "jaw"
About "all men alike in the eyes of the law"
And many a similar canting old saw—
My Lord Gomorrah smiled.

Englishmen, men of cash, class, and clan,
Who can say of yourselves, at least,
Your vices bear the stamp of the man,
And not the mark of the beast,
Will you suffer that justice stint its stroke,
Or speak out strong as you oft have spoke?
Or do you, mes amis, relish the joke?—
My Lord Gomorrah smiles.[103]

The West End scandals provide a wealth of material for any inquiry into
the social expressions of male homoeroticism and the politics surrounding

the legal enforcement of sexual morality. Public discussion constructed the participants primarily in terms of their age, social status, and economic condition; their sexual desires and activities were interpreted and judged in relation to more complex identities and forms of life. The "sodomite" was embodied quite differently in the representation—and experience—of John Saul and in that of Lords Euston and Arthur Somerset, the subject known as "Lord Gomorrah" in the lines cited above. The figure of the "homosexual" or "invert," defined by his sexual desires for member of his own sex, does not appear in the press accounts or in the court proceedings. Neither medical nor psychiatric expertise was deemed relevant. (This fact contrasts with the Boulton and Park case, where contested medical evidence, however different from the psychiatric, played a central role.) Of course, the only actual trial in the Cleveland Street was Euston's libel case against Ernest Parke.

The only contemporary efforts to interpret the affair in terms of pathology appear in private correspondence that did not see the light of day until 1976. In a letter to Prime Minister Lord Salisbury that also confirms suspicions of a cover-up, Sir Dighton Probyn, a high official in the Prince of Wales's household, expresses his concern about the impact of prosecution on Somerset's family and adds: "For the man, in his defense, I can only trust that he is mad." Similarly, after hearing details of the case against his equerry, the Prince of Wales writes the prime minister about "the 'unfortunate Lunatic' (I can call him nothing else)."[104] However, these judgments are not very specific and avoid the language of psychiatry. In public, moral fervor against sodomy combined with civic republican discourse to condemn aristocratic corruption and challenge the government's complicity with social privilege.

As in the campaigns around female prostitution, an ethic of middle-class respectability was used to condemn both upper-class decadence and lower-class brutishness. The West End scandals mobilized this assertive public morality: aristocratic clients ready to pay for favors were portrayed as preying on the sons of working-class families eager to improve their lot. Much was made of the youths' employment as uniformed messengers in the postal service; the implication was that their corrupters posed a threat to the nation itself. The press distinguished the situations and character of the male prostitutes and their clients. At the same time, among the prostitutes, the telegraph delivery boys were represented quite differently from John Saul, who himself expressed resentment toward them. The young men already had full-time jobs and social roles, which marked their sexual activities as mercenary and their prostitution as temporary. Saul identified himself as a "Mary-ann" "walking the streets" in search of other men willing to pay for sex; he inhabited fully a stigmatized social role and a sexualized personal identity. In less obvious ways, the two noble lords named in the press complicated the image of the sodomite as upper-class sexual predator. Whereas the absent Somerset was matched with the telegraph boys and systematically represented as their corrupter, Lord Euston had been confronted by an unrepentant but marginalized Saul. Not surprisingly, Euston emerged the victor in the legal proceedings and in the court of public opinion, while Somerset lived out his life in exile and died in disgrace. Although the poem in the *North London Press* explicitly targeted Somerset's escape to France, it was Euston who "got over" while "my Lord Gomorrah" had little cause to smile.

Somerset was linked to Euston in the radical press and in the gossip generated by the West End scandals. He was not happy to have the affair prolonged by the libel trial, writing to Regy Brett: "I am sorry that Euston has been obliged to go to law. It will keep up the gossip such a time and may even do worse."[105] Parke's lawyer was eager to keep the connection between noble lords in the jury's mind. One paper reported the following exchange between Lockwood and Euston:

> Is Lord Arthur Somerset a friend of yours? — I know him. When did you see him last? — Last summer some time. During the season, in society. I kept meeting him constantly.
> Have you seen him since? — No.
> Do you know where he is? — I do not know where he is.[106]

Somerset wrote Regy again: "I hope they will not drag me into it more than necessary. I thought Lockwood dragged my name in very unnecessarily the other day. It will worry my poor old mother so."[107] Evidently he suffered rather more as a result of the Cleveland Street affair than Euston, whose vindication at the libel trial permitted him to get on with the business of his life, whatever that may have been. Euston remains an opaque figure. We may speculate about his activities at Cleveland Street, but we cannot determine finally the meaning of his behavior, much less his desires or self-understanding. Lord Arthur left rather more in the way of correspondence with friends and family, which, though governed by concerns of prudence and propriety, provides a glimpse of his own experience of the affair. Even without this valuable material, the evidence in the case provides a profile of his behavior somewhat different from that of Euston.

If we take Saul's word for it, Euston visited the brothel at least twice. He had sex with Saul only once, and cautioned the "Mary-ann" not to approach him on the street. Saul testified that he had frequently seen Euston around

Piccadilly and Leicester Square. The second time he was at the brothel, he went off with a different man. Neither that man, Charles Hewitt, nor Newlove testified at the libel trial, but both told the police they had seen Euston at 19 Cleveland Street. If we accept all this, we can conclude only that Euston occasionally engaged in sexual contact with other men: "He was not an actual sodomite, he liked to play with you and 'spend' on your belly." In contrast, if we accept Euston's account of his one admitted visit, he had gone there in search of illicit but heterosexual pleasures and demonstrated indignation at having his desires misunderstood. As some of the newspapers commented, even this conduct fell outside the publicly accepted norms for respectable gentlemen. Although his social status protected him from ostracism and he had no political ambitions, Euston certainly failed to meet the standards of the increasingly powerful moral purity lobby. If not "actually a sodomite," Lord Euston played the role of the "libertine," displaying the casualness in sexual matters associated with a licentious aristocracy.

The evidence against Lord Arthur Somerset paints a different picture, that of a character altogether more complex in his desires and sense of self. Not only was the evidence strong enough to lead to his indictment, but it led Somerset to conclude that he could not face down the charges; hence he fled to France. During the pendency of the court proceedings, Regy Brett acted as a liaison between the Somerset family and Arthur Newton, the solicitor retained to look after their interests. Regy also received a number of letters from young men in government and the professions seeking advice about how to conduct themselves in relation to the investigation of 19 Cleveland Street. Many of these expressed considerable anxiety about their positions and asked Brett to destroy their letters after responding. Regy did not keep copies of his replies, nor does he refer directly to the West End scandals in his journals, except for the cryptic inscription already quoted. However, not only did he keep the letters he received, he also had them bound in a leather volume he called "The Case of Lord Arthur Somerset."

In an early letter, the Duke of Beaufort reveals something important about the familial and social context. The duke reports his efforts not to upset his wife, who suspected that something was very wrong. Since Arthur first had gone to stay with his brother Henry in Monaco, their mother feared that Henry might have been sick. After being reassured on that score, she focused her anxiety on Arthur. The duke later wrote: "I had to tell her more than I wished because first she said, 'Of course he will face any accusation,' and then she said, '*No entanglement with a woman would oblige him to go abroad and give up his Regiment.*'" Beaufort then spun a "cock-and-bull story" of his own: "I told her we thought he had been decoyed to a House by some woman and the people of the House threatened him, and having no rebutting evidence to bring *against any accusations they chose to make* would not face the horrors of a trial" (emphasis added).[108] Although the press did not mention it, sex scandal was not new to the Somerset family. The duke himself had quite a reputation as a womanizer.[109] The duchess may not have needed quite so much protection from unpleasant realities as her husband thought. One anecdote reveals her aplomb in circumstances that would daunt a lesser soul. In the course of a luncheon party, the butler announced that a new painting had arrived. The entire party trooped to view the acquisition, which proved to be the portrait of a beautiful young woman known to be the duke's mistress. After wondering aloud where it might best be hung, the duchess is said to have decided, "His Grace might like it in his own room perhaps. You had better hang it there."[110] In 1877, their second son, Henry, known as "Penna," ignored the advice of his family and sued his wife, Isabella, for custody of their son after she left him after five years of marriage. Lord Henry Somerset lost his suit. Under the law at that time, husbands were presumed to be the legal custodians of their children. Isabella, something of a puritan and opposed to divorce, claimed she had left the conjugal household because of her disapproval of Lord Henry's unorthodox and homoerotic sexual tastes. The Duchess of Beaufort wrote her daughter-in-law at the time, "We have nothing whatever to say in defense of Penna and unless he is mad cannot understand his behavior."[111] The custody contest did no one any good. The disgraced Penna went into exile, first in Monaco, later in Florence; shunned socially for breaking the code of marital silence, Isabella devoted the remainder of her life to good works.

As the duke's concocted story reveals, Lord Arthur's family and friends suspected that the evidence against him was strong. Others who seemed to have some connection with Cleveland Street recognized that Somerset was the one most directly jeopardized by the investigation: "We cannot blind ourselves to the fact that he is primarily in this mess and that principally through his own act. We are only hangers-on and there is only a distant probability involving an immense stirring up of mud of our being injured."[112] The waters were considerably muddied by the rumors about Prince Albert Victor. Whether there was any truth to them at all, it is clear that Charles Hammond, proprietor of the house, was "stirring up" mud, prepared to make allegations against the heir presumptive. Many of Lord Arthur's friends believed that his refusal to face the charges against him had been partially motivated by a desire to protect the royal family. Somerset felt compelled to write them that he knew nothing whatever about Prince Eddy's activities and that he had not told

Sodom on the Thames

members of his family that he was acting to protect him. Apparently, some in court circles saw his failure to offer a public rebuttal of the stories as a betrayal of his duties to the Prince of Wales. Although speculation about Prince Eddy's involvement fascinated and continues to fascinate royal watchers and conspiracy theorists, Lord Arthur had strong motives of his own to take flight. He faced overwhelming evidence that he had committed acts of "gross indecency" with a number of young men whom the police had interviewed and who were available to testify against him. The stories they told are richer and more interesting than the case against Euston.

Lord Arthur Somerset was named by Newlove immediately after his arrest and was subsequently identified by two of the telegraph delivery boys as a frequent client at 19 Cleveland Street. The case against him grew with the discovery of Algernon Edward Allies, whose letters had been found on Veck after his arrest. Allies was the son of a coachman in service in Suffolk. He had been employed as a houseboy at the exclusive Marlborough Club, founded by the Prince of Wales, where Somerset was a member. When Allies was convicted of stealing at the club, Lord Arthur appeared on his behalf and secured his release on "good behavior." He promised the boy he would help him find work and arranged temporary accommodation for Allies—at 19 Cleveland Street. The youth had already returned to his parents' home when Newlove was arrested. However, he remained in touch with both Veck and Somerset. When the police tracked him down, Allies admitted that the generous "Mr. Brown" with whom he had a long-term association was actually Lord Arthur. Tipped off ahead of time, Allies had destroyed Somerset's letters the day before P. C. Hanks arrived to question him. Still the police were able to retrieve from the post office three money orders of one pound each, issued from Knightsbridge and cashed by Allies. (The money orders would be important corroboration of Allies's story if the case went to trial.) As the Cleveland Street affair continued to develop, Allies was brought by the police to live in London at government expense. The solicitor Newton got into legal troubles of his own as a result of his efforts to persuade Allies to resettle outside Great Britain with financial assistance from the Duke of Beaufort. The young man would become a principal witness against the solicitor. The radical press treated this prosecution as an attempt to find a scapegoat for their own mishandling of the case. The summary of Allies's testimony in the *North London Press* reveals more about his connection with Lord Arthur: "He is a good-looking, curly-haired youth of twenty, who at one time was employed at the Marlborough Club. He was convicted of dishonesty, but was saved from imprisonment by the intérposition of a friend . . . Lord Arthur Somerset. The intimate relations thus established between the page boy and the peer subsequently became of a character that cannot be particularized."[113] Although his conduct during the investigation raised questions about his motives, there can be little doubt that Allies had been involved in a relationship with Somerset that went beyond the casual encounters reported by the telegraph boys.

In his correspondence with Brett, Lord Arthur allowed himself some irony regarding Allies: "I trust [Chief Detective Inspector] Abberline is seeing that A. is comfortable for the rest of his life, and the other youths. I am quite surprised that they have not applied to me for pensions." In fact, Allies did try some months later. In a letter to the Duke of Beaufort written July 6, 1890, he asked for Somerset's address and for help from the duke himself: "I am solely destitute and should be glad if anything could be done to help me." The tone of the letter, though importunate, is not simply that of a failed blackmailer:

> You must understand that when the effort was made to get me to go away I knew it was too late. I had given evidence which I knew I was compelled to give and his Lordship knows it was his mistake. . . . I am sorry for his Lordship. Also you. But now I am Destitute. I ask you kindly to do something for me. And if this does not meet with approval, I shall not ask anything more because I shall think you blame me for what has been done. But I am sure his Lordship would help me a little.[114]

Allies may have been right about Lord Arthur. His letters to Brett reveal a sentimental side to his attachments. Even in his most self-pitying moments, he expressed concern for the servant who had accompanied him into exile: "I can not bear to think of parting with him, but he would be miserable living abroad with one always without a soul to speak to. . . . If his wife were alive I would take a lodging somewhere, and they should do for me, but she died 3 years ago. He would be so lonely by himself out in these parts." The most gentle and disinterested manifestation of his care for younger men from the working classes appears in relation to a youth who worked in the regimental stables. On October 21, 1889, Somerset wrote Brett:

> Then by the bye there is a boy in my stable in Barracks named Barrett. He comes from Little Bad Minton and his parents are wretchedly poor and I took him because he was so starved. I wish you or [illegible] would take him and keep him as a helper or get him a place. He is very willing but not very smart to look at. The farmer I took him from was very much annoyed at my taking him because he was so useful to send out the carts etc.

On November 29, Lady Blanche informed Brett: "The small boy, Barrett, has got a place, which I have told Podge—and he will be glad."

Sodom on the Thames

14. *"Podge," Lord Arthur Somerset,* Vanity Fair, *1887*

Somerset's letters from exile chronicle his considerable suffering. He was very reluctant to leave: "I am afraid things look as black as it is possible for them to do . . . so much so that Newton is very anxious that I should go abroad again for a good long while. But of course I might as well cut my throat at once."[115] Although coming from a family of wealth and status, as a younger son he had only limited means. Work was an issue from the beginning. His difficulties were complicated by social ostracism: "I have wandered about all day for two days trying to think what employment I am fit for and am still undecided. You see, if I got a promise of any employment, I should require a reference. To whom am I to refer?"[116] Somerset traveled to Constantinople in the hope of being hired to help the sultan with his horses. Failing there, he went to Budapest, Vienna, and eventually back to France. It gradually became clear that no one associated with his regiment or with the household of the Prince of Wales would intervene on his behalf. As one whose life was shaped by the institutions and associations of aristocratic birth, Lord Arthur Somerset had become a man without a place. Publicity about the scandal followed him to Continental Europe, where he adopted pseudonyms and avoided others from home for fear of being shunned or worse. He wrote of his efforts to hide the day's *Figaro* from an American guest at a hotel where he had stayed because it contained "miles of Labouchere, Euston, and Somerset—all about a '*tendresse étrange pour les jeunes télégraphistes*' which I was supposed to have." In Vienna, he felt harassed by the police and believed they were having him followed by street boys to provoke an incident.

The recurrent tone of his letters is an abiding loneliness with little prospect of relief: "Constantinople was very interesting, but I rather wanted a friend to go with me to see all the things. Can not I find any luckless devil like myself who wanted a friend to talk to?" Although his brother Henry was in Monaco and Lady Blanche traveled to visit him, he felt cut off from his family: "My poor father and mother, it is too awful for them and I suppose I shall never see them again nor shall I see any of my many friends." To the later consternation of Labouchere and the radical press, Somerset had in fact returned once after his initial flight in August 1889. In early October, he attended the funeral of his grandmother, the dowager duchess of Beaufort, at the family estate of Badminton. The police went so far as to send an officer to look for him there, but higher authorities refused to authorize his arrest. By late October, Somerset had returned to Europe, having resigned his commission in the regiment and his position in the Prince of Wales's household. On November 12, 1890, a warrant was finally issued for his arrest. Lord Arthur Somerset remained in exile until his death in 1926 at Hyères on the French Riviera, where he was

Sodom on the Thames

buried. During the West End scandals, his treatment by highly placed officials and courtiers was taken as primary evidence of their complicity in protecting aristocratic malefactors from the full measure of legal punishment. However, it is hard to maintain that Lord Arthur got away with anything. His life was ruined as a result of his desires to have sex and establish friendships with young men from the lower classes. No doubt it would have been even worse had imprisonment been added to his disgrace. Still, did "my Lord Gomorrah" smile? As Shaw's Eliza Doolittle might say, "Not bloody likely!"

4. ON THE TOWN

Neither Euston nor Somerset left anything like a candid account of their experiences at 19 Cleveland Street. In his care to preserve correspondence about Lord Arthur's legal troubles, Regy Brett chose not to keep any such reports, if in fact he had them. To get a fuller sense of what clients might have found in such venues, we must return to John Addington Symonds's *Memoirs*. It has been read as a tale of unnecessary suffering and as a salutary progress toward sexual liberation, interrupted by an untimely death.[117] Symonds lived to overcome the anxiety and self-laceration crystallized in the two early encounters on the London streets discussed in my prologue. As he grew older, he became progressively more open with his friends, more adventurous in seeking sexual satisfaction, and more fully engaged in efforts at law reform. However, self-division and moral conflict ran as deep within him as his desires for other men. In one episode, Symonds more fully explicates the policing of his own desires as he reflects on his own experience in a setting similar to the house on Cleveland Street. Returning from Switzerland to London to lecture in 1877, he accompanies a friend to a male brothel near the Regent's Park barracks. Once again the object of his desire is in uniform: "Moved by something stronger than curiosity, I made an assignation with a brawny young soldier for an afternoon to be passed in a private room at the same house."[118] Their meeting becomes another turning point in Symonds's erotic journey:

> We came together at the time appointed; the strapping young soldier with his frank eyes and pleasant smile, and I, the victim of sophisticated passions. For the first time in my experience I shared a bed with one so different from myself, so ardently desired by me. . . . For him . . . it involved nothing unusual, nothing shameful; and his simple attitude . . . taught me something I had never before conceived about illicit sexual relations.

What lesson does he draw from the encounter? "Instead of yielding to any brutal impulse, I thoroughly enjoyed the close vicinity of that splendid naked piece of manhood; then I made him clothe himself, sat and smoked and talked with him, and felt, at the end of the whole transaction that some at least of the deepest moral problems might be solved by fraternity."[119] The two meet again several times during the London visit, but "without a thought of vice," as Symonds insisted. He concludes: "The physical appetite of one man for another may be made the foundation of a solid friendship, when the man drawn by the friendship exhibits a proper respect for the man who draws."[120] Ambivalence and asymmetry mark Symonds's account of his breakthrough. He emphasizes not only the social difference between himself and the soldier but also an asymmetry in their interests: he is moved by passion, the other by economic need and sociability. For Symonds, sexual expression remains in tension with fraternity. Respect for his partner restricts the range of permissible sexual practices. Although he does not specify the practice, anal intercourse would seem to be precluded regardless of the roles taken; it is somehow "brutal" and "vicious." Further, he adopts a notion of erotic complementarity that reflects conventional oppositions between masculine and feminine, active and passive, lover and beloved. These divisions apply to feelings as well as sex roles. Reciprocity of same-sex desire is a threat to masculinity. Symonds seems never to have found an acceptable model of mutual male love.

Symonds's ambivalence extends to the venues where he found the cross-class intercourse he celebrated. The male brothel provides an environment free from conventional barriers to social interaction and the expression of manly desire. Symonds draws an astonishing comparison: "I also seemed to perceive that, within . . . that lawless godless place, permanent human relations—affections, reciprocal toleration, decencies of conduct, asking and yielding, concession and abstention—find their natural sphere: perhaps more so than in the sexual relations consecrated by middle-class matrimony." He found no violation of "natural sentiments" here but only a collision with the constraints of law and convention. His mood swings violently within a single paragraph: "Was this a delusion?" He acknowledges that he left the place with a sense of "disgust" but insists he felt the same way when he visited brothels that housed women. However, he had failed to find there the satisfaction offered by that "strapping young soldier with his frank eyes and pleasant smile." Symonds insists: "From him I learned that natural male beings in the world were capable of responding to my appreciation of them. A dangerous lesson, perhaps."[121]

What about Symonds's marriage? Like Brett and Cory, he had established a family and remained married until his death in 1893. Still it is hard to miss personal implications in the claim that the male brothel is a more fertile setting for natural feeling than middle-class marriage. The complexity of his relationship with Catherine North cannot be explored here in detail, but the couple seem to have enjoyed a significant friendship for much of their lives. His letters to her appear frank and soul-searching. Among the texts assembled for his memoirs he includes several of hers to him as well as passages from her diaries.[122] Her account of their courtship reveals she was deeply and romantically in love with "Johnny," who was three years her junior. Symonds's candid description of the early nights of their marriage stands as a stinging rebuke to sex education as it existed among the Victorian middle classes. Soon after the incident in the London brothel and after the birth of four daughters, the couple ceased to have sexual relations entirely. It is possible that Catherine shared her husband's difficulties integrating love and lust:

> I separated from my wife with her approval; for the sexual side of marriage had never been for her more than a trouble. She disliked childbirth, and had, I think, no constitutional difficulties to overcome. In truth our married life had long been ill-arranged upon the ordinary basis of cohabitation. We had taken precautions against pregnancy; and our intercourse in this respect was by the need I felt for sexual outlet.[123]

Symonds acknowledges that the denial of this "outlet" caused him considerable anguish, but he insists that the decision strengthened their marriage ties: "It placed me upon a sound and true relation to my wife—that of pure and faithful friendship." The tension between comradeship and sexual intercourse applied to Symonds's relations with both sexes. He was capable of friendship with women and sometimes turned to female prostitutes for sexual satisfaction. Despite intensive efforts early in his life, Symonds never felt the passion for women that even casual encounters with men excited in him. Shortly after his decision to stop having sex with his wife, he reports how powerfully his desires were stirred by the sight of a tipsy "Tyrolese pedlar" urinating by the road: "Desire . . . shot through me with a sudden stab. . . . If only I could follow him, and catch him there, and pass this afternoon with him upon the sweet new hay."[124]

Symonds continued to insist that sexual expression of his desires for other men should be integrated into fuller personal and social relationships. His failing health had led him and his family to move to Switzerland, where he devoted considerable energy to the development of erotic relations with European men. Like Regy's friend Chat, he traveled regularly to Italy, where he found the men especially attractive. These adventures "abroad" recall those of earlier aristocratic figures such as Beckford and Byron, who traveled to the

Mediterranean to satisfy desires forbidden at home. Symonds was conscious of the risks of exploitation in these relations and worked to establish ongoing friendships, often colored by financial patronage. He helped the family of a Swiss friend through business difficulties and later developed a long-term friendship with one Angelo Fusato and his family. These relations, though they flourished, were never free from anxiety. Explicitly contrasting the Swiss Christian Boul and the soldier in the London brothel, Symonds wrote: "I have never enjoyed a more sense-soothing and more elevated pleasure than I had with him—sex being nowhere. . . . A spy might have looked through cracks in the doors upon us; and the spy would have seen nothing reprehensible."[125]

Despite his insistence on forming long-term friendships and taking on social obligations toward his lovers, he remained keenly aware of the role that fantasy played in shaping these connections. He describes a glimpse of Christian: "When he rode towards me, standing erect upon an empty wood-sledge and driving four stout horses at a brisk trot down a snow slope, I seemed to see an ancient Greek of the Homeric age, perfect in *sophrosyne* and unassuming power."[126] Of his first meeting with Angelo Fusato, he writes: "This love at first sight . . . was an affair not merely of desire and instinct but also of imagination."[127] Symonds imaginatively transforms his sense of himself as well: "In these waking dreams I was at one time a woman whom he loved, at another a companion in his trade—always somebody and something utterly different from myself."[128] As Symonds charts his erotic odyssey, his moralizing drive to domesticate desire coexists with the persistent elaboration of fantasies, both romantic and transgressive.[129]

5. PORNOTOPIA

The Sins of the Cities of the Plain; or, Confessions of a Mary-ann, from which I have drawn a sexually explicit counterpoint to the histories in this book, was privately printed in London in 1881. According to a French bookseller named Charles Hirsch, he sold Oscar Wilde "certain licentious works of a special genre which he euphemistically called 'socratic'. Most of these were in French, but at least one, he recalled was in English. This was *The Sins of the Cities of the Plain*."[130] The novel opens with the narrator's account of his encounter with "John Saul" of Lisle Street, the eponymous "Mary-ann," whom he met in Leicester Square. The succeeding chapters purport to be based on Saul's account of his life. As we have seen, a man named John Saul became a central figure in the West End scandals. On the witness stand, defending Ernest Parke against Lord Euston's libel action, he described himself as a "professional sodomite." The resemblance between the historical individual portrayed in

Sodom on the Thames

15. *"The Mower," Hamo Thornycroft (1882–1894)*

press accounts and police reports and the character in the pornographic novel written almost a decade earlier is undeniable. However, *The Sins of the Cities of the Plain* is probably not the story of anyone's "real life." In mapping a Victorian sexual underworld, it shows how hard it may be to separate vivid projections of personal fantasy from documentary representations of social reality. At the same time, its publication demonstrates the existence of an audience willing to pay well to share the fantasies it retails.

Sins does not conform to canons of literary unity. Although it starts out traditionally enough, with the narrator providing a frame that introduces the recollections of the male prostitute who is its central figure, that structure breaks down as Saul interpolates the stories of others he has met along the way. At the end of the book, "essays" are tacked on without connection to the picaresque narrative: "The Same Old Story: Arses Preferred to Cunts," "A Short Essay on Sodomy etc.," and, perhaps surprisingly, "Tribadism."[131] The introduction resonates with the urban encounter that so disrupted Symonds's equilibrium in 1865. It allows us to imagine what might have happened had a less timid Symonds acted on the impulses from which he fled and which remain sublimated in his visit to the brothel near the Regents Park barracks years later. The narrator's pickup of the "Mary-ann" also provides a mirror image to the historical Saul's account of his meeting with Lord Euston in Piccadilly. More generally, the scene is a plausible rendering of male cruising in a London setting where similar encounters may still be observed today. Let me quote this passage at length, repeating some phrases cited earlier:

> The writer of these notes was walking through Leicester Square one sunny afternoon last November, when his attention was particularly taken by an effeminate, but very good-looking young fellow, who was walking in front of him, looking in shop-windows from time to time, and now and then looking around as if to attract my attention.
>
> Dressed in tight-fitting clothes, which set off his Adonis-like figure to the best advantage, especially about what snobs call the fork of his trousers, where evidently he was favoured by nature by a very extraordinary development of the male appendage; he had small and elegant feet, set off by pretty patent leather boots, a fresh looking beardless face, with almost feminine features, auburn hair, and sparkling blue eyes, which spoke as plainly as possible to my senses, and told me that the handsome youth must indeed be one of the "Mary-Ann's" of London, who I had heard were often to be seen sauntering in the neighborhood of Regent Street, or Haymarket, on fine afternoons or evenings.[132]

The erotics are unambiguously homosexual and phallic. The "Mary-ann" is descended from the "molly" of earlier decades, but the full feminine drag that marked her appearance—like that of Fanny and Stella—has been reduced to the more discreet "pretty patent leather boots" that show off "small and elegant feet." (The "Piccadilly Vulture" depicted in figure 13, above, displays remnants of cross-dressing absent from both the novel and the historical record.) Otherwise the Mary-ann's effeminacy is linked to his youth. Saul might be the androgynous ephebe so admired in Hellenizing pederasty, but with one important exception. The bulge in the fork of his trousers commands attention. Saul combines features of femininity and hypermasculinity. This combination may express a Victorian tendency to see flagrant sexuality as itself a feminine characteristic. (Debates about prostitution often divided women between asexual "angels in the house" in need of protection and "fallen" women who carried the contagion of sexual excess and venereal disease.) A later comment by Freud on Greek love suggests another way of taking this configuration: "The sexual object is not someone of the same sex, but someone who combines the character of both sexes; there is, as it were, a compromise between an impulse that seeks for a man and one that seeks for a women, while it remains a paramount condition that the object's body (i.e., genitals) shall be masculine."[133] The account in Sins displays further ambiguity on this score. The very prominence of the bulge, first announced as a natural endowment, leads the narrator to wonder if it is real: "That lump in his trousers had quite a fascinating effect upon me. Was it natural or made up by some artificial means?"[134]

The perspective shifts unsteadily between Saul's attributes and their effect on the cruising gaze. The ambiguous bulge works primarily to mobilize the narrator's interest: "All this ran through my mind, and determined me to make his acquaintance, in order to unravel the real and naked truth."[135] He follows his quarry into a store that displays photographs of scantily clad females. (Remember the "picture shops" mentioned by The Yokel's Preceptor.) Here the narrator makes his move: "I asked him if he would take a glass of wine. He appeared to comprehend that there was business in my proposal, but seemed very diffident about drinking in any public place."[136] Saul knew the game: "Why do you seem so afraid to say what you want?"[137] Like Symonds's grenadier, he prefers a direct approach. Soon they are off in a cab to the narrator's chambers. (The historical Saul testified that Lord Euston took him in a cab to 19 Cleveland Street after picking him up in Piccadilly.) Their meeting is free from the constraints of social class and economic status; it occurs in a largely male world, where each is free to gaze openly on the other and act on agreements negotiated between them. The narrator conflates his sexual interest with the pursuit of truth, which shifts from getting a look and feel of that endowment to discovering what makes the Mary-ann tick. Eventually he will pay Saul to write the story of his life. This move resonates with Foucault's contention that "modern sexuality" is believed to hold the key to the "inner truth" of an individual life. We might also read the passage as a parody of Symonds's insistence that he meet subsequently with the soldier from the brothel for fraternal conversation rather than sex. Such sublimation is quite alien to the pornographic vision of *Sins*. In the privacy of his rooms, the narrator (named "Mr. Cambon" according to the "little plate" on his door) can witness the truth of the matter firsthand:

> "You seem a fine figure, and so evidently well hung that I had quite a fancy to satisfy my curiosity about it. Is it real or made up for show?" I asked.
>
> "As real as my face, sir, and a great deal prettier. Did you ever see a finer tosser in your life?" he replied, opening his trousers and exposing a tremendous prick, which was already in a half-standing state. "It's my only fortune, sir; but it really provides for all I want, and often introduces me to the best of society, ladies as well as gentlemen. There isn't a girl about Leicester Square but what would like to have me for her man, but I did find it more to my interest not to waste my strength on women; the pederastic game pays so well, and is quite as enjoyable. I wouldn't have a woman unless I was well paid for it."[138]

As a sexual "professional," Saul is available to both men and women, constrained only by spermatic and monetary economy. The fictional Mary-ann clearly takes pleasure in his work. Further, it introduces him into "the best of society." He appears proud of his contacts with "gentlemen and ladies." In response to Cambon's interest, Saul agrees to write the story of his life over several weeks at "a fiver a week" for "thirty or forty pages . . . tolerably well written."[139] The two conclude with an evening of sexual gymnastics described in detail; these include masturbation and fellatio, Saul's beating Cambon with a birch, and the narrator's anal penetration of the Mary-ann. Although Cambon assumes the dominant position suggested by his greater age and social superiority, the flagellation is more ambiguous. The other practices are mutual, with Cambon taking considerable interest in Saul's phallic satisfaction. The feminization of the Mary-ann in the original encounter is undercut by the reciprocity and versatility of their sexual engagement.

The Mary-ann's titillating narrative moves from the country and suburbs to the city, presenting its hero in ever more complex and transgressive situations. Recall Cambon's story about the origin of Saul's "confessions": "At each visit we had a delicious turn at bottom-fucking, but as the recital of the same kind of thing over and over again is likely to pall upon my readers, I shall omit a repetition of our numerous orgies of lust, all very similar to the foregoing, and content myself by a simple recital of his adventures."[140] The novel's distinctively urban settings include a private membership club where wealthy patrons and cross-dressed male prostitutes with feminine names celebrate sex with multiple partners; the drag ball where Boulton and Lord Arthur Clinton play starring roles and the belles and their admirers eventually share in their own "orgies of lust"; and streets and squares where "rough lads" and soldiers sell sexual services for money and occasionally rob or blackmail their clients. Just as the transvestite prostitutes and Mary-anns mimic and confound expectations of feminine behavior and desire, so do the soldiers in relation to masculinity. Fred Jones, whom Saul meets as a fellow prostitute at "Mr. Inslip's" establishment in the novel, emphasizes the links between prostitution and the military that were also displayed in Symonds's *Memoirs:*

> "We all do it. . . . It's the commonest thing possible in the Army. As soon as or (before) I had learned to goose-step, I had learned to be goosed, and enjoy it, my dear, don't you, Jack?" he said, slapping his thigh and passing his hand over my most interesting member. "Now, I'll tell you all about it. We'll keep ourselves fresh for tonight, but another day I mean to both fuck you and have you fuck me."[141]

As his proposition to Jack reveals, Jones's sexual interests in other men are not simply mercenary. Symonds reached similar conclusions about the soldiers he enjoyed. Writing to Carpenter in 1893, he reported: "I made the acquaintance last autumn in Venice with a Corporal of the 2d Life Guards who was traveling with a man I knew. He gave me a great deal of information. But it all pointed to the mercantile aspect of the matter. However, he said that some men 'listed on purpose to indulge their propensities. An Italian Colonel told me . . . that young men of the best families, after serving as volunteers or in the natural course of conscription, would sometimes remain on in the ranks with a view to the opportunities afforded by barracks."[142] The role-switching in anal intercourse that Jones proposes to Saul does not sit easily with standard images of "butch" guardsmen penetrating their clients or permitting themselves to be fellated. We can only speculate about what actually went on between them. Jones proves as adept at the erotics of narrative as Saul himself, continuing his seduction of our hero with the tale of his own initiation into sex with men by his colonel. The former guardsman claims his experience reflects standard practice:

> When a young fellow joins, someone of us breaks him in and teaches him the trick; but there is very little need of that, for it seems to come naturally to almost every young man, so few have escaped the demoralization of schools or crowded homes. . . . Although we all do it for money, we also do so because we really like it, and if gentlemen gave us no money, I think we should do it all the same. Many of us are married but that makes no difference. . . . All the best gentlemen in London like running after soldiers, and I have letters from some of the very highest in the land.[143]

The personnel in the armed forces are devoted to prodigious sexual activities among themselves and for pay, while schools and slum housing provide excellent preparation for the life. Special venues facilitate the exchange: "There are lots of houses in London where only soldiers are received, and where gentlemen can sleep with them."[144] Fred Jones's self-portrayal is complex: "I have had lots of women, but do not care so much for them, for they do not make half so much of us as gentlemen do, although of course they always pay us. You can easily imagine it is not so agreeable to spend half-an-hour with a housemaid when one has been caressed all night by a gentleman." Partly the difference is in capacity to pay, the men being better off, but the social distance is eroticized as well. Is there also inversion in the suggestion that our macho guardsmen really want to be "caressed all night by a gentlemen"? The text emphatically underlines the gender-bending: after proposing mutual anal intercourse to Saul and regaling him with tales of social climbing, Jones takes on the role of lady's maid and helps him get dolled up for Mr. Inslip's party before donning drag himself. The soldier displays the same versatility as the transvestite; Jones is both.

The Sins of the Cities of the Plain moves through scenes of increasingly exotic and transgressive activity, adding incest, miscegenation, pedophilia, and bestiality to those already enumerated. Many of these scenes include both men and women; there is even one with a cow. Clients of apparent respectability mix with male prostitutes, who may wear full feminine drag or military uniform—or, like Jones, both. Most of these scenes cross boundaries defining gender roles and sexual propriety, age cohorts and social classes. Schoolmasters have sex with their pupils; employers with servants; customers with clerks; brothers with sisters; noble lords with rough lads; respectable bourgeois with drag queens. However fantasmatic the elaboration, the landscape is recognizably late Victorian London. *The Sins of the Cities of the Plain*

Sodom on the Thames

portrays a number of specific locales and social venues familiar from the *Yokel's Preceptor,* Symonds's *Memoirs,* the Boulton and Park case, and the West End scandals. The erotic imaginary it maps cannot be simply assimilated to today's highly visible gay culture.

In 1992, Masquerade Books published a book in its Badboy Series of pornography for gay men called *Sins of the Cities of the Plain.* The author was anonymous. Although an editor is nowhere identified or a source acknowledged, the novel is for the most part an adaptation of the 1881 text. It maintains the original structure and most of its language, adding a few scenes here and there and changing details in some of the original episodes. One revision, consistently made, stands out: all the women are changed into men. Maids become handymen; secretaries, clerks; stepsisters, brothers. Even the milliner who thinks she is having a lesbian encounter with Laura is transformed into a man. The contemporary version of that scene includes some very puzzling details, given the sex change: the prospect of a big belly is omitted entirely. The publishers seem to find the Victorian novel just too queer for today's market in gay pornography. The original is an epic of polymorphous pansexuality and gender fuck.

PART FOUR 🎭 WILDE'S TIME

DRAMATIS PERSONAE

Oscar Wilde, *playwright, poet, aesthete, celebrity*
Lord Alfred Douglas, *aka Bosie, Wilde's lover*
Constance Lloyd, *Wilde's wife*
Robert Ross, *Wilde's devoted friend*
Marquess of Queensberry, *Bosie's father*
Lord Rosebery, *Liberal foreign minister, then prime minister*
Lord Drumlanrig, *Bosie's late brother, secretary to Rosebery*
Alfred Taylor, *Wilde's friend and codefendant, charged with procuring*
Sir Edward Carson, *Queensberry's attorney at the libel trial*
Charles Gill, *prosecutor at Wilde's first trial*
Sir Frank Lockwood, *attorney general, prosecutor at Wilde's second criminal trial*
Alfred Wood, *a would-be blackmailer*
Fred Atkins, *an extortionist, Wilde's companion on a trip to Paris*
Charles and Frank Parker, *an unemployed valet and groom*
Alfonso Conway, *a newsboy, "dressed in public school colours"*
Edward Shelley, *a publisher's assistant and aspiring writer*
Sidney Mavor, *a witness who changes his story*
Walter Grainger, *a waiter too plain to be kissed*
Maurice Schwabe, *Wilde's friend and Lockwood's nephew*

The love that dare not speak its name in this century is such a great affection of an older for a younger man as there was between David and Jonathan, such as Plato made the very basis of his philosophy, and such as you find in the sonnets of Michelangelo and Shakespeare. It is that deep spiritual affection that is as pure as it is perfect. — Oscar Wilde, in the dock (1895)

People thought it dreadful of me to have entertained the evil things of life, and to have found pleasure in their company. But they, from the point of view through which I, as an artist in life approached them, were delightfully suggestive and stimulating. It was like feasting with panthers. The danger was half the excitement. I used to feel as the snake-charmer must feel when he lures the cobra to stir from the painted cloth or reed-basket that holds it, and makes it spread its hood at his bidding, and sway to and fro in the air as a plant sways restfully in a stream. They were to me the brightest of gilded snakes. Their poison was part of their perfection. — Wilde to Lord Alfred Douglas (1897)

Some might say that the West End scandals culminated with the trials of Oscar Wilde in 1895. Nothing in the historical record links Wilde or his friends to the house on Cleveland Street, but a hostile reviewer in 1890 already had sex scandal in mind when he suggested that *The Picture of Dorian Gray* was fit only for "outlawed noblemen and perverted delivery boys."[1] When Wilde was finally driven to take legal action against the Marquess of Queensberry, he confronted charges of sexual misconduct linking him to male prostitutes and petty criminals who inhabited a demimonde similar to that exposed in the earlier scandal. Queensberry's lawyers explicitly invoked Cleveland Street, portraying one of Wilde's friends as a procurer who plied his trade from a sinister apartment in Westminster. Radical newspapers seized on the precedent, demanding that this time the government not let privileged wrongdoers escape justice. Some editorials and letters to the editor reached as far back as the Boulton and Park scandal, in a litany accusing the defender of the new aestheticism of promoting urban decadence. Wilde's novel created quite a stir, with its suggestions of aristocratic libertinism, ill-defined secret immorality, and a background of London vice. By the time of his trials, detectives employed by Queensberry's solicitor had no trouble finding evidence that the writer himself had descended into such an underworld.

However, to see the episodes in this book as previews of the Wilde affair is to read history backward, as if his punishment were the end toward which they had been headed all along, the terrible moral of these tales. The characters introduced here lived their own lives, experienced unorthodox desires, and contended in their own ways with pressures to conform. Their stories suggest some of the possibilities that Wilde faced and the cultural context he had to negotiate. In this part of the book, I revisit the trials of 1895 in light of those episodes. How is Wilde's situation illuminated by the promenades of Fanny and Stella, the marriage of Lord Arthur Clinton, the romantic attachments of William Cory and his friends, the enterprise of the telegraph delivery boys, the legal troubles of Lord Arthur Somerset, or the camp defiance of John Saul? Rereading the Wilde scandal is like looking into a kaleidoscope where elements of these narratives are reconfigured with a few shakes of the hand, the new pattern enlarged by extraordinary publicity. Familiar figures and themes are realigned; the increase in scale generates dramatic, sometimes unnerving effects.

Many individuals and institutions formed the new constellation: the celebrated writer and his fans and detractors; intense friendships and divided families; a press and public eager for fresh meat; innovations in criminal law and procedure; a politics fueled by scandalous accusations and moral controversy;

changing conventions of gender and social class. Wilde's fate was determined by no single act or author, but there can be little doubt as to his own agency or that of his implacable adversary, the Marquess of Queensberry. Wilde's "feasting with panthers" involved him with young men from the urban underclass whom bourgeois society would regard with fear or contempt. However, unlike Dorian Gray, who pursued vaguely defined vices in the dark enclaves of London's East End, Wilde performed his snake-charming act out in the open at West End restaurants, clubs, and hotels. The writer and his circle advertised themselves in extravagant dress with lilies or green carnations in their buttonholes.

Wilde promoted an aesthetic approach to life hostile to middle-class respectability. The theatricality of his public performances surrounded by admiring young men recalls the promenades of Fanny and Stella. These links were reinforced by evidence that some of his friends may have dressed "in women's attire" or cavorted with those who did. Whereas the cross-dressers successfully defended themselves as actors who played women's parts, the playwright's associations with the theater were exploited to increase suspicion of his moral nonconformity. However, when challenged to defend "the love that dare not speak its name" at his trial for "gross indecency between men," Wilde invoked a more traditional model of male friendship. He was defending the connection with Lord Alfred Douglas to which his father, the "scarlet Marquess," had responded with such vehemence. One of the most distinguished products of the Oxford "Greats" curriculum, Wilde invoked the tradition of pedagogical eros, emphasizing its spiritual purity. However, as Cory and Browning had already discovered, one could get into trouble for pursuing the Greek ideal too intensely. Wilde combined high culture with the low life in a mix that proved explosive when mercilessly exposed at the Old Bailey and in the press.

The facts of the case are well known and amply documented and commented on. Wilde's trials progressed through three phases: the action for criminal libel he initiated against the Marquess of Queensberry; his prosecution for sexual offenses as codefendant with Alfred Taylor, which ended in a hung jury; and a second trial of him alone leading to his conviction for "gross indecency" and imprisonment for two years at hard labor. Two aspects of Wilde's case distinguish it from the earlier scandals involving love between men: his memorable writing and his extraordinary celebrity. The effective efforts, first of Queensberry's defense, then of the public prosecutors, to link these factors marked the trials as events of political and cultural importance. They associated Wilde's aestheticism with the social phenomenon of effeminacy and with the private indulgence of prohibited desires. Carson blurred the boundaries between literature and life, using Wilde's writing to cast him as a corrupt poseur from whom Douglas's father worked to save the young nobleman. The lawyer painted the lower-class youths connected with Wilde as at once utterly unsuitable companions and as innocents seduced by the older man. Most of the press eagerly followed Carson's lead, portraying the writer as a symbol of cultural decadence, sexual exploitation, and dangerous deviance. The scandal shaped attitudes toward homosexuality for generations to come.[2] Images of the male homosexual, whether dangerous or persecuted, coalesced around Wilde's personality and fate. However, the contemporary debate about the affair's broader social significance aired diverse and conflicting interpretations.

1. "FEASTING WITH PANTHERS"

Wilde was a star, perhaps the first modern celebrity. He was a poet, playwright, novelist, and editor. From the beginning of his literary career, Wilde promoted himself not only as a poet and playwright but as the spokesman for a new approach to art and to life: "I think I may say without vanity—though I do not wish to appear to run vanity down—that of all men in England I am the one who requires least advertisement."[3] Wilde's father had been a distinguished physician and folklorist; his mother, a poet and campaigner for the Irish nationalist cause. After two years at Trinity College, Dublin, Wilde won a fellowship to Magdalen College, Oxford, where he excelled academically while making a name for himself as a witty and extravagant defender of the new aestheticism. When he arrived in London, he was already recognized as an up-and-coming literary figure and something of a character. Lecturing widely in England and in the United States, Wilde was both celebrated and reviled as the embodiment of a doctrine of "art for art's sake" opposed to late Victorian moralism. Young Wilde was caricatured as the poet Bunthorne in Gilbert and Sullivan's operetta *Patience* (1881); later, he became the model for Cyprian Brome in André Raffalovich's *A Willing Exile* (1890) and for Mr. Amarinth in Robert Hichens's *The Green Carnation* (1894).

As he became increasingly successful, Wilde married Constance Lloyd and established a household at 16 Tite Street, where he and his wife often entertained friends and raised their two sons. Still, by 1890 rumors about his personal life had begun to circulate. Even Symonds, to whom Wilde sent a copy, had reservations about *The Picture of Dorian Gray:* "It is an odd and very audacious production, unwholesome in tone, but artistically and psychologically interesting. If the British public will stand this, they can stand anything.

However, I resent the unhealthy, scented, mystic, congested touch which a man of this sort has on moral problems."[4] Wilde had been introduced to sex between men as late in his life as 1886 by Robert Ross, then seventeen and preparing to enter Kings College, Cambridge, where his tutor would be Oscar Browning. Ross precociously affirmed his love for other men, getting into trouble with both family and fellow students. He left the university prematurely after being thrown into the college fountain by a group of hostile undergraduates. "Robbie" would remain a lifelong friend and would devote himself to restoring Wilde's estate and reputation until his own death in 1918. After discovering the pleasures of male love, Wilde reveled in the company of young men. He spent more of his time away from home, entertaining at various venues in the West End. The writer attracted a following among aspiring litterateurs, while at the same time courting men of a rougher sort. The publication of *Dorian Gray* much enhanced his reputation among aesthetically inclined undergraduates. One of these was Lord Alfred Douglas, known as "Bosie," a student at Wilde's alma mater, Magdalen College, Oxford. The youngest son of the Marquess of Queensberry, Bosie eagerly sought an introduction to the writer. After their meeting in June 1891, nothing would ever be the same for either man.[5]

By the spring of 1895, Wilde's ascent appeared unstoppable. He had found his métier in drawing room comedies sparkling with witty conversation. *An Ideal Husband* was playing to full houses in the West End, with *The Importance of Being Earnest* about to open. The events leading to Wilde's disgrace, imprisonment, and early death were set in motion when Queensberry left a card at the Albemarle Club on February 18, 1895. It was inscribed: "For Oscar Wilde, posing [as a] somdomite [*sic*]."[6] This gesture was the last in a deliberate, sustained campaign of harassment. The marquess would defend his conduct as an effort to separate Lord Alfred from a corrupting influence, since Lord Alfred was unwilling to do so himself. Queensberry was no paragon of Victorian family values. Divorced by his first wife in 1887, he married a much younger woman in 1893 only to have that marriage annulled. The marquess had a succession of mistresses and was estranged from his five children. An enthusiastic sportsman, Queensberry gave his name to the rules for amateur boxing. He was also no stranger to scandal. He had created quite a fuss when his son was appointed to the House of Lords where he could no longer sit himself. His eldest son had been parliamentary private secretary to Lord Rosebery, then Liberal foreign minister. As a Scottish peer, Queensberry could sit in the British House of Lords only if elected by his fellow peers, who declined to reelect him in 1880 because of his professed atheism.[7] After the

Sodom on the Thames

government appointed his son Lord Drumlanrig to the House of Lords, the resentful marquess pursued Rosebery to Hamburg armed with a dog whip. Only the intervention of the Prince of Wales kept the peace.[8]

Queensberry then turned his attention to his youngest son, threatening to disinherit Lord Alfred if he did not break off his connection with Wilde. When Bosie's mother supported the pair, Queensberry wrote to her father, Alfred Montgomery, that Wilde was "a damned cur and coward of the Rosebery type," denouncing his ex-wife for complicity in "the Rosebery-Gladstone-Royal insult that came to me through my other son."[9] When Drumlanrig died in October 1894 from a gunshot wound that may have been self-inflicted, there were rumors that blackmailers had threatened to expose his affair with Rosebery.[10] Queensberry certainly was suspicious, writing to his former father-in-law of his son's death: "It is a *judgment* on the whole *lot of you*. Montgomerys, The Snob Queers like Roseberry [*sic*] & certainly the Christian hypocrite Gladstone, the whole lot *of you*."[11]

The marquess stepped up his pressure to end the friendship between Wilde and Bosie. Calling on the writer at 16 Tite Street, he stopped just short of accusing them of sodomy: "I don't say you are it, but you look it . . . and you pose as it, which is just as bad."[12] Queensberry's insults and threats led Wilde to show him the door. When *The Importance of Being Earnest* opened on February 14, 1895, the marquess planned to create a scene, as once he had disrupted a performance of Lord Tennyson's *The Promise of May*.[13] This time the police stopped him from entering the theater. Queensberry left behind "a grotesque bouquet of vegetables" for the author.[14] After he received the offensive card left at his club, Wilde decided to take action. Despite an expense that he could ill afford and risks of exposure that he managed to ignore, Wilde decided to prosecute Queensberry for criminal libel.[15] A conviction might have resulted in the marquess's imprisonment. Perhaps the writer recalled the success of Lord Euston in his prosecution of Ernest Parke. However, this time it was the defendant who had the title. Worse yet, Queensberry consulted Wilde's friend, Sir George Lewis, who had advised the defendants in the Dublin Castle case to hire a private investigator.

Despite his reputation as a libertine and an atheist, the marquess would cast himself as a devoted father protecting his son's moral welfare. Whereas in 1871 Ernest Boulton's mother successfully defended her son's friendships against accusations of sexual impropriety, Queensberry would claim to be fighting to save Lord Alfred from the older Wilde. Regy Brett wrote to a friend that it would be hard to find a "dirtier scoundrel" to present himself as a "champion of public morals." In his journal, he described Wilde as "a man of genius behaving like a fool." Later he wrote Rosebery: "What a fool was Oscar Wilde."[16] Wilde later described himself as a casualty in the warfare between Lord Alfred and the marquess:

> Then when his father saw in me a method of annoying his son, and the son saw in me the chance of ruining his father, and I was placed between two people greedy for unsavoury notoriety, reckless of everything but their own horrible hatred of each other, each urging me on, the one by public cards and threats, the other by private, or even half-public scenes, threats in letters, taunts, sneers . . . I admit I lost my head.[17]

In the letter he wrote Douglas from prison, later known as *De Profundis,* Wilde would comment: "Blindly I staggered as an ox into the shambles."[18] He lamented an outcome that had come to seem inevitable:

> At the end, I was of course arrested and your father became the hero of the hour; more indeed than the hero of the hour merely: your family now ranks, strangely enough, with the Immortals, for . . . your father will always live among the kind pure-minded parents of Sunday-school literature, your place is with the Infant Samuel, and in the lowest mire of Malebolge I sit between Gilles de Retz and the Marquis de Sade.[19]

However complex Wilde's motivations (and many scholars have tried to plumb their depths), his decision to prosecute Queensberry led to personal disaster.

The case fully occupied newspapers across the political spectrum, offering a confrontation between two of Victorian Britain's most conspicuous figures. It offered the spectacle of courtroom drama while allowing the press to moralize about life and art, family and friendship, aristocracy and celebrity. The libel trial was fueled from the start by charges of harassment and persecution and countercharges of criminal sexuality. The first count of the indictment charged that leaving the card at the Albemarle Club amounted to publishing a "false scandalous malicious and defamatory libel." Queensberry had implicitly claimed that Wilde "had committed and was in the habit of committing the abominable crime of buggery with mankind to [his] great damage scandal and disgrace."[20]

Much of the argument at trial revolved around the significance of the word "posing": the marquess's attorney alleged that Wilde's literary work was evidence of such a pose. At Queensberry's first appearance in criminal court, his attorney stated that his client had "thought it well for the morality of his son to put an end to the relations between the parties." The marquess testified: "I

Sodom on the Thames

wrote that card simply with the intention of bringing matters to a head having been unable to meet Mr. Wilde otherwise, and to save my son, and I abide by what I wrote."[21] These statements adumbrate the plea of "justification" by which the defense undertook to prove that the accusation was true and that the public benefited from its publication. Queensberry's private investigators covered the West End in search of men willing to reveal their relations with the writer. The formal plea, filed on March 30, 1895, went far beyond the marquess's initial provocation. In nineteen paragraphs, it presented a devastating indictment of Wilde that the legal language could not obscure. A plea of justification turns the tables on the "prosecutor" in a libel case, who must defend himself against the evidence introduced by the "defendant." Queensberry's plea enumerated specific incidents, times, and places where Wilde was said to "solicit," "incite," and even commit sodomitical or "indecent" acts with ten named individuals and "other boys" who had not been identified. The locations ranged from London to Paris to Brighton, including the Savoy Hotel, the Albemarle Hotel, the lodgings of one of the men, Wilde's home at 16 Tite Street, and his rooms at 10 St. James Place, as well as vacation rentals in Goring and Worthing. The episodes were alleged to have occurred on specific dates between February 1892 and September 1894. Given how publicly Wilde had entertained these young men, they had not been hard to find. Would they appear to testify against him in court? The two parties to acts of sodomy or "gross indecency" were equally guilty in the eyes of the law. Would the witnesses risk being prosecuted for sexual offenses? Or had Queensberry's lawyers made a deal with the public prosecutor to protect them?

The concluding paragraphs of the plea of justification focused on literary matters. They charged Wilde with publishing "a certain immoral and obscene work in the form of a narrative entitled *The Picture of Dorian Gray* . . . designed and intended . . . and understood by the readers thereof to describe the relations intimacies and passions of certain persons of sodomitical and unnatural habits tastes and practices." More controversially, Queensberry claimed that Wilde "joined in procuring the publication" of *The Chameleon,* which included "divers obscene matters and things relating to the practices and passions of persons of unnatural habits and tastes" and as "its first and principal contributor" published "certain immoral maxims" entitled "Phrases and Philosophies for the Use of the Young." Wilde would eloquently defend *Dorian Gray* against his adversary's characterization and deny responsibility for anything other than his own piece in *The Chameleon.* However, Queensberry's lawyers linked the literary to the criminal allegations against the writer.

The plea alleged that

> before and at the time of the said alleged libel the said Oscar Fingal O'ffla-
> hertie Wills Wilde was a man of letters and a dramatist of prominence and
> notoriety and a person who exercised considerable influence over young
> men that . . . Wilde claimed to be a fit person and proper person to give
> advice and instruction to the young and had published the said maxims
> . . . in the magazine . . . for circulation amongst the students of the Uni-
> versity of Oxford and that the said works entitled *The Chameleon* and *The
> Picture of Dorian Gray* were calculated to subvert morality and to encourage
> unnatural vice and that [Wilde] had corrupted and debauched the morals of
> the said Charles Parker, Alfonso Harold Conway, Walter Grainger, Sydney
> Mavor, Frederick Atkins, Ernest Scarfe and Edward Shelley . . . and [Wilde]
> had committed the aforementioned and the said sodomitical practices for a
> longtime with impunity and without detection.[22]

The public interest required that Wilde's "true character and habits" be exposed
to deter him from further offenses and from "further corrupting and debauch-
ing the liege subjects of our said Lady the Queen." Forewarned by the marquess's
vigilance, they might "avoid the corrupting influence" of the writer. Wilde's
works are said to "subvert morality." His status as a public figure transforms a
series of sordid sexual allegations into a trial for "corrupting the youth"—the
ancient, and lethal, charge for which the Athenians condemned Socrates.

2. "CORRUPTING THE YOUTH"

When the trial opened, the prime attraction proved to be the confrontation
between Wilde and Carson. The writer recounted the history of his friendship
with Bosie and Queensberry's campaign of harassment against them. Importantly, he portrayed himself as a friend of the family—of Lord Alfred's mother
and brothers. He recounted his stays at Lady Queensberry's houses and Bosie's
visits to the Wilde household.[23] The writer testified that his first meetings with
the marquess had been friendly as well: he had tried to reconcile the quarrel-
ing father and son. Wilde reflected Bosie's picture of Queensberry as the odd
man out in his own family. In fact, Lord Percy Douglas would be one of the
writer's sureties when he was finally released on bail during his criminal trials.
As these drew to a close, Queensberry and his oldest son were arrested for disturbing the peace on Piccadilly when they refused to stop fighting.[24]

Perhaps to deflect the element of surprise, Wilde's lawyer had placed in evidence a letter from the writer to Alfred Douglas that had been part of a failed

Sodom on the Thames

blackmail attempt and which had circulated in theatrical circles. The prosecution would introduce another letter from Wilde to Bosie. As a result, the "literary" dimension of the case would include not only Wilde's publications but also his private correspondence. As in the case of Boulton and Park, the case would require a jury to decide the permissible forms of expression between men. Wilde famously defended one letter as a work of art, a prose poem that had been translated into French and published. He had written it in response to some poetry from Bosie. Their shared commitment to writing helped shape the friendship. (Douglas had edited *The Spirit Lamp,* the journal that had published the translation of Wilde's letter.) These facts increased the urgency of issues about the relations between literature and life, ardent prose and indecent conduct.

Carson pressed Wilde vigorously on his conception of art and its relation to morality, relentlessly implying that the writer's aestheticism masked a thoroughgoing immoralism. The lawyer interrogated the writer about *Dorian Gray* and about *The Chameleon,* which did not survive the notoriety it achieved in the trials. The greatest trouble came from "The Priest and the Acolyte," a story that chronicled with apparent sympathy a doomed affair between the title characters. Carson pressed Wilde about the meaning of Lord Alfred's poems "In Praise of Shame" and "Two Loves," which had also appeared in *The Chameleon.* Wilde distanced himself totally from the story, which was "from a literary view highly improper," though he refused to label it "blasphemous" as Carson insisted. However, he described Bosie's work as "exceedingly beautiful poems." Carson implied that they contained "improper suggestions," quoting the last line of "Two Loves": "I am the love that dare not speak its name." Asked about its meaning at his first criminal trial, Wilde would rise to heights of eloquence. Here he simply denied the suggestion of impropriety.[25] Although the conflicting interpretation of private letters resonates with the Boulton and Park trial, Wilde's and Douglas's publications added a more explicitly ideological tone to the literary debate.[26]

Observers could differ as to whether the writer or the lawyer gained the upper hand in their exchanges, but there was little question that the pair were evenly matched. Papers reported with relish the thrust and counterthrust of question, aphorism, and insinuation. Carson's strategy was to blur the borders between the aesthetic and the moral, undermining Wilde's attempts to draw a clear line. He turned the writer's use of paradox against him, taking it as a sign of the ridiculous extremes to which his position led. The lawyer's unrelenting literalism in the face of Wilde's subversive playfulness may have established the courtroom as an irony-free zone for some time to come.

Wilde's carelessness, recklessness even, contributed to his undoing. At the very beginning of his sworn testimony, Wilde had testified that he was thirty-nine years old.[27] Having been Wilde's classmate at Trinity College, Dublin, Carson immediately challenged him. An apparently indifferent Wilde had to admit he was over forty: "I have no intention of posing as a younger man at all."[28] Queensberry's counsel immediately asked the age of Lord Alfred Douglas: Wilde stated clearly that Bosie was twenty-four but had been twenty-one when they first met. Wilde appeared to have misrepresented his age to minimize the gap between the two men. Carson questioned the writer about their friendship and the marquess's efforts to end it. Later the lawyer would press Wilde on the age difference between him and the various men named in the plea of justification. Most of them had been under twenty and of suspect social position. Carson telegraphed his major themes early in his cross-examination, confronting Wilde with a review of *Dorian Gray:*

> The story—which deals with matters only fitted for the Criminal Investi-gation Department or a hearing in camera—is discreditable alike to author and editor. Mr. Wilde has brains, and art, and style; but if he can write for none but outlawed noblemen and perverted telegraph boys, the sooner he takes to tailoring (or some other decent trade) the better for his own rep-utation and the public morals.[29]

Wilde replied in detail to the attack on the morality of his writing. However, the reference to the Cleveland Street scandal introduced questions about male prostitution and the sexual exploitation of working-class youth. These impli-cations, which Carson drew in his cross-examination, would be supported by evidence at Wilde's criminal trials. His young companions were identified as servants or clerks, often out of work; some of them would admit to occasional blackmail as well as prostitution.

Although Wilde consistently denied any sexual improprieties, he passion-ately defended his attraction to youth: "I like the society of young men. I de-light in it."[30] Still he tended to overestimate the men's ages, placing them at between twenty and twenty-two, when some had been in their teens when he met them. The writer used wit to deflect Carson's efforts to pin him down: "I don't keep a census."[31] In response to further pressure: "I have never asked him his age. It is rather vulgar to ask people their ages. (*Laughter.*)"[32] In the background, of course, was another youth outside the writer's social class. When Wilde admitted taking eighteen-year-old Alfonso Conway to Brighton for a stay at the Albion Hotel, Carson asked if he had ever taken "another boy" to that hotel. Wilde replied he had stayed there with Lord Alfred Douglas.[33]

Sodom on the Thames

The lawyer relentlessly exposed and underlined class differences. Conway had either sold newspapers or just hung around at the pier in Worthing; Charles Parker and his brother were an unemployed valet and groom; Edward Shelley was described as an "office boy." Wilde rejected these characterizations, insisting that Parker (like others among his young companions) had aspired to perform in music halls and Shelley (uniquely among them) to pursue a literary career. However, Carson continually referred to them in invidious terms. The writer defended his literary work against prurient and moralizing interpretation by insisting on the distance between those who appreciate art and an uncultivated philistine majority. Now Carson asked again and again what the aesthete might find to discuss with youths who were mostly idle and uneducated. Wilde did not deny that he had sought out these young men, wining and dining them at restaurants and clubs in Soho and the West End, lavishing gifts on them, and occasionally giving them money. Pressed to say what enjoyment he could find with men whose interests were neither literary nor artistic, Wilde affirmed: "The pleasure of being with those who are young, bright, happy, careless, and amusing." When Carson interrupted, he went on "(emphatically): I don't like the sensible, and I don't like the old."[34] The questions ended with this famous exchange:

> Wilde: Well, I will tell you Mr. Carson, I delight in the society of people
> much younger than myself. I like those who may be called idle and
> careless, I recognize no social distinctions at all of any kind and to me
> youth—the mere fact of youth—is so wonderful that I would sooner
> talk to a young man half an hour than even be, well, cross-examined
> in court. (*Laughter.*)
> Carson: Then, do I understand that even a young boy that you would
> pick up on the street would be a pleasing companion to you?
> Wilde: Oh, I would talk to a street Arab if he talked to me, with
> pleasure.
> Carson: And take him to your rooms?
> Wilde: If he interested me.[35]

In protesting so vigorously, the writer may have revealed too much.

Carson was more interested in houses of ill repute than in street pickups. In his opening statement, Queensberry's counsel argued that "Alfred Taylor is the pivot of this case." Throughout his cross-examination, he repeatedly questioned Wilde about the character of their relationship. The writer admitted that he had visited Taylor's rooms at 110 College Street for tea parties with his friends. When Carson claimed that Taylor was "notorious for introducing younger men to older men," his response seemed lame: "No, I never heard that in my life. He has introduced young men to me." Wilde admitted that he had met as many as seven or eight men through Taylor, including five named in Queensberry's plea as his partners in "indecent practices." The writer insisted that Taylor was "a young man of great taste and intelligence, and brought up at a very good English public school." Unlike the men to whom he introduced Wilde, "he was very artistic, extremely intellectual, and clever, and pleasant."[36] Taylor had inherited and quickly run through a large fortune from the family cocoa business. Wilde denied that his friend had been expelled from prestigious Marlborough School, though he had not graduated. His accomplishments included playing the piano for his friends. When Carson sought to exploit Taylor's "artistic" propensities in decorating his rooms, Wilde defended his "good taste," denying that they were luxurious or that dark curtains were always drawn against the light of day. Carson sought to portray the apartment where Wilde met his young companions as exotic, even sinister, "strongly perfumed." For Wilde, it was "charming perfume": "He was in the habit of burning perfume, as I am in my rooms."[37] As he brought the two men into ever closer proximity, Carson established that they had met again just before the trial began. Taylor's unorthodox style associated him with Fanny and Stella: "Did you know whether Mr. Taylor had a lady's costume there? . . . Did you ever see him with a costume on—a lady's fancy dress?"[38] Wilde denied ever having seen or heard of such a thing. At the first criminal trial, Charles Parker would testify that Taylor "had gone through a form of marriage with a youth named Mason, that Taylor had worn a woman's dress, and that they had a wedding breakfast."[39] By Taylor's second trial, the prosecutor had found a letter from Mason asking for money and urging: "Come home soon, dear, and let us go out sometimes together." It was signed "with much love."[40]

Carson used reports of a police raid on a house in Fitzroy Square to invoke both the Boulton and Park trial and the Cleveland Street affair; the links were pursued enthusiastically by the press, which had made so much of the earlier scandals. Wilde did not deny he had known that Taylor and Charles Parker had been among twenty men arrested in August 1894. Carson alleged that these men had been charged with "felonious practices." Apparently some of the men had been fined, but as Wilde's counsel pointed out, that could hardly have been the penalty for the serious offenses that Carson had mentioned. Here is the writer's account of what he had read in *The Daily Chronicle:* "Two men in women's clothes drove up to the house—music hall singers it was stated—and . . . they were arrested outside the house, but whether there was

Sodom on the Thames

anybody in woman's clothes at this house or entertainment, whatever it was, I don't know." Wilde admitted he had been distressed when he learned of his friends' trouble, but concluded, "The magistrate seems to have taken a different view because he dismissed the case."[41] No evidence was introduced to contradict this innocuous account.

Despite Wilde's distance from the house at Fitzroy Square, Carson ran through the published names and occupations of all the arrested men, asking whether the writer had known or "heard of" any of them before. Wilde denied knowing anything about any of them, but the lawyer's questions underlined the issue of social class. The men included waiters, valets, servants, clerks, a tobacconist, a costumier, a fishmonger, a fruiterer, and several men of "no occupation." Carson implied that Wilde was guilty by association: "Did you never hear of Preston in connection with the Cleveland Street scandals?" and "Isn't Marley a notorious sodomite?" When the writer denied having heard of either of them, Carson took another tack: "Now, I ask you: when you saw that Taylor was arrested in the company of these varied people, did it make any difference in your friendship toward Taylor?" The party had been more diverse than those in Taylor's rooms. (Neither Wilde nor Carson mentioned the men's ages: of the twenty men arrested, only three were between seventeen and twenty; three were between twenty and thirty; the rest over thirty, including three men over forty years old.)

The press listed the incriminating evidence: "Beer, spirits, and mineral water . . . dresses, fans, corsets and women's underclothing . . . a hare's foot with orange and powder upon it, powder puff, Vaseline, glycerine, a pair of curling tongs, box of powder, a necklet and pendant." The defense argued that these materials were "used in theatrical making up." On his arrest, Marley claimed he had been asked "to sing a few songs in female attire. He said it was his profession to appear in music halls as a female impersonator."[42] Both the initial accusations and the defense resonate with the story of Fanny and Stella. When Charles Parker testified at Wilde's first criminal trial, he was asked about the house in Fitzroy Square: "Orgies of the most disgraceful kind used to happen there?"[43] Those familiar with central London would know that the square was not far from 19 Cleveland Street.

Wilde's "feasting with panthers" had occurred on his own terrain. It is unlikely that the writer would have appeared at anything like the party that the police had raided. Although he admitted to attending Taylor's tea parties, more often he had entertained his young friends at restaurants and hotels in the West End: the Café Royal, the Florence, Kettner's, Solferino's. Occasionally he would take one of them for special treats to such places as the Crystal

Palace, invite him to the theater or to his house at Tite Street or his rooms at St. James Place. When Carson pressed him as to whether he had visited Parker's room, the writer insisted he had seen him only in public or at his own place: "Well it wouldn't interest me very much to go and see him. It would interest him very much to come and see me." He tried to deflect a question about whether the youth had moved to a house "ten minutes walk away" with another joke: "I never walk. (*Laughter.*)" Carson pursued the point, getting Wilde to assert that he always took cabs and that he would have them wait when he paid a call. The lawyer confronted the writer with very specific allegations about the date and time of a visit to Parker, which Wilde denied. (At his criminal trials, a fellow lodger would testify that she had seen Wilde pay a call at Parker's room while the cab waited outside.)

As Carson interrogated the writer about his encounters with the men listed in the plea of justification, Wilde began to falter. Perhaps flustered by recognition of the dangers ahead, he tried to deflect the questions with one witticism too many. Asked if he had kissed a youth working as a waiter at one of his private dinners, Wilde replied: "Oh, no, never in my life; he was a peculiarly plain boy."[44] The lawyer leaped on the implication; Wilde was unable to explain himself. For the first time, he lost his composure, acknowledging the costs of Carson's cross-examination: "Pardon me, you sting me, insult me, and try to unnerve me in every way. At times one says things flippantly when one should speak more seriously, I admit that, I admit it—I cannot help it. That is what you are doing to me."[45] For audiences in search of dramatic reversals, this has been a moment to savor. It seems a classic case of the hero undone by his own overreaching. However, Wilde's libel case was guaranteed to fail once it became clear that some of the men he had so publicly entertained were prepared to testify against their patron. Queensberry's detectives had found witnesses willing to support his defense.

Carson wove the potential evidence about Wilde's conduct and associations, together with a reading of his letters and publications, into a net with which to snare the writer. It is hard to imagine Wilde would have escaped even if he had not adopted such a provocative "pose" in court. The lawyer's speech made explicit the strategy that had guided his cross-examination, moving deftly back and forth between Wilde's work and his life. Carson portrayed his client as being in the right in his efforts, however extreme, to end the friendship between Wilde and Lord Alfred. Again and again, the lawyer asked the all-male jury: what would you have done if you had been a father in Queensberry's position? Wilde's writings were used to support the charge of "posing," independent of any testimony as to the writer's sexual conduct. Carson

Sodom on the Thames

argued their author must have been "either in sympathy with, or addicted to, immoral and sodomitical habits."[46]

The lawyer capitalized on Wilde's insistence that the interpretation of literary works depended on the literacy and the aesthetic or moral positions of the audience. The writer had to admit that Dorian Gray's sins *might* be read as including sodomy or that Basil Hallward's adoration of Dorian *might* be read as sexual desire. Carson implied that the young and impressionable men who admired Wilde might be especially prone to these readings. The lawyer emphasized the widespread distribution and sale of the novel regardless of the cultural qualifications of its readers. Similarly, he argued that *The Chameleon* was directed at inexperienced undergraduates who would read "Phrases and Philosophies for the Use of the Young" alongside "The Priest and the Acolyte" and Douglas's poems praising "the other love." Wilde's "prose poem" addressed to Bosie encouraged the production of his questionable verse. Thus, Wilde's publications, even if they were ambiguous as their author asserted, should sound the alarm for an attentive parent.

Carson found a single thread running through the fiction, letters, and poetry: "a man using towards a man the language which men sometimes use, and perhaps legitimately use, towards women."[47] Equally damaging, he described another theme common to "The Priest and the Acolyte," *Dorian Gray,* and Wilde's letters: the domination of a younger by an older man. Carson argued that this was the key to the writer's connection with Bosie: "Have you the slightest doubt that the same kind of mind that wrote this *Chameleon* wrote these letters to Lord Alfred Douglas?"[48] The lawyer read the jury an extended passage from the novel about the impact on "this innocent young man" of Dorian's first conversation with the worldly and cynical Lord Henry Wotton: "Life suddenly became fiery coloured to him. It seemed he had been walking in fire. Why had he not known it?" Watching, the older man "was amazed at the sudden impression that his words had produced."[49]

For Carson, *Dorian Gray* prefigured Wilde's influence on Douglas: "It is the story of a man corrupted by another man and who by such corruption is brought to commit, or the book suggests he has committed, this sodomitic vice of which we will hear a good deal more, probably, before this case closes."[50] Bosie's poem "The Two Loves" might stand alone as justification for Queensberry's "frightful anticipation":

There is no difficulty in seeing in it that the whole object and the whole idea of it is to draw the distinction between what the world calls "love" and what the world calls "shame," one being the love that a man bears toward a woman, and the other being the unholy shame that a man ought to have if he ventures to transfer that kind of love and that kind of passion to a man. That is the idea all through Lord Alfred Douglas's poem, and is it not a terrible thing to think that a young man, upon the threshold of his life, having been these several years in the company, aye, under the domination of and adored by Oscar Wilde as would appear from these letters that have been given here—is it not a horrible thing to think that there to the public he makes known the results of his education and the tendencies of his own mind upon this subject, the frightful subject of the passion of man for man?[51]

For Carson, Wilde's letter to Bosie expresses his "vile abominable passion towards this young man": "I want to know, when that letter has been written by Wilde to Lord Queensberry's son and Lord Queensberry protests, are you going to send Lord Queensberry to gaol?"[52] In uttering the marquess's title three times, Carson underlines the improbability of this outcome to the libel trial.

Wilde's own road to "gaol" may have been paved by his literary production, but he traveled it because of his conduct and associations. Early in his speech, Carson targeted Alfred Taylor as "the pivot of the case," "practically the right-hand man of Wilde in all these orgies with artists and valets." Carson uses Taylor's rooms to evoke the brothel on Cleveland Street and to suggest the perils of aestheticism: "You will hear the kind of life this man Taylor lived, the extraordinary den that he kept in Little College Street with its curtains always drawn, the luxurious hangings of his windows, the rooms gorgeously and elaborately furnished with the perpetual changes of varied perfumes and the altogether extraordinary life that he was leading there; the daylight never admitted: always the shaded light of candles or of lamps or gas."[53] This characterization suggests the steamier passages in *Dorian Gray*. Carson identifies contradictions between Wilde's pronouncements on art and on social class:

> When you come to confront him with these curious associates of a man of high art, which no one can understand but himself and the artistic but his case is that he has such a magnanimous, such a noble, such a democratic soul (*laughter*) that he draws no social distinctions, and it is exactly the same pleasure to him to have a sweeping boy from the street—if he is only interesting—to lunch with him, as the best educated artist or the greatest *littérateur* in the whole kingdom.[54]

Carson characterizes the writer's position as "utterly irreconcilable" but offers his own damning resolution of the apparent paradox: "something unnatural, something unexpected" in the writer's relations with these young men.[55] Wilde had met the Parker brothers when Taylor brought them to share his birthday dinner. Carson was unrelenting in his insistence on the "unnaturalness" of this cross-class socializing. Why did Taylor bring as his guests "a groom and a valet . . . if he knew that Wilde was moral and upright and the artistic and literary man that he undoubtedly was"? The lawyer's answer is that Taylor was Wilde's procurer. His ridicule is as much social as sexual: "Wilde addressing the valet as Charlie, and Parker addressing Wilde, the distinguished dramatist—whose name was being mentioned, I suppose, in every circle in London for the distinction he had gained by his plays and by his literature—and, just fancy, the valet at the dinner addressing him as 'Oscar.'"[56]

Carson portrays Wilde's transgression of social boundaries as a pursuit of personal pleasure rather than an expression of altruism or solidarity. The lawyer walks a fine line between treating the writer's companions as symptoms of his degradation and regarding them as victims of his influence: "Let those who are inclined to condemn these men for allowing themselves to be dominated, misled, corrupted by Mr. Oscar Wilde, remember the relative positions of the two parties and remember that they are men who have been more sinned against than sinning."[57] He underlines the asymmetries in these relationships: "They were not one of them really educated parties with whom he would naturally associate; they were none of them his equal in years; and there was . . . a curious similarity in the ages of each and every one of them." Acknowledging the writer's fascination with the young, the lawyer asks: "Has Mr. Wilde been unable to find more suitable companions . . . in youths of his own class?"[58]

Then Carson closes in for the kill. Referring to his "theories of putting an end to social distinctions," he argues that Wilde was not motivated by "a very noble and a very generous instinct." If he had wanted to help his young associates, he could have found work for them or assisted in their education. Instead, Wilde bought them silver cigarette cases and entertained them in a fashion they could never have afforded. Carson insists that when the writer gave money to some of the men, he was paying for incriminating letters or buying silence about his sexual conduct. When Wilde admitted he had given Alfred Wood money to move to the United States, Carson treated it as an attempt to get the blackmailer out of the way. (In the Cleveland Street affair, Lord Arthur Somerset's lawyer was convicted of attempting to pay the tele-

16. *"The Wilde v. Queensberry Case, and How It Ended,"* Illustrated Police News,
April 1895

graph delivery boys to emigrate before the case came to trial.) Carson depicts
the new clothes Wilde bought Alfonso Conway for a trip to Brighton as an
effort to disguise the youth's status: "He dresses him up like a gentleman and
he puts some of these public school colours on his hat and he makes him look
as if he were a proper person to be associating with him." Queensberry's attorney condemned the writer for taking his young friends out of their "proper
sphere" in a way that "in the future [they] could never expect to live up to."[59]
By the conclusion of his speech and the introduction of his witnesses, Carson
had outlined a damning indictment. Wilde was guilty of "corrupting the
youth"—not only through sexual misconduct and literary subversion but also
through exploitation of the working classes.

3. "GROSS INDECENCY"

Wilde did not appear in court on the third day of the trial, when his lawyers
tried to withdraw the case with the least damage to their client. They con-
ceded that, based on the literary evidence alone, the defense had shown that

Sodom on the Thames

Wilde had *posed* as a sodomite, but they admitted no sexual wrongdoing. However, Queensberry stood firm: the judge directed a verdict in his favor, a finding that his accusation was true and had been published in the public interest. The press, which had done so much to promote Wilde's reputation, now trumpeted his fall and the end of the aesthetic movement:

> The obscene imposter, whose prominence has been a social outrage ever since he transferred from Trinity Dublin to Oxford his vices, his follies, and his vanities, has been exposed, and that thoroughly at last. But to the exposure there must be legal and social sequels. There must be another trial at the Old Bailey, or a coroner's inquest—the latter for choice; and the Decadents, of their hideous conceptions of the meaning of Art, of their worse than Eleusinian mysteries, there must be an absolute end.[60]

As soon as the verdict was announced, Queensberry's solicitor wrote the director of public prosecutions: "In order that there may be no miscarriage of justice, I think it my duty at once to send you a copy of all our witnesses' statements together with a copy of the shorthand notes of the trial."[61] To make sure the government did not mistake *their* duty, he sent a copy of the cover letter to the London papers as well. After consultation with the Home Secretary and the law officers, Director of Public Prosecutions Hamilton Cuffe decided to proceed immediately. He had been second in command during the Cleveland Street affair, when he insisted on the distinction between acts affecting consenting adults and those involving the exploitation of youth. Carson had succeeded in shaping both the criminal prosecution and opinion among the political elite.

George Wyndham, a Conservative MP, relation and friend of Alfred Douglas, reported the talk at Westminster to his father: "W[ilde] is certain to be condemned, and . . . the case is in every way a very serious one, involving the systematic ruin of a number of young men. Public opinion is fiercely hostile to [Wilde], among all classes." As to Bosie, "[they] are unanimous in saying that he had better go abroad for a year or two" Wyndham concluded: "Whatever is proved, it is common knowledge in London that there was a sort of secret society around the man Taylor"[62] The Liberal government was eager to avoid a repeat of the accusations of cover-up with which radicals had dogged the Conservative administration in 1889–1890. However, the magistrate to whom they had applied for an arrest warrant deferred the matter until later in the afternoon. Although the indignant editorialist quoted above implied that Wilde should kill himself, some in authority would have settled for his exile. It has been reported that the judge fixed the time for handing down his decision only after asking his clerk when the last boat train departed for France. Despite the delay and his friends' urging that he flee the country, Wilde was arrested at the Cadogan Hotel the evening of April 5, 1895, and charged with multiple counts of gross indecency.[63]

The evidence gathered by the marquess's private investigators would now be aired in open court and retailed in the newspapers as the government's case against the writer. The young men named and described by Carson in his cross-examination would appear in person to tell their sordid stories. Alfred Taylor would stand in the dock beside Wilde, having refused to "turn Queen's Evidence" and testify against him.[64] In addition to separate charges of "gross indecency" with various men, the two were charged with "conspiracy" to induce others to commit indecent acts with Wilde. Taylor was also charged with procuring and with attempted sodomy with two of the men to whom he had introduced Wilde.[65] The prosecution reflected the press coverage in treating the affair as one with broader social implications: "[Although] it was a most unpleasant case to go into . . . it was enormously important that it should be known to those young men the Prisoner had come into contact with that there was only one end to such a life as that of the prisoner Wilde, and that was at the hands of justice."[66]

The two men were to be tried together on all charges, a fact that worked to Wilde's disadvantage. As in the case of the men accused of conspiring with Boulton and Park, evidence incriminating only one defendant could prejudice the jury against the other. (This cut both ways: Taylor might well have avoided prosecution if he had not associated with the celebrated writer.) When Parker testified about Taylor's "wedding" to Mason, one headline inadvertently reflected the general impact of the joint trial:

WILDE & TAYLOR
Committed for Trial
"A Mock Marriage"
The Scene in Court[67]

The efficacy of Carson's strategy was displayed further when the prosecution entered into evidence his cross-examination of the writer about his publications and the letters to Douglas. The press commented that dullness descended on the court as a stenographer read the once-lively exchange into the record. Wilde visibly sagged during the reading. The defendants faced a procession of accusers from the working classes or lower—valets, grooms, unemployed clerks, a newspaper boy—a number of whom had been part-time prostitutes and blackmailers. Since their testimony about sexual misconduct would inculpate themselves as well, the witnesses had been granted immunity against prosecution. However, the law requires corroboration of evidence from accomplices in a crime, so they were followed by a series of landladies, waiters, hotel maids, and bellboys, who could attest to Wilde's presence at the times and places indicated if not always to his indecent acts.

Perhaps most damaging was the testimony of personnel from the Savoy Hotel. A maid and masseur testified that they had seen a naked youth in Wilde's bed, "a common boy, rough looking about 14 years of age." The head of housekeeping confirmed that the bed linen from his room had been especially soiled. Statements to Queensberry's detectives had been explicit: the sheets "were always in a most disgusting state . . . with traces of Vaseline, soil and semen."[68] (Commenting on this evidence at Wilde's second criminal trial, Judge Sir Alfred Wills might have stolen his line from Lady Bracknell: "It is a condition of things that one shudders to contemplate in a first-class hotel.")[69] The intense surveillance at places generally considered private recalls the conflicting testimony about the living arrangements of Stella and Lord Arthur Clinton at the Boulton and Park trial.

Despite the plethora of evidence against Wilde and Taylor, things did not go according to the prosecution's plan. The Criminal Law Amendment Act of 1885, which included Labouchere's amendment, permitted those charged under its provisions to testify on their own behalf. (The general disqualification of criminal defendants would not be lifted until 1898.) Wilde was able to speak personally in response to the charges. Asked once again to explain "the love that dare not speak its name," he reached heights of eloquence describing the tradition of pedagogical eros (see the first epigraph above). Wilde concluded his reply:

> It is in this century misunderstood . . . and, on account of it I am placed where I am now. It is beautiful, it is fine, it is the noblest form of affection. There is nothing unnatural about it. It is intellectual, and it repeatedly exists between an elder and a younger man, when the elder man has intellect, and the younger man has all the hope, joy, and glamour of life before him. That it should be so the world does not understand. The world mocks at it and sometimes puts one in the pillory for it.[70]

The judge admonished the audience for the outburst of applause—mixed with a few hisses—that greeted these words. They may well have moved some jurors to support the writer. The jury could not agree to convict either man on any of the charges against him. Instead, they acquitted both of the charges relating to Fred Atkins. He had accompanied the writer on a trip to Paris but had been caught by Wilde's attorney lying about his involvement in a scheme involving extortion of money from a man with whom he had had sex. The judge had already dismissed allegations involving Sidney Mavor, one of the more respectable prosecution witnesses, who denied on the stand that Wilde had ever committed or suggested any sexual indecencies with him. Later Alfred Douglas would claim he had persuaded Mavor to change his story at the last minute with this argument: "Remember you are a gentleman and a public school boy. Don't put yourself on a level with scum like Wood and Parker. When the counsel asks you the questions, deny the whole thing, and say you made the statement because you were frightened by the police. They can't do anything to you."[71] Whatever the reasons, the trial of Wilde and Taylor was something of a shambles for the prosecution. This outcome led to Wilde's eventual release on bail pending a second criminal trial.

It was a short-lived victory. Despite the dismissal of the conspiracy charges and the severing of the cases of the two defendants, the government signaled its seriousness by naming the solicitor general, Sir Frank Lockwood, to present the case. He prosecuted with even more vigor and vehemence than in the first trial. This time the defendants were tried separately. Over the objections of Wilde's counsel, Taylor was tried first and convicted. Even the most hostile papers commented on Wilde's evident exhaustion when he appeared in the dock. He would not rise again to the rhetorical peaks that may have swayed his first jurors. Still Wilde's attorney managed to undermine some evidence from the Savoy Hotel staff. Edward Shelley, the single surviving accuser untainted by criminality, showed himself so emotionally unstable that the judge dismissed his allegations for lack of corroboration.[72] Observers in the courtroom thought the outcome a close question, despite the general expectation that Wilde's conviction was inevitable. In the end the jury convicted the writer of all the remaining counts. They had accepted the flawed accounts of the incidents at the Savoy Hotel. However, the conviction rested primarily on the evidence of Charlie Parker and Alfred Wood, admitted prostitutes and blackmailers. In his closing statement, the solicitor general suggested that the desire to commit "acts of indecency" was the cause of both prostitution and blackmail: "Were it not that there are men willing to purchase vice in the most hideous and detestable form, there would be no market for such crime and no opening for these blackmailers to ply their calling."[73] Charging the jury, Judge Wills demonstrated the continuing impact of the libel trial: "It is in my opinion impossible . . . for twelve intelligent, impartial and honest gentleman to say there was no good ground for an indignant father, a loving and affectionate parent, to charge Mr. Wilde with having posed as the Marquess

Sodom on the Thames

of Queensberry suggested."[74] Further: "The whole of this lamentable inquiry has arisen through the defendant's association with Lord Alfred Douglas."[75] Notoriously, Wills sentenced both Wilde and Taylor to two years' imprisonment with hard labor, complaining that the legal maximum was inadequate to the gravity of their offense:

> It is of no use for me to address you. People who can do these things must be dead to all sense of shame, and one cannot hope to produce any effect upon them. It is the worst case I have ever tried. That you, Taylor, kept a kind of male brothel it is impossible to doubt. And that you, Wilde, have been the centre of a circle of extensive corruption of the most hideous kind among young men, it is equally impossible to doubt.[76]

Queensberry could not have wished for a more powerful vindication of his lawyers' strategy. And yet, after the hung jury, Sir Edward Carson himself had approached the solicitor general, urging him to "let up on the fellow now" on the grounds that Wilde had already suffered enough.[77]

17. *"Closing Scene at the Old Bailey Trial of Oscar Wilde,"* Illustrated Police News, *May 1895*

Why did the government pursue the writer with such ferocity when the scandal alone had already discredited him with the public and destroyed him socially and financially? Lockwood answered Carson that the government "dare[d] not" drop the case because "it would at once be said both in England and abroad that owing to the names mentioned in Queensberry's letters we were forced to abandon it."[78] (Recall that the marquess had inveighed against Gladstone, Rosebery, even the queen, for elevating his eldest son to the House of Lords.) The papers in both the Boulton and Park trials and the Cleveland Street affair had been rife with speculation about aristocratic personages who were being protected by the government of the day against legal proceedings and popular scandal. The naming of the late Lord Arthur Clinton and the self-exiled Lord Arthur Somerset—both younger sons of dukes—had only fueled rumors that even more highly placed personages may have been implicated. The widespread rumors about Prince Albert Victor's involvement in Cleveland Street had informed deliberations at the highest level, despite repeated assurances that no evidence supported such charges.

At Wilde's second criminal trial, the foreman of the jury actually interrupted the judge's charge to ask: "In view of the intimacy between Lord Alfred Douglas and Mr. Wilde, was a warrant ever issued for the apprehension of Lord Alfred Douglas?"[79] Douglas himself wrote to a French journal a year later to claim that the "extraordinary animosity" of the government resulted from warnings by the prime minister that "if a second trial was not instituted and a verdict of guilty obtained . . . , the Liberal Party would be removed from power." It was necessary to obtain the "sacrifice of a great poet to save a degraded band of politicians." Bosie claimed that the "maniacs of virtue" had threatened legal action to create "an unprecedented scandal in Europe" by exposing "a large number" of men with tastes similar to Wilde's unless the writer was convicted.[80] By the time Douglas wrote, the Liberals had already been roundly defeated in the parliamentary elections of 1895. One recent scholar has argued that Queensberry himself threatened to release evidence implicating Rosebery in a homosexual affair with his late son Drumlanrig unless Wilde was punished and Lord Alfred protected.[81] However, a memorandum from Charles Gill, who prosecuted the first criminal trial, to the director of public prosecutions suggests Douglas had not been in any danger. The strategy of Queensberry's lawyers had already carried the day: "Having regard to the fact that Douglas was an undergraduate at Oxford when Wilde made his acquaintance, the difference in their ages, and the strong influence that Wilde

Sodom on the Thames

has obviously exercised over Douglas since that time, I think that Douglas, if guilty, may fairly be regarded as one of Wilde's victims." Moreover, the evidence against Lord Alfred amounted at best to a "grave suspicion." Only Wood and Parker attested to his sexual misconduct and their evidence could not be corroborated.[82] Ironically, Wilde would claim later that the testimony from employees of the Savoy Hotel about soiled linen and a boy in bed had actually described conditions in Bosie's room. The writer blamed Queensberry and his agents for this "deliberate, plotted, and rehearsed" displacement.[83]

Whether as a result of Carson's rhetorical strategy or Queensberry's subornation of perjury, Alfred Douglas was safe from prosecution. In addition, the marquess's defense in the libel trial had done more than enough to secure Wilde's prosecution. The Cleveland Street affair had demonstrated a government's vulnerability to charges of cover-up regardless of the merit of the underlying charges. Rosebery's party was already in trouble as he sought to govern with a deeply divided cabinet. Moreover, as the Dilke and Parnell scandals had demonstrated, the Liberal Party with its moral reform wing was especially vulnerable to being torn apart by allegations of sexual impropriety. Was there anything to cover up? Rosebery's name had already been mentioned at the libel trial. Both the Queensberry defense and criminal prosecution teams went to some length to keep another name out of the public record. In cross-examining Wilde and presenting the case against him, lawyers asked witnesses to respond to questions about a man whose name had been written on a piece of paper rather than pronounced aloud. Maurice Schwabe, who had first introduced Taylor to Wilde and had been familiar with his associates, had spent time in Paris with the writer and Fred Atkins. Indeed, Atkins testified that he had found Wilde and Schwabe in bed together committing "indecencies." Carson referred to him as a "missing witness" used by the writer to explain away inconvenient facts, like the trip to Paris with Atkins. Why was he not produced in court to testify on the writer's behalf? However, when Wilde stood in the dock, the government could only lose by emphasizing Schwabe's role. His aunt was married to Sir Frank Lockwood, the solicitor general so relentless in his prosecution of Wilde.

What about the prime minister? Although Wilde's biographers have recognized Queensberry's resentment of Rosebery and his influence on Drumlanrig, no evidence has emerged to substantiate the marquess's supposed beliefs that a homosexual relation existed between the two or that the young man killed himself to protect his patron. No doubt Queensberry had hounded Rosebery, but Carson insisted that his grievance was political, a response to his son's elevation to the House of Lords. The marquess's accusations of a "queer" conspiracy against his sons prove no more than their author's homophobia and paranoia. However, during the winter and summer 1895, Rosebery had suffered enormous strain, almost a breakdown. Fear of new accusations from the "scarlet Marquess" may have contributed, but the prime minister's difficulties antedate the Wilde affair and even the death of Drumlanrig. Regy Brett had been an acquaintance of Rosebery since their Eton days. The future prime minister, who was five years older than Brett, had been "Joab," a great favorite of Cory's. After they became political allies and personal friends, Brett wrote him: "One of my earliest recollections is the stress laid upon your name by one who had the greatest influence over my youth."[84] The prime minister drew on Brett's friendship during his depression of 1895, often inviting him for late-night talks when he could not sleep. Brett does not mention the Wilde trials in this connection, analyzing his friend's condition as an inability to recover from the loss of his wife in 1890. Regy informed Chat in March 1895:

> He complains of loneliness. Marriage frightens him—he cannot believe in a fresh disinterested affection. As if that matters to anyone who understood love! I tell him he dried up the fount by becoming a man too soon. . . . You know I disapprove of second marriages but I suppose that the P. Minister cannot in these days have a mistress. Certainly he requires intimate friends, or he will die.[85]

He commented in his journal: "His intimacies are intermittent. He ought to marry again. He requires companionship."[86] Brett had no need for discretion in his journal or a letter to Chat. He is likely to have mentioned the fact if love between men or sexual scandal had been involved. Instead, he attributes Rosebery's troubles to flaws in his character: "His rapid and early growth into manhood with the aloofness entailed by it, and that necessary element of what is called 'pose' in everyone who is a man at an age when others are boys, fitted him for oligarchic rule but not to be Chief of a Democracy. He is curiously inexperienced in the subtler forms of happiness which come from giving more than one gets."[87]

Wilde's trials crystallized anxiety about the reach and limits of male friendship in both pedagogical and political contexts. The idiosyncratic and independent W. T. Stead, leader of the campaigns against child prostitution and against the Liberal leader Dilke, reflected these concerns in the *Review of Reviews*, the journal he founded after leaving the *Pall Mall Gazette*. Acknowledging that same-sex desire might well be "natural for the abnormal person who is in a minority of one," he worried that its acceptance might cast a pall over all friendships between men. However, he condemned the unequal treatment that convicted Wilde and Taylor while indulging men who seduced girls or women: "If Oscar Wilde instead of indulging in dirty tricks of indecent familiarity with boys and men, had ruined the lives of half-a-dozen innocent simpletons of girls, or had broken up the home of his friends by corrupting the friend's wife, no one would have laid a finger on him. The male is sacrosanct; the female is fair game." Pursuing an old obsession, Stead deplored the inconsistency that "sends Oscar Wilde to hard labour and places Sir Charles Dilke in the House of Commons." However, his most stunning rebuke targeted "the tacit universal acquiescence of the very same public in the same kind of vice in our public schools." Famously, he wrote: "If all persons guilty of Oscar Wilde's offences were to be clapped into gaol, there would be a very surprising exodus from Eton and Harrow, Rugby and Winchester, to Pentonville and Holloway."[88] A complex figure, Stead would later write to Robbie Ross: "[Wilde] always knew that I at least never joined the herd of his assailants. I had the sad pleasure of meeting him by chance afterwards in Paris and greeted him as an old friend."[89]

Reynolds's Newspaper, which had covered the earlier scandals extensively from a radical republican viewpoint, devoted several front-page commentaries to the Wilde trials and opened their correspondence columns to wide-ranging debate. From the beginning, they linked the scandal to broader social tendencies, not only aestheticism but also male prostitution, "immorality in public schools," and "sex-mania." The editorials and correspondence reiterate themes that cut across the central episodes in this book, while also introducing for the first time an explicit antifeminism and terms of the "new sexology." In "The Notorious Mr. Wilde," the paper telegraphs its major concerns. Wilde's position as writer and celebrity plays a minor part. The editorialist links the affair to what we know as the "first wave" of feminism: "As the times the fashion in scandal changes, and in the era of the 'new woman,' it is not surprising that the sex-problem is putting on a new face, and marking out a rich course for itself." He quickly shifts from the distinctively modern to parallels from "ancient Rome in the days of its idle and wealthy classes" and those "Oriental countries" where "similar practices are carried out daily, in an intensely grosser form, under the eyes almost of English tourists." In London, money has immunized these practices against the police and the Vigilance Society: "The reason doubtless is that the sinners and lawbreakers have, in the past, been such as could afford the costly orgies of the Cleveland Street Bacchanalia." The editorial exposes and condemns the protection that wealth and position bring. Its author urges the authorities prosecuting Wilde to avoid "any concealment of names of 'exalted' or other personages" as in the Queensberry libel trial.

This editorial transports the origins of sexual irregularity from the urban underworld exposed in Wilde's trials to "the great public schools of England." The press has avoided "the real lesson taught by the recent appalling revelations," failing to identify "the sources of the abominations which contaminate the minds of thousands of lads yearly." England's youth are corrupted by the prevalence "at certain educational establishments of the highest class" of "the traditional vices of the schools and colleges." Indeed, "the morality of the students is past praying for." Rich parents who indulge their sons with extravagant allowances pressure school authorities to overlook the vices that inevitably develop. The schools are further deterred from harsh action by their awareness of "the patronage and influence which the future might place at the disposal of their aristocratic pupils." The paper calls for "drastic measure of reform to be taken to purge these schools from the peculiar forms of iniquity which poison the social life of England at its very fountain head."[1] (Of those publicly implicated in the Wilde affair, only Taylor and Bosie had attended public schools.)

In "Sex-Mania," its next front-page editorial, *Reynolds's* casts an even wider net. Described as a terrible plague that has "seized hold of the nation," "this prevailing lunacy of sex" is caused by "a violent reaction from the Puritanical restraints and artificial upbringing of both sexes." The piece is ambivalent about the modernization of sex already noticed in earlier references to the "new woman": "To repress every manifestation of passion is the cardinal directive of English home-training. The result is that schools of both sexes have become hot-beds of vice." For the first time in the debate, women appear outside the opposing roles of wife and prostitute. However, the paper links the risk of female same-sex desire to feminist aspirations: "The 'New Woman' is, to a certain extent, a development of sex-mania: the male decadent is its victim, and the rising population are being affected physically and mentally by symptoms of the same disease."

Antifeminism is conjoined with the new sexology: "Pederasty, Sadism, Masochism, Fetishism, Androgyny, Gynandry, are forms of madness which drive the sufferers to lunatic asylums or to suicide." The language of psychiatry supplements moral and political condemnation of sex scandal: "To rave at their infamies is not to understand the disease." The editorialist argues that the followers of Sade and Sacher-Masoch and "the Messalinas of social life" "need to be treated medically and placed under restraint." He cites Kraft-Ebbing's claim that "excessive devotion to religion" is itself a form of sex mania resulting from a displacement of libido. Apparently, medical discourse had already entered the courtroom. According to *Reynolds's*, "the defense of uncontrollable sex tendency, amounting to partial lunacy" was offered as a plea to certain criminal offenses: "If the truth were known, Jack the Ripper was nothing but a sex maniac, in the sense that we have been using." The paper embeds psychiatric diagnosis in a republican indictment of the "luxury," "idleness," "decay," and "corruption" that are "the forerunner of the downfall of nations." History offers the lessons of Greece, Rome, the Italian Republics and Old Regime France. There is "no example to the contrary": "So we may take it that the shocking depravity of the English idle classes is a symptom of our approaching dissolution."

In a striking conclusion, the editorial links male effeminacy and the "new woman" in a critique of upper-class marriage: "A feature of the low state of morals among the patrician class has been that the most conspicuous devotees of unnatural offences have been persons already married." These men are motivated by the desire for money, position, or influence rather than "natural affection": "They have simply gone into the marriage mart and bought a female for commercial reasons." For these men, "there are the consolations of Cleveland Street and Pimlico." What about their wives? The editorial concludes with a specific example combining "excessive devotion to religion" with feminist concerns. The paper rejects Lady Henry Somerset's campaign to alleviate the effects of "compulsory motherhood," suggesting that its leader would be better off "making jam." The editorial does not engage the issues she raised. Its dismissive reference to her suggests that readers might recall the scandalous custody battle that led her husband to take refuge in Florence after his wife's accusations of sodomitical vice. The earlier mention of Cleveland Street would certainly remind them of his brother Lord Arthur Somerset, driven into exile by that affair.[2]

The following week, *Reynolds's* returned to the particulars of "Oscar's Wilde's Case." Their front-page editorial emphasizes that the prosecution depended on witnesses who were "social parasites of the worst type, living by preying on the weaknesses and follies of others." Published after the hung jury in the first criminal trial, the editorial acknowledged that "it is certainly not easy to convict any man of shameful crimes on the testimony of despicable creatures like these unless it is so absolutely proven that no man can doubt it." Despite criticizing the fairness of the trial, the paper for the first time attacks Wilde's influence as a cultural figure. The editorialist characterizes the "kind of literature with which his name is identified" as "pernicious" and "one of the most diseased products of a diseased time." Citing Max Nordau's "powerful book" *Degeneration,* he treats the writer's work as symptomatic of a more general cultural malaise: "We do not know where we should find all the worst characteristics of our decadent civilization—its morbidity, its cold heartless brilliance, its insolent cynicism, its hatred of all rational restraint, its suggestiveness—more accurately mirrored than in the writings of Oscar Wilde." The urgency of the diagnosis is underlined by the report from an anonymous "assistant surgeon at one of the great London hospitals" that "the increase of immorality in the metropolis, especially among the young, is assuming alarming proportions." Still, the republican paper condemns the prosecutor's suppression of names as providing "one law for the rich and another for the poor": "The memory of the escape of the Cleveland Street gang with—as was freely

Sodom on the Thames

asserted and believed at the time—the connivance of the authorities, makes us believe that because persons are in a high social position, the government ordered their suppression."[3]

After Wilde's conviction, *Reynolds's* is one of the very few papers to sympathize with the writer, refusing "to gloat over the ruin of the unhappy man." Its lead editorial announced the broader theme of "Male Prostitution": "Every person with any feeling will feel sorry that a man of such eminent parts as Oscar Wilde could have so far degraded himself and outraged the ordinary instincts of humanity, as to seek an outlet for his passions in male prostitution." Reiterating its claim that "sexual offences between males is a common practice among our leisured and cultured classes," the paper gives the earlier scandals an explicitly political inflection:

> Many of our readers may not remember the Boulton and Park scandal, but all are familiar with the Cornwall and French case in Dublin, the Cleveland street atrocities, the conviction of De Cobain. These came to the surface, but the police were perfectly aware of their existence long previously, and of the existence of many similar cases, as to which they had a difficulty of obtaining legal proof. The offenders in all these cases were men of social position . . . and, curiously enough, all were Tories.

As for "the infamous crew" of prosecution witnesses, the editorialist insists, "It did not require Wilde to degrade them. They were brutes before he ever set eyes on them." The verdict would have been supportable had it been based on evidence that Wilde seduced innocent men, but the court had dismissed the charges of Edward Shelley, the publisher's assistant with literary aspirations, leaving only "the testimony of notorious harlots and blackmailers." The ostensibly egalitarian *Reynolds's* remains troubled by the contradiction between Wilde's cross-class associations and his manner on the witness stand:

> How is it to be explained that this man of supreme talent should have, for his companions, grooms and valets and the half-baked riff-raff of shop assistants and social parasites. Wilde gave no satisfactory explanation of the strange society in which he was found, and his ornate and gushing language, his bastard affectation of literary culture, did him as much harm as anything else with the jury.

The paper explicitly criticizes "the unnecessary virulence in the tone of the Solicitor-General" and the continuing influence of the personal quarrel that started it all: "And certainly we think it was indecent for the Marquis of Queensberry to remain in court a spectator of one of the most painful scenes that the historic Old Bailey has ever witnessed." The editorial directly condemns the conduct of the Scottish peer: "He may have rendered a public service; but the means were very questionable and undoubtedly as vulgar as can be conceived by which he initiated the proceedings which have led to Wilde's conviction."[4]

The readers of *Reynolds's Newspaper* display an even wider range of response than its editorials. Under the headline "Puritanism and Democracy," one reader urges fellow Radicals to abandon the Liberal Party, which has become "the party of cant and humbug" under the influence of nonconforming Protestantism and "the fanatical among the Temperance Party." A letter signed "Anti-Puritan" denounces moralism about sex as a hypocritical betrayal of reform, linking the criminalization of "gross indecency" with the opposition to birth control: "What use to talk of poverty when the neo-Malthusianism which is to my mind the only cure cannot be discussed. The unnatural practices now being exposed are the result of unnatural restraints and those who commit them are really insane. We need social and sexual freedom." "Anti-Puritan" proposes an alternative creed for the Liberal Party to that espoused by Stead, "the fanatics of dissent, and the Salvation Army": "The true radical wants liberty all round."[5] One of the few correspondents who signs his own name rather than a nom de plume quotes at length passages on the need to eliminate poverty from "The Soul of Man under Socialism." He argues that the editors' "sense of justice" should revise their "sweeping denunciation of Mr. Wilde's writings." Roy's letter appears under the heading "Oscar Wilde and the Democracy."[6]

The attack by *Reynolds's* on "immorality in public schools" hit home in many quarters. It generated a debate that, according to one "new reader," displayed unprecedented candor on a subject he had never before seen publicly addressed. Public school graduates attest to their own "corruption" by fellow students or that which they witnessed. Some testify to the great difficulties they faced in later life overcoming the long-term effects of schoolboy indulgence, finding help at last in religious discipline, conjugal happiness, or hypnosis. A few writers strike a more worldly and tolerant note, pointing to historical evidence that some men have always preferred sex with their own kind, while most outgrow their adolescent indulgence. "Experto Crede" urges a more sober assessment of the criminal law in light of such facts, distinguishing sex between consenting adults from that involving force or the abuse of children.

"Ethicus" canvasses the arguments of several professionals about criminalizing sex between men. He accepts a medical doctor's claim there is no

Sodom on the Thames

physical injury involved, while rejecting a lawyer's citation of the state's interest in maintaining population growth and a clergyman's description of pederasty as "unnatural, disgusting, degrading." The writer argues: "Surely it would be no good for the State, even if it were possible, that every single spermatozoa should fertilize every single ovum." Anyone with more than "a schoolboy's knowledge of history" recognizes the tendency as "common to all men and all classes of men at all times and in all countries." Since it is found in animals also, he asks: "In what sense, then is it unnatural?" Pederasty had been practiced by some very accomplished men: "It is not so debilitating as masturbation or sexual excess, nor so degrading as prostitution or adultery." As for its being "disgusting," "It evidently does not disgust those who practice it. On what is the principle founded that what is disgusting to some is illegal for all?" "Ethicus"'s critique of the laws against same-sex conduct is more radical than that of Symonds in his private publications or Shaw in his unpublished letter about the Cleveland Street affair.

Some of the letters provide more personal testimony about contemporary anxieties. "An Old Boy" worries about the long-term effects of widespread schoolboy tolerance. He describes the scene at one "middle-class" public school when several boys were expelled before dawn for indulging in "immorality": fifty boys gathered at the windows in their nightshirts to "cheer them as they went." In this "hotbed of vice," the prefect system supposed to enforce discipline perpetuates the problem: "As they—the older boys—were the very ones who incited the younger ones to vicious practices, the authorities of the school were encouraging the very evil they wished to suppress." "Old Boy" passes over "the influence which salacious classical authors may have had in producing this state of affairs," but hopes that Wilde's conviction will help dispel the tolerance of criminality and vice.[7]

"A School Boy" reports leaving his father's rectory at fourteen for "a certain well-known school in the South of England," where he quickly lost his innocence: "Even amongst the youngest boys, sexomania was rampant. Every one had his stock of filthy French novels and Belgian photographs. Conversation ever turned on the same topic—sex and the sexual passions." Not much had changed since Symonds complained of his fellows at Harrow in the 1850s: "At night, when masters slept, the most revolting unnatural practices were engaged in. In the study hall, in the classroom—nay, at very prayers—I have known masturbation to be carried on." School authorities failed to act despite evidence of "soiled bed clothes and torn trousers pockets, apart from the pimpled foreheads and emaciated appearance of the boys."[8]

Another writer, "X.Y.Z.," reports that he was seduced by the headmaster on his first night at school. Subsequently changing schools, he went on to seduce "the youngest usher" and to join in the initiation rites inflicted on new boys. His report suggests a scene from *Sins of the Cities of the Plain:* "When a new and big lad came to this school, four of us, who were in the secret, would lay ourselves out to 'break him in' as we called it. Having succeeded, we would learn from him which usher he liked best, and the one he named set about to acquire him." His life, however, turns out differently from John Saul's. "X.Y.Z.," now forty-nine, is married, the father of three sons, and owner of a prosperous business. He has continued to struggle all these years against the "sex-mania" he contracted at school: "Let a boy once get a taste of such practices, and nothing you can do, so say, will kill the evil."

"Experto Crede" writes again in reply to "Schoolboy"'s account of his corruption. He argues that "boys find no vices at public school that they do not take there": "Human nature is not nice, and boys' nature not at all nice." In replying to another correspondent's suggestion that the Wilde trials offer the public a morally beneficial lesson, he offers a skeptical assessment of earlier scandals. Although the Boulton and Park trial may have helped "clean up the streets" of the West End for a while, Dublin Castle was pure political opportunism. Worst of all, the Cleveland Street affair may have promoted male prostitution and blackmail by showing how easily a willing youth might profit in the urban marketplace.[9]

Another correspondent, "Homo," attributes the prevalence of "unnatural vice" to the lack of satisfactory sexual outlets for men not yet in a position to marry. He describes brothels as likely to lead to "loathsome and perhaps fatal disease" as well as personal shame and social disgrace: "As for seduction, rape, etc., I need not speak of them and their consequences." Sex between men may be the least harmful option. (Recall the *Daily Telegraph*'s defense of female prostitution during the Boulton and Park affair.) "Homo"'s remedy, however, is widespread acceptance of sex as a natural, beneficial, and necessary function that will lead to the alleviation of many social maladies, including the elimination of child murder.

On June 2, 1895, the editors of *Reynolds's Newspaper* bring the debate to an end. They hope that the "astounding facts" revealed by the letters will contribute to a "more healthy tone" among "those classes that are, or may be affected by these vices." Despite the wide range of views expressed by their correspondents, the editors maintain the subject of the debate is "one of the greatest evils of our time." Still they express pride in breaking the silence that generally prevails. They admit they touched on one related subject only very

Sodom on the Thames

briefly: "the position of affairs in girls' boarding schools, which as many people know, are by no means above the gravest suspicion." On this topic they are reticent: "That, however, is a subject too delicate for treatment in a public journal, although we deem it right merely to call attention to the matter."

"An Old Boy" declares that Wilde has been made a scapegoat while the practices in which he engaged remain widespread at Oxford. Wilde's visits to his old college, where he was the center of a wide circle of admiring undergraduates, led to gossip before he was accused. But sexual irregularity was not restricted to his followers. Sexual practices learned at school often continue at university, especially given the lack of other outlets. The colleges carefully regulate student behavior, on the alert for female prostitutes from town. "An Old Boy" reports seeing on the Oxford High Street a "catamite" similar to the "Mary-anns" who plied their trade beside the women at Piccadilly. The writer reports with apparent approval an incident involving undergraduates whose exercises in "Socratic love" had been discovered by fellow students. The head of the college refused to take official action for fear of scandal but implied he would not object if the students took matters into their own hands. The result was a late-night dunking in the fountain followed by an early morning departure from the college in disgrace. (Something similar had happened to Robbie Ross at Cambridge.)

A few writers explicitly condemn the double standards that led to Wilde's imprisonment:

> What for? For being immoral? No. A man may commit adultery with another man's wife or fornication with a painted harlot who plys her filthy trade in the public streets unmolested with impunity. It is because this man has dared to choose another form of satisfying his natural passions the law steps in. Yet he has not injured the State or anyone else against their will. Why does not the Crown prosecute every boy at a public or private school or half the men in the universities?

"Crede Experto" offers a final reflection: "This passion is not a fashion or a passing craze, it is universal in all ages and in all countries. . . . It would be strange if anything so usual were without a purpose. It would be inconsistent with all experience if such an inclination were without advantage." He speculates that same-sex activity may be an instrument of population control. Most importantly he urges: "It is not wise to treat with contempt a human passion that has survived the rigour of the most ruthless laws, that has defied the ordnances of religion, and is so irresistible as to have conquered sometimes the very ministers of religion themselves." This writer welcomes the fact that in his lifetime the punishment was reduced from death to two years' imprisonment with hard labor: "Thank God for that improvement. Our sons may see wiser and more humane measures yet."

Another correspondent, "M.A. Oxon," emphasizes the distinction between juvenile practices and those that endure throughout life. He argues that for most boys "spooning" with their fellows is a rehearsal for the love of women, "Venus trying her 'prentice hand." The continuation of a preference for one's own sex is "an abnormal, if not a rare, perversion of the sexual instinct." The severe legal penalties for sodomy are "a legacy from the Pentateuch,": "the same superstitious regard for supposed 'Word of God' which sent so many women to the stake as witches for long centuries and made adultery a capital crime at so many periods of English and Scottish history." Less sanguine and better informed about the law than "Crede Experto," this correspondent recognizes that the sodomy laws were not replaced but supplemented by the prohibition of gross indecency. The penalty of ten years to life in prison remained available "out of all proportion to the heinousness of the offence where it is not accompanied with violence or committed on a child." In such cases, "It is a vice more than a crime, or, perhaps, a disease rather than a vice."

Voices in the *Reynolds's* debate not only sympathize with Wilde but also offer a sustained critique of the laws under which he was condemned. Their invocation of history, psychiatry, or liberal political principle had some resonance. Over a year later, Regy Brett writes his old Eton boyfriend Chat: "I return to you the Reynolds correspondence. It may do some good but I doubt anyone having the courage to undo the Labouchere clause except Labby himself."[10] That law would remain in effect until 1967, when sexual conduct between two men in private was decriminalized by Parliament pursuant to the recommendations of a royal commission. The Wolfenden report itself was guided by considerations much like those initially aired in the 1895 debate.

More was at stake in the Wilde trials than the legal regulation of male homosexuality. Max Nordau, cited in a *Reynolds's* editorial, identified Wilde as an emblematic figure of modernity. In *Degeneration,* published in Germany in 1893 and translated into English early in 1895, Nordau devotes an entire chapter to the leading English exponent of aestheticism. He analyzes the aesthetic movement as a symptom of decadence. Before the Wilde trials had even begun, Regy Brett noted in his journal: "I finished Max Nordau's brilliant invective against everything and everybody modern."[11] For Nordau, the celebration of art for art's sake and the promulgation of a "softer" model of masculinity undermined the "social health" of European nations. He added a general cultural critique to the diagnosis of degeneration promoted by such Continental thinkers as Lombroso, whose primary concerns were criminality and sexual deviance. Nordau's polemic targeted an individualist ethic that undermined social cohesion and national values. Even after the trials had begun, Regy would write to Chat: "Don't forget Nordau—he will amuse you by his violence and philistinism."[12] The chapter on Wilde did not touch on sexual irregularity but rather on conceptions of masculinity. Alan Sinfield points out that there is only one (almost passing) reference to same-sex desire in *Degeneration*: "Vice looks to Sodom and Lesbos, to Bluebeard's Castle and the servants' hall of the 'divine' Marquis de Sade's *Justine* for its embodiments."[13] Nordau is not primarily concerned with sexuality. He almost regrets Wilde's conviction:

> My readers will surely know the shocking fate that befell this unfortunate man in 1895. I should have preferred to have avoided making any mention of Oscar Wilde [rather than seeming to] be placing my foot upon a vanquished man who [already] lay on the floor but although he was sentenced to hard labour . . . the English may have banned his plays from their theatres and his books from their bookshops, it is not so easy to erase his name from the social history of our time. Oscar Wilde remains the most informative embodiment of a mentality which has placed a part in modern spiritual life and which is still embraced by no small number of degenerates and their imitators. Consequently it seemed impossible to pass him by in silence and with an averted gaze.[14]

Wilde himself agreed with Nordau's estimation of his importance: "I was a man who stood in symbolic relations to the art and culture of my age. I had realized this for myself at the very dawn of my manhood, and had forced my age to realize it afterwards. Few men hold such a position in their own lifetime and have it so acknowledged."[15]

The writer saw his trials not as a fulfillment of this "symbolic relationship" but as its antithesis. He wrote Douglas: "The one disgraceful, unpardonable, and to all time contemptible action of my life was my allowing myself to be forced into appealing to Society for help and protection against your father." He accepted some responsibility for the processes he had initiated. "Of course once I had put into motion the forces of Society, Society turned on men, and said: 'Have you been living all this time in defiance of my laws, and do you now appeal to those laws for protection? You shall have those laws exercised to the full. You shall abide by what you have appealed to.' The result is that I am in jail."[16] The writer blames neither the men who testified against him nor himself for having associated with them: "I don't feel ashamed of having known them. They were intensely interesting. . . . Clibborn and Atkins were wonderful in their infamous war against life." Taking Queensberry to court was not an act of resistance to Victorian society but rather its triumph:

> I found myself obliged to send long lawyer's letter to your father and constrained to appeal to the very things against which I had always protested. . . . What is loathsome to me is the memory of interminable visits paid by me to the solicitor Humphreys in your company, when in the ghastly glare of a bleak room you and I would sit with serious faces telling serious lies to a bald man, till I really groaned and yawned with *ennui*.

As for his performances on the witness stand: "At the end I had to come forward, on your behalf, as the champion of Respectability in conduct, of Puritanism in life, and of Morality in Art."[17] These statements cannot be taken as Wilde's final judgment, since they appear in *De Profundis,* the hyperbolic long letter to Douglas that Wilde wrote from prison. It is informed partly at least by the grief and rage he felt because Bosie had not written him. Still there is a measure of objectivity in these passages.

Despite his celebration of "feasting with panthers," Wilde is ambivalent about his "walk on the wild side": "Tired of being on the heights I deliberately went to the depths in the search for new sensations. What the paradox was to me in the sphere of thought, perversity became to me in the sphere of passion. Desire, at the end was a malady, or madness, or both. I grew careless of the lives of others. I took pleasure where it pleased me and passed on."[18] He appears to regret having put only his talent into his work, no longer convinced that he put his genius into his life: "I became the spendthrift of my genius and to waste an eternal youth gave me a curious joy."[19] In letters to the Home Office, Wilde would describe himself as suffering from an erotomania that imprisonment could only exacerbate. His adoption of the language of psychiatry was no doubt informed by a sense of what might persuade officials to relieve his suffering. Still, the self-diagnosis turns not on same-sex desire but on obsessive sexuality.

It is not easy to say how Wilde's "genius," the "indicative" relation he once enjoyed to modern art and culture, relates to his "homosexuality," his love for other men and the pursuit of sexual pleasure with them. His impact in shap-

Sodom on the Thames

18. *"An Athlete Wrestling with a Python," Frederic Leighton (1874–1877)*

ing conceptions of male same-sex desire well into the twentieth century is beyond doubt. When the eponymous hero of E. M. Forster's novel *Maurice*
finally consults a medical specialist about his attraction to other men, he
describes himself as "an unspeakable of the Oscar Wilde sort." That legacy is
not so negative as one might have predicted on the basis of Wilde's disgrace.
Havelock Ellis famously observed in *Studies in the Psychology of Sex* that the

scandal may have allowed more Englishmen to accept their homosexuality: "No doubt the celebrity of Oscar Wilde and the universal publicity given to the facts of the case may have brought conviction of their perversion to many inverts who were only vaguely conscious of their abnormality and, paradoxical though it may seem, have imparted greater courage to others."[20]

This project was initially animated by questions in queer theory, particularly those that arise from recent efforts to "historicize" sexuality, to situate forms of desire and their expression within specific cultural contexts at definite periods of time. Those questions may have been eclipsed by the extended narratives that make up this book. As I argued in the introduction, the turn to storytelling does not entail ignorance of the discursive constraints and institutional contexts against which individual lives and relationships are played out. I have tried to display concretely the vicissitudes of same-sex desire among groups of men in a particular time and place.

In these concluding comments, I hope to indicate several ways in which "telling tales" brings about a more general understanding of desire and its place in individual and social life. Theory and history must be placed in continuing dialogue, each challenging the perspective and assumptions of the other. In particular, storytelling provides a vehicle for comprehending the interplay among the diverse social categories that intersect in the formation of individual desires and identities; it may illuminate the diversity of discursive frameworks that coexist in a particular period and that offer competing templates of social ascription and self-understanding. The combination of thick description of earlier forms of life and attention to the dynamics of interpretive conflict allows us to reconsider accounts of the emergence of distinctively modern "homosexual" desires and identities. It may provide concrete examples of a broader erotic life than do contemporary conceptions of sexuality that reduce desire to specifically genital urges and their satisfaction. Finally, we must maintain some critical awareness of our own interests as writer and readers in shaping the hermeneutic context from which we approach historical forms of desire.

Some recent queer theory and feminist thought have insisted on the importance of the intersection between sexuality and gender and of both with other social forms such as race, class, religion, ethnicity, and nationality. Storytelling allows us to go beyond listing these categories to show how they mutually inflect each other in specific situations. Certainly the episodes examined in this book demonstrate the centrality of social class as a determinant of individual life and political conflict. It is unlikely that Fanny and Stella would have appeared even as footnotes in social history were it not for their families' status and economic capacity to provide them with high-powered legal counsel and expert witnesses. The publicity surrounding their case was fueled by the links discovered between these sons of the professional classes and Lord Arthur Clinton, son of a duke. There was continuing speculation that their circle included other members of the aristocracy. The radical press treated the emergence of the "hermaphrodite clique" as symptomatic of upper-class corruption linked to urban decadence. The prosecution tried to establish Boulton's and Park's déclassé status as male prostitutes; the defense portrayed them as high-spirited sons of the bourgeoisie. The presiding judge worried that they displayed less than proper respect for their noble friend.

Fanny's and Stella's cross-dressing flouted gender norms inseparable from their social position. The trial failed to establish a connection between their affront to "public decency" and sexual conduct; the romantic effusion of their admirers could not simply be seen as an indication of sexual desire. Even today it is not easy to say whether Boulton and Park acted on homosexual desires or whether they are better understood as expressing a transgendered refusal of normative masculinity. Public anxiety certainly focused as much on gender as on sexuality. Witness the letters to the *Times* about the dangers of having boys play girls' roles in theatrical performances at school. Gay writers of an earlier generation tended to treat the pair contemptuously as "narcissists" or "exhibitionists." It has occurred to me more than once that Stella was something of a "cock tease." The systematic point may be that the ambiguous fascination of Ernest Boulton's gender performance and the opacity of his desires are more instructive than any reductive categorization.

Gender transgression among the young is also manifest in the practice of calling some boys by girls' names, mentioned in the Boulton and Park trial, Symonds's *Memoirs,* and the letters and journals of William Cory and Regy Brett. In all these cases, gender is inflected by both social class and age. As Park's attorney insisted, most boys outgrow their youthful deviations. Moreover, the arena of these concerns is public schools for the sons of the upper and aspiring classes. The privileged status of Regy and his friends makes their sentimental attachments more ambiguous than the friendships among women that have been so well detailed in recent histories. Whereas Martha Vicinus can persuasively portray the associations promoted by girls' schools and women's colleges as sources of resistance and pressure for change, the relations fostered among these young men reinforced patterns of male dominance. Although Cory's students may have developed alternative forms of

Sodom on the Thames

masculine desire, most of them remained comfortably at the heart of the British establishment; only Chat seems to have dropped out.

Social position also emerges as the dominant theme in the Cleveland Street affair and may have been decisive in Wilde's fall. John Saul's déclassé status contributed to the hostility with which he was received, whereas the young men employed at the post office were treated as ambitious but randy sons of the working class. Lord Arthur Somerset was portrayed as an aristocratic exploiter of the young and economically vulnerable; Wilde, as a hypocrite when he professed socialism. Cross-class relations were as threatening as deviant desires, especially when paraded in public. Equally important, for Somerset, Symonds, and Wilde, youth and social difference were part of the attraction of telegraph delivery boys, soldiers, or hustlers, just as the privileged position of Cory's and Brett's protégés attracted the older men. I am not arguing that social class is always and everywhere more fundamental than gender or sexuality, but its centrality is evident in these stories of late Victorian London.

Class conflict is culturally mediated: the sexual and gender nonconformity displayed here was interpreted through competing lenses of moral and political judgment. Radical working-class politics; movements for moral purity; defenses of the bourgeois family; opposition to urban culture, modernism, and feminism: all converged in condemning the scandalous behavior recounted in these stories. These frameworks offered distinct grounds for stigmatizing manifestations of same-sex desire: as aristocratic corruption, individual sinfulness, aesthetic libertinism, cultural decadence. Equally important, these discourses were articulated with reference to specific institutional contexts, such as school, university, household, theater, clubs, government, or metropolitan capital. They were developed, promulgated, and maintained by the press, public opinion, legislation, judicial hearings, and gossip. Sexual conduct was not considered in isolation but as symptomatic of more general tendencies. Public controversy was accompanied by ambiguity regarding the underlying acts; the medical evidence in the Boulton and Park trial failed signally to establish the proof of anal intercourse required for a sodomy conviction. In the Cleveland Street affair, only John Saul dared speak openly of sex. Fanny's and Stella's cross-dressing and the interactions at 19 Cleveland Street could be condemned for indicating a range of social ills.

Moreover, dominant norms did not simply define standards by which to judge individual acts of transgression. They defined kinds of individuals who threatened the social and moral order: the sodomite, rake, libertine, effeminatus, decadent, aesthete. These character types, if not sexual identities, in all their variety were linked to same-sex desire but grounded in the worldviews that condemned them. Such ascriptions could also be appropriated and transformed by individuals in search of self-understanding. These stories provide evidence of alternative discourses in which male same-sex love could be defended: pedagogical pederasty, Hellenistic citizenship, romantic friendship, and even sodomitical rebellion. The men who loved men in these stories used a variety of terms for their shared erotic disposition, if they named it at all: Uranian, Socratic, Greek, Arcadian, *l'amour de l'impossible*. Cross-dressers might be "mollies"; male prostitutes, "poofs" or "Mary-anns." John Saul described himself as a "professional sodomite." The erotics and politics of naming were also individualized, as with Fanny and Stella, or the nicknames at Eton, not only "Tute" and "Chat" and "Beak" but also "Ivy" for Bickerstaff and, briefly, "June" for Regy Brett. Cory referred to two of his young friends as "Phaedrus." What's in a name? Quite a lot for late Victorians: Lord Chief Justice worried about how Park addressed Lord Arthur Clinton and Sir Edward Carson cast suspicion on the famous writer because he was called "Oscar" by an unemployed valet and groom. Wilde displayed the power of a counterdiscourse, enunciated by Cory and Symonds as well, when he defended "the love that dare not speak its name," in the names of David and Jonathan, Socrates and Plato, Michelangelo and Shakespeare.

To what extent do these figures resemble the modern male homosexual or contemporary gay man? Michel Foucault importantly linked historical and theoretical claims when he argued that sexuality as such, understood as an autonomous domain yielding the "truth" about individuals, first emerged in the medical and psychological discourses of the nineteenth century. More specifically, some argue that Foucault believed that the homosexual as a "new species," a distinctive identity grounded in same-sex desire, appeared only as a subsequent construct of that discourse. My research for this book began in part to test the validity of the latter claim, at least insofar as it applied to Britain in the late nineteenth century. Strikingly, the language of sexology does not appear until the Wilde case in 1895. Even then, it is in the service of a diagnosis of "sex-mania" that links same-sex desire to aestheticism and feminism. At the same time, we have encountered a proliferation of discourses defining men who loved men, whether to condemn or defend them.

The question of the emergence of a distinctive "modern homosexuality" implicates forms of historical periodization as well as self-understanding and social ascription. Symonds introduced Continental sexology to Anglophone readers in *A Problem in Modern Ethics*, privately published in 1883. *Sexual Inversion*, on which he collaborated with Havelock Ellis, was published in England in 1897 but was quickly withdrawn under the threat of an obscenity prosecution. Writing to the Home Office in an effort to secure early release or at least an improvement in his treatment, Wilde claimed he suffered from mental illness, an erotomania that could only be exacerbated by the conditions of his confinement. The invocation of medical discourse was necessitated by the constraints on penological discretion, but even here the terms are broader than same-sex desire. Facts like these complicate both sexual typologies and genealogies. The question of when distinct forms emerged may be less salient than the movement within discursive formations and the interaction among them.

As Foucault himself demonstrates, most of the diagnostic categories of late nineteenth-century sexology have long since disappeared. The staying power of "homosexuality" must be explained separately from its emergence. Furthermore, it may be no more coherent a category than the confusing term "sodomy" it is said to displace. "Sexual inversion" was defined by the "inner androgyny" to which Foucault refers, but many of the men portrayed here shared Symonds's view of a male comradeship that verges on hypermasculinity. Freud's distinctions among sexual urge, object, and aim made it possible to further disarticulate same-sex sexuality and gender. The taxonomies of sexual science developed within the field of professional debates and in continuing interaction with the social phenomena they purported to explain. Given the plurality of discourses already on offer, it is hard to see any one simply displacing the others, as opposed to expanding the repertoire of terms available for continuing deployment and contestation. In 1980s London, the British writer and director Neil Bartlett wrote movingly about many of the figures in this study in an unabashed pursuit of gay ancestors. My own research is refracted through a queerer prism that highlights the multiple differences among these men and between them and us. Their own self-understandings were subject to ongoing revision over time, as witnessed by the lifelong reflections of Symonds and the correspondence of Brett and his friends. There is no reason to believe that "we" are immune to the proliferation of perspectives or vicissitudes of time.

Narrative challenges theory by juxtaposing sexual taxonomies with a more nuanced social phenomenology that displays social types and discursive formations overlapping, occasionally colliding or dividing, in ongoing metamorphoses. Storytelling in itself offers no theoretical resolution. Narrative too comes in many forms. There are sweeping narratives and omniscient narrators as well as grand theories and universal speculations. Contemporary historians of sexuality such as Halperin and Sinfield have used specific research to expand the typologies through which we understand same-sex desire. Local stories aware of their limited points of view, open to differing perspectives and continuing revision, focus instead on the dynamics of diversity. Such storytelling may capture more of the flavor of erotic life. Perhaps ambiguity, vacillation, and opacity are inherent in desire. Narratives may also remain more faithful to the piecemeal and often inconclusive character of historical evidence. At the same time, they may remind us of the point of view from which stories are told: we too are situated historically and approach the past from our own personal and political positions. Greater awareness of the perspectival character of historical knowledge may lead us to question the drive for closure in both theory and narrative. What desires, what interests are served by the development of comprehensive schemes of categorization? What might we gain by accepting an irreducible dimension of opacity in our efforts to comprehend differences? Our contemporaries in different social positions may be no more transparent than historical "others."

Some of us will insist on translating the tales of late Victorian London and its queer inhabitants into more familiar categories, often imposing our own judgments along the way—sympathizing with persecuted gays, deploring the effects of gender hierarchy, or condemning the abuse of advanced age or superior position. One additional aspect of these stories returns to my starting point and leaves me wondering further about the adequacy of our own understanding. Eros appears in these tales in many guises. We do well to avoid the quick translation of the intense emotions and relations among these men into the terms of contemporary sexuality. Sentimental attachments that include physical admiration and warm embraces often stopped short of genital sexuality. It is too easy to assume this sublimation was simply the effect of social constraint or psychological repression. *The Sins of the Cities of the Plain* exhibits the wide range of explicit expression available to the unfettered imagination. Does the pornographic novel display the underlying truth of these men's desires? Or did some of them find in the more diffuse and ambiguous manifestations of the erotic a fulfillment beyond the grasp of our own sexual imaginary?

ACKNOWLEDGMENTS

This book got its start at a summer seminar titled "The Culture of London, 1850–1914," sponsored by the National Endowment for the Humanities in 1995. I am extremely grateful to Director Michael Levenson and my fellow Londonists for the stimulation and encouragement they provided. Some have continued the conversation, especially Heidi Holder, Pamela Gilbert, and Joseph McLaughlin. Archival research was a new undertaking for me; I was launched with generous help from Purchase College colleagues Geoffrey Field and the late Michael O'Loughlin and from William A. Cohen. I have been further assisted by a summer research grant from NEH, annual grants from Purchase College, and a generous leave policy. I appreciate the support of Provost Gary Waller and Dean of the School of the Humanities Gari LaGuardia. My colleagues in the School of Humanities, the Philosophy Board of Study, and the Lesbian and Gay Studies Program have been an ongoing source of support, friendship, and inspiration. I spent my sabbatical year 2001–2002 as visiting fellow at the Birkbeck College Law School, University of London. I am very grateful to the faculty and staff who welcomed me warmly and provided a stimulating and congenial intellectual environment. I have been very lucky in my affiliations.

My research has benefited considerably from conversation with other scholars currently working in the field who shared with me their unpublished work, especially Paul Robinson, Matt Cook, Harry Cocks, Chris Waters, Matt Houlbrook, and Matt Stone. (See the "Suggestions for Further Reading" for references to their subsequent publications.) Other friends have also been generous in discussing the project over the years: Ed Stein, Gari LaGuardia, Frank Farrell, Garrath Williams, Jamie Mayerfeld, Peter Mack, Carolin Emcke, Seyla Benhabib, Alan Ryan, Judith Butler, Les Moran, and Elena Loizidou. Two friends went well beyond the call of duty in helping with this work. Michael Levenson provided a detailed critique of this manuscript at almost every stage of its development. Bill Torbert spent part of his vacation reading the entire penultimate draft to offer invaluable advice from the perspective of the elusive "general reader." I am indebted to them for some of the book's best qualities; the faults remaining are my own.

I could not have pursued this work without the opportunity to lecture and publish along the way. I feel enormously indebted to the interdisciplinary community of scholars from whom I have learned so much. This list can be only a partial record of my debts. Thanks to: Elizabeth Emens, Jeffrey Weeks, Joseph Bristow, Judith Walkowitz, Lynda Nead, Lynne Segal, John Howard, Harry Hirsch, Peter Stansky, Davina Cooper,

Carolyn Dinshaw, David Halperin, Pericles Lewis, Oliver Philips, Nancy Tuana, Tracy Strong, Alison Shonkwiler, George Robb, Patrick Hanafin, Adrian Rifkin, Irit Rogoff, Didi Herman, Peter Fitzpatrick, Regina Kunzel, Deborah Amory, James Thompson, Randolph Trumbach, Eugene Rice, Nicola Lacey, and Martha Vicinus.

This work would not exist without the archival material on which it is based. Many institutions made available their resources, including books, newspapers, manuscripts, and images. I am grateful for their assistance to members of the staff at: Churchill College, Cambridge; the British Library and the BL Newspaper Collection, Collindale; the Public Records Office, now the National Archive, Kew; the London Library; Tate Britain; the Victoria and Albert Museum; the National Museums, Liverpool; and the Essex County Records Office. I am especially grateful to the Hon. Christopher Brett for permission to quote extensively from the Esher Archive at Churchill College.

I would like to thank those who invited me to present my research and to those who responded to my presentations at the following colleges and universities: Columbia University; Kings College, Cambridge; Goldsmiths College, London; Birkbeck College, London; Stanford University; University of California, San Diego; University of California, Berkeley; South Bank University; University of Oregon; University of Washington; Yale University. Thanks also to the organizers and audiences at the following conferences: "Old Boys and New Women," Clark Library, UCLA; "Gender, Sexuality, and the Law," Keele University; "Queer Matters," Kings College, London; National Conference on British Studies; Middle Atlantic and Pacific Conferences on British Studies; American Political Science Association; Western Political Science Association; International Association for the Study of Sexuality and Culture; and Metropolitan New York Lesbian and Gay History Group.

Thanks to the staff at Cornell University Press for their assistance in producing this book, especially Bernie Kendler and Ange Romeo-Hall. Jane Marie Todd provided excellent copyediting and David Prout prepared the index.

Passages from previously published articles have been incorporated at various points throughout the book. "Did 'My Lord Gomorrah' Smile?" appeared in *Disorder in the Court,* ed. Nancy Erber and George Robb (London and New York, 1998). "Who's Afraid of John Saul? Urban Culture and the Politics of Desire in Late Victorian London" was published in *GLQ: A Journal of Lesbian and Gay Studies* 5, no.3 (1999). "'Men in Petticoats': Border Crossings in the Queer Case of Mr. Boulton and Mr. Park" appeared in *Imagined Londons,* ed. Pamela Gilbert (Albany, 2001). "Literature in the Dock: The Trials of Oscar Wilde" was published in *Journal of Law and Society* 31, no. 1 (2004): 113–30. The material is used with permission of the publishers.

The frontispiece and figure 18 are reproduced with permission of the Tate Museum, London; figures 4, 12, and 14 with the permission of the British Library (1414K10, Vanity Fair LD61 November 7, 1874, 257; November 19, 1884, 323); figures 1–3, 5–7, that of the Essex County Records Office; figures 8, 13, 16, and 17 from *Illustrated Police News,* courtesy of the British Library Newspaper Collection, Collindale; figures 9 and 11 with the permission of the Victoria and Albert Museum, London; figures 10 and 15 with permission of the Lady Lever Art Gallery and of the Walker Galleries at the National Museums, Liverpool.

Closer to home, my friends and family have been wonderful as I have divided my time increasingly between New York and London. I am especially grateful to my sisters, Susan Rosenberg and Barbara Kaplan, for their general support and for not complaining about my being away so much during the years of our mother's decline. Very special thanks to Marin and Lauren Haythe for opening their home in London to me over these last years. I cannot imagine being able to complete this work without their generosity. My stays in London have been very much enriched by the hospitality of a diverse community of engaged intellectuals who have welcomed me and made me feel at home. My dear friend Robin Faine shared her home while I waited to repossess my apartment in New York.

Three very special people who contributed so much to my life and work are not here to see this book. My teacher Don Gifford has been much in my mind throughout this endeavor: he gave me a model of eclectic, imaginative, and humane scholarly engagement. My friend Mary Lawrence encouraged my efforts with curiosity, sympathy, and the occasional nudge to get on with it. My mother did not flag in her support of my commitment to lesbian, gay, and queer studies; she seemed especially proud that this research led me to spend so much time in London. This book is dedicated to the memory of these three, with love and gratitude.

NOTES

EROS IN THE ARCHIVES

1 Merlin Holland, *Irish Peacock and Scarlet Marquess* (London, 2003). The authoritative text for the two criminal trial remains the reconstruction by H. Montgomery Hyde, *The Trials of Oscar Wilde* (New York, 1973; originally published London, 1948).

2 Christie's, *Valuable Printed Books and Manuscripts,* London catalog for June 6, 2001.

3 Neil McKenna, *The Secret Life of Oscar Wilde* (London, 2003).

PROLOGUE

1 John Addington Symonds, *Memoirs,* ed. Phyllis Grosskurth (Chicago, 1984), 186.

2 See Symonds, *Memoirs;* and Phyllis Grosskurth, *The Woeful Victorian: A Biography of John Addington Symonds* (New York, 1974). See also Paul Robinson, *Gay Lives* (Chicago, 1999).

3 Symonds, *Memoirs,* 116.

4 Ibid., 129–33; Grosskurth, *Woeful Victorian,* 65–68; Oliver Buckton, *Secret Selves: Confession and Same-Sex Desire in Victorian Autobiography* (Chapel Hill, 1995), 91–96. This affair, along with a similar controversy regarding Walter Pater, is also treated in Linda Dowling, *Hellenism and Homosexuality in Victorian Oxford* (Ithaca, 1994), 86–89.

5 Symonds, *Memoirs,* 187.

6 Ibid., 187n.

7 Ibid., 187–88.

8 Ibid., 188.

9 Ibid., 106.

10 *The Letters of John Addington Symonds,* ed. Herbert M. Schueller and Robert L. Peters (Detroit, 1967), 1:446. Throughout this book, I will preserve the punctuation and spelling used in the original texts. Although both are different from current conventions and sometimes idiosyncratic to the writers, I have chosen to avoid cluttering the text with *sic* except where necessary to avoid confusion.

11 Symonds, *Memoirs,* 187.

12 Symonds, *Letters,* 1:444.

13 Ibid., 1:446.

14 Ibid., 2:43.

15 John Addington Symonds, typescript from the original manuscript of *Memoirs,*

London Library, 1:218. Grosskurth does not include this passage in her edition, from which she omitted about one-fifth of the material. A severely truncated version of this letter appears in Symonds, *Letters,* 1:718–20.

16 Symonds, *Letters,* 1:722.

17 See Dowling, *Hellenism and Homosexuality.*

18 For a fuller discussion of Symonds's Hellenism, see Morris B. Kaplan, *Sexual Justice: Democratic Citizenship and the Politics of Desire* (New York, 1997), chap. 2.

19 John Addington Symonds, "The Dantesque and Platonic Ideals of Love," in *The Key of Blue and Other Essays* (1892; New York, 1970).

20 Symonds, *Memoirs,* 100–102. See also the response of Norman Moor, a former boyfriend, to Symonds's warning, in Symonds, *Memoirs,* 295–97.

21 Symonds, *Letters,* 3:808.

22 Ibid., 1:460.

23 Letter from Reginald Brett, Lord Esher, to Charles Williamson, Esher papers, Churchill College, Cambridge, vol. 1, ESHR 8/3, November 17, 1892, February 1, 1893. See part 2 of this book for a detailed account of Brett's friendship with Williamson.

1. SEX IN THE CITY

1 See generally Rictor Norton, *Mother Clap's Molly House: The Gay Subculture in England 1700–1830* (London, 1992). See also Alan Bray, *Homosexuality in Renaissance England* (London, 1982), 81–114; and Randolph Trumbach, "The Birth of the Queen: Sodomy and the Emergence of Gender Equality in Modern Europe 1660–1750," in *Hidden from History: Reclaiming the Gay and Lesbian Past,* ed. Martin Duberman, Martha Vicinus, and George Chauncey (New York, 1989), 129–40.

2 Quoted in Norton, *Mother Clap's Molly House,* 55.

3 Quoted in Bray, *Homosexuality in Renaissance England,* 87.

4 Norton, *Mother Clap's Molly House,* 100.

5 Ibid., 66.

6 Quoted in ibid., 192.

7 Norton, *Mother Clap's Molly House,* 187–98.

8 Quoted in H. Montgomery Hyde, *The Other Love: An Historical and Contemporary Survey of Homosexuality in Britain* (London, 1970), 120.

9 Ibid., 120–21.

10 See William Roughead, *Bad Companions: Lives of Criminals* (Edinburgh, 1930); Neil Bartlett Weeks, *Who Was That Man? A Present for Mr. Oscar Wilde* (London, 1988), 129–43; and William A. Cohen, *Sex Scandal: The Private Parts of Victorian Fiction* (Durham, N.C., 1996), 73–129.

11 See Frank Mort, *Dangerous Sexualities: Medico-Moral Politics in England since 1830* (London, 1987), 69–76; and Judith Walkowitz, *Prostitution and Victorian Society: Women, Class, and the State* (New York, 1980).

12 Walkowitz, *Prostitution and Society,* 69–89.

13 Hyde, *The Other Love,* 92.

14 See Harry Cocks, *Nameless Offenses: Speaking of Male Homosexuality in Nineteenth-century England* (London, 2003).

15 See Norton, *Mother Clap's Molly House,* 130–33, 191–94; and Louis Crompton, *Byron and Greek Love: Homophobia in Nineteenth-century England* (Berkeley, 1985), 21–22, 158–71.

16 *Times,* April 30, 1870, 11.

17 *Daily Telegraph,* May 7, 1870, 3.

18 *Times,* May 7, 1870, 11.

19 Ibid., May 14, 1870, 10.

20 Ibid., May 21, 1870, 11.

21 Ibid., May 30, 1871, 13.

22 The records of the Boulton and Park case are found in two separate files. The transcript of the trial in May 1871 is found in DPP 4/6 at the National Archives, Kew, along with copies of thirty letters offered into evidence. The signed depositions reflecting testimony offered at Bow Street are in KB 6/3. I have modernized the punctuation but otherwise left the texts unaltered.

23 KB 6/3, 10.

24 KB 6/3, 12.

25 KB 6/3, 16.

26 KB 6/3, 21.

27 *Reynolds's,* May 15, 1870, 5.

28 KB 6/3, 1.

29 James Lees-Milne, *The Enigmatic Edwardian: The Life of Reginald Brett, 2nd Viscount Esher* (London, 1986), 60.

30 KB 6/3, 5.

31 KB 6/3, 6.

32 KB 6/3, 7.

33 KB 6/3, 39.

34 KB 6/3, 40.

35 KB 6/3, 40–41.

36 KB 6/3, 42.

37 KB 6/3, 43.

38 Ibid.

39 Erika Diana Rappaport, *Shopping for Pleasure* (Princeton, N. J., 2000), 151.

40 KB 6/3, 53.

41 *Reynolds's,* May 22, 1870, 5.

42 KB 6/3, 49–51.

43 KB 6/3, 49.

44 KB 6/3, 52.

45 *Reynolds's,* May 8, 1870, 5.

46 Ibid., May 29, 1870, 5.

47 *Oxford English Dictionary,* 2nd ed. Oxford, 1989), s.v. "drag."

48 *Reynolds's,* May 29, 1870, 5.

49 Ibid.

50 *Times,* May 23, 1870, 13.

51 *Reynolds's,* May 29, 1870 5.

52 Ibid., June 5, 1870, 5.

53 KB 6/3, 162.

54 *Reynolds's,* June 5, 1870, 5.

55 Ibid.

56 KB 6/3, 169.

57 KB 6/3, 171.

58 *Reynolds's,* June 5, 1870, 5.

59 KB 6/3, 172.

60 Ibid.

61 *Reynolds's,* June 5, 1870, 5.

62 Ibid.

63 Ibid.

64 Ibid.

65 *Times,* May 23, 1870, 13.

66 Ibid., 266.

67 *Reynolds's,* May 22, 1870, 5.

68 Ibid.

69 Ibid.

70 *Reynolds's,* May 8, 1870, 5.

71 *Daily Telegraph,* May 16, 1870, 2.

72 *Reynolds's,* May 8, 1870, 5.

73 Ibid.

74 KB 6/3, 129–32.

75 *Reynolds's,* May 29, 1870, 5.

76 KB 6/3, 133.

77 *Reynolds's,* May 29, 1870, 5.

78 *Times,* May 12, 1870, 11.

79 *Reynolds's,* May 22, 1870, 5.

80 *Times,* May 21, 1870, 11.

81 *Reynolds's,* May 29, 1870, 5.

82 *Reynolds's,* June 5, 1870, 4.

83 Ibid.

84 Ibid.

85 *Daily Telegraph,* May 16, 1870, 2.

86 Ibid., May 21, 1870, 6.

87 KB 6/3, 80.

88 *Reynolds's,* May 29, 1870, 5.

89 *Daily Telegraph*, May 21, 1870, 6.

90 KB 6/3, 84.

91 *Daily Telegraph*, May 21, 1870, 6.

92 *Reynolds's*, May 29, 1870, 5.

93 KB 6/3, 73.

94 *Reynolds's*, May 15, 1870, 6.

95 Ibid., May 29, 1870, 5.

96 Ibid., June 5, 1870, 4.

97 Ibid.

98 Ibid.

99 Ibid.

100 *Daily Telegraph*, May 30, 1870, 5.

101 KB 6/3, 135.

102 KB 6/3, 137.

103 *Reynolds's*, May 29, 1870, 5.

104 DPP 4/6, 1:36–37.

105 *Oxford English Dictionary*, s.v. "camp."

106 *Reynolds's*, May 14, 1871, 6.

107 *Times*, May 16, 1870; *Reynolds's*, May 22, 1870, 5.

108 *Daily Telegraph*, May 16, 1870, 2.

109 Ibid.

110 *Reynolds's*, May 22, 1870, 5.

111 DPP 4/6, 6:97–98.

112 Jonathan Ned Katz, *Love Stories: Sex between Men before Homosexuality* (Chicago, 2001).

113 KB 6/3, 88.

114 Ibid., 89.

115 *Reynolds's*, May 29, 1870, 5.

116 *Illustrated Police News*, May 28, 1870, 1.

117 KB 6/3, 90.

118 Ibid., 90–91.

119 *Illustrated Police News*, May 28, 1870, 1.

120 KB 6/3, 91.

121 Ibid., 92.

122 *Reynolds's*, May 29, 1970, 5.

123 Ibid.

124 *Daily Telegraph*, May 23, 1870, 2.

125 *Reynolds's*, June 12, 1870, 1.

126 Ibid., June 5, 1870, 5.

127 *Times*, June 20, 1870, 7.

128 Ibid., May 7, 1870, 11.

129 Ibid.

130 Ibid., May 31, 1870, 9.

131 Ibid.

132 *Penny Illustrated Paper,* June 4, 1870, 354.

133 *Times,* May 31, 1870, 9.

134 Ibid.

135 *Pall Mall Gazette,* May 31, 1870, 5.

136 *Reynolds's,* June 5, 1870, 5.

137 Ibid.

138 Ibid.

139 *Daily Telegraph,* May 31, 1870, 4–5.

140 Ibid., 5.

141 "The Lives of Boulton and Park: Extraordinary Revelations," penny pamphlet published anonymously, May 1870, 1.

142 Ibid., 8.

143 *Times,* June 2, 1870, 8.

144 Ibid., 8.

145 *Pall Mall Gazette,* June 8, 1870, 1–2.

146 *Times,* June 4, 1870, 11.

147 *Daily Telegraph,* May 23, 1870, 2.

148 Ibid., June 1, 1870, 3.

149 Ibid., June 3, 1870, 3.

150 Kings College Archives, OB 1/1531.

151 *The Correspondence of Algernon Swinburne,* 6 vols., ed. Cecil Lang (New Haven, 1959–62), 3:143–44.

152 *Reynolds's,* June 12, 1870, 1.

153 Ibid., July 10, 1870, 4.

154 Ibid.

155 *Daily Telegraph,* May 10, 1871, 5.

156 See Charles Upchurch, "Forgetting the Unthinkable," *Gender and History* 12, no. 1 (April 2000): 127–57, for the argument that these changes reflected a deliberate strategy to efface the larger queer community revealed by the Bow Street hearings and to treat Boulton and Park as exceptional cases.

157 *Reynolds's,* May 29, 1870, 5.

158 DPP 4/6, 641.

159 DPP 4/6, 595.

160 Ibid.

161 Ibid.

162 Ibid., 598.

163 Ibid., 597.

164 Ibid., 599.

165 Ibid., 610.

166 KB 6/3, I, unpaginated.

167 DPP 4/6, 600.

168 Ibid., 610.

169 Ibid., 601.

170 Ibid., 604.

171 Ibid.

172 Ibid., 607.

173 Ibid., 604–5.

174 Ibid., 609.

175 Ibid., 603.

176 Ibid., 604.

177 Ibid., 605.

178 Ibid., 622.

179 Ibid., 612.

180 Ibid., 614.

181 Ibid., 608.

182 Ibid., 608.

183 Ibid., 616.

184 Ibid., 617.

185 Ibid.

186 Ibid., 617–18.

187 Ibid., 618–19.

188 Ibid., 180.

189 Ibid., 199.

190 Ibid., 200.

191 Ibid., 823.

192 Ibid., 868.

193 Ibid.

194 Ibid.

195 DPP 4/6, 869.

196 Ibid., 870.

197 Ibid., 877.

198 Ibid., 872.

199 Ibid., 30.

200 Ibid., 32–33.

201 Ibid., 33.

202 Ibid., 32.

203 Ibid., 37.

204 Ibid., 37.

205 Ibid., 39.

206 Ibid., 40.

207 Ibid., 6–7.

208 Ibid., 29.

209 Ibid., 15.

210 Ibid., 16.

211 Ibid., 19.

212 Ibid., 28.

213 Ibid., 38.

214 Ibid., 36–37. See Paul Fussell, *The Great War and Modern Memory* (New York, 1975), 277–78.

215 DPP 4/6, 23.

216 Ibid., 46.

217 Ibid., 443.

218 Ibid., 461.

219 Ibid., 462.

220 Ibid., 411.

221 Ibid., 415.

222 Ibid., 413–14.

223 Ibid., 431.

224 Ibid., 825.

225 Ibid., 436.

226 Ibid., 426.

227 Ibid., 433.

228 Ibid., 530–31.

229 Ibid., 535.

230 Ibid., 536.

231 Ibid., 538.

232 Ibid., 544.

233 Ibid., 842.

234 Ibid., 471.

235 Ibid., 499–500.

236 Ibid., 481–82.

237 Ibid., 483.

238 Ibid., 503.

239 Ibid., 494.

240 Ibid., 510.

241 Ibid., 513.

242 Ibid., 516.

243 Ibid., 579.

244 Ibid., 584–85.

245 Ibid., 860.

246 Ibid., 590.

247 Ibid., 585.

248 Ibid., 587.

249 Ibid., 591.

250 Ibid., 914.

251 Ibid., 911–13.

252 Ibid., 917.

253 Ibid., 921.

254 Ibid., 916.

255 Ibid., 930–31.

256 Ibid., 933.

257 Ibid., 948.

258 Ibid.

259 Ibid., 951.

260 Ibid.

261 Ibid., 952.

262 Ibid., 953.

263 Ibid., 936.

264 Ibid., 955.

265 Ibid., 964.

266 Ibid., 997.

267 *Penny Illustrated Paper,* May 20, 1871, 31.

268 *The Sins of the Cities of the Plain,* 2 vols. (London, 1881), 96 [89]. The page numbers in brackets refer to analogous passages in the Badboy edition (New York, 1992). Badboy omits the definite article from the title; it is necessary to locate the original in the British Library.

269 H. Montgomery Hyde seems to me to be far off the mark when he writes, regarding the historical John Saul who testified at the Euston libel case in the Cleveland Street affair: "He had given a detailed account of his homosexual activities to the author of *The Sins.*" (Hyde, *Their Good Names,* [London, 1970], 107).

270 A French bookseller named Charles Hirsch said he had sold Oscar Wilde "certain licentious works of a special genre which he euphemistically called 'socratic.' Most of these were in French, but at least one, he recalled was in English. This was *The Sins of the Cities of the Plain.*" (Hyde, *The Other Love,* [London, 1970], 141).

271 Quoted in Colin Simpson, Lewis Chester, and David Leitch, *The Cleveland Street Affair* (Boston, 1976), 59.

272 *Sins,* 1:97 [89].

273 Ibid., 98 [90].

274 Ibid., 100 [91].

275 Ibid., 105 [93].

276 Ibid., 106 [94].

277 Ibid., 2:8 [94].

278 Ibid., 2:20, [103].

279 Ibid., 2:14 [97].

280 Ibid., 2:19–20 [100].

281 Ibid., 1:7 [7].

282 The historical Saul testified at Ernest Parke's libel trial in the Cleveland Street affair that Lord Euston took him in a cab to the male brothel at 19 Cleveland Street after picking him up in Piccadilly. See part 3 below.

283 *Sins,* 1:25–26 [23].

2. LOVE STORIES

1 Benjamin Disraeli, *Coningsby,* ed. Asa Briggs (New York, 1962), vii.

2 *Sins* (London, 1881, 1:27; rpt. New York, 1992, 41).

3 Ibid., 1:28; rpt., 42.

4 Ibid., 1:28; rpt., 43.

5 Ibid., 150; rpt., 171.

6 Ibid., 152; rpt., 172.

7 Symonds, *Memoirs,* 97.

8 Ibid., 98.

9 Ibid., 96–98, 112–16; Grosskurth, *Woeful Victorian,* 30–41.

10 Symonds, *Memoirs,* 94.

11 Quoted in Faith Compton Mackenzie, *William Cory: A Biography* (London, 1950), 42.

12 George N. Curzon to OB, July 20, 1874, British Library, Mss. Eur/f/112/327.

13 Scarborough to OB, July 14, 1874, ibid.

14 William Johnson Cory, "Academicus," quoted in Jonathan Gathorne-Hardy, *The Old School Tie: The Phenomenon of the English Public School* (New York, 1978), 180.

15 From *Ionica* (1858), in Brian Reade, *Sexual Heretics: Male Homosexuality in English Literature from 1850 to 1900* (London, 1970), 68.

16 Quoted in Gathorne-Hardy, *Old School Tie,* 188.

17 Quoted in Gathorne-Hardy, *Old School Tie, 186.*

18 Quoted in Lees-Milne, *Enigmatic Edwardian,* 8.

19 See especially Arthur C. Benson, biographical introduction to William Cory, *Ionica* (London, 1905), and the response of Mackenzie, *William Cory,* 17–18.

20 Benson, biographical introduction, xix–xx.

21 Reade, *Sexual Heretics,* 10.

22 Timothy d'Arch Smith, *Love in Earnest: Some Notes on the Lives and Writings of English Uranian Poets from 1889 to 1930* (London, 1970), 9.

23 Symonds, *Letters* 1:178.

24 The Journal of William Johnson Cory, October 16, 1868, 1 vol., ESHR 9/1, Esher Archives, Churchill College, Cambridge, hereafter WJC journal.

25 Symonds, *Letters,* 3:412.

26 Symonds, *Memoirs,* 109–10.

27 Ibid., 110. Greek in original; translation in brackets is by the editor.

28 *Letters of Swinburne,* 2:202.

29 Reginald Brett to Charles Williamson, January 5, 1892, 2 vols., ESHR 8/3–8/4, Esher Archives, hereafter RB to CW. Not paginated.

30 RB to CW, October 27, 1892.

31 RB to CW, October 31, 1892.

32 WJC journal, July 19, 1868.

33 Ibid.

34 Quoted ibid.

35 Ibid.

36 William Johnson Cory to Reginald Brett, July 1868, ESHR 9/3, 11–12; 10 vols., ESHR 9/3–9/12, Esher Archives, hereafter WJC to RB. Paginated.

37 Ibid., 19–20. June 30, 1808.

38 Ibid., 40.

39 Ibid., 22.

40 Ibid., 33.

41 Ibid., 38.

42 Ibid., 41.

43 Ibid., 42.

44 Ibid.

45 WJC journal, August 12, 1868.

46 Ibid., August 23, 1868.

47 Ibid., August 26, 1868.

48 WJC to RB, July 23, 1868, ESHR 9/3, 44–45.

49 WJC journal, August 23, 1868.

50 Ibid., August 26, 1868.

51 Ibid., August 27, 1868.

52 Ibid.

53 Ibid., September 10, 1868.

54 Ibid., September 2, 1868.

55 Ibid., "Today (Sunday)" between September 27 and October 4, 1868.

56 WJC to RB, December 31, 1868, ESHR 9/3, 58.

57 Reginald Brett journals, October 16, 1875; 10 vols., ESHR 2/1–2/10, Esher Archives, hereafter RB journals, not always paginated.

58 Ibid.

59 WJC journal, September 5, 1868.

60 Ibid., October 16, 1868.

61 Ibid.

62 Ibid., n.d., between October 16 and 21, 1868.

63 Ibid.

64 Ibid., September 27, 1868.

65 Ibid.

66 Ibid., October 4, 1868.

67 Ibid.

68 Ibid., October 8, 1868.

69 Ibid., October 21, 1868.

70 Ibid., October 25, 1868.

71 Ibid., October 29, 1868.

72 WJC to RB, July 23, 1868, 51–52.

73 Ibid., 55.

74 Ibid., 57.

75 Ibid., 61–62.

76 Ibid., 64.

77 Ibid., 65.

78 Ibid.

79 Ibid.

80 Ibid.

81 Ibid., 63.

82 Ibid.,67.

83 Ibid.

84 Ibid.

85 Ibid., 69.

86 Ibid.

87 Ibid., 70.

88 Ibid., 70–71.

89 RB journals, April 4, 1870.

90 Ibid.

91 RB journals, October 28, 1868, quoted in Lees-Milne, *Enigmatic Edwardian,* 13.

92 RB journals, April 9, 1870.

93 RB journals, January 1877, quoting FE to WJC, July 21, 1869.

94 Lees-Milne, *Enigmatic Edwardian,* 17.

95 RB journals, April 3, 1871 .

96 Ibid., April 5, 1871.

97 Ibid.

98 Ibid., April 18, 1871.

99 Ibid., July 1871.

100 Ibid., March 29, 1872.

101 Ibid., April 9, 1872.

102 Ibid., April 14, 1872.

103 Ibid., April 26, 1872.

104 Ibid., May 14, 1872.

105 Ibid., May 15, 1872.

106 Ibid., May 18, 1872.

107 Ibid., n.d., ESHR 9/4.

108 RB to CW, February 22, 1893.

109 RB to CW, January 24, 1893.

110 RB journals, August 4, 1872, 49.

111 WJC to RB, August 11, 1872, 2.

112 Ibid., August 22, 1872, 4–5.

113 RB journals, August 9, 1872, 49–51.

114 Ibid., August 28, 1873, 94.

115 Ibid., 100.

116 WJC to RB, October 19, 1872, 15–16.

117 Ibid., n.d., 69.

118 Ibid., November 2, 1874, 151.

119 Ibid., December 6, 1874, 165.

120 Ibid., November 2, 1874, 152–53.

121 Ibid., July 31, 1873, 71.

122 Ibid., July 31, 1873, 72–73.

123 Ibid., 74.

124 Ibid., November 29, 1872, 20.

125 Ibid., December 27, 1872, 28.

126 Ibid., January 13, 1873.

127 Ibid., April 20, 1873, 43–44.

128 Ibid., February 7, 1877.

129 Ibid., February 26, 1874, 124.

130 Ibid., February 7, 1877.

131 Ibid., November 19, 1877.

132 RB journals, February 12, 1875, 91.

133 Ibid., 92.

134 Ibid., March 24, 1875, 114.

135 Ibid.

136 Ibid., April 9, 1875, 145.

137 Ibid., November 20, 1875.

138 Ibid.

139 Ibid., July 27, 1876.

140 Lees-Milne, *Enigmatic Edwardian,* 29.

141 RB journals, March 6, 1875, 106.

142 Ibid., February 16, 1875, 97.

143 Ibid., March 6, 1875, 106.

144 Ibid., March 8, 1875, 108.

145 Ibid., April 9, 1875, 145.

146 Ibid., June 1, 1877; quoted in Lees-Milne, *Enigmatic Edwardian,* 41.

147 RB journals, November 11, 1875.

148 Ibid., November 17, 1875.

149 Ibid., December 2, 1875.

150 Ibid., December 31, 1875.

151 Ibid., November 29, 1872, 20.

152 Ibid., November 2, 1874, 151.

153 Ibid., 152.

154 WJC to RB, n.d. [1875], ESHR 9/5, 103–4.

155 Ibid., 135.

156 Ibid., 74.

157 Ibid., 135.

158 WJC to RB, March 2, 1876.

159 RB journals, September 26, 1876.

160 Howard Sturgis to RB, January 10, 1877, ESHR 10/17.

161 RB journals, September 26, 1876.

162 Ibid.

163 George Binning to RB, December 17, 1877, ESHR 10/13.

164 RB journals, September 26, 1876.

165 George Binning to RB, December 17, 1877, ESHR 10/13.

166 WJC to RB, November 3, 1876.

167 Ibid.

168 RB journals, December 31, 1878; January 6, 1877.

169 Ibid., June 8, 1877.

170 Quoted in Mackenzie, *William Cory,* 96.

171 Ibid., 97.

172 Quoted in Lees-Milne, *Enigmatic Edwardian,* 42.

173 WJC to RB, March 3, 1878.

174 WJC journal, July 19, 1868.

175 WJC to RB, Eve of St. Mark, 1868.

176 Ibid., September 25, 1878.

177 Ibid., March 28, 1879.

178 Ibid., July 31, 1879.

179 RB journals, August 4, 1877.

180 RB to Curzon, February 14, 1878, BL Mss. Eur/f/112/327.

181 RB journal, September 12, 1878.

182 RB to Curzon, December 4, 1878, BL Mss. Eur/f/112/327.

183 RB journals, November 22, 1878, 83.

184 Ibid., January 6, 1878.

185 Ibid., November 3, 1878, 90–91.

186 Ibid., August 13, 1878.

187 Ibid., September 12, 1878.

188 WJC to RB, June 3, 1877, quoted in Lees-Milne.

189 Ibid.

190 Nelly Brett to RB, quoted in Lees-Milne, *Enigmatic Edwardian,* 48.

191 RB to Nelly Brett, ibid., 49.

192 Ibid.

193 Ibid.

194 Lees-Milne, *Enigmatic Edwardian,* 48.

195 WJC to RB, July 31, 1879. The typescript of Cory's letter was torn to omit the long

Notes to Pages 143–151

discussion of marriage, but the intact autograph remains in the archive, ESHR 9/2.

196 WJC to RB, September 9, 1879. The top portion of this letter, preceding the quoted passage, was torn off.

197 RB journals, October 24, 1879, 85.

198 RB journals, October 20, 1879, 83.

199 RB to Curzon, October 24, 1879, BL Mss. Eur/f/112/327.

200 Ibid., August 14, 1879.

201 RB journals, November 3, 1879, 90.

202 Quoted in Mackenzie, *William Cory*, 141.

203 Ibid., 150.

204 Ibid., 141.

205 RB to CW, January 5, 1892.

206 Ibid., January 22, 1892.

207 RB to CW, February 6, 1892.

208 Ibid.

209 Ibid.

210 RB to CW, August 25, 1892.

211 Ibid., October 23, 1892.

212 Ibid., October 31, 1892.

213 Ibid., January 24, 1893.

214 Ibid., February 8, 1892.

215 Ibid., February 1, 1893.

216 Ibid., July 24, 1893.

217 Ibid., September 24, 1893.

218 Ibid., February 8, 1892.

219 Ibid., September 20, 1892.

220 Ibid., February 2, 1893.

221 Ibid., February 12, 1893.

222 Ibid., April 6, 1893.

223 Ibid., April 10, 1893, emphasis in original.

224 Ibid., April 11, 1893.

225 Ibid., April 6, 1893.

226 Ibid., July 6, 1893.

227 Ibid., July 7, 1893.

228 Ibid., July 11, 1893.

229 Ibid., January 12, 1893.

230 Ibid., August 21, 1893.

231 Ibid., September 3, 1893.

232 Ibid.

233 Ibid., August 19, 1894.

234 Ibid.

235 Ibid., January 12, 1893.

236 Ibid., January 24, 1893.

237 Ibid., November 13, 1892.

238 Ibid., October 18, 1893.

239 Ibid., January 18, 1896.

240 Ibid.

241 Ibid.

242 Ibid., March 20, 1896.

243 Ibid.

244 Ibid., April 6, 1897.

245 Symonds, *Memoirs,* 272.

246 RB to CW, October 31, 1892.

247 Ibid.

248 Ibid.

249 Ibid., November 17, 1892.

250 Ibid., January 1, 1893.

251 Ibid., January 24, 1893.

252 Ibid.

253 Ibid., February 1, 1893.

254 Ibid., February 22, 1893.

255 Ibid.

256 Ibid, May 22, 1893.

257 Ibid., January 11, 1895.

258 Ibid.

259 Ibid., March 18, 1895.

260 Ibid., January 12, 1893.

261 Ibid., September 22, 1897.

262 Ibid., July 23, 1897.

263 Ibid.

264 Ibid.

265 Mackenzie, *William Cory,* 42.

266 RB to CW, September 9, 1997.

267 Quoted in Lees-Milne, *Enigmatic Edwardian,* 352.

3. WEST END SCANDALS

1 RB journals, ESHR 2/8, flyleaf.

2 Quoted in Simpson et al., *Cleveland Street Affair,* 68. This part of the book is based on my own investigation of the primary materials at the Public Records Office, the Esher papers in the archives at Churchill College, Cambridge, and the newspaper collection of the British Library at Collindale. Wherever possible I have referred readers to quotations from already published sources. If not indicated, the quotations are taken from the archival files. Most of the documents in ques-

tion are to be found in the files at the Public Records Office, London, DPP 1/95, 1–7.

3 Quoted in H. Montgomery Hyde, *The Cleveland Street Scandal* (New York, 1976), 30.

4 Quoted in Simpson et al., *Cleveland Street Affair,* 74.

5 Hyde, *Cleveland Street Scandal;* and Simpson et al., *Cleveland Street Affair.*

6 I owe this observation to Michael Levenson.

7 *Echo,* November 11, 1989.

8 *Truth,* November 14, 1989.

9 Quoted in Simpson et al., *Cleveland Street Affair,* 105.

10 Ibid., 106.

11 *Pall Mall Gazette,* July 6, 1885, 5.

12 For a detailed analysis of "Maiden Tribute" and its effects, see Judith Walkowitz, *City of Dreadful Delight: Narratives of Sexual Danger in Late Victorian London* (Chicago, 1988), 81–134.

13 *Pall Mall Gazette,* July 6, 1885, 2.

14 Ibid.

15 RB journals, July 15, 1885.

16 Ibid.

17 Ibid.

18 Ibid.

19 RB journals, April 3, 1891.

20 Frank Harris, *My Life and Loves* (1922–27; New York, 1991), 144.

21 *Hansard Parliamentary Debates;* 3d series (London, 1890), August 6, 1885, 1397.

22 *Reynolds's,* July 19, 1885. Quoted in Walkowitz, *City of Dreadful Delight,* 278–79 n. 123.

23 Louise A. Jackson, *Child Sexual Abuse in Victorian England* (New York, 2000), 100–101.

24 Quoted in Hyde, *The Other Love,* 128. I rely on his account of this affair, 128–33.

25 Quoted in ibid., 129.

26 *Times,* July 3, 4, 5, 7, 8, 1884.

27 Quoted in Hyde, *The Other Love,* 130.

28 Ibid., 132.

29 Hyde, *The Other Love,* 132.

30 Ibid., 133.

31 Ibid., 132–33.

32 *Hansard Parliamentary Debates,* 3d series (London, 1890), 341:1534.

33 Ibid., 1535.

34 Ibid., 1541.

35 *North London Press,* September 28, 1889.

36 Ibid.

37 *Reynolds's,* September 29, 1889.

38 Ibid.

39 Ibid., emphasis in original.

40 Hyde, *Cleveland Street Scandal*, 112.

41 Ibid.

42 *Truth,* January 2, 1890.

43 See Joseph Bristow, *Vice and Vigilance: Purity Movements in Britain since 1700* (Dublin, 1977).

44 Harris, *My Life and Loves,* 640.

45 RB journals, January 18, 1886.

46 Ibid., February 19, 1886.

47 Ibid., February 24, 1886.

48 Ibid., July 31, 1892.

49 Ibid.

50 H. Montgomery Hyde, *A Tangled Web: Sex Scandals in British Politics and Society* (London, 1986), 111–45.

51 Ibid., 126–45.

52 Lord Durham to RB, November 11, 1890, quoted in Lees-Milne, *Enigmatic Edwardian,* 83.

53 RB journals, November 19, 1890.

54 Ibid., November 25, 1890.

55 Ibid., November 27, 1890.

56 Ibid.

57 RB journals, December 1, 1890.

58 See Harry Cocks, *Abominable Crimes: Sodomy Trials in English Law and Culture, 1830–1889,* Ph.D. diss., Department of History, University of Manchester, 1998.

59 See Crompton, *Byron and Greek Love;* and Norton, *Mother Clap's Molly House.*

60 See the data collected in the early chapters of Crompton, *Byron and Greek Love.*

61 Recent empirical work has challenged the frequent assertion that the 1885 amendment effectively transformed the legal treatment of same-sex conduct. Patterns of police and judicial enforcement did not substantially change after its passage. See Cocks, *Abominable Crimes.*

62 Michel Foucault, *The History of Sexuality,* vol.1, *An Introduction* (New York, 1976), 43.

63 Simpson et al., *Cleveland Street Affair,* 68.

64 Ibid., 123.

65 The reference to "perverted telegraph boys" in the *Scots Observer*'s review of Wilde's *Dorian Gray,* quoted in the epigraph to this section, is the only one I found.

66 Simpson et al., *Cleveland Street Affair,* 131.

67 Hyde, *Cleveland Street Scandal,* 53.

68 Smith, *Love in Earnest,* 29.

69 An aversion to anal penetration, whatever the role played, appears in Symonds's *Memoirs* as well.

70 Bray, *Homosexuality in Renaissance England;* Trumbach, "Birth of the Queen."

71 The sodomite is a close relative of the rake, virtually indistinguishable from him, in fact. And the rake is godfather at least to the nineteenth-century dandy. See Trumbach, "Birth of the Queen."

72 Symonds, *Letters,* 3:554.

73 George Bernard Shaw, *Collected Letters* (New York, 1965), 1:230.

74 Ibid., 131.

75 Quoted in Simpson et al., *Cleveland Street Affair,* 73.

76 Ibid., 123.

77 Ibid., 130.

78 A difficult question about the conduct of Parke's defense is why it failed to call Newlove, who had named Euston and who should have been available, since he had pleaded guilty and was in jail.

79 Harris, *My Life and Loves,* 336.

80 Quoted in Simpson et al., *Cleveland Street Affair,* 153.

81 Ibid.

82 Ibid., 144.

83 *Truth,* January 23, 1890.

84 Quoted in Hyde, *Cleveland Street Scandal,* 159–60.

85 Ibid., 156.

86 Ibid., 158–59.

87 Ibid., 158. Hyde writes that these passages came from the same editorial. In fact, the first appeared on January 23, 1890, 156–57; the second, on January 30, 204.

88 Quoted in Hyde, *Cleveland Street Scandal,* 160.

89 *Truth,* January 23, 1890.

90 Harris, *My Life and Loves,* 337.

91 Quoted in Simpson et al., *Cleveland Street Affair,* 163–64.

92 Ibid., 164.

93 Ibid., 163.

94 Ibid.

95 Ibid., 164–65.

96 Quoted in Hyde, *Cleveland Street Scandal,* 157.

97 *Morning Post,* January 16, 1890.

98 Smith, *Love in Earnest,* 169.

99 Saul statement, PPP 1/95, National Archives, Kew.

100 *Prostitution and Victorian Society* (Cambridge, UK, 1980), Judith Walkowitz stresses that one of the effects of the Contagious Diseases Acts was to transform prostitution from an occasional activity of hard-pressed working-class women into a full-time "profession" with stigmatized social status.

101 He referred to a recent stint at the Drury Lane Theater in connection with "The Royal Oak," but did not say what his work had been.

102 I owe this insight to Tracy Strong.

103 *North London Press,* January 11, 1890, 8. The first two stanzas are reprinted in Simpson et al., *Cleveland Street Affair,* 117–18.

104 Quoted in Hyde, *Cleveland Street Scandal,* 96.

105 Lord Arthur Somerset to RB, December 3, 1889, ESHR 12/3. Not paginated.

106 *St. James Gazette,* November 26, 1889.

107 LAS to RB, December 5, 1889.

108 Quoted in Hyde, *Cleveland Street Scandal,* 101.

109 Ibid., 43.

110 Ibid., 43.

111 Ibid., 43–44.

112 Hugh Wequelin to RB, September 9, 1890, quoted ibid., 42.

113 *North London Press,* January 11, 1890.

114 Quoted in Hyde, *Cleveland Street Scandal,* 214.

115 Ibid., 87.

116 Ibid., 99.

117 See Grosskurth, *Woeful Victorian.*

118 Symonds, *Memoirs,* 253.

119 Ibid., 253–54.

120 Ibid., 254.

121 Ibid., 255.

122 It is puzzling that while Grosskurth includes some shorter extracts from this material she omits entirely Catherine's account of their courtship and first year of marriage, which Symonds included in full. See the Symonds manuscript, London Library.

123 Symonds, *Memoirs,* 260–61. Symonds does not quote Catherine's words on this matter, as he so frequently does elsewhere in his memoirs.

124 Ibid.

125 Ibid., 266.

126 Ibid., 263.

127 Ibid., 272.

128 Ibid., 273.

129 For a more systematic examination of the role of fantasy in constructing sexual subjects and the objects of their desire, see Kaplan, *Sexual Justice,* chap. 4.

130 H. Montgomery Hyde, *A History of Pornography* (London, 1964), 149–50.

131 *Sins,* 2:100–107, 107–17, 118–22. All quotations are from the 1881 edition, a copy of which I examined at the British Library and which I quote with permission. In brackets I will provide references to comparable passages when they occur in the 1992 Badboy version, which is more easily accessible but not reliable.

132 *Sins,* 1:7–9 [7–8].

133 Sigmund Freud, *Three Essays on the Theory of Sexuality* (New York, 1975), 10.

134 *Sins,* 1:9 [8].

135 Ibid. [9].

136 Ibid., 10.

137 Ibid., 11 [11].

138 Ibid., 12–13 [12].

139 Ibid., 19 [16].

140 Ibid., 25–26 [23].

141 Ibid., 83–84 [80].

142 Symonds, *Letters,* 3:813.

143 *Sins,* 1:86–87 [82].

144 Ibid., 89 [83].

4. WILDE'S TIME

1 *Scots Observer,* July 5, 1890, quoted in Holland, *Irish Peacock,* 77.

2 See especially Alan Sinfield, *The Wilde Century: Effeminacy, Oscar Wilde, and the Queer Moment* (New York, 1994).

3 Oscar Wilde, *The Complete Letters,* ed. Merlin Holland and Rupert Hart Davis (London, 2000), 321.

4 Symonds, *Letters,* 3:477.

5 Richard Ellmann, *Oscar Wilde* (London, 1987), 324–25.

6 Hyde, *Trials,* 76.

7 Ellmann, *Oscar Wilde,* 365.

8 Hyde, *Trials,* 69–70.

9 Quoted in Holland, *Irish Peacock,* 216.

10 Ellmann, *Oscar Wilde,* 402.

11 Ibid., italics and punctuation in original.

12 Holland, *Irish Peacock,* 58.

13 Ibid., 36, 58.

14 Ibid., 59.

15 Hyde, *Trials,* 77–78.

16 Lees-Milne, *Enigmatic Edwardian,* 98.

17 OW to Robert Ross, November 1896, in Wilde, *Complete Letters,* 670, ellipsis in original.

18 OW to AD, January–March 1897, in ibid., 690.

19 Ibid., 691.

20 Holland, *Irish Peacock,* 285–86.

21 Quoted in ibid., 22.

22 Ibid., 290–91.

23 Ibid., 29–30, 47–50.

24 Hyde, *Trials,* 232–33.

25 Ibid., 67–68.

26 See Cohen, *Sex Scandal,* chap. 6.

27 Holland, *Irish Peacock,* 45.

28 Quoted in ibid., 64.

29 Ibid., 77.

30 Ibid., 164.

31 Ibid.

32 Ibid., 165, parentheses and italics in original.

33 Holland, *Irish Peacock,* 151.

34 Quoted in ibid., 166, parentheses and italics in original.

35 Ibid., 175, parentheses and italics in original.

36 Ibid., 159.

37 Ibid., 156.

38 Ibid., 158.

39 Hyde, *Trials,* 173.

40 Quoted in ibid., 229.

41 Quoted in Holland, *Irish Peacock,* 180.

42 *Daily Chronicle,* August 14, 1894.

43 Quoted in Hyde, *Trials,* 173.

44 Quoted in Holland, *Irish Peacock,* 207.

45 Ibid., 209.

46 Ibid., 255.

47 Ibid., 256.

48 Ibid., 257.

49 Ibid., 260.

50 Ibid., 261.

51 Ibid., 257–58.

52 Ibid., 270.

53 Ibid., 253.

54 Ibid., 254.

55 Ibid., 274.

56 Ibid., 275.

57 Ibid., 273.

58 Ibid., 274.

59 Ibid., 279.

60 *National Observer,* April 6, 1895, quoted in Hyde, *Trials,* 156.

61 Quoted in Hyde, *Trials,* 151.

62 Ibid., 161–62.

63 Ibid., 151–52.

64 Hyde, *Trials,* 159n.

65 Ibid., 167.

66 *Evening Standard,* April 6, 1895, quoted in Ed Cohen, *Talk on the Wilde Side: Toward a Genealogy of a Discourse on Male Sexualities* (New York, 1993), 175.

67 *Reynolds's,* April 21, 1895, 4.

68 *Observer,* May 6, 2001, 12, reporting on the newly discovered witness statements made to Queensberry's detectives. The courtroom testimony was not quite so vivid in contemporary reports.

69 Quoted in Hyde, *Trials,* 268.

70 Ibid., 201.

71 Hyde, *Trials,* 190, quoting Lord Alfred Douglas, *Autobiography,* 2nd ed., 119.

72 Hyde, *Trials,* 239–40.

73 Quoted in ibid., 259.

74 Ibid., 262.

75 Ibid., 263.

76 Ibid., 272.

77 Ibid., 224.

78 Ibid.

79 Ibid., 164.

80 Ibid., 346.

81 Michael S. Foldy, *The Trials of Oscar Wilde: Deviance, Morality, and Late Victorian Society* (New Haven, 1997), 21–30.

82 Holland, *Irish Peacock,* 294–95.

83 Wilde, *Complete Letters,* 714.

84 RB to Rosebery, June 2, 1895, ESHR 10/10.

85 RB to CW, March 14, 1985, ESHR 8/3.

86 RB journals, March 14, 1895, ESHR 2/10.

87 Ibid.

88 Quoted in Hyde, *Trials,* 340–41.

89 Wilde, *Complete Letters,* 788n. 2.

EPILOGUE

1 *Reynolds's,* April 14, 1895, 1.

2 Ibid., April 21, 1895, 1.

3 Ibid., May 5, 1895, 1.

4 Ibid., May 26, 1895, 1.

5 Ibid., April 28, 1895, 5.

6 Ibid., May 12, 1895, 5.

7 Ibid., April 21, 1895, 5.

8 Ibid., May 12, 1895, 2.

9 Ibid., May 26, 1895, 5.

10 RB to CW, July 11, 1896, ESHR 8/3.

11 RB journals, March 21, 1895, ESHR 2/10.

12 RB to CW, May 1895, ESHR 8/3.

13 Quoted in Sinfield, *The Wilde* Century, 96.

14 Ibid., 97. The additions in brackets are Sinfield's.
15 Wilde, *Complete Letters,* 729.
16 Ibid., 757–58.
17 Ibid., 759.
18 Ibid., 730.
19 Ibid.
20 Quoted in Sinfield, *The Wilde Century,* 125–26.

SUGGESTIONS FOR FURTHER READING

The impulse and inspiration for this book came from an essay by Jeffrey Weeks, "Inverts, Perverts, and Mary-annes: Male Prostitution and the Regulation of Homosexuality in the Nineteenth and Early Twentieth Centuries," in *Hidden from History: Reclaiming the Gay and Lesbian Past,* edited by Martin Duberman, Martha Vicinus, and George Chauncey (New York, 1989). That collection also includes relevant essays by Duberman, Vicinus, and Randolph Trumbach. Weeks's *Coming Out: Homosexual Politics in Britain from the Nineteenth Century to the Present* (London, 1977), remains the best general introduction. His *Sex, Politics, and Society: The Regulation of Sexuality Since 1800* (London, 1981), situates homosexuality in the context of broader issues.

Many of the figures considered here appear in Neal Bartlett's *Who Was That Man? A Gift for Mr. Oscar Wilde* (London, 1988), a brilliant essay from the perspective of a gay Londoner in the 1980s. Two very recent books importantly expand our knowledge of nineteenth-century British homoeroticism: Harry Cocks's *Nameless Offenses: Homosexual Desire in the Nineteenth Century* (London, 2003), explores patterns of law enforcement earlier in the century and cultural contexts outside London; Matt Cook's *London and the Culture of Homosexuality, 1885–1914* (Cambridge, 2003), examines literary works and makes illuminating use of personal diaries and notebooks. Matt Houlbrook's *Queer London* will extend the story into the first half of the twentieth century (Chicago, forthcoming 2005).

Graham Robb's, *Strangers: Homosexual Love in the Nineteenth Century* (London, 2003), offers interesting perspectives on France especially, but is superficial and derivative in its treatment of Britain. An earlier generation of historiography, sometimes still useful, is represented by H. Montgomery Hyde, *The Other Love: An Historical and Contemporary Survey of Homosexuality in Britain* (London, 1970), and Rupert Croft Cooke, *Feasting With Panthers: A New Consideration of Some Late Victorian Writers* (London, 1967).

Alan Sinfield's *The Wilde Century: Effeminacy, Oscar Wilde and the Queer Moment* (New York, 1994), explores the ways that the events of this period affected understandings of homoeroticism well into the twentieth century. Joseph Bristow's *Effeminate England: Homoerotic Writing after 1885* (Buckingham, U.K., 1995) has chapters on Symonds, Wilde, Firbank, and Forster; Richard Dellamora's *Masculine Desire: The Sexual Politics of Victorian Aestheticism* (Durham, N.C., 1990) is especially good on Pater. Linda Dowling's *Hellenism and Homosexuality in Victorian Oxford* (Ithaca, 1994), illuminates the curricular and pedagogical contexts shared by Pater, Symonds, and Wilde.

Eve Kosofsky Sedgwick's *Love between Men: English Literature and Male Homosocial Desire* (New York, 1985), is a groundbreaking study with an important appendix on the cult of Whitman in nineteenth-century England.

For an earlier period in Britain, the classic study is Alan Bray, *Homosexuality in Renaissance England* (London, 1982). See also Seth Koven, *Slumming: Sexual and Social Politics in Victorian London* (Princeton, 2004). Rictor Norton's *Mother Clap's Molly House: The Gay Subculture in England, 1700–1830* (London, 1992), presents a great deal of useful material, though its interpretive framework is problematic and the writing often over the top. Louis Crompton's *Byron and Greek Love: Homophobia in Nineteenth-century England* (Berkeley, 1985), encompasses more than its title suggests. It is gracefully written and includes an important discussion of Jeremy Bentham's unpublished writings on sodomy. Cynthia Herrup's *A House in Gross Disorder: Sex, Law, and the 2nd Earl of Castlehaven,* is an exemplary treatment of the micropolitics of the Castlehaven sodomy trial in 1631 and its reception in subsequent periods.

For a more general treatment of the intersections of sexuality and urban culture in late nineteenth-century London, see Judith Walkowitz, *City of Dreadful Delight: Narratives of Sexual Danger in Late Victorian London* (Chicago, 1988). Her more specialized study, *Prostitution and Victorian Society: Women, Class, and the State* (Cambridge, U.K., 1980), is especially good on the Contagious Diseases Acts. She makes convincing links among sexuality, gender, and social class. Two important studies of women, prostitution, and urban culture are: Amanda Anderson, *Tainted Souls and Painted Faces: The Rhetoric of Fallenness in Victorian Culture* (Ithaca, 1993), and Deborah Epstein Nord, *Walking the Victorian Streets: Women, Representation, and the City* (Ithaca, 1995).

Edward Bristow's *Vice and Vigilance: Purity Movements in Britain since 1700* (Dublin, 1977), provides a good account of the moral reform movements, while Frank Mort links them to developments in public health in *Dangerous Sexualities: Medico-Moral Politics in England since 1830* (London, 1987). The Dublin Castle and Parnell affairs are well treated in H. Montgomery Hyde, *A Tangled Web: Sex Scandal in British Politics and Society* (London, 1986). Roy Jenkins's *Sir Charles Dilke: A Victorian Tragedy,* is a sympathetic and detailed account of its subject.

For the general linkage among homosexuality, modernity, and urban culture, see Henning Bech, *Where Men Meet* (Chicago, 1999). An excellent specific study that also illuminates this theme is George Chauncey, *Gay New York: Gender, Urban Culture, and the Makings of the Gay Male World, 1890–1940* (New York, 1994).

The phenomenon of romantic friendship and its relation to sexual intimacy has been a formative topic in lesbian history. For Britain, see Lillian Faderman, *Surpassing the Love of Men* (New York, 1981), and Martha Vicinus, *Independent Women: Work and Community for Single Women, 1850–1920* (Chicago, 1985) and *Intimate Friends: Women Who Loved Women, 1778–1928* (Chicago, 2004). For the United States, see Carroll Smith-Rosenberg, "The Female World of Love and Ritual," in *Disorderly Conduct: Visions of Gender in Victorian America* (New York, 1985).

Romantic friendships between men have received less attention. For the nineteenth-century United States, see Jonathan Ned Katz, *Love Stories: Sex between Men before Homosexuality* (Chicago, 2001), which includes not only such icons as Walt Whitman and Abraham Lincoln but also John Safford Fiske in the years after the Boulton and Park trial. For eighteenth-century Britain, see George E. Haggerty, *Men in Love: Masculinity and Sexuality in the Eighteenth Century* (New York, 1999).

Fanny and Stella do not fare well in William Roughead's *Bad Companions: Lives of Criminals* (Edinburgh, 1930), Peter Ackroyd's *Dressing Up: Tranvestism and Drag. The History of An Obsession* (London, 1979), or Croft Cooke's *Feasting with Panthers*. Far more sympathetic is Lawrence Senelick, *The Changing Room: Sex, Drag, and Theatre* (London, 2000), who claims to have discovered evidence that Boulton eventually pursued a theatrical career in the United States. The best recent treatments are Bartlett's *Who Was That Man?* and William A. Cohen's *Sex Scandal: The Private Parts of Victorian Fiction* (Durham, N.C., 1996). Cohen makes good use of *The Sins of the Cities of the Plain* and has a concluding chapter on Wilde as well.

The Eton scandals of the 1870s have not received much attention from recent historians of male homoeroticism. James Kincaid, *Child Loving: The Erotic Child and Victorian Culture* (New York, 1992), offers a provocative discussion of Browning and Cory but makes stronger assumptions about their sexual conduct than the evidence will bear. Both men, along with the Harrow headmaster Vaughan, appear in W. C. Lubenow, *The Cambridge Apostle, 1820–1914: Liberalism, Imagination, and Friendship in British Intellectual and Professional Life* (Cambridge, UK, 1998), but their scandalous departures are veiled in discretion.

Faith Compton Mackenzie's *William Cory: A Biography* (London, 1950), is traditional and respectful with a selection of his poetry. Ian Anstruther's *Oscar Browning: A Biography* (London, 1983), is candid about sexual matters, though the author's dislike of his subject is too evident. James Lees-Milne's *The Enigmatic Edwardian: The Life of Reginald Brett, 2nd Viscount Esher* (London, 1986), is comprehensive and treats Brett's erotic life with considerable candor. Both Brett and Cory appear in Timothy d'Arch Smith, *Love in Earnest: Some Notes on the Lives and Writings of English Uranian Poets from 1889 to 1930* (London, 1970). Paul Fussell illuminates the influence of pastoral elegy and Uranian love poetry on Wilfred Owen and Siegfried Sassoon in *The Great War and Modern Memory* (New York, 1975).

The West End scandals received extensive treatment in two books when the files were opened to scholars for the first time: H. Montgomery Hyde, *The Cleveland Street Scandal* (London, 1976), and Colin Simpson, Lewis Chester, and David Leitch, *The Cleveland Street Affair* (London, 1976). Both studies, written immediately after the Watergate scandals, are more concerned with the cover-up and political scandal than with the sexual narratives. Neither considers John Saul in any detail. Hyde appears to have had access to materials from the Somerset family, which increase his study's human interest. The affair is also discussed in Richard Dellamora, *Masculine Desire*.

Phyllis Grosskurth's *The Woeful Victorian: A Biography of John Addington Symonds* (New York, 1974), is groundbreaking and detailed but suffers from the assumption embedded in her title. Grosskurth's edition of his *Memoirs* (Chicago, 1984), remains the best source, along with *The Letters of John Addington Symonds,* edited by Herbert M. Schueller and Robert L. Peters (Detroit, 1967), in three volumes. Symonds receives sympathetic treatment in Paul Robinson, *Gay Lives* (Chicago, 1999).

Symonds's writings receive critical attention in: Oliver Buxton, *Secret Selves: Confession and Same-Sex Desire in Victorian Autobiography* (Chapel Hill, 1995); Eric A. Clarke, *Virtuous Vice: Homoeroticism in the Public Sphere* (Durham, N.C., 1999); Ruth Vanita, *Sappho and the Virgin Mary: Same-Sex Love and the English Literary Imagination* (New York, 1996); Wayne Koestenbaum, *Double Talk: The Dynamics of Male Literary Collaboration* (New York, 1989); and Scott Bravmann, *Queer Fictions of the Past: History, Culture, and Difference* (Cambridge, U.K., 1997).

The classic analysis of Victorian pornography is Steven Marcus, *The Other Victorians* (New York, 1966). However, his neglect of *The Sins of the Cities of the Plain* allows him to argue that sex between men is not explicitly portrayed but displaced onto scenes of flagellation. William Cohen makes effective use of *Sins* in his chapter on Boulton and Park, but it has otherwise eluded scholarly attention. Although not completely faithful to the 1881 edition in the British Library, the Badboy edition of the text (New York, 1992) is the best way to learn more about it.

There is an enormous body of literature on Oscar Wilde's life and work. *The Complete Letters,* edited by Merlin Holland and Rupert Hart Davis (London, 2000) is invaluable and a great read. Richard Ellmann's *Oscar Wilde* (London, 1987), is comprehensive and detailed. Neil McKenna's *The Secret Life of Oscar Wilde* (London, 2003), uses the statements made by witnesses to Queensberry's detectives and has unearthed correspondence and diaries of a number of Wilde's associates. However, McKenna has a tendency to treat every allegation as fact, even from people he characterizes as proven liars. Douglas Murray's *Bosie: The Life of Lord Alfred Douglas* (London, 2000), is scrupulously researched but suffers from an uncritical admiration of its subject.

Merlin Holland's *Irish Peacock and Scarlet Marquess: The Real Trial of Oscar Wilde* (London, 2003), is the most detailed record of the libel trial, though it does not give the provenance of the transcript used. H. Montgomery Hyde's *The Trials of Oscar Wilde* (London, 1948; New York, 1973), remains the best account of the criminal trials. Ed Cohen, *Talk on the Wilde Side: Toward a Genealogy of a Discourse on Male Sexualities* (New York, 1993), focuses on the moral panic around sexuality and representations of Wilde in the press accounts of the trials. Regenia Gagnier's *Idylls of the Market Place: Oscar Wilde and the Victorian Public* (Stanford, Calif., 1986), deals more broadly with Wilde's relations to commodity culture. Michael S. Foldy's *The Trials of Oscar Wilde: Deviance, Morality, and Late Victorian Society* (New Haven, 1997), probes the cultural context but is unpersuasive in portraying Wilde as a Sadean rebel. Foldy pays close attention to the crisis within the Liberal Party, making the best case yet for Rosebery's personal stake in the prosecution.

Recent work in the history of sexuality has been profoundly influenced by theory.

The issues raised by Michel Foucault's *The History of Sexuality, vol. 1, An Introduction* (New York, 1976), have dominated discussions of the late nineteenth century. However, my research shows the continuing relevance in this period of the ancient sexual ethics Foucault sympathetically anatomizes in *The Uses of Pleasure* (New York, 1985) and *The Care of the Self* (New York, 1986). Foucault's perspective is defended and extended by David Halperin, *One Hundred Years of Homosexuality* (New York, 1989), and *How to Do the History of Homosexuality* (Chicago, 2003).

Eve Kosofsky Sedgwick's *The Epistemology of the Closet* (Berkeley, 1990), is essential for understanding the interplay between a dominant homosociality and a stigmatized homosexuality so often exemplified here; her treatment of the intersections among gender, sexuality, and social class is exemplary. Judith Butler's *Gender Trouble: Feminism and the Subversion of Identity* (New York, 1990), remains indispensable for anyone interested in reflecting on the complexities of same-sex desires and identities. Important for thinking about social responses to diverse marginalized sexualities is Gayle Rubin's "Thinking Sex" in *The Lesbian and Gay Studies Reader,* edited by Henry Abelove, David Halperin, and Michele Barale (New York, 1990), which also includes Adrienne Rich's "Compulsory Heterosexuality and Lesbian Existence" and useful selections from Butler, Halperin, and Sedgwick.

Friendship as a distinctive form of relationship has not received much attention from theorists of sexuality. Jacques Derrida's *Politics of Friendship* (London, 1997), offers an original and provocative engagement with canonical texts by Plato, Aristotle, Cicero, and Montaigne and with more recent thinkers such as Carl Schmitt and Maurice Blanchot. Alan Bray's "Homosexuality and the Signs of Male Friendship in Elizabethan England," in *Queering the Renaissance,* ed. Jonathan Goldberg (Durham, N.C., 1994), 40–61, placed friendship at the heart of studies of early modern sexuality. His posthumous book, *The Friend* (Chicago, 2003), linked friendship with mourning and inspired the collection "The Work of Friendship: In Memoriam Alan Bray," ed. Jody Greene, special issue, *GLQ: A Journal of Lesbian and Gay Studies* 10, no. 3 (2004).

INDEX

Note: Page numbers in bold with an *f* indicate illustrations.

Index

Index

Index

Index